Religion and Philosophy in the U.S.A.

Arbeiten zur Amerikanistik

Herausgegeben von Peter Freese

Band 1

2. Teilband

Peter Freese
(ed.)

Religion and Philosophy in the United States of America

Proceedings of the German-American Conference
at Paderborn, July 29 – August 1, 1986

vol. II

verlag
DIE BLAUE EULE
essen

CIP-Kurztitelaufnahme der Deutschen Bibliothek

Religion and philosophy in the United States of America : proceedings of the German American conference at Paderborn, July 29 – August 1, 1986 : vol. I. vol. II / Peter Freese (ed.). – Essen : Verlag Die Blaue Eule, 1987.

(Arbeiten zur Amerikanistik ; Bd. 1)

ISBN 3-89206-149-1

NE: Freese, Peter [Hrsg.]; GT

These volumes were printed with
the financial support of the:

Universität-Gesamthochschule Paderborn;

Minister für Wissenschaft und Forschung
in Nordrhein-Westfalen;

Universitätsgesellschaft Paderborn.

ISBN 3-89206-149-1

printed in germany

herstellung:
horn-satz, essen   druck: difo-druck, bamberg

Contents

Volume I

Volume II

Samuel S. Hill

Providence and Provision: Economics and Religion in the South

The relation between economics and religion is actually very close. This is true notwithstanding their apparent disparity - as reflected in such corny puns as the contrast between "profits" and "prophets" - and the general inattention to their correlation.

In the West, the historic connection between economics and religion has been rather firm, owing to the strength of the biblical notion of Providence. For centuries everyone believed that the God above and over history provided for it, that is, guided it and his human creatures in ways and toward goals consistent with his eternal purpose. Daily occurrences, petitionary prayer, miracles, and theodicy are only some aspects of Christian and Jewish teaching that express this.

Modern intellectual developments have been playing havoc with that construction of things for four centuries now. But Providence and provision, that is, religion and economics, are co-implicated whether or not it is fashionable so to note. At the most fundamental level, we must acknowledge that both religion and economics are basic. Religion deals with meaning, responsibility, and personal identity. Economics deals with the providing of food, shelter, clothing, other necessities, and much else thought to be desirable for the good life.

At another level, religion recognizes the significance of economics by treating it as one of the "orders of creation." The placing of this arena of human activity alongside the state and the family points to God's authorship of it. Economics, politics, and the family exist by divine intention for the nourishment of constructive living; they are not accidents, or simply the fruits of much experience, or in any way man-made creations. In other words, the economic order is an indispensable féature of human life, hence is an arena of direct concern to the One who creates and governs all life. He created the economic order just as he creates individual people.

The concern of this paper is the interaction within culture of these two basic dimensions of life, economics and the divine government of the historical process. Christian views toward property, usury, and charity, for example, are not examined. Instead, human beings' everyday economic affairs are related to the overall supervision that God gives to history in general and to individuals in particular.

And this paper focuses upon a particular culture at that: the American South. Religiously speaking, the culture of the South is Protestant. The meanings of that assertion are manifold. Centrally important is the issue associated with the theological doctrine of assurance: that is, since the advent of Protestantism, the questions of how to be certain of what you know, how to be sure who you are, and how to ascertain why things happen as they do, have permeated western understanding. Once the ramifications of the Reformation took hold in western society, and most surely in the American South, assurance became a vital, gnawing concern. The principal intersection of economics and religion occurred at the point that assurance became a Protestant doctrine. It was especially prominent in Calvinist theology with its emphasis on election, which by all rights should have deemphasized assurance but, paradoxically, called keener attention to it. Quite specifically, one's job, financial capability, and place in society were seen as truly important and somehow bound up with religion. In one historian's words, "Calvin's comforting, mysterious providence became a means to read God's will; secular history became divine revelation."[1]

Southern Christians have by and large accepted the view that economics is an order of creation, something basic and inherently good that is meant to sustain life and foster the good life. They have rarely been monastic; taking a vow of voluntary poverty is foreign to regional religious understanding. Nor have the churches challenged the orders of creation concept, not even particular systems of economics and politics prevalent in the society. During the past two centuries, slavery and plantation economics often occasioned struggles of conscience, but no one argued that economics as such was of no moral or practical importance. In this century capitalist economics and democratic politics, and particular local variations of each, have been affirmed, indeed taken for granted.

Long before there was an America, European societies respected an institutional church that taught that people do not need to know more than is available through the Church. Accordingly, the assurance issue with its implications for economics and religion did not stand out. Protestantism undermined that conviction and disrupted that consensus. If one accepts Max Weber's interpretation that the Protestant ethic contributed to the rise of the spirit of capitalism, the impact of the new theology was still greater. In the Protestant understanding, no society and no individual can know much for sure, most certainly not by taking comfort in the appearance of a single grand eschatological institution. Instead, the touch-point is either or both: (1) the mystery of the divine election; (2) the Eschaton, history's conclusive and decisive event, which lies in the future. What is one to do between now and then in an effort to discern the will of God, to be clear on one's identity, and to perceive why things happen as they do? The exciting force of this study is how uncritically accepting of the status quo in economic issues and attitudes southern Christianity has been at the same time that it was seeking to transform the world. "Radical" and "restless" are terms that characterize its theological rhetoric and churchly action, but "quiet" and "accepting" apply to its policies toward regional economic life. And this coincidence is dramatized by the absolute centrality of ASSURANCE as a theological theme. Millions of southern Christians are eager to know how they stand with God. Historically for Puritans, close ties have bound this need to be assured with observation as to one's success in the daily walk of providing and making profits. Not so in the South - not so much, any way. In the South, assurance is a vital concern, and the belief is widespread that God governs the economic arena, but the two are not viewed correlatively. Among other topics, we need to examine the particular role that religious assurance has played in "secular" (economic) society.

In many forms of Protestantism, eschatology becomes individuated and the indeterminate future is foreshortened. Calvinism began with an emphasis on Aufgabe (duty, alongside Gabe, gift or grace). In the Puritan outlook, obedience in Calvinist thought was sharpened to answerability. This in turn was modified by revivalism, where answerability acquired a highly individualistic meaning - I am answerable to God for my sins which he offers to forgive. In formal theological terms, most Protestant traditions long ago opted for a posture of responsible indifference to the matter of one's eternal destiny. By contrast, the popular religion of the American South has preferred precision - individual certainty - and has found a way to attain it by means of a datable conversion experience and in concomitant murmurs of the heart. Having answered the question of each person's eternal destiny, Southern Christians want to be sure of proximate destiny as well. Being consumers, spenders, workers, providers, parents, victims of circumstance and guests of opportunity, they yearn for guarantees and certainties in the work-a-day world, with family and friends, in the marketplace. What happens after death is one thing and important; the present state of affairs is another thing and important. Not many Protestant theologies have addressed the pair in combination very well. But in practice, many Protestants have reconciled proximate destiny and Providence to their satisfaction, usually by turning to the economic sphere. Weber argued thus, vis-a-vis Calvinism. In certain respects so have southern Protestants, as we are now ready to examine.

In the Old South, especially after 1830, Evangelical religion and sectionalism emerged as dominant social forces. Both required and provided for assurance: one for the person's eternal and proximate destiny, the other for the regional society's legitimation. During the antebellum period, for the first time, a regional religious consensus prevailed. Evangelicalism in Methodist, Baptist, and Presbyterian forms overturned a nominally establishmentarian pattern that first was supplemented and later supplanted by a variety of enthusiasms and ethnic faiths. At the heart of this dynamic expression of vital piety lay a conviction that one could be sure of his eternal standing before God; indeed for most the claim ran, "If you're not sure, you're not saved." Heaven and earth had drawn quite close; divining eternal mysteries had moved into the realm of possibility.

Those who know so much about their salvation often are in position to fathom much about ordinary events in the secular sphere. Old South citizens, the saved, the churched, and many others as well, attributed secular happenings to the divine handiwork. They saw daily affairs as governed not by the fates but by the Almighty. One lives by reliance on the Lord. As Anne C. Loveland has recently shown, Old South Evangelicals believed in the "sovereignty and omnipotence of God and the dependence of man." Indeed the central thesis of her 1980 book is that this attitude "informed the whole of their thinking, and more than any other single element, contributed to the distinctiveness of southern evangelical thought in the nineteenth century." This view of Providence affected southern positions on the sectional controversy, the slavery question, and temperance reformation, even going so far as to enable Southerners to "accept secession."[2]

Assurance was widely believed to be accessible for what one wanted to know about self and God, the events of daily life, and the welfare of the society. Moreover, if things were going badly, the remedy was obvious: penitence and prayer. Human strivings and accomplishments are vain; our help comes from the Lord. Dependence on Him and righteousness in His ways avail sufficiency.

What of economics and religion under these ideological conditions? At least four systems have to be taken into account: the plantation as a moon with satellites, subsistence farming, the emergent capitalism of towns and cities concentrated on getting cotton and tobacco to market, and commercial agriculture. The first two predominated, with the consequence that traditional economics prevailed - hardly that liberal innovation called "free-enterprise capitalism." The plantation system after all was an arrangement that kept things in place and people in their places. The planter class was content with things as they were. That was Providence. God willed that some be at the top with all others beneath them and left to their care. Relatively little currency changed hands in this early form of welfare capitalism. Economic providentialism, then, took the shape of something that might under other conditions be thought of as fatalism or resignation. This is not fatalism but submission, a different thing; submission is taking one's place in a hierarchical structure superintended by the boss but designated by the Lord. Consenting to subjection to the powers that be, while more medieval than modern, more European than American, hardly fell outside biblical or traditional Christian modes of thought.

In a different way, subsistence farming blocked the raising of modern, free-enterprise capitalism kinds of questions and, as well, theological issues in the sphere of economic activity. Thus a majority of Old South Christians largely ignored the economic dimensions of Providence. We all have noticed that religious people characteristically ask more questions about isssues for which there are already incipient answers – that is, about matters that are on principle solvable – than on those theological concerns largely confined to theory.

The mention of Evangelical suggests to most hearers a radical form of Christianity - perhaps the more so when Evangelicalism has the strength of consensus in the culture. The South became a stronghold of Evangelical Christianity in the antebellum period, but that did not mean that a radical social movement had emerged – at least not in the economic and most public areas. Asceticism, the spirit of self-denial and world-renunciation that was present in so much of Calvinism, was a stranger to southern Evangelicalism. Moreover, nothing akin to the Catholic "counsels of perfection" had currency in the southern regimen. Vows of poverty, chastity, and obedience, or an Evangelical counterpart to them, might have been expected among such intense and certain Christians, but they did not appear. A sense of the disciplined life did grow out of this Evangelical understanding in such areas as personal sobriety, education, the family, and relations to slaves, as Donald Mathews' studies have shown. But southern religion was not ascetic. In fact its actual rhythm was the episodic. One lives on high moments, through occasional emotional episodes that punctuate life. It is illuminating to ponder how a radical social ethic powered by asceticism might have affected a conservative South in comparison with the impact actually made on medieval European societies by the monastic tradition.

It appears that religion reinforced traditionalist economics in the Old South, doing as little in that city of human endeavor as in most others to foment serious change. Beyond that fact the relation of economics to Providence seems to have been ignored or was viewed as inalterable, whereas in political, racial, sectional, and other moral areas, the role of Providence was more apparent and more directly appealed to.

At all events, we know that the churches did not encourage the faithful Christian to withdraw from the economic sphere. Various spokesmen offered instructions. One "must labor and take care; he must buy and sell; he must advance his interest in some way, if he maintain a reputable stand in society ..." The problem, of course, was "how to do this and sin not." Several observed that "... following the Bible did not prevent one from being successful in worldly business." Another put it pithily: "The gospel not only justifies but requires the pursuit of wealth. It is not the possession, nor the proper appropriation; but the 'love' of money, that the apostle pronounced 'the root of all evil.'" Temptations are present, it was allowed, but that fact does not make it sinful to be rich. Principles must be honored, in particular integrity, diligence, and moderation. On one specific issue, question was raised by some as to the moral rightness of bankruptcy. Yet, despite a diversity of utterances about the relation of faith to economic matters, historian Loveland concludes that "economic matters did not bulk large in the social thought of southern Evangelicals." Their thinking was "generally superficial and even naive. Moral exhortation substituted for informal analysis. They were chiefly concerned with the conduct of individuals, rather than entities like corporations or government." [3]

Providence and provision were different in the New South - or were they? Truth to tell, for most people down to the 1940s the continuities with the Old South mentality were more striking than were any new departures. The New South boosters began to make their voices heard during the last quarter of the century but encountered difficulty in making their ideas work. They preached that only a radical discontinuity with past economic practices would rescue the South from its impoverished condition and put it on course toward modernity, a modernity that was industrial and urban like the North's and Western Europe's. While the future was broadly to lie with that point of view, southern economic life went on relatively unaffected.[4] We must note how curious it is that the South's most backward and awkward economic era coincided with the Progressive era of the North. It is by now well known that the decades before and after 1900, not the Old South years, are the period which gave the South its reputation as poor and regressive.

Even so, despite the so-called "colonial" or "tributary" economics of the South from Reconstruction to World War II, important changes were taking place. Relatively, the South's economic picture was steadily improving. The region continued poor as compared with the more industrialized North, but rather well off when set alongside most of the rest of the world including Canada. Also, while southern capital was in short supply, necessitating financing through northern institutions, that capital was obtained in surprising and growing proportions. This economic progress was undergirded by a widespread "growth psychology" that persisted and won wide support. [5] With hindsight, we may opine that the incorporation of the South into the national economy was inevitable, being only a matter of time. The South and the North may have been strangers to each other economically, religiously, politically, and all the rest, but they were parts of the same household.

What of religion; how do Christian belief and church life fit in this picture of economic backwardness punctuated by hope for growth? Drawing the distinction between Providence and fatalism is illuminating. "Reliance on the Lord," the providential ideology of the

Old South, shaded into a moderately different outlook among New South citizens. The difference may seem trivial since both refer historical action to sources outside history that are beyond effective human control. In the setting of the Old South, at least, the providential philosophy existed in a public-minded society which lived with confidence in its point of view and some hope that its position would flourish and even be taken up by other societies. There was about the Old South, after all, a genuine and positive conviction that the region's arrangements for living were defensible and constructive, even worth exporting.[6] The people of the Old South knew who they were and made the case for theirs as a highly developed civilization. More precisely of course, it was those for whom the system was beneficial, those whose perspectives facilitated public-mindedness and hopefulness, who "knew" and who were assured.

By contrast the fatalism of the New South was a far more private-minded theology of Providence. The South as a region had been ravaged, its way of life discredited both psychologically and economically. Its people needed assuring, its public life needed bolstering. In the Old South, fatalism may have functioned for some within the under-class, white and black alike in their private lives, but they lived in a society whose leaders believed it had a place in the sun and, withal, the South was a proud society. In the New South, there was little evidence either to leaders or to ordinary citizens that they had much of anything to give anybody else – except religion. With glass-shattering vibrancy, the southern religious declaimed the superiority of regional religion. "Isms," including pluralism, may have taken over elsewhere, but not in the South where pure, faithful, God-fearing, Bible-believing religion held fast. That should be marketed to the whole wide world, a conviction that generated much talk and, additionally, a great deal of action in the formation of missionary societies devoted to worldwide evangelization. Southerners somehow knew that their religion was a treasure they could recommend to the whole world.

In their personal lives, the southern faithful were affected by a fatalistic perception. Wayne Flynt captured this outlook in his description of life in the Appalachian subculture.

> No aspect of mountain culture ran more counter to the main stream of American values than fatalism. Most Americans were achievement oriented, and few ideas had such universal support in the nation's past as the work ethic ... The willingness of the mountain people to reconcile themselves to deprivation and to passively accept it as fate and 'God's will' was both frustrating and inscrutable to the bureaucrats who administered government programs. 7

What Flynt says of Appalachian people applies to many other Southerners as well. Modern society was not going, or coming, their way.

In the face of such unpromising circumstances, what can people do? There are several possibilities: (a) they can ignore the harsh realities, that is, in a phrase of Wilbur Cash's, refuse to acknowledge the ugly; (b) they can sidestep any effort to reconcile a loving Providence and a dark or desperate plight; or (c) they can resign themselves to their lot in life, which inevitably means to relinquish their homeland's place in the world. Religious faith seems to have prompted one or more of these forms of inaction. As a consequence, the governing forces of the universe were bifurcated, held to be two: the first is the personal God who is the source of all beneficence, the second is the devil who is the agent not only of evil, but also of the unexplainable or unspeakable.[8] Not good theology, and indeed no formulated theology, this outlook seems to have been widespread among the lower classes and perhaps unspokenly present in the understanding of the better-off. Complicating this philosophy of fatalism in New South society was the legal and social dismantling of the old hierarchical social structure resulting, in theory at least, in opening doors for everyone. This was furthered by a stark awareness that other Americans were experiencing an improved life; these developments issued in rising expectations for people in a South that had tried to secede but really could not manage it. The South may have been the nation's number one economic problem, but it belonged inescapably to the national society, hence shared its dreams, hopes, and expectations.

The peculiar character of the industrialization that occurred in the South had a great deal to do with the prevalent attitudes toward how Providence interacts with economics. Most of it featured low-paying jobs for people from farm backgrounds in nonunionized plants. In some cases welfare capitalism operated so that the entirety of a family's life was lived out in a community dominated by the mill and its ownership.

For such industrial workers, the message of religion framed a context. "God's involvement in all human affairs" was taught, and this meant that, broadly speaking, things are as God means for them to be. Both the ruling and the working classes are to accept their lot in life. Such a philosophy discouraged social activism and doing much reflecting on one's location in a particular social class. For the workers, humility was a virtue, one's own unworthiness a fact that he or she ought to admit. Too much concern about material progress was judged unbecoming since real gratification comes beyond the grave. Moreover, as historian James C. Cobb observes, most were doing well enough to think that they were better off than they had been on the farm. "Was it reasonable, or even 'Christian,' to expect more?" Buying a house, a car, and modern appliances should surely be sufficient to keep workers and their families satisfied. One should always remember that it is Christian to accept your lot in life. Underscoring this entire way of responding to their economic condition was the view, carried over from pre-industrial Gemeinschaft societies, that you are given your job by an individual to whom you are responsible, a man who already has his own lot and enough problems of his own. But, in one novelist's words: "It was still difficult for them to realize that they were not working for any individual as an individual - that they were working for a corporation, complicated and technical and highly organized and involved."[9]

The shift from Old South to New South did show more continuity than discontinuity but, even so, many circumstances worsened in the short run. Religion's role became more passive in both public and private dimensions, but its significance increased in keeping with the rapid expansion of the number of church members. However, a major change has taken place between the old New South and the new New South, that is, the "recent and contemporary" or the "much-less-southern" South. From the theological standpoint one has to say that religion's role is less pure, somewhat more crass, except perhaps in the black community. From the standpoint of capitalist economics, religion's role is more prominent and more positive.

We have noted how very Protestant the South is and how direct the relation that links Protestantism with economics. In a civilization where consensus and cohesiveness had given way to diversity and atomization, Protestant theology made assurance an issue and a triumph. It raised the questions of how to be sure of what you know, who you are, and why things happen as they do, and it answered them. Providence and provision came together. In this treatment of religion and economics in the South, the argument has been made that assurance has indeed been a significant force in the private and public life of Southerners. Yet one branch of the "Protestant ethic," the so-called "work ethic," has been conspicuous by its absence. If this contention is correct, we have here another instance of the South's distinctive history and culture. It appears that the Providence-provision issue has been resolved in a way that is unconvential for America both religiously and economically. In the main, the religious impact of assurance has been private, consisting in the good news for the individual that all is well with his/her Maker, irrespective of public circumstances. And the economic impact has come in a sense of satisfaction that things are as they are, and that they are as they are meant to be. Of such the aggressive entrepreneurial initiative is not made. In other words, the wide sea of Protestantism bounded by the Atlantic on the east, the Gulf of Mexico to the south, and one or another border on the north and the west, has not been the oyster bed manufacturing the pearl of capitalist economics - until the past four decades or so, that is.

Entrepreneurial initiative and commercial expansion in industry, business, and complex organizations have indeed marked the southern economic picture since World War II. The pitch made by the Twelve

Southerners who took their stand in 1930 for the agrarian style of life made some difference but has largely been superseded in favor of modernity. William Nicholls' appeal of 1960 that the South acknowledge the impossibility of having it both ways, that is, a traditional economic-social system and a prosperity resulting from a commitment to modern methods and advanced technology - "tradition" and "progress" are his terms - was in fact an encouragement to accelerate the pace of modernization.[10] In most basic respects now it is difficult to distinguish the economic life of the South from that of the rest of the country. A convergence is occurring between the South's and that of the nation as a whole.

Has religion played a part in this coming together of the nation's one idiosyncratic region with the society at large? At the very least, we must acknowledge that prosperity is greater than it used to be and that progressive measures are subscribed to, at least in theory, by almost everyone. The lower classes are still large and often very poor, but the enlargement of the upper class has been dramatic. Also the so-called "work ethic" has become a vital force; the notion that hard work is an end in itself and some kind of altum bonum is taken for granted. As an example, opposition to welfare programs believed to excuse the lazy and foster indolence may be more extensive in the South than elsewhere; it is hardly less so. The ultimate inference from the "work ethic" has been made in the South (as elsewhere): those who are successful have worked hard and those who are not successful have not.

Have the churches and religious values inculcated the work ethic, fairly recently come to prominence in the South? Probably not. More likely, the expansion of initiative, corporate and private, has been directly responsible. There are more resources available, some regionally generated and some invested from outside the region. Capital and capitalism are on the scene everywhere. In addition it must be noted that recent cultural changes have stripped religion of leverage to make heavy impact on any other basic dimension of the society. Such is the nature of complex modern societies. Social-structural differentiation is now a fact of regional life. That means that dimensions or aspects of society are simply less susceptible to impact by others. Religion's influence was more widely felt in previous eras in a pre-modern South than it can be today or for the foreseeable future. In their Gastonia-revisited study, Earle, Knudsen, and Shriver found that religion had made more difference in interracial attitudes between 1940 and 1970 than it had in economic attitudes and behavior, very little surfacing in the economic area. But chiefly they concluded that the new social complexity - "modernization" - prevented much flow of influence from religion toward any other dimension.[11]

We have observed that southern religion's intention to be radical does not carry over into its economic ethic. Indeed we may question whether southern religion has realized its desire to be radical in very many public or social ways. The economic ethic connoted by the churches cannot be fairly described as capitulatory or accommodationist. Instead they have attended to another agenda, principally the conversion and sanctification of individuals. They have been urged to "honor the Lord in every area of live." That has meant in practice that certain values and virtues - integrity and industry, for example - have been brought to bear on their natural participation in the current economic system. The prevailing "economic ethic," then, has influenced the religious ethic more than the other way around.

An occasional dissenting voice has been heard from some pulpit or religious visionary. One penetrating prophetic witness stands out, the Koinonia Farms community of Sumter Country, Georgia. A communal farm colony, it was founded in 1942 by the Rev. Dr. Clarence Jordan, a Baptist New Testament scholar. It flourishes to this day, in its spirit and with economic success, as a group of people who own nothing individually and "hold all things in common." Through the 1960s it was the frequent target of gunfire, harassment, and economic boycott. Its biracial makeup surely contributed most to its hostile reception. But its economic communalism and its pacifism also stamped it as radical and could hardly have been minor factors in its rejection by fellow countians, not all of them Klansmen by any means.

The denominations too have adopted the prevailing economic models and goals. The Southern Baptist Convention and the United Methodist Church, two of the largest and most efficient industries in Nashville, have become very big business indeed. For one thing, they are large and wealthy; for another they employ the latest business practices and technology. If when traveling one stops in at the First Baptist Church in any southern town, he is apt to find a progressive, heavily staffed, and highly productive organization. How good these patterns, features, and values are for the Christian faith and cause is an issue for debate, but that economic models govern a great deal in contemporary church life is beyond dispute.[12]

Now to rehearse the argument: We have noted that the Protestantism of the American South is as keen on the issue of assurance - how can I be sure how I stand with God - as historic Protestantism was. But the meaning and role of assurance differs in the two cases owing to the influence of revivalism in the South. For classic Calvinism and Puritanism, there was a riddle to be solved, namely, how to fathom the divine election. Demystification took the form of looking to the secular sphere of economics to figure out how one was faring with the Almighty. An ascetic, hyper-industrious life style accompanied this approach. Cause-effect ways of thinking emerged; a rational coordination of the spiritual and the mundane came about.[13] In the South, the focus shifted from the mundane to the spiritual for ascertaining whether one were saved or not. If your own heart told you that you had been converted, then you had been. This approach is no less rationalized, that is, demystified, for being emotional and private. In the two quite different cases, turning a mystery into a question produced an answer.

Beyond the experience of conversion, and indeed throughout a southern Christian's life, the economic sphere was basic to living. Each was expected to put personal Christian principles into practice. But the system of economics operating in the society was permitted to go on, was honored as the framework for carrying on the commerces of life. Instead of challenging systems, one was expected to take his place in them - and generally accept his lot in life, whether as slave, plantation overlord, factory foreman, loom operator, field hand, or entrepreneur. This kind of passive accommodation to reality held on throughout the Old and New South periods. Lately, it has been significantly diffused by the deep incursions of modernization into southern society and by much improved economic conditions for many classes and groups in the society. Assurance remains a matter of personal spiritual confirmation and the economic sphere remains largely sacrosanct, the faithful Christian being expected to bring something to it but not really to raise questions about it, or about his or her place within it.

Anyone addressing the topic of economics and religion in the setting of southern culture should say a great deal more than I have said or close his account, yet I have already gone on too long. I conclude with some teasers, a brief list of items that might have been treated: boycotts, Sunday blue laws, communitarianism, single tax towns, and welfare capitalism whether in mill villages, coal mining camps, utopian communities, or Delta plantations. It is indeed a marvelous amalgam of economics and religion that we have here in the South.

NOTES

[1] Ronald J. Van der Molen, "Providence as Mystery, Providence as Revelation: Puritan and Anglican Modification of John Calvin's Doctrine of Providence," Church History, 47 (March 1978), 47.

[2] Anne C. Loveland, Southern Evangelicals and the Social Order, 1800–1860 (Baton Rouge: Louisiana State University Press, 1980), pp. 265, 263.

[3] Ibid., pp. 107, 108.

[4] Paul M. Gaston, The New South Creed (New York: Alfred A. Knopf, 1970), Epilogue.

[5] George B. Tindall, The Emergence of the New South, 1913-1945 (Baton Rouge: Louisiana State University Press, 1967), chapter 14, pp. 462, 463, 470-472.

[6] Louis Hartz, The Liberal Tradition in America (New York: Harcourt, Brace and World, Inc., 1955), chapter 6.

[7]J. Wayne Flynt, Dixie's Forgotten People (Bloomington: Indiana University Press, 1979), p. 147. See also pp. 150-154.

[8]Charles Hudson, "The Structure of a Fundamentalist Christian Belief-System," in Religion and the Solid South, ed. Samuel S. Hill (Nashville: Abingdon Press, 1972), chapter 5.

[9]James C. Cobb, Industrialization and Southern Society, 1877-1984 (Lexington: University Press of Kentucky, 1984), pp. 94-95.

[10]William H. Nicholls, Southern Tradition and Regional Progress (Chapel Hill: University of North Carolina Press, 1960).

[11]John R. Earle, Dean D. Knudsen, and Donald W. Shriver, Spindles and Spires (Atlanta: John Knox Press, 1975), pp. 304-307.

[12]See "On Jordan's Stormy Banks: Religion in the South," Southern Exposure, Vol. IV, no. 3 (1976), 83-103.

[13]For a classical analysis of this development, see Jacob Viner, Religious Thought and Economic Society (Durham, N.C.: Duke University Press, 1978), especially chapter 4.

Eugene Kelly

Pragmatism and Platonism in Santayana's Philosophy of Religion

It has been observed that philosophers, unlike scientists, disdain membership in a community, even a community of philosophers; and rather, renouncing all allegiance to nation, tradition, and native gods, pursue the free inquiry into truth in a vocabulary and in forms of speech congenial to their own natures. Others may warn that one cannot escape the influences of one's culture; but the philosopher, aspiring to "stand naked beneath the open sky," wrings out the ultimate criteria of truth from the depths of skepticism, and pursues knowledge and blessedness alone.

George Santayana's life in philosophy represents such a cosmopolitan ideal, much as do external facts of his life, which extended from 1863 to 1952. He rejected any fixed locus to his wanderings, except, as he once put it, the world of English letters. Santayana was not an American, for he was born in Spain, and never formally renounced his allegiance to that country, even after forty years of life in America, which were followed by twelve in England, and the final twenty-seven in Rome. He is claimed as an American by those of us who love him. Moreover, he cannot be called an adherent of that supposedly prototypical American philosophy called pragmatism, which had been developed by C.S. Peirce and William James at Harvard during Santayana's years there as a student and teacher, for he rejected pragmatism wholeheartedly. Nor, despite the title of this paper, was he a Platonist, for he rejected what is a prime contention of Plato, that ideas, rather than matter, control and oversee the world of experience. And, although he spent two student years in Germany, returning to Harvard to write a dissertation on Lotze, he found no spiritual home nor intellectual community here. For despite the acknowledged influence of Hegel in the plan of The Life of Reason, and his profound appreciation of the genius of Goethe, he denounced German transcendental philosophy as "barbarous", and its inherent pantheism as "idolatry." His closest sympathies seem to be, apart from the "ultimate religion" we shall discuss later, with the Catholic Church, of which he was not a member, and with a Mediterranean civilization that was long dead, except, as he might put it, to the imagination.

I would like to take time to follow with you the life and culture of this unusual man, for I believe that he is not well known in Germany, although many critics in America consider him to be a great philosopher, representing, with James and Dewey, the highest level which the philosophical spirit in America has yet attained. Lacking time, I will deal instead with this apparent paradox: how can a man incorporate in a life of thought two modes of thought, so foreign to each other, as pragmatism and Platonism? Then, from this perspective, we may see how Santayana attained a profound understanding of the function of religion in what he called the Life of Reason, and thereby achieved a philosophical vision that itself may be called "religious."

The Nature of Religion

The textbook account of Santayana's philosophy of religion reduces to the theory that religion is essentially poetry. In Skepticism and Animal Faith, he writes, "There are two stages in the criticism of myth, or dramatic fancy, or the sort of idealism that sees purposes and intentions and providential meanings in everything. The first stage treats them angrily as superstitions; the second treats them smilingly as poetry."[1] Despite Santayana's deep-seated atheism and materialism, and his clear awareness of the abuses of religious fanaticism, he rarely denounced religion as superstition, nor did he display condescending toleration of its abuses by protesting the benefits these superstitions afford to the masses by rendering their ignorance harmless and their fears defeatable. Nor, when he praised religion, did he limit himself to an appreciation of its practical value in support of public morality, although this, too, is a position that persons who dismiss religion as mere poetry are wont to take. He suggests merely that by adopting a poetic attitude towards religion and removing it from the arena of literal truth, we may eliminate the dangerous fanaticism it sometimes inspires, and liberate the profound humanity it conceals.

But in what sense is religion poetry? There is poetry, of course, in the notion of God as our divine friend, as he appears in the great traditions. The poetry of the Greek myths, and their ability to inspire fresh poetry even in our own day, is remarkable. The Old Testament continues to be read as great literature in our schools where it is no longer taught as true religion, and the Christmas story still delights and uplifts us every year. However, that religion is poetry is in another sense quite false, for the adherents of a religion do not perceive themselves as poets, but rather as being in the hands of a living God, whose Word, though it be expressed in beautiful language, is not true poetically, but literally. Nevertheless, those believers whose faith is instinctive and whose need for God is genuine and profound, rarely demand good scientific proof for their beliefs; rather what they require in most instances is in fact good poetry. For example, Santayana notes that most Christians today are repelled by the traditional Christian doctrine of Hell as a place where men suffer unending tortures for a few wretched sins.[2] Their rejection of doctrine on this point is not due to any new discoveries as to the nature of damnation, but because they find the idea of hellfire aesthetically revolting; their nerves have become too weak for such grotesque dramas. Religious truth, Santayana concludes, always contains the element of "imaginative rightness" or aesthetic value, where empirical fact is lacking.

On a deeper level than the aesthetic and imaginative, religious poetry may be found to have moral elements. For religion is the primary means by which the human heart first formulates its ideals, in an effort to transcend or perhaps correct what it finds lacking in this world. It postulates an absolute distinction between right and wrong, and tells of its morality in the tales of Heaven and Hell, where it is given its final corroboration and seal; it imagines the completion and perfection of the ideal tendencies inherent in all things, and sings the poetry of it in tales of the New Jerusalem.[3] That all men will not be saved, and even that innocents may be damned to eternal torments, placed a poetically terrifying stamp of eternity and absoluteness upon good and evil which, alas, we experience only as relativities in this incomplete and imperfect world. Such visions are obviously empirically false, but they have a moral rightness about them that appealed, at first, to the spiritual needs of disenfranchised persons adrift in an evil world and at the mercy of their rulers, and, ultimately, to the majority of mankind in the West.

The divine personalities are themselves ideally human, in Greek religion even more than in the Christian; the moral role of these poetic figures is to exert a "formative influence upon all cultivated minds,"[4] and thus, by expressing the inarticulate needs of strong hearts, help them find their own perfection. Their effect upon the imagination is thus not gratuitous, but based in the demands of the imagination for symbols to represent its inmost longings. That they become objects of literal belief should not be surprising, Santayana notes; for "if we are hopeful, why should we not believe that the best we can imagine is also the truest?"[5]

The term "moral" may seen ambiguous in Santayana's usage, for he appears to distinguish it only slightly from the aesthetic realm, much as was the practice of the ancients: beauty and goodness, although not one, are closely connected in Santayana's view. Both emerge from the life of reason itself, which he defines as the attempt to give unity to all existence by a mind in love with the good.[6] "The good," in this general context, is the harmony of all our wants and desires, a harmony that is merely ideal, insofar as all our wants and needs cannot be simultaneously satisfied. "Goodness" itself is the term we give to whatever satisfies these wants and needs. In a perfect world, every physical, moral, and aesthetic desire, even that of the least of creatures, would be satisfied in a way compatible with every other desire.[7] The sphere of religion, like the other spheres of art, common sense, society, and science is a place where the mind discovers the elements of unity and order in the world that are a promise, but not a guarantee, of such an ultimate harmony and fulfillment.

This search for unities is thus imposed upon us by our wants and needs themselves, and, ultimately, by our instinct for survival; it attempts to satisfy not only our need to know, but our fear of chaos; it promises us that there is an order to the world in which our most pressing needs, at least, have a chance of being met. Religions arose out of that practical desire: The ultimate proof of the existence of God, according to Santayana, is in our hunger and its satisfaction by the powers that do not deny us the fruits of the fields; that our worst fears are only rarely realized, and we continue to live despite the dangers about us. This need for unity or order in a sea of chaos, which gave rise to the impulse to seek our satisfactions in a rational way, is thus based in animal hunger and fear; and Santayana notes very truly that "water is not more grateful to a parched throat than a principle of comprehension to a confused understanding."[8] But this water slakes a thirst that is also moral and aesthetic, although founded in our animal natures, and it is capable, in its time, of giving rise to a poetry that gives voice to our ideals. It offers principles of comprehension, although, perhaps, less to a confused understanding than to a confused imagination. It gives voice to our moral sense; it interprets the human heart, and helps it make "peace with reality." Here mankind's deepest aspirations for an understanding of life that will satisfy the yearnings of his soul for harmony, beauty, and order, in a world that all too often shows itself to be chaotic, uncaring, and fearsome, are given expression. We shall learn more from it than mere delight, or, worse, the misuses of reason. We shall learn something of the human heart, where the secret of all religion lies.

If religion ultimately fails to unify our experience, and make good upon its promises of final satisfaction, this failure is due not to the quality of its poetry, nor to the moral aspiration that gives it wings, but to its confusion of imagination and science, of poetry and fact, of ideals and realities. Its principles of comprehension do not remain moral and aesthetic, but aspire to truth. But where poetry portrays the "ideals of experience and destiny,"[9] in a way that is "fitter to the primary tendencies of our nature, truer to the ultimate possibilities of the soul,"[10] religion adds the false assurance that these moral needs are not mere ideals, but realities, and that these ultimate possibilities will in time be realized. Its failure, indeed, soon turns reason against itself, and fancy becomes aggressive, as in fanaticism, or turns away from the life of reason entirely, as in mysticism.

In order not simply to <u>understand</u> religion, but to regain the moral freedom that these confusions have cost us, such that knowledge may be put to rational use in the achievement of those ends that are practically possible in this world, we must seek out the secret of the gods' inspiration, of their sway over the moral imagination. The needs that give rise to otherworldly hopes are indeed genuine, and if we are to fulfill these same needs in a more rational way, we must first understand "what an undisciplined soul in the first instance desires; and in this way we may trace her chastening and education, observing the ideal compensations which may console her for lost illusions."[11] Thus, the recovery of our moral freedom seems to depend upon a scholarly reduction of religion, reminiscent of Feuerbach, into its natural and moral constituents. And this is one of the chief tasks of <u>Reason in Religion</u>.

Santayana's Pragmatism

For Charles Darwin, whose influence weighed upon the minds of Santayana's generation like an ambiguous revelation, man is in his origins and nature a biological organism. Reason itself is an adaptation to massive biological needs; the need, first, to survive, and, secondly, to establish an equilibrium: to be, as it were, at peace with the indifferent world that bore us. Reason is hence an instrumentality, a weapon in the struggle for survival, and not the disinterested organ of truth, as it was in its Greek origins. The American pragmatists were among those to conclude that the human mind ought to liberate itself from the dream of objective and absolute truth, and rededicate itself, as its primary occupation, to the pursuit of scientific knowledge and the transformation thereby of the physical environment. The fine arts, speculative philosophy, and religion were interesting phenomena to be sure, and worthy leisure-time activities when the energies placed in the service of continent-building needed renewing, but they are fundamentally childish, like play itself.

Santayana retained one important element of this pragmatic vision of emancipated knowledge: he agrees that the value of ideas consists in the satisfactions they achieve. Values are generated by need: what other kind of value could we understand? We think of values otherwise only because they seem to have been imposed upon us from without, as it were, when we are children; we do not understand that they were once derived from some unity of satisfactions achieved somewhere in human experience. Thus every child knows that sugar is good, but he may not know why it is also good to learn to play the piano; the exercises at the piano that are forced upon him will hence appear to him as alien, and if accept them he must, he will attribute their goodness to a higher power, perhaps ultimately to one lying somewhere beyond the clouds, which even imposes itself upon his parents. And, if he or his race have imagination, they will make that imagined power palatable to themselves by rendering it personal, and depicting its glories and its benevolence.

However, Santayana believes that the pragmatists made two central mistakes. The first was to imagine that the human mind, even when applied to the sphere of fact, possesses the power to direct our action. Reason itself is an impulse that emerges from the activity of our brains; its function is to perceive an order and coherence in our sense experience that enable us to take account of our environment and adjust ourselves to it. But it is not capable of establishing its own ideal ends and then pursuing them. The human spirit that arises upon this biosphere, as it were, is hence by no means an autonomous entity; its thoughts and even its highest ideals reflect the rumblings of our animal nature, without having any power to alter the nature or the direction of the wants, needs, and longings that beset it. The technical name for this doctrine is epiphenomenalism, a philosophy of mind that developed in Europe after the midpoint of the previous century.

That ideas - or their expression in such works of art, religion, and philosophy as Santayana cites - have no efficacy within the course of historical events at all is, of course, a commonplace of certain forms of materialism or naturalism, such, say, of historical materialism, but by no means of all. Ideas may be granted an independent and irreducible role in the course of nature or of individual destiny, although mind may still be viewed as an emergent entity. It is this latter possibility that Santayana seems, however, to be at pains to deny in most of his references to the topic, asserting instead not only the derivative but dependent role of mind and its merely expressive and appreciative function in the human economy. The peculiar beauty of such frail vehicles of spirit that we call works of art, and their extraordinary power over the imagination, is founded in the impulses of matter which fester in the peculiar organization we call the human body, and in the "trope," or regular organization of those impulses, that Santayana calls the psyche - impulses that the realm of spirit expresses but does not in any way determine. In this way, undoubtedly, Santayana wished to free the spirit from any role in the life of the body so as to value it all the higher; the appreciation of such finely-wrought essences as those encountered in art, religion, and philosophy is what makes life valuable, and not simply an affair of dumb survival. It is an accidental and incidental affair in the realm of matter, but it opens to us the imaginative or spiritual life. Thus, in what John Herman Randall[12] calls one of Santayana's "unforgettable metaphors," he writes "there are not two parallel streams [psyche and spirit], but one stream which, in slipping over certain rocks, or dropping into certain pools, begins to babble a wanton music; not thereby losing any part of its substance or changing its course but unawares enriching the world with a new beauty." Yet spirit cannot act back upon matter; matter is the only substance that is an agency or power in the universe. Spirit, on the contrary, is a mere "lyric cry" of the flesh,[13] without force or potency.

The emphasis in Santayana's pragmatism is not, therefore, upon the uses of knowledge, but upon the aesthetic enjoyment of the rational poetry that is generated in the spirit by the efforts of reason to discern an intelligible order in things. And this is the second point at which he breaks with pragmatism. The issue hangs upon the specific dispute between James and Santayana concerning the former's criticism of Santayana's Interpretations of Poetry and Religion for holding that the aesthetic contemplation of ideal forms is a good in itself, rather than deriving its value from the action to which it prompts. In return, Santayana criticizes pragmatists such as James for neglecting those needs that are spiritual or ideal in character: those needs of the soul for harmony, order and purpose that give rise to the activity of the imagination. The pragmatists seek, he seems to suggest, to build an imposing edifice of brick and steel for men to live in, while their souls are like an unadorned hut; they create a desert, and they call it civilization.

No, says Santayana, the products of the imagination may be unreal; they may be totally without efficacy in the stream of events, but it is they alone that make life worth living, indeed, they justify what would otherwise be a mad, lamentable, and generally painful animal existence. For man is throughout a poetic creature, whose life of reason "may be generated and controlled by the animal life of man in the bosom of nature,"[14] but whose poetry resounds throughout nature. Good poetry does not oppose our animal nature, it is its unexpected fulfillment, and speaks in a new language the tale of man's most sublime needs. Science itself is a kind of poetry, expressive of a human perspective upon the world, and acceptable to us because it makes possible a close and prosperous adjustment to environing matter, much as religion may make possible a successful adjustment to our moral nature. It is this moral and aesthetic rightness that Santayana speaks of when he writes that "what is false in the science of facts may be true in the science of values."[15]

In sum, then, it is the concept of truth itself that becomes subject to a pragmatic evaluation: true are those propositions that have predictive qualities: they enable us to adjust to the environing world. Belief in material substance, to be sure, is imposed upon us by animal need; the hungry dog must believe, says Santayana, that the bone before him is real, and not a mere illusion. However, the knowledge we have of the real is at best partial and in any case inadequate; truth is itself not a thing, but an ideal: the ideal that at least some of our experiences may not simply be wild imaginings, but are of what in fact happens independently of our experience of it. Thus the most we can say of our propositions is that they yield a "constant, sufficient, and consistent object,"[16] but not that they are certain. For these reasons, Santayana's later works have been interpreted as leading towards a metaphysics of transcendental subjectivism. However, the significance of Santayana's pragmatism lies less in his metaphysical theories of the status of mind as in his moral repugnance at the view of idealists that the world must correspond to our moral conceptions of it. Since James appeared to have arrived, before his death, at the view that the world revealed in human practice is the real world, Santayana broke with him.[17] "The world" surpasses immensely our conceptions of it. We deal with it as best we can, finding in it the potential for satisfactions that our needs demand, and our moral nature requires, but a wise man will take his own pet metaphysical theories "cum grano salis," and with a certain measure of irony: for the ways of nature are ultimately unfathomable. But although the world may rarely correspond to our idea of how it ought to be, our spirit can imagine the objects it encounters in the world in a more perfected state. And thus the spirit, propelled by need, gives rise to the Ideal.

Santayana's Platonism

If the pragmatic element in Santayana's thought reveals him as a naturalist, who, in religion, seeks to unfold the history of the mind's creation of eternal things, the Platonic element reveals him as a man actively striving towards a kind of salvation, one that is worthy of a free and honest man who offers allegiance to nothing. This Platonic element consists in Santayana's identification of the proper object of aesthetic and moral contemplation with ideal essences. This edifying thought, so different from the pragmatists' glorification of rational action as the proper pursuit of the mind, is founded in a highly complex and, I believe, ultimately obscure and perhaps incoherent metaphysics of essence that differs from Plato's in substantial ways. Nevertheless, his thought is at least metaphorically Platonic.

Santayana rarely attempts an analysis of specific ideal essences, a fact that makes it difficult to grasp the nature of these entities; indeed, despite the affinities, admitted to by Santayana himself, of his doctrine of essence to that of Husserl, the style of his writing is more poetic than analytic, more general then thematic, more insightful than descriptive; it seems to float above the phenomena with which it deals. Nevertheless, we make take, as a brief example of his procedure, his observations on Platonic love.[18] In a sonnet of Guido Cavalcanti, a Florentine poet and friend of Dante, we hear of the poet in a French town, where he finds a young girl whose features remind him of his true love back home, la Donna mia. His heart is wounded by an arrow shot from her eyes not, as Santayana would have it, because the lady rebuffed the invitation that Guido's eyes made to her, nor because Guido felt remorse at such unfaithfulness to his Lady, but because in her merely physical presence there was a rebuke to the ideal love that he had formed in his heart. No real woman could ever live up to the ideal that his true love had inspired in his heart, perhaps not even the original girl herself. For the ideal love incorporates all real love, and yet transcends them; as with all Platonic ideals, the gap between the ideal and the real is unbridgeable, although the ideal is, as it must be, founded upon the real. That is why Cavalcanti could love and even marry other women while yet bearing his ideal love in his heart. The ideal is the imagination's way of completing the realities that it suffuses, as it were, with its light; it rebukes the world that fails to measure up to its demands, and yet it remains the happy object of the soul's - if not the body's - deepest aspiration. A mind that regularly encounters such ideals is perhaps not wise, but is certainly spiritual. It is not fanatical, for it recognizes its ideal love as peculiarly its own, and sees no need to impose it upon others: it is not mystical, for it has made its peace with the world, and carries its ideal with it as its secret joy, the source of its inner longing, and its taskmaster in affairs of worldly love.

The ideal love of Guido, although imaginatively projected upon the figure of a particular woman, involves the Platonic ideas of beauty and spiritual purity, and shares their absoluteness and immateriality. To the spiritual mind, such a love does not inspire disaffection with the things of this world, nor does it necessarily arise out of disillusion, for its objects are the things of this world themselves, but seen now in the light of their possible perfection. Through such love, the mind discovers the essences that, for Santayana as for Plato, are the adequate objects of contemplation by the spirit. For the spirit in us is essentially aspiration, not achievement;[19] the spiritual mind aspires naturally to perfection, and nothing in this world of change and relativity can satisfy it ultimately.

These similarities with Plato, however, make the contrasts with Santayana's doctrine all the more striking. For, in the first place, Santayana insists that Plato's ideas do not exist: as we have seen, Santayana's metaphysics is naturalistic and materialistic: "existence" applies to material things alone. Poets and religious men fancy that the ideal perfection that every experience vaguely suggests to the spirit must therefore exist in itself, if not in this world, then in some other; but the wiser and more honest man will refrain from such inferences. The error inherent in all such Platonizing tendencies, when they seek to become more than aesthetical or spiritual as in Cavalcanti, but rather metaphysical and literal, is that they introduce a permanence into change and an absoluteness into relativities that are simply not there.

Nevertheless, the motivation behind such illicit Platonizing is understandable and noble. It is the desire to give this world of moral relativities and meaningless change a kind of moral stewardship that is guiding all things to their ideal ends. It holds that the ideals we perceive as inherent in the indifferent individual objects of this world are in fact the ideal ends that guide the actual processes of nature. Such a view is necessarily parochial and narrow, Santayana believes. When it becomes a fanatical insistence upon a single set of ideals that dictate their laws to dead and uncaring matter, it excludes or inhibits the natural aspirations of other sentient creatures towards their own ideal satisfactions. It is symptomatic of this view that the Good only flowers under specific forms and types (which, at bottom, are the moral counterparts of the spiritual needs of some specific persons or races) that Plato's ideal state requires guardians:[20] desiccated sages and astrologers who, fearing the intuitive and truant poetry of youth, attempt perforce to retain the State beneath a single pantheon of ideals. This belief that the good could and must manifest itself in a single way does an injustice, Santayana believes, to the human heart, which is capable of loving the good in an infinite variety of manifestations. That Plato was led in life to such conclusions, more melancholy than extravagant, is tragic in a man whose love of the ideal was so great; but again, it is understandable when one considers that the claim of the ideal upon our hearts is absolute. If that love of an ideal is great, then, like the Hindu god to whom the worshipper is devoted, it begins to appear as if it were the only ideal. Thus Plato, who banished poetry and art from his ideal state, although they are in fact the only means we have for expressing the ideal, chose instead the poetic notion that the ideals of Socrates were the true rulers of the world. A politics based on these notions would necessarily have become fanatical, and philosophy, for its part, would have become idolatry.

Thus Santayana is only metaphorically Platonic; his ideals emerge from the material world rather than stand over against matter as its magnet and its target. And yet his idealism is nonetheless Platonic, for it insists that the spiritual life must have as its object ideals that are absolute and perfect, and, as such, beyond the things of this world. Indeed, he insists, the ideal is the only rational foundation of religion, and it is in fact the only thing that can satisfy the craving of the human soul for the transcendent. To make God and His angels in Heaven physically real is precisely to do injury to the human spirit, and is a concession of coarser and more superstitious persons to the fears and cravings of their animal natures. Religion begins in such fear and craving, but it is the function of the spirit to liberate the mind from these natural religions and seek solace in aspirations that reconcile the mind to its material embodiment. Such a spirituality would be salutary; it prepares the mind for its ultimate disillusionment, and teaches it to aspire without hope of tangible reward; it gives expression to our deepest needs without ensnaring the mind in vain hopes. It is a true piety, for it respects the unfathomable processes that give us birth, but is yet a piety that, in the realm of ideas, if not in matter, is active rather than passive, creative rather than contemplative, for it directs us to seek the natural excellence in all things, as well as in ourselves. It is, in fact, based in traditional piety, and is closer to it than that of the theological religions. Santayana writes:

> Whatever is serious in religion, whatever is bound up with morality and fate, is contained in those plain experiences of dependence and of affinity to that on which we depend. The rest is poetry, or mythical philosophy, in which definitions not warranted in the end by experience are given to that power which experience reveals. To reject such arbitrary definitions is called atheism by those who frame them; but a man who studies for himself the ominous and the friendly aspects of reality and gives them the truest and most adequate expression he can is repeating what the founders of religion did in the beginning. He is their companion and follower more truly than they are. 21

"Ultimate Religion"

To "study for oneself the ominous and friendly aspects of nature" may give rise to an idealism such as Cavalcanti's, in whom the stirrings of his animal lust ultimately produced an outpouring of poetry expressive of them, now spiritualized, absolute, and more truly beautiful. All things in this world, indeed, are capable of being perfected, and are hence capable of being idealized; piety consists in a respect for what the world can be, as well as for what it is. But although elements of the ideal can be found everywhere in life, there are, for Santayana as for Plato, certain overarching ideals which, for the former, are the central focus of the spiritual life, and which constitute an ultimate religion, that is, one for the liberated mind. The first is sympathy. This ideal is precisely what Plato's vision lacks: a sense of the good, perhaps quite different from one's own conception, to which all sentient creatures are incessantly striving. The Good, as such, would be the harmonious realization of all these disparate, individual goods, much as, for Santayana, the Truth is the sum of all propositions that are true of reality. The attainment of this vision is, as we have seen, the object of the life of reason itself.

A further overarching ideal is that of charity, which, we might say, is sympathy extending its good will indifferently to all goods, and working to realize them. For all goods are truly good to the heart to whom they belong; and if honesty compels us to the conclusion that all goods are not equally good, this is only because we know that real existence forces us to make compromises, sacrificing some smaller goods for the sake of more encompassing ones. But to the human spirit, whose region is the thinner air of ideals, sympathy can be extended to all. To imagine the Good realized in fact would be an illusion that renders hopes painful; to worship it would be an idolatry that might be brutally physical or dreamily mystical; but to love it in spirit is to enter upon a religion of health and understanding. It is a religion of health, for it reconciles us with the lost illusions of our natural religions; it is a religion of understanding, for it teaches us to extend our ideal goods beyond the loves of our own hearts.

The sublime prophet of ultimate religion, which saves us from illusion, idolatry, otherworldliness, and the worship of our own petty loves, was Spinoza. Santayana's own appreciation and correction of Spinoza is revealing. Santayana has, of course, much in common with the great Jewish thinker: both men were seekers after a personal salvation that they find in a kind of love that comes from contemplation within, rather than from grace granted from without; both men sought this blessedness in reclusive, independent lives. For both, the world is indifferent to human ideals: they rejected all notions of natural teleology in favour of a mechanistic naturalism. They believe that our values are founded first in the simple desire for life, and, as refined by reason, in the desire for the health of the soul. For both, that health consists in the achievement of a conformity between our soul and nature. They are thus both adherents of the life of reason, that is, of a life in which reason formulates the ideals and creates the harmonies that are a condition of human blessedness. The chief enemy of this blessedness is an idolatrous fanaticism that reads into nature as its telos the moral demands of the imagination. And finally, the affinity between them that is perhaps most profound, they believe that it is only when religion passes into contemplation that it becomes at all efficacious; that is, becomes the poetry of the soul, and has the power to create the inner joy that makes life worth living.

Santayana's only essay on Spinoza, written in 1933 on the occasion of a celebration of Spinoza's three-hundredth birthday,[22] begins with a question that, at bottom, appears to be the one that pursued both men throughout their lives: how does a truly free man make his peace with reality, and stand "naked under the open sky," steering a middle course between a dreamy mysticism that loses the world, and a nervous fanaticism that is too narrow to understand the world? What religious attitude pins its hopes on nothing, nor loves in such a way that its love binds it to the world? Surely it is Spinoza, he says, who has come closest to such an ultimate religion. This key question, however, cannot be appropriately answered, according to Santayana, until we measure two central errors of his mentor.

The first error consists in Spinoza's pantheism. This doctrine is attacked by Santayana most vehemently where it is found in the German transcendental idealists, among whom it takes a particularly egregious form, dissolving, as it were, all of reality into an absolute mind that reflects the categories of human reason, and then

442

calling it God. Spinoza's pantheism is, similarly, a worship of reason - reason writ large and placed within the Ground of Being: Deus sive natura. And so Santayana says of Spinoza:

> The sun [he] tells us, seemed to be about two hundred feet away: and if his science at once corrected this optical illusion, it never undermined his conviction that all reality was within easy reach of his thought. Nature was dominated, he assumed, by unquestionable scientific and dialectical principles; so that while the forces of nature might often put our bodily existence in jeopardy, they always formed a decidedly friendly and faithful object for the mind. There was no essential mystery. ... Every man had a true and adequate idea of God: and this saying, technically justified as it may be by Spinoza's definitions of terms, cannot help surprising us; it reveals such a virgin sense of familiarity with the absolute. ... Yes, although the dead cannot change their minds, I would respectfully request the shade of Spinoza himself to suspend for a moment that strict rationalism, the jealous, hard-reasoning, confident piety ... and to imagine - I do not say admit - that nature may be but imperfectly formed in the bosom of chaos, and that reason in us may be imperfectly adapted to the understanding of nature. Then, having hazarded no favorite postulates and invoked no cosmic forces pledged to support our aspirations, we may all quietly observe what we find, and whatever harmonies may then appear to subsist between our spirits and the nature of things will be free gifts to us and, so far as they go, unchallengeable possessions. 23

When we thus stand before life, it reveals itself to us simply as power, a power that assaults us with its unfathomableness, and mocks the goods we pursue with its indifference. If we overcome the revulsion at our state that has become so prominent in the works of the existentialists and accept our childish disillusionment, our religion will be one that is based in our joy at what little natural excellence some few things are able to achieve, and what even greater perfections they suggest to the mind. This religion will love the ideal essences of Plato cleansed, however, of their pretension to power over nature; it will be otherworldly only in the sense that what it rejoices in will not be ideals mistakenly thought to be real, but realities transformed by the mind into ideals worthy of the spirit's deepest aspirations. Such a religion accepts the world as unintelligible, and it not only disdains to hope that its own values are realized in this world, it disclaims all values that are based upon anything other than the needs of its own spirit. To this moral renewal, at which Santayana appears to be aiming, of a mankind for whom God is truly dead, or at least should be put to rest, there are indeed great hinderances, for men seem incapable of accepting a moral authority that is merely their own, or an ultimate benefit that is of this world only.

The notions of sympathy and charity are the basis of Santayana's second correction of the Spinozistic religion. For Spinoza's religion sees its only good in the love of the intellect for the logical necessity of things and events. This rarified air, which only few are able to breathe, fears and despises all engagement in the world that is not one of reason, and turns over the passions to the sovereignty of the mind. But for Santayana, the life of reason, as we have seen, is nothing more than the search for harmonies among our vital needs and passions, which are sovereign over themselves. He does not imagine that reason is able to comprehend all of reality, or that reality is rational. Reason is only one of the passions, and it would be again idolatry to elevate reason to honorary status as the only worthy passion. All passions, be they human or otherwise, seek their own good; reason is different in respect only of the fact that it seeks the harmony of all goods, and as such is again an ideal of life, not its foundation. Charity extends the love of the good of all creatures, and a love that rejoices in the imagined good of all things would be precisely more poetical than the rigorous religion of Spinoza, which, as the intellectual love of all things, extends itself only to things as they are, and not to things as they might have been.

To live spiritually in an ideal that has no other authority than the moral and aesthetic truth that becomes visible through it, is Santayana's religion of naturalism – a religion that is a necessary antidote, perhaps, to an American pragmatic naturalism that had liberated itself from Christian myth, but, like Spinoza, not from the worship of reason, which, in America, was the reason that takes the part of practical efficiency and technical efficacy.

NOTES

[1] *Scepticism and Animal Faith* [1923] (New York: Dover, 1953), p. 247.

[2] *Interpretations of Poetry and Religion* [1900] (Gloucester, MA: Peter Smith, 1969), pp. 94-95.

[3] *Ibid.*, pp. 99ff.

[4] *The Sense of Beauty* [1896] (New York: Random House, Modern Library, 1955), p. 184.

[5] *Ibid.*, p. 186.

[6] *The Life of Reason, or, The Phases of Human Progress* [1905-06]. One-Volume Edition, ed. D. Cory (New York: Charles Scribner's Sons, 1954), p. 7.

[7] That reason and imagination are instruments in the search for the good suggests, indeed, a value theory very close to that of his pragmatist associate William James. Cf. William James, "The Moral Philosopher and the Moral Life," in *William James: Essays in Philosophy*, eds. P.H. Burkhardt et al. (Cambridge, MA: Harvard University Press, 1978).

[8] *The Sense of Beauty*, p. 96.

[9] *Interpretations of Poetry and Religion*, p. 286.

[10] *Ibid.*, p. 270.

[11] *The Life of Reason*, p. 284.

[12] John Herman Randall, Jr., in *Animal Faith and the Spiritual Life*, ed. John Lachs (New York: Appleton, 1967).

[13] "The Efficacy of Thought," *Journal of Philosophy*, Vol. 3 (1906), p. 411.

[14] *The Philosophy of George Santayana*, ed. P.A. Schilpp [The Library of Living Philosophers, Vol. II] (La Salle, IL: Open Court, 2nd ed., 1951), p. 14.

[15] *Interpretations of Poetry and Religion*, p. 91.

[16] *The Life of Reason*, pp. 188-89.

[17] *The Philosophy of George Santayana*, pp. 498-99.

[18] *Interpretations of Poetry and Religion*, Chapter V: "Platonic Love in Some Italian Poets."

[19] "Platonism and the Spiritual Life," [1927] in Platonism and the Spiritual Life and Winds of Doctrine (Gloucester, MA: Peter Smith, 1971), p. 291.

[20] For Santayana's interpretation of Plato's ideal state, cf. The Philosophy of George Santayana, pp. 546ff.

[21] The Life of Reason, p. 193.

[22] "Ultimate Religion," [1933] in Obiter Scripta, eds. Buchler and Schwartz (New York: Charles Scribner's Sons, 1936).

[23] Ibid., paragraphs 2-3.

Ernest Kurtz

Alcoholics Anonymous: A Phenomenon in American Religious History

Rarely must a scholar defend his choice of topic, and it is of course impolitic to begin with an apologia, but a decade's experience has taught that approaching Alcoholics Anonymous as an historically significant phenomenon requires such an introduction. In the context of this conference, if my topic needs defense, I would point less to the over one million now living human beings who attest that A.A.'s fellowship and program have enabled them to find and to live the meaning of their humanity - sheer numbers, after all, mean little - than to two other realities that it seems irresponsible to ignore.[1]

First, despite wide-ranging developments both philosophical and theological, we still live in the shadow of Bonnhoeffer's call for a "religionless Christianity." Although the writings of theologians over the last forty years have failed to concretize that reality, the same forty years have witnessed A.A.'s claim to be "spiritual rather than religious" find resonance both in the minds of a surprisingly large smattering of intellectuals and - even more surprisingly - in the experience of an ever more diverse spectrum of ordinary people.[2] Second, for whatever reasons of health-care economics or valid re-evaluation of the role of professional expertise in treating chronic illness, the burgeoning spread of "self-help mutual aid groups" that enable the healing and the recovery of human dignity is too obvious - and too obviously significant - to ignore. Such groups virtually all use Alcoholics Anonymous as model, and most of them adopt or adapt the "Twelve Steps" that are the core of A.A.'s program as their own modality of healing.[3]

What is Alcoholics Anonymous?

Alcoholics Anonymous is a fellowship of men and women who share their experience, strength and hope with each other that they may solve their common problem and help others to recover from alcoholism.

The only requirement for membership is a desire to stop drinking. There are no dues or fees for AA membership; we are self-supporting through our own contributions. AA is not allied with any sect, denomination, politics, organization or institution; does not wish to engage in any controversy, neither endorses nor opposes any causes. Our primary is to stay sober and help other alcoholics achieve sobriety 4

That "Preamble," the reading of which begins most meetings of Alcoholics Anonymous, well summarizes the thrust of A.A.'s significance in American Religious History. Two points stand out. First, note the idea of a "fellowship," a Gemeinschaft, a fraternité, within which one seeks self-healing through sharing one's own "experience, strength and hope" - that is, telling one's story. Second, mark the wariness of the usual trappings of religion in the succinct detailing of the membership requirement, the attitude to money and to controversy, the explicit denial of belief-based or cause-based affiliation.

Although my approach to describing A.A.'s significance will be historical, it seems better to use the alloted time to analyze that significance rather than to detail its historical development. Thus, to frame understanding, let me merely list the conscious, explicit, and well-documented sources of the ideas embodied and enacted within Alcoholics Anonymous and then briefly sketch how those ideas got there.[5]

A.A.'s explicit sources are three: (1) the psychology of Dr. Carl Jung and most particularly his insistence on the importance of "religious experience;" (2) the Oxford Group (later Moral Re-Armament) vision of "First Century Christianity" as promulgated by the Pennsylvania-born Lutheran minister, Frank Buchman; and (3) William James's portrayal of The Varieties of Religious Experience and especially his description of the "conversion" experienced by the "twice-born" or the "sick-soul."

The story of A.A.'s shaping by these sources can be told briefly. Over several month in 1931, Roland Hazard, a Connecticut businessman, sought treatment for his alcoholism from Dr. Jung, who suggested that his only hope was "a religious experience." Rowland joined the Oxford Group and carried that message of Jung to his friend, also alcoholic, Edwin Thatcher. Thatcher in turn, in November of 1934, conveyed it to the most hopeless drunk he knew, his old drinking-buddy William Griffith Wilson, a former Wall Street hustler. Scant weeks later, Wilson, while being detoxified in Towns Hospital in New York City, underwent a "spiritual experience" that his physician, Dr. William Duncan Silkworth, helped him to understand in Jamesian terms.

Upon his release from the hospital, Wilson for four months tried to carry the same message to others, both within the Oxford Group and at Towns Hospital, but without any success beyond the fact that he himself stayed sober. In May of 1935, Bill traveled to Akron, Ohio, in pursuit of a business opportunity that promptly failed. Fearing that he would again turn to alcohol, Wilson sought out another alcoholic not for the purpose of saving that alcoholic but to save himself. The alcoholic Bill found turned out to be a physician, a surgeon, Dr. Robert Holbrook Smith, and so rather than tell him about the disease, alcoholism, Wilson told Smith about himself, the alcoholic. Although familiar with Oxford Group ideas, Smith heard something different in Wilson. The date of Smith's last drink, June 10, 1935, is celebrated within Alcoholics Anonymous as its birthday, and "Bill W. and Dr. Bob" are revered as A.A.'s co-founders.

Mindful of those sources, some dismiss Alcoholics Anonymous as another example of the crutch that simplistic evangelical religion affords the intellectually deficient, seeing little difference between attending A.A. meetings and joining some revivalist congregation.[6] Others find in Alcoholics Anonymous more of a "mind-cure" or "positive thinking" approach, and of course Donald Meyer has taught us to see through all the heirs of William James.[7] Still others, perhaps more respectfully but no less reductively, concentrate on the "mysticism" of Jungian thought and present A.A. in terms of Aldous Huxley's "perennial philosophy" as updated by Milton Berman or, more fashionably, in the concepts of Gregory Bateson's "Cybernetics of Self."[8] Most recently, in response to A.A.'s continuing success, we find deeper psychological yet still religiously lacking analyses in the work of Harvard psychiatrists John Mack and Edward Khantzian in their explorations of "narcissism" and "The Governance of the Self."[9] Yet all these analyses of Alcoholics Anonymous, whether contemptuous or appreciative, overlook the same two things: A.A.'s context and A.A. practice.

My point in this paper is that in order to understand the religious and philosophical significance of Alcoholics Anonymous and its offspring in American history, two simple facts must be kept in mind. First, Alcoholics Anonymous came into being and attained final form in the decade between 1935 and 1945. Second, from its beginning and still today, the philosophy and the spirituality – the healing – of Alcoholics Anonymous is transmitted by the practice of storytelling, of telling a particular kind of story the very format of which inculcates a way of thinking that shapes a particular way of life.

First, the context. Ideas, perhaps especially if borrowed from varied sources, have implicit as well as self-conscious roots. There is both a climate and a soil of opinion. The years between 1929 and 1945 mark the dawn of a renewed awareness of human limitation. Less significant, for our purposes, than the Great Depression, the revelations of Auschwitz, and the use of atomic weapons, are the permeation of American thought by existentialist philosophy and neo-orthodox theology. However, confusedly, Americans in this era found themselves confronting "the experience of nothingness" and distinguishing not only between doing and having but between doing and being.[10]

The earliest members of Alcoholics Anonymous, like most of their successors, were not readers of Heidegger and Sartre, nor even of Paul Tillich and the brothers Niebuhr. And although there is evidence of subtly shaping influence by the thought of Karen Horney and Harry Stack Sullivan, I prefer to rest my claim for affinity on the recognition of it by Reinhold Niebuhr in his 1960 "Letter to A.A.," in which he marked precisely the "acceptance of failure and limitation" as the key to A.A.'s success.[11]

The personal acceptance of human essential limitation permeates the whole A.A. program. It comes through most clearly in the

Alcoholics Anonymous understanding of the "alcoholic" as someone who cannot safely drink any alcohol at all. The acceptance of that "cannot" does not take away freedom but bestows it. For if there is a not at the very core of one's being, then embrace of that not fulfills one's being. Guided by an insight far older than the fifty or two hundred years usually accorded it by the historically naive, the A.A. member views his or her disease as an inherent attraction to the self-destructive - in psychological terms, as an obsession-compulsion. In a theological vocabulary, Alcoholics Anonymous understands alcoholism not as actually sinful but as a manifestation of "original sin." In the acknowledgment "I am an alcoholic," then, one professes less "I cannot drink" than "I can not-drink" - no small freedom for the obsessive-compulsive, for the addict.

A.A.'s focus on the "not-ness" of human essential limitation suggests a vision of human both-and-ness, of the human as a mixture or a meeting point of being and non-being. Because that concept is so abstract, let me break off from this exploration of what A.A. drew from the context of its formative decade and turn to how this abstract vision is conveyed within the very concrete format of an A.A. meeting - by the practice of storytelling.

The bridge between context and practice, between the abstract and the concrete, may be found in two understandings that undergird Alcoholics Anonymous as both program and fellowship. According to a key passage of the A.A. "Big Book": "Selfishness - self-centeredness! That, we think, is the root of our troubles."[12] That self-centeredness, which attempts to deny human both-and-ness, manifests itself in especially two ways in the drinking alcoholic. First, there is the claim and the demand to be in control, signaled by the way the alcoholic uses both alcohol and other people. Second, there is the denial of all dependence - again, both on alcohol and on others.

In reality, of course, as A.A. recognizes, the actively drinking alcoholic is both totally out of control, addicted, and utterly dependent on the chemical alcohol. A.A.'s prescription, the fundamental message of all the stories told at its meetings, is the middle course of limited control and limited dependence. "You can do something, but not everything." "You alone can do it, but you cannot do it alone." These acceptances, conveyed by the telling of stories, shape the nature of the A.A. fellowship.

The telling of stories. Recall A.A.'s "Preamble": "share their experience, strength and hope." How is it that personal narrative – telling stories that "disclose in a general way what we used to be like, what happened, and what we are like now"[13] – can prove healing not only of chronic disabilities such as alcoholism but of one's humanity itself? For the answer, it seems most helpful to turn first not to the context of scholarly discussion in the fields of philosophy, theology, literary theory and historiography, but to the context of A.A.'s own history.[14]

When the fledgling fellowship left the Oxford Group – in 1937 in New York, in 1939 in Akron – its first one hundred members did so precisely because they objected to the Group's explicit religiosity. Philosophically, the Oxford Group's insistence on its "Four Absolutes" did not fit the emerging program's focus on essential limitation. Theologically, the Oxford Group practice of narrating tales of conversion offended the sensibilities of both the agnostics and the Roman Catholics who made up a significant part of early A.A. membership. But what, then, were they to do at their own meetings?

Newcomers attended those gatherings, and the neophytes had questions. They had failed at earlier efforts to avoid drunkenness, how was A.A. different? What did it mean when one suffered memory-loss? How complete need be the "inventory" and the "amends" spoken of in the Twelve Steps? Was wanting to get even the same thing as "harboring a resentment"? These and a hundred other questions were raised: no one is more skilled in denial, in finding a reason to drink again, than the newly dry alcoholic. But those sober for a year or two were not philosophers, theologians, psychologists, nor physicians – even Dr. Bob, after all, was a proctologist. And so they could answer only by telling of their own experiences with the same or similar concerns.

Thus developed the A.A. modality of story-telling: a modified "conversion narrative" that contained echoes of the classic story motifs of the hero and the pilgrimage. The themes explored by Joseph Campbell in his studies of heroic myth shed much light on A.A. stories.[15] Each teller, in the pursuit of "more," had entered the outer darkness and had explored the pit; now, having surmounted its dangers, he had returned, wiser and witnessing to hope. But the heroic plot of separation-initiation-return is leavened by another, deeper, theme - that of the pilgrimage.[16] A.A. storytellers are still "on the way," for they are ever mindful that A.A.'s promise is "spiritual progress rather than spiritual perfection,"[17] and the very fact that they are present testifies that they too need help.

"What we used to be like, what happened, and what we are like now" thus describes a dialectical process of both being changed and changing. Or, to put it another way, in the A.A. modality of storytelling, one is "saved," but not completely. Salvation - sobriety - remains operative only so long as one makes it available to others by telling the story of one's own.

Having limned A.A.'s context - the existentialist and neo-orthodox sense of limitation - and the implications of the A.A. practice of storytelling, it is now time to bring these together in a deeper unity. Through the program and within the fellowship of Alcoholics Anonymous, human beings are healed not by technique but by practice, not by science but by art. For A.A. has discovered - and tells and implements - a larger story.

One corollary of essential limitation, and therefore of the context of the sense that marks the post-modern sensibility, is the rediscovery of the ancient distinction between techne and phronesis, between knowledge and wisdom.[18] Perhaps the greatest significance of Alcoholics Anonymous in the history of ideas consists in its practical implementation of a mode of thinking that leads to a way of life that values the claim of wisdom without rejecting the validity of knowledge.

For those unfamiliar with or perhaps unsympathetic to the rediscovery of phronesis, let me suggest ten distinctions in an attempt not to explain but to describe the significance of the fundamental distinction and therefore of Alcoholics Anonymous.

1. Knowledge seeks to collect facts, data; concerned with technique, it hears the question "Why?" as asking "How?" Wisdom is concerned with meaning and thus with value; seeking reasons rather than causes, it hears the question "Why?" as inquiring "Wherefore?" Research demonstrates that A.A. stories offer better raw material for philosophy than for sociology.[19]

2. Knowledge is primarily a method; it seeks truth by experiments that aim at exactness. Knowledge focuses on quantity, and the mastery of knowledge produces experts. Wisdom is a vision; it seeks truth by understanding, which is concerned with adequacy. Wisdom focuses on quality: immersion in wisdom produces artists. There are no experts in Alcoholics Anonymous.

3. Knowledge can and must be added to, even replaced; it comes to us in textbooks and articles that we read once and then "refer to." Wisdom is less added to than deepened; it comes to us in "classics" - works that we re-read and ponder because we change more than they do. As its nickname hints, A.A.'s "Big Book" falls in the latter category.

4. Knowledge gives answers: one possesses knowledge and therefore can sell it. Wisdom suggests new perspectives on ultimate questions; one does not possess wisdom but is rather possessed by it, and thus any claim to "sell" wisdom signals the charlatan. No one can "buy" Alcoholics Anonymous.

5. In the ancient classical understanding, the source of knowledge is leisure, either the possession of it or the desire for it. A.A. stories witness to what Edith Hamilton has suggested was a core Greek insight: "Wisdom's price is suffering, and it is always paid unwillingly although sent in truth as a gift from God."[20]

6. Knowledge attends to realities as things: biochemists and neurologists can offer us much knowledge about alcoholism. Wisdom attends to realities as personal: Alcoholics Anonymous is interested only in the alcoholic.

7. Knowledge locates human uniqueness in the capacity to think. Wisdom locates human uniqueness in the capacity to love. A.A.

presents itself as both program and fellowship.

8. Knowledge, rejecting story for analysis, insists on the separation of "fact" and "value." Wisdom finds truth in stories because of its insistence that "What can I know?" and "How shall I live?" are not two unrelated questions.

9. Knowledge is fascinated by the new; it is at least tempted to give the presumption of validity to novelty. Wisdom encourages mindfulness of the old, offering the presumption of value to that which has endured the test of time. The truest statement about Alcoholics Anonymous is that it is nothing new.

10. Knowledge accepts as reality only that which has been or at least can be proven. Wisdom acknowledges the possibility of the existence of that which escapes strict proof, holding that there are some realities, such as love and sobriety, in the existence of which one must believe before one can see them.

Now let me blur those distinctions: according to the point of view represented by Alcoholics Anonymous, to be human is to be both scientist and artist, for to live humanly requires both knowledge and wisdom. If, as we have been warned and have even experienced in some modern cult and drug experiences, "Knowledge separates while mysticism unites," it is also true that wisdom distinguishes without either separating or uniting.

Wisdom's key distinction and the message of all storytelling concerns the complexity of human being. To be human is to be both a unique, individual self and somehow part of reality greater than the self. This insight underlies all religion, art, and love. To be human is thus also at the same time to be both more and less than merely human: it is to exist, essentially, in a mixed, middle, paradoxical condition. Over Emerson Hall, the philosophy building in Harvard Yard, there is inscribed the Judaeo-Christian version of one-half of that ancient wisdom: "You have made him a little less than the angels." The ancients knew that we are also a little more than the beasts, or, better, that to be human is to be neither beast nor angel yet somehow also to be both. Wisdom's vision is of human both-ness.

All comedy and all tragedy - all storytelling - witness to that vision. The core of comedy is the embrace of human both-and-ness. Tragedy details the effort to deny that same both-and-ness. And what of Alcoholics Anonymous, wherein the way in which tragic tales are met with laughter confuses so many observers? Long before A.A., some alcoholics - "compulsive drunkards," they were called in American colonial times - recovered. Until Alcoholics Anonymous, they thought of themselves as "ex-alcoholics," or perhaps as "reformed drunkards."[21] Now I am sure you know that the customary introduction of any storyteller within Alcoholics Anonymous runs: "My name is ..., and I am an alcoholic." Refer to an "ex-alcoholic," and most members of Alcoholics Anonymous will begin searching the obituary pages.

Wisdom's paradox of human both-and-ness, then, is contained in and taught by the very concept "sober alcoholic." That is why a recovering member need not even speak at all to tell his story at an A.A. meeting: simply <u>being there</u> as a sober alcoholic, tells the story ... although it is of course useful and helpful to hear some of the details of each particular heroic pilgrimage quest. To accept the possibility of being a "sober alcoholic" is to accept the reality of human both-and-ness, and in the wake of that acceptance comes wisdom itself.

Does this embodiment of "wisdom" make Alcoholics Anonymous a philosophy or a religion? No, but A.A.'s claim to be a "way of life" does appear validated.[22] Remember Bonhoeffer's call for a "religionless Christianity." Both philosophy in the classical sense and theological religion have suffered eclipse in modern times, especially in the Anglo-American world that gave birth to Alcoholics Anonymous and first witnessed its widespread impact.[23]

My point in this paper concerns the significance for the story of wisdom of the story of Alcoholics Anonymous. For at least a millennium, until some time in the seventeenth or eighteenth century, human beings preferred wisdom to knowledge. Then, for some two or three centuries, they pursued knowledge at the expense of wisdom. In both contexts, some sought to reverse the trend, but almost always in an either-or, all-or-nothing fashion. The modern drug cult, and even some therapies, evidence that tendency. The significance of Alcoholics Anonymous, lies in its attempt to regain wisdom without sacrificing knowledge, in its witness to their complementarity, in the reality that the A.A. fellowship and program have transcended the religious "problems" of the past two or three centuries in a way that again makes Wisdom and its insights available to large numbers of very ordinary people without requiring them to reject knowledge.

But wisdom - phronesis, sapientia - is not the same as "religion" nor even as the reality for which Bonhoeffer called. Alcoholics Anonymous presents its fellowship as "spiritual rather than religious," and co-founder Bill Wilson was wont to parry challenges to its program by those who wanted it to be "more" by referring to A.A. as "a spiritual kindergarten." Mindful that "only what does not have a history can be defined,"[24] I would suggest that no better description of wisdom can be found than A.A.'s portrayal of itself as "way of life."

My second contention in this paper, then, involves the claim that Alcoholics Anonymous is also significant because of what its way of life teaches, enables, and inculcates: an attitude - a posture before reality - that is at the same time both profoundly philosophical and deeply religious.

How describe such an attitude? Of what might it consist? Argument, although inevitable, proves fruitless. Rather than beginning with a definition and proceeding deductively, then, let me begin with A.A. practice, seeking to derive an at least possible model. To what does research indicate the practice of the A.A. program leads in the daily life of its members?

The literature on Alcoholics Anonymous recognizes four attitudes as characteristic of A.A.'s sober members.[25] Feeling a sense of release for which they are profoundly grateful, members of Alcoholic Anonymous in embracing their own both-and-ness as "sober alcoholics" reveal a humility from which flows profound tolerance - a joyous willingness to accept others' limitations. Would it be too much to claim that it is precisely these qualities - releasement and gratitude, tolerance and humility - that characterize any really "religious" attitude?

You will note that something is apparently missing. A philosopher has recently insisted that the core of religion is to be found in worship.[26] But is "worship" so different from the "attitude of awe in the face of the universe" that the psychiatrist, John Mack, remarked in A.A. - especially if that attitude of awe be celebrated communally?[27] Alcoholics Anonymous not only has a program; it _is_ a "fellowship." Releasement and gratitude, tolerance and humility, although A.A. members attempt to practice them "in all our affairs," are celebrated at A.A. meetings - celebrated _by_ the telling of stories.

Often, religious professionals see in those meetings either too much or too little. In A.A.'s early years, Catholic clergy scented in its Oxford Group origins and in its usual use of "the Protestant Lord's Prayer" a forbidden communicatio in sacris. More recently, other clerics have more pragmatically resented the fact that at least some alcoholics seem to substitute going to A.A. meetings for attendance at church. Similarly, most non- religious professionals tend to view Alcoholics Anonymous as "just another form of religion," just another "church."

But these objections must be balanced by criticisms from the opposite direction. Others, beginning with the Jesuit theologian John Ford in the 1940s, have found A.A.'s claim to be "spiritual rather than religious" all too true, or even too much. They fault Alcoholics Anonymous less for its failure to worship than for its absence of theology. Some social scientists follow the same tack, viewing A.A. as primarily group socialization - but Durkheimian religion is not religion in any usual sense.[28]

Where does such disagreement leave the observer concerned primarily with A.A.'s continuing history? The revivification of religion, like the rebirth of philosophy, is of course beyond A.A.'s scope. Sober alcoholics are not that grandiose. But I would suggest that any interested in either question - and perhaps especially any scholars fascinated by the current revival of interest in story-telling among philosophers and theologians, critics and historians, might find suggestive hints in the ongoing story of Alcoholics Anonymous.

The significance of Alcoholics Anonymous as a phenomenon in American Religious or Philosophical History is quite simply that for the past half-century it has been in the center of a mainstream that most scholars have been led by ideological blinders to ignore. Two current revivals of interest render the continuation of that ignorance unconscionable. Within Alcoholics Anonymous and its Twelve-Step offspring, more and more people are asking more and more explicitly for guidance in spirituality. Indeed, "spirituality" bodes to become the next fad in an already over-fadded field. That outcome will be sad, for it will steal from all of us yet another important word. When a culture does not accept the existence of some reality, whatever term those who experience that reality use to name it quickly becomes debased, its original meaning perverted and lost.

Perhaps the second revival, then, can offer hope - if those engaged in it can prove more open-minded than their predecessors. The revival of interest in narrative, in storytelling, might learn much from the experience, strength and hope of Alcoholics Anonymous. I commend to you that task in the words of the only italicized sentences that appear in the book, Alcoholics Anonymous: "Willingness, honesty and open mindedness are the essentials of recovery. But these are indispensable."[29]

A.A.'s experience proves that that holds true for recovery from alcoholism. May I suggest that it might hold equally true for scholarship's recovery of humanity?

NOTES

[1]Current membership figure by private communication with A.A.'s General Service Office, 10 January 1986; on the accuracy of such figures, cf. Barry Leach and John L. Norris, "Factors in the Development of Alcoholics Anonymous," pp. 441-543, in Benjamin Kissin and Henri Begleiter, Treatment and Rehabilitation of the Chronic Alcoholic (New York: Plenum, 1977), pp. 443-451.

[2]"More of the Young and Cross-Addicted Now in A.A., Survey Reveals," Box 459, Vol. 29 (1984), no. 5, 1; similar articles on other diversity can be found in almost every issue.

[3]Leonard D. Borman, ed., Explorations in Self-Help and Mutual Aid (Evanston, IL: Northwestern University, 1975); Alan Gartner and Frank Riessman, eds., The Self-Help Revolution (New York: Human Sciences Press, 1984); Daniel J. Anderson, Living With Chronic Illness (Center City, MN: Hazelden, 1985).

[4]May be found on p. 3 of any issue of the A.A. Grapevine.

[5]The history of Alcoholics Anonymous is recounted in two of its own publications: Alcoholics Anonymous Comes of Age (New York: A.A. World Services, 1957) and "Pass It On" (New York: A.A.W.S., 1984). Full sources for all the detailed points that follow may be found in my own study, Not-God: A History of Alcoholics Anonymous (Center City, MN: Hazelden, 1979).

[6]R.K. Jones, "Sectarian Characteristics of Alcoholics Anonymous," Sociology (Oxford) 4:181-195 (1970).

[7]Donald Meyer, The Positive Thinkers (Garden City, NY: Doubleday, 1965), pp. 315-324.

[8]Morris Berman, The Re-Enchantment of the World (Ithaca, NY: Cornell University Press, 1981); Gregory Bateson, "The Cybernetics of 'Self': A Theory of Alcoholism," in Bateson, Steps to an Ecology of Mind (New York: Ballantine, 1972), pp. 309-337.

[9]John Mack, "Alcoholism, A.A., and the Governance of the Self," pp. 128-162; E.J. Khantzian, "Some Treatment Implications of the Ego and Self Disturbances in Alcoholism," pp. 163-188, both in Margaret H. Bean and Norman E. Zinberg (eds.), Dynamic Approaches to the Understanding and Treatment of Alcoholism (New York: Free Press, 1981); cf. also George E. Vaillant, The Natural History of Alcoholism (Cambridge, MA: Harvard University Press, 1983).

[10]William Barrett, Irrational Man (New York: Doubleday, 1958).

[11]"Letter to A.A. from Reinhold Niebuhr," Thirty-Five Years (New York: A.A.W.S., 1960), p. 65; on the claim to influence by Horney and Sullivan, cf., e.g., Dr. Esther Richards (Baltimore) to Wilson, 18 July 1938.

[12]Alcoholics Anonymous (New York: The Alcoholic Foundation, 1939), p. 74; in the more readily available 2nd and 3rd editions (New York: A.A.W.S., 1955 and 1976), p. 62.

[13]Alcoholics Anonymous, 1st ed., p. 70; 2nd and 3rd eds., p. 58.

[14]The recent literature on story is vast; I rely especially on: Stanley Hauerwas, Truthfulness and Tragedy (Notre Dame, IN: University Press, 1977); Alasdair MacIntyre, After Virtue (Notre Dame, IN: University Press, 1981); Terry Eagleton, Literary Theory: An Introduction (Minneapolis: University of Minnesota Press, 1983); Paul Ricoeur, Time and Narrative, Vol. 1, trans. Kathleen McLaughlin and David Pellauer (Chicago: University Press, 1984); Paul Veyne, Writing History, trans. Mina Moore-Rin-volucri (Middletown, CT: Wesleyan University Press, 1984); Arthur C. Danto, Narration and Knowledge (New York: Columbia University Press, 1985).

[15]Joseph Campbell, The Hero With A Thousand Faces (Princeton, NJ: Princeton University Press, 1949).

[16]Concerning pilgrimage, cf. MacIntyre, pp. 203–204.

[17]Alcoholics Anonymous, 1st ed., p. 72; 2nd and 3rd eds., p. 60.

[18]In addition to the sources cited in note 14, cf. Richard J. Bernstein, Beyond Objectivism and Relativism (Philadelphia: University of Penn. Press, 1983); also Robert N. Bellah, Richard Madsen, William M. Sullivan, Ann Swidler, and Steven M. Tipton, Habits of the Heart (Berkeley: University of Cal. Press, 1985).

[19]Why this is true may perhaps best be grasped from a very insightful anthropology dissertation: Mary Catherine Taylor, Alcoholics Anonymous: How It Works (University of California at San Francisco, 1977), University Microfilms *79-13241.

[20]Edith Hamilton, The Greek Way (New York: Norton, 1930), p. 59.

[21]Cf. Mark Edward Lender and James Kirby Martin, Drinking in America (New York: Free Press, 1982), pp. 9–21.

[22][William G. Wilson], Twelve Steps and Twelve Traditions (New York: A.A.W.S., 1953), p. 15; [Wilson], As Bill Sees It: The A.A. Way of Life (New York: A.A.W.S., 1967).

[23]Cf. Kurtz, Not-God, pp. 113, 185.

[24]Attributed to Friedrich Nietzsche by Susan Sontag, "When Writers Talk Among Themselves," The New York Times Book Review, 5 January 1986, p. 22.

[25]The pre-1979 literature is best perused in Kurtz, Not-God; more recently, cf. especially Vaillant, Natural History, pp. 197–208 and also "Dangers of Psychotherapy in the Treatment of Alcoholism," pp. 36–54, in Bean and Zinberg (eds.), as well as Mack, pp. 160ff., and Khantzian, p. 172, as cited. A less technical and more comprehensive view is offered by Milton A. Maxwell, The

Alcoholics Anonymous Experience: A Close-Up for Professionals (New York: McGraw-Hill, 1984), especially pp. 70-128.

[26]Leszek Kolakowski, Religion (New York: Oxford University Press, 1982), pp. 175ff.

[27]Mack, "Governance," p. 144.

[28]For an early example, cf., e.g., R.F. Bales, "The Therapeutic Role of Alcoholics Anonymous as Seen by a Sociologist," Quarterly Journal of Studies on Alcohol 5:267-278 (1944); further references on this and the preceding points may be found in Kurtz, Not-God, pp. 306, 314.

[29]Alcoholics Anonymous, 1st ed. (after the 1st printing), p. 400; 2nd and 3rd eds., p. 570.

Bernhard Lang

Burial in America: From Colonial Public Grave to Modern Private Shrine

"A bombshell of a book," wrote a reviewer in the New York Times; "crowded with facts every American should know," and therefore, of course, every student of American culture should know as well. The book thus acclaimed is Jessica Mitford's American Way of Death.[1] Published in 1963, it has nothing to do with the now fashionable interest in "death and dying" inspired by the Swiss-American psychologist Elizabeth Kubler-Ross. Jessica Mitford did not write about death as the process of passing away; her book is on the undertaking trade. More precisely, she blended three different themes: an ethnography of what undertakers do to make a living; an aggressive critique of the questionable ways that trade makes money, and in fact makes too much of it; and, third, she explains how to escape from the undertaker's snares - for example by donating one's body to medical research.

With seven editions in the year of publication, this was indeed a bombshell of a book. Reading it twenty years later makes us aware, however, of its limited approach. Jessica Mitford did not tell the whole story. As a matter of fact, her analysis consists in the simple and somewhat naive statement that undertakers (and florists, too) are merciless money-makers "die über Leichen gehen" as the German idiom has it (trampling corpses under foot). When people recover from the first shock of bereavement, they find at least two bills in the mail box: one sent by the undertaker and one by the cemetery management. Arguing that undertakers exploit the helplessness of mourning Americans, Mitford sets her journalistic mind at rest. Preoccupied with blaming the professionals (whose professional status is questioned), she forgets the patrons who rely on their services. She forgets to ask why mourning Americans actually pay the bills they get.

To study this question means to study aspects of human behavior that transcend the economic level and are more complex than greed and exploitation. With categories borrowed from sociology and anthropology we can speak of ancestor worship, cult of the dead, and conspicuous waste in sacrifice. Despite their exotic and "primitive" overtones, the use of these labels can be justified, and I will try to do so in the rest of this paper. First, I will discuss the establishment of the burial plot as a privately-owned shrine; second, the hope of being reunited with the deceased; and third, the conspicuous gifts presented to the deceased relative or friend.

From Communal Burial Ground to Privately Owned Grave

Today, it is nothing special to own the plot in which one's parents or relatives are buried. When we look back in history, we can see that private plot-ownership in a cemetery is actually a recent institution. In colonial New England, for example, the dead were buried in the churchyard or in a burial ground situated in the town commons at the edge of the settlement.[2] The public character of the town commons is evident, and so is the communal quality of the churchyard. In neither case were the burial plots privately owned. Its very location defines the churchyard as an extension of the church itself. Being buried at a place of public worship the dead still belong to the worshiping community of which they mystically form a part. This is the time-honored Christian idea of the "communion of the saints," the idea that living and dead members of the church belong together and form one community. The public character of the cemetery is further enhanced by its actual appearance. Cluttered with virtually identical, indistinguishable gravestones it reminds us of the Puritan congregation whose identically dressed members met in their meeting house. In the graveyard the dead Christians form a silent, petrified congregation. It replicates the living church members who worship their God in the church, and the departed souls standing around the divine throne in heaven.

The corpse, therefore, does not belong to the family of the

deceased, but to the community. Even more than during life, when a man or woman could be excluded from the church or resign from membership, he or she is the inalienable property of all. One could also say that the corpse belongs to God and, therefore, to the church as his earthly representative. Both explanations amount to the same, to saying that the dead are lost to their relatives, but not to the community as a whole.

It is in keeping with this that in the eighteenth century the bier and the pall that covered the coffin during the procession were usually either the property of churches, and under their management, or belonged to the community and were in the hands of the civil authorities. More importantly, this was true of New England cemeteries which were typically owned by the town.[3] In spite of the fact that many New England burial grounds are adjacent to the sites of old meeting houses and churches, they were legally unrelated. While the church would receive only its members, the civic graveyard would eventually accommodate everyone – saint and sinner, Christian and atheist, and cover the deceased's coffin with its communal pall. In either case the cemetery and the interred bodies belong to the realm of the communal and public rather than that of the family.

During the nineteenth century, all of this changed. The rapid growth of the population necessitated the establishment of new and considerably bigger burial grounds. Between 1790 and 1830, for instance, Boston's population grew from 18,000 to some 61,000 inhabitants. The churchyards and the urban burial grounds of the eighteenth century were overcrowded and seemed not only too small and unsightly, but also offended the growing sense of hygiene. People felt that they were a menace to public health.

The solution were the so-called rural cemeteries established outside of the cities.[4] Boston's Mount Auburn cemetery was opened in 1831 and soon became the model of a "rural cemetery" that every decent American city should have. In 1836, Philadelphia established its Laurel Hill cemetery, and Brooklyn's Greenwood followed in 1838. By 1861 there were at least sixty-six garden cemeteries in the United States.

Rural cemeteries imply a significant modification of the eighteenth-century idea and practice of burial. While the colonial grave belonged to the community, and was typically near the meetinghouse in town, the Victorian American's grave was owned by the family. Dead bodies, too, were owned by families and were legally treated as the property of the surviving spouse and the next of kin.[5] The grave was situated in a suburban area considered ideal for living. Just like the ideal home the ideal grave should be outside of the busy, noisy, and often industrial city. In the wake of the industrialization Americans began not only to romanticize nature, but also claimed it as the proper location of homes for the living as well as the dead.

Rural cemeteries do not belong to churches or towns, but are owned and operated by non-denominational, private companies. These sell individual lots as real estate property. Individuals would normally acquire lots of about 300 square feet that are neatly marked off as private property, often by fences. Within their lots, they would build subterranean vaults, a stylish house-vault above the ground, a little mausoleum, or just inter their relatives in individual graves. The character of the cemetery as an assemblage of individually or family owned memorial places is enhanced by the extreme variety of decorative art which was unknown before. "In the office of the cemetery will be found a large selection of photographs of burial monuments in the modern cemeteries of Italy, recently collected," say the 1887 Regulations of Philadelphia's West Laurel Hill Cemetery; "from which new designs can be selected. It is very desirable to avoid, as far as possible, duplicating styles of monuments already in the grounds."[6]

A visit of the still-existing rural cemeteries conveys an impressive contrast with the older churchyards: colonial uniformity and simplicity gives way to varied and elaborate, if not excessively luxuriant monuments. By the end of the nineteenth century, the idyllic gravestone hidden under the shade of a tree is replaced by an impressive monument. The cemetery, once a Puritan place of meditation on the vanity of life, has become a place of Victorian pomposity and display of monumental vanities. It is not surprising, then, that rural cemeteries became open-air museums attracting numerous visitors.

The private character of the cemetery, however, was secured and protected in the bylaws: "Sundays. Admittance can only be granted on this day of the week to funerals, and to the relations and friends accompanying them; or to lot-holders on foot with their tickets, (which are in no way transferable) with members of their families, or friends in company."[7]

Like the burial ground, the corpse of the dead had moved from communal into family property. Consequently, the cemetery should be a place "where the smitten heart might pour out grief over the grave of the cherished one, secure from the idle gaze of heartless passengers."[8] Even inside the cemetery itself people with "a cultivated and refined taste" preferred a secluded spot for their burials to one that was too visible. "Seclusion," explained one cemetery guide, "is more in unison with the feelings of many friends of the dead than publicity, glare, and notoriety."[9] The Victorians were torn between the ideas of sepulchral privacy and monumental display. The private ownership of corpse and burial plot allows for both possibilities.

From the Beatific Vision to Heavenly Reunion

At the colonial grave the minister said a prayer and sometimes gave an address that extolled the known, or not-so-known, virtues of the passed member of his flock. More frequently, the funeral sermon was delivered at the next regular Thursday or Sunday service. In his address the minister might recall what the catechism of the New England Primer taught about the body's and soul's fate after death. "The souls of believers are at their death made perfect in holiness," wrote the Primer, "and do immediately pass into glory, and their bodies being still united to Christ, do rest in their graves till the resurrection."[10] Death involved the separation of body and soul; the former would stay in the grave, while the latter might pass either into heavenly glory or into the torment of hell, whichever was deserved.

If they could afford to do so the relatives marked the grave with a simple headstone that indicated the name of the dead, the date of passing, the age, and occasionally some more information about the life of the interred person. Sometimes the personal data were followed by a lyrical epitaph addressed to the reader, reminding him or her of the inevitability of death, as well as the Christian duty to be well-prepared. A typical epitaph reads, "Come mortal man/ and cast an eye/ come read thy doom/ prepare to die." (1740)[11] More effusive texts praised the moral and religious qualities of the deceased, but rarely referred to private virtues. One epitaph from 1709 which called a pastor not only "a fruitful Christian," but also "a tender husband, and a parent kind, a faithful friend" is the exception rather than the rule.[12] On early eighteenth-century gravestones a stern and icy tone prevails.

During the eighteenth century, especially after the "Great Awakening" of religious emotion and sentiment in the 1740s, the ice melts. Epitaphs increasingly suggest the idea of heavenly ascension, with the old Puritan doubts cast aside or simply forgotten.[13] The new optimism was also expressed in iconography: the winged skull was replaced by a winged head, reminding the onlooker of angelic existence in heaven rather than putrefaction in the grave.[14] Toward the end of the century, the right to shed tears is recognized. Lamentation is not hidden, but engraved in stone, and often the misfortunes of the deceased, shared by the family, are tearfully chronicled. When one member of the family suffers from illness or bad luck, the whole group is emotionally involved. The family group, at times enlarged to include friends or fellow-citizens, made its entry into the epitaph. It affirmed the affection felt or recognition of those who erected or dedicated the monument. With the emergence and appreciation of the deceased as "private person," the "public person," whose professional career many colonial epitaphs had dutifully recorded, faded away. This is the age of an affective revolution that restructured love, life, and family in both America and Europe.[15]

Heaven did not remain uninfluenced by the surge of sentiment. For epitaph writers, heaven is not a place for the beatific vision of

God, but a place where one would find and rejoin one's beloved. This new idea emerged shortly before 1800, and soon gained currency as expressed by grieving spouses and despairing parents. The innovation can be found on several gravestones of 1797. The rector of the Swedish churches in Pennsylvania, for instance, dedicated an inscription to his deceased wife. "He erected," it says, "this monumental record of her piety, kindness, economy, neatness; her faithful affection to him in many trying scenes; of his grief, which shall not cease until they meet in the land of the living" (1797, Philadelphia).[16] Another stone, dedicated to a widow who had died soon after her husband, celebrates her day of passing as the time when "she commenced her inseparable union with her much beloved consort" (1800).[17] To the readers of Emanuel Swedenborg's Delights of Wisdom Concerning Conjugial Love (Philadelphia, 1796) and A Treatise Concerning Heaven and Hell (Baltimore, 1812) these ideas sounded thoroughly familiar. The Christian Examiner of 1824 refers to the expectation of meeting friends in the other world as a matter of fact.[18] Starting in 1833 America's bookstores were flooded with popular and semi-popular books on the social aspects and joys of life after death. Between 1833 and ca. 1900, at least fifty such titles were published, and many of them went through numerous editions. The authors were Reformed or Evangelical ministers, Episcopalian priests, Unitarians, Moravians, Swedenborgians, and Spiritualists. A Catholic version was also available.[19]

There are differences among these authors. Unitarians do not distinguish between God and Jesus as the focus of heavenly existence, and they believe in eternal spiritual activity and progress rather than rest. Catholics have their purgatory as a place of the soul's preparation before its eventual admission to paradise. Swedenborgians repeat, with great rhetorical skill, their master's assertion that married life in heaven will include carnal joys.

Despite such peculiarities, nineteenth-century popular literature on heaven conveys the impression of a vague yet perceptible consensus. Both theological and popular authors emphasized the social enjoyments of heaven as well as its domestic nature: friends and relatives would be reunited, mothers would find their lost children, wives their husbands - and so on. Some of the more daring authors, including the Anglican bishop Mant and the French Jesuit Blot, suggested that the marriage bond would continue beyond the grave. The New Testament assertion that there would be no "marrying and being given in marriage" in heaven, was given rather doubtful new meanings. Conjugal love conquered the biblical text.[20]

The divine center, so prominent in the Puritan concept of the other world, was also modified. In the final analysis, people were less interested in meeting God or Jesus than in being reunited with their lost parents, children, or spouses. "As you know," mused John Beecher in a letter, "to me Heaven is where Father and Mother and Aunt Esther are, rather than or I should say, more than where God is. For God is here, they are not."[21] Heaven has become anthropocentric - man-centered rather than God-centered, and thus as un-Puritan as conceivable. For nineteenth-century spiritualists and liberal Christians, heaven could be without God, but certainly not be without deceased friends. Father, mother and aunt Esther can even replace the divine. "God, as fearsome judge," explains the historian Laurence Moore with tongue in cheek, "abdicated the role of public enforcer of morality to an assorted set of relatives and human dignitaries hovering about sixty miles out beyond the earth's atmosphere."[22] There is more truth in this arrogant caricature than we would expect.

From Colonial Gift-Giving to Sacrifice for the Dead

The death of a child or a stranger may go almost unnoticed. The death of an adult, however, upsets the balance of family life, rents the social fabric, and disrupts the order of a community. Samuel Willard, a prominent Puritan divine of the seventeenth century, heaps biblical metaphor upon metaphor when lamenting the death of a friend. "When the pillars are gone," he says, "how shall the building stand? When the watch-men are asleep, who shall descry, and warn us of the enemy's approach? When the wall is plucked down, and the hedge is removed, who shall keep the boar of the wilderness?" - and there are three more biblical metaphors to follow, all illustrating the experience of loss and unsheltered exposure to danger.[23]

The damage done by a death must be carefully repaired. In colonial New-England society, this "repair" involved ritual activities that did in no way reflect the spirit of simplicity and frugality that one might expect. More than once sumptuary laws attempted to restrict funeral expenditures because they were held responsible for the "impoverising of many families."[24] Even in the cases of the wealthiest individuals, it was not uncommon for the funeral expenses to consume twenty per cent of the deceased's estate.[25] What, then, was so expensive? The early American's funeral bill did not come from the undertaker but from the tailor and the goldsmith. Upon the death of a family member, colonial Americans sent scarves or gloves to friends and acquaintances, both men and women, as a gesture of invitation to the funeral. The number of such invitations often ran into the hundreds. Since ministers were always invited to funerals, most of them acquired enormous quantities of gloves. One minister reputedly maintained a record of the gloves he was sent, and in thirty-two years collected close to three thousand pairs. He finally sold them for the equivalent of seven hundred dollars.[26] People who attended the funeral would wear the gloves or scarves that accompanied the invitation.

After the interment, the members of the procession returned to the church or the house of the deceased where they feasted. They also received funeral rings to mark their esteemed attendance. As was the case with the invitational gloves, the rings accumulated. Samuel Sewall in time acquired almost threescore of them, and we know of individuals who left their heirs tankards full of such rings. The rings were fashioned of gold and were often inlaid with delicately carved black enamel death's heads, skeletons, coffins, and other reminders of the frailty of life. The ring itself, however, retained its standard meaning as a symbol of union - of union with the bereaved family.

Like any gift we give for birthdays or Christmas, the giving of costly rings and gloves is meant to create or cement social ties. The disruption caused by death was to be repaired. Far from being simple tokens of invitation and attendance, these gifts invite reciprocity. Everyone who attended the funeral should be indebted, at least symbolically, to the mourning family and must give back benefits. At the death of one of its members, the family invested in a ritual creation or re-creation of social ties. By giving gifts, the social solidarity should be restored.

While the giving of gloves continued well into the nineteenth century, it disappeared in the twentieth. Now the family arranging for a funeral no longer engages in the distribution of symbolic gifts. This disappearance is only part of a whole new set of ideas. Now people prefer private funerals in which only a small circle of family and relatives participate. The custom of wearing mourning garb also disappeared. Mourners, especially women, no longer appeal to a wider public by making their grief visible.[27]

The new style in funeral custom is not less expensive than the earlier colonial burial. What is different, however, is the recipient of the gifts. Gifts, formerly distributed in the surviving community, are now lavished upon the deceased person. Flowers increasingly invade the ritual. When the noted liberal theologian Henry Beecher died in 1887, his casket lay buried "in a mound of blossoms."[28] Funeral directors as well as florists were quick to exploit the new possibilities of business. Flowers, bouquets, and wreaths have soon become a regular feature of burials. Other gifts given to the deceased are both more enduring and more expensive: the burial plot or vault as well as the gravestone or any other form of monument. The dead person is worshiped at a shrine belonging to him or her. "The final rites, memorial tributes, the hallowed pageant of the funeral service," explained a Symposion on Sentiment, sponsored by the Society of American Florists, "all speak for the dignity of man ... Memorialization is love. It records a love so strong, so happy, so enduring that it can never die. It is the recognition of the immortality of the human spirit, the rightful reverence earned by a good life. It is the final testimony of the dignity of man."[29]

Thus worshiped, the deceased and dignified human person has become divine like an ancestor of native religions. As a shrine, the grave is religiously visited even by people of no religious persuasion. In the words of the late Philippe Aries, now an ancestor himself: "Those who no longer go to church, still go to the cemetery."[30] The most religious people of the world, some seventy per cent of the Americans believe in life after death.[31] They worship their dead – at least by respectfully paying the bill they get from the funeral director.

NOTES

[1] Jessica Mitford, The American Way of Death (Greenwich, Conn.: Fawcett, 1964). Original ed. published in 1963.

[2] Allen I. Ludwig, Graven Images: New England Stonecarving and Its Symbols 1650-1815 (Middleton, Conn.: Wesleyan University Press, 1966), p. 54; Gordon E. Geddes, Welcome Joy: Death in Puritan New England (Ann Arbor, Mich.: UMI Research Press, 1981), pp. 133, 145-147.

[3] Cf. note 2.

[4] James J. Farrell, Inventing the American Way of Death, 1830-1920 (Philadelphia: Temple University Press, 1980), pp. 99-113.

[5] Perceval E. Jackson, The Law of Cadavers and of Burial and Burial Places (New York: Prentice-Hall, 1936), p. 116.

[6] West Laurel Hill Cemetery, Philadelphia: Description and Regulations, ed. Office of the West Laurel Hill Cemetery Company, 11th ed. (Philadelphia, Penn.: Office of the Company, 1887), p. 17.

[7] Guide to Laurel Hill Cemetery Near Philadelphia (Philadelphia, Penn.: Treasurer of the Cemetery, 1851), pp. 43f.

[8] Guide to Laurel Hill Cemetery, pp. 15f.

[9] Adolphus Strauch, Spring Grove Cemetery (Cincinnati: Robert Clarke, 1869), p. 9.

[10] The New England Primer, 1727, ed. Paul L. Ford (New York: Dodd, Mead & Co., 1899) – facsimile reprint without pagination.

[11] Dickran Tashjihan and Ann Tashjihan, Memorials for Children of Change. The Art of Early New England Stonecarving (Middleton, Conn.: Wesleyan University Press, 1974), p. 279.

[12] David H. Watters, With Bodilie Eyes: Eschatological Themes in Puritan Literature and Gravestone Art (Ann Arbor, Mich.: UMI Research Press, 1981), p. 110.

[13] Michel Vovelle, "A Century and One-Half of American Epitaphs 1660-1813," Comparative Studies in Society and History 22 (1980), 534-547.

[14] Edwin Dethlefsen and James Deetz, "Death's Heads, Cherubs, and Willow Trees: Experimental Archaeology in Colonial Cemeteries," American Antiquity 31 (1965/66), 502-510.

[15] Cf. Edward Shorter, The Making of the Modern Family (New York: Basic Books, 1975).

[16] Timothy Alden, A Collection of American Epitaphs and Inscriptions, 5 vols. (New York: J. Seymour, 1814), no. 974.

[17] Ibid., no. 618.

[18] "On the Future Life of the Good," The Christian Examiner 1 (1824), 350-357 (without author).

[19] Cf. Marie Caskey, Chariot of Fire: Religion and the Beecher Family (New Haven: Yale University Press, 1978), pp. 249-302; Ann Douglas, "Heaven Our Home: Consolation Literature in the Northern United States 1830-1880," in Death in America, ed. David E. Stannard (Philadelphia, Penn.: University of Pennsylvania Press, 1975), pp. 49-68.

[20] Cf. Luke 20: 34-36: "And Jesus said to them, The sons of this age marry and are given in marriage; but those who are accounted worthy to attain to that age and to the resurrection from the dead neither marry nor are given in marriage ... because they are equal to angels." (Revised Standard Version)

[21] Caskey, Chariot of Fire, pp. 290f.

[22] R. Laurence Moore, In Search of White Crows: Spiritualism, Parapsychology, and American Culture (New York: Oxford University Press, 1977), p. 60.

[23] David H. Stannard, The Puritan Way of Death (New York: Oxford University Press, 1977), p. 130.

[24] Ibid., p. 129.

[25] Ibid., p. 113.

[26] Ibid., p. 112.

[27] Farrell, _Inventing the American Way of Death_, pp. 180f.

[28] Ibid., p. 82.

[29] Mitford, _The American Way of Death_, p. 86.

[30] Philippe Aries, _Western Attitudes toward Death_ (Baltimore: Johns Hopkins University Press, 1974), p. 73.

[31] Cf. Andrew Greeley, _Death and Beyond_ (Chicago, Ill.: Thomas More Press, 1976), pp. 58-72; George Gallup and William Proctor, _Adventures in Immortality_ (London: Transworld Publishers, 1982).

Bill J. Leonard

Southern Baptists and Southern Culture: A Contemporary Dilemma

During the late 1970's, historian Martin E. Marty described the Southern Baptist Convention as one of the most "intact" Protestant subcultures in contemporary America. This intactness meant that a religious group exercised continuity with its past, and provided a unifying sense of identity for its constituents. In Marty's words, it revealed "regularities of behavior and consistent norms for evaluation."[1] Intactness provided Southern Baptists with a denominational stability which many mainline groups had been unable to sustain.

Marty also insisted that this distinct Southern Baptist identity was so closely linked with Southern identity that it was possible to describe the convention as "the Catholic church of the South."[2] Not only did Southern Baptists represent the de facto "established" church of the South, but under the huge umbrella of denominational unity there was great diversity of theology and practice. Within the cultural security of Southernness, was a theological/spiritual unity based on "the primacy of experience in religion."[3] Generally speaking, therefore, the diverse elements of America's largest Protestant denomination were held together by common cultural, organizational, and religious experiences.

Marty was correct in his evaluation of Southern Baptist intactness, at least for a moment. Yet almost simultaneously with the publication of his analysis, forces long present within the convention developed a prominence which threatened to destroy the uneasy alliance of culture and experience which for years had kept the denomination intact. It began with the effort of right wing/fundamentalist elements to gain control of convention boards and agencies. Through the election of convention presidents sympathetic to their cause, these fundamentalists hoped to use the appointive power of that office in securing their goals. Disturbed by what they believed to be the leftward drift of denominational institutions and emboldened by the impact of other new political/religious right forces in the nation, they sought to turn the convention toward a particular doctrinal uniformity which they believed to be "historically Baptist." As so-called denominational "moderates" reacted to this effort, the convention has become increasingly factionalized over questions of what actually constitutes "historic Baptist doctrine."[4]

There is no question that Southern Baptists are facing a crisis in their denominational life. The thesis of this essay is that while theological tensions must not be overlooked, they must be viewed as symptoms of a wider and more complex identity crisis in both the denomination and the culture. It suggests that the Southern Baptist convention formed a denominational unity based less on elaborate theological uniformity than on denominational and Southern identity. As cultural pluralism challenges the remaining myth of Southernness and religious pluralism presents new alternatives to denominational programs, an identity crisis is bound to occur. Theological debates must be understood in light of cultural and organizational disfunction. Questions of theology cannot be separated from parallel issues of cultural and denominational instability.

The relationship between church and culture is an increasingly important topic for scholars of American religion. Numerous studies have recently examined that relationship in the South. Many turn for definition to Clifford Geertz's now classic work, The Interpretation of Cultures, and the idea that culture "denotes an historically transmitted pattern of meanings embodied in symbols, a system of inherited conceptions expressed in symbolic forms by means of which men communicate, perpetuate, and develop their knowledge about and attitudes toward life."[5] Through culture a people establishes norms for behavior, values, meaning, and other aspects of common life. As M. J. Herskovits writes, "a society is composed of people; the way they behave is their culture."[6]

Geertz's belief that culture patterns are transmitted by means of symbols or myths is extremely important in an analysis of Southern religion. For it is by means of common symbols/myths that diverse, highly pluralistic segments of the South were united. Through cultural symbols Southerners developed a means for combining the collective data of their existence. Myths were a way of defining the whole identity of the Southern people. The issue is not whether details of the myths were entirely factual, but whether they became an effective, and in that sense true, way of defining collective existence. As Mark Shorer suggested, "a myth is a large, controlling image that gives philosophical meaning to the facts of ordinary life; that is, which has organizing value for experience."[7] Through its myths a society gives meaning to the actual empirical events of its history. Those myths thus provide cultural identity and are perpetuated by the culture they help define. The American South has been one region where myths and symbols have provided a major source of cultural unity and security. Paul Gaston writes, "what does distinguish the South, at least from other parts of the United States, is the degree to which myths have been spawned and the extent to which they have asserted their hegemony over the Southern mind."[8]

The significance of myth in defining the nature of Southern culture is illustrated in Charles R. Wilson's recent work, Baptized in Blood, The Religion of the Lost Cause, 1865-1920. Wilson shows how Southern churches utilized the myth of The Lost Cause – the idealization of the Southern heritage even in defeat – to rebuild the South's spiritual and moral identity following the Civil War. In an effort to help a vanquished people overcome their despair, Southern churchmen provided a theological explanation for secular and political events. Wilson writes that Southern ministers "saw little difference between their religious and cultural values, and they promoted the link by constructing Lost Cause ritualistic forms that celebrated their regional, mythological and theological beliefs."[9] What was the great Southern myth: the people who had lost the war retained the vision. Even in defeat Southern regionalists would demonstrate greater piety and deeper spirituality than their Northern conquerers. For Wilson's purposes, the actual events of defeat were less important than the way in which they became symbols of and for Southern culture.

Baptized in Blood represents but one effort on the part of recent historians to demonstrate the powerful relationship between Southern religion and culture. Certainly it is dangerous to generalize about the cultural and religious homogeneity of an entire region, even the South. W. J. Cash's famous work, The Mind of the South, is a case in point. Cash generalized provocatively about the Southern "mind" but not without over-stepping his bounds or failing to acknowledge significant exceptions to his theses.[10] This brief analysis is no less prone to similar generalizations. They are made with caution. Nonetheless, it does suggest that a distinct Southern culture did exist, and that it is in a state of transition. Current tensions within the Southern Baptist Convention, that denomination most identified with Southern culture, illustrate the dilemma of an institution caught in the midst of cultural upheaval. Southern Baptist controversies - institutional, theological, and ideological - cannot be understood apart from a consideration of Southern culture.

The intricate relationship between cultural and religious forces in the South continues to be a prominent theme of historical studies. In discussing the antebellum South, Donald Mathews suggested that "religion and the American South are fused in our historical imagination in an indelible, but amorphous way."[11] Mathews observed that evangelical religion enabled both blacks and whites to understand their place in Southern culture. Each appropriated a religious experience which provided adherents with "a sense of personal esteem and liberty."[12] Mathews insisted that even before the Civil War, Southern religion was closely identified with "social solidarity." Thus church attendance was both a "religious act" and "a civic responsibility."[13]

Liston Pope, in the well known sociological analysis, Millhands and Preachers, published in 1942, contended that Southern churches were among the most powerful social forces in continuing a spirit of isolation and "idealizing antebellum civilization."[14] Samuel Hill, Jr., whose numerous works on the South have made him a major analyst of that culture, insists that the "religion of the Southern people and their culture have been linked by the tightest bonds. That culture, particularly in its moral aspects, could not have survived without a legitimating impetus provided by religion ... For the South to stand its people had to be religious and its churches the purest anywhere."[15] As Southerners struggled with their identity following the Civil War and the humiliation of Reconstruction, Southern Baptists set themselves to the task of reclaiming their region and distinguishing themselves from the separated brethren in the North. The distinctiveness was characterized by close identification with Southern culture and the development of a denominational program.

The late John Lee Eighmy acknowledged that during the first sixty years of its history, the Southern Baptist Convention "assumed the role of a cultural establishment by sanctifying a secular order devoted to states' rights, white supremacy, laissez faire economics, and property rights."[16] Eighmy believed that Southern churches were in cultural captivity since they required a consensus of distinct values which validated their existence as a separate body from Northern Baptists.[17] Eighmy concluded that while elements of the social gospel philosophy were present in the SBC, they were not the dominant theological force. Rather, a majority of Southern Baptists focused attention on individualistic issues of personal conversion and morality, not on the corporate sins of the Southern society. In the epilogue to Eighmy's work, Samuel Hill observed that Baptist evangelical individualism served as a way of preserving and perpetuating certain qualities of Southern culture. He called this "a primary means of preserving the region's cultural unity." He further suggested that

> In the process of holding on to the individualistic theology of saving souls, the churches have served, usually unwittingly as agents of [social] reinforcement. This has been the case because both Christianity and Southernness have been effective frameworks of meaning – cultural symbols for communicating, perpetuating, and developing knowledge and attitudes. 18

Eighmy's study does show that the SBC was influenced by the Social Gospel in the early twentieth century and that questions over the corporate and personal implications of evangelism were represented in segments of the denomination.[19] These diverse approaches have become more pronounced as the convention has become more pluralistic.

Other scholars agreed with Eighmy that Southernness was a significant factor in determining Baptist response to social issues. Rufus Spain observed that Southern Baptists were limited in their social awareness in part because of their "intensely 'Southern' outlook." He concluded that "Northern-born social Christianity had first to overcome Southern sectionalism before it could find acceptance among Southern Baptists."[20] Even in matters of personal morality about which Southern Baptists were outspoken, they continued to reflect the existing mores of Southern culture. Spain claimed that Baptist "significance in Southern life consisted not in their power to mold their environment to conform to their standards. Rather their importance as a social force was in supporting and perpetuating the standard of the society at large."[21]

Southern Baptist identification with Southern society developed alongside another important source of identity, the denomination. This denominational consciousness provided an increasing sense of unity and uniqueness for churches affiliated with the SBC. It served to distinguish Southern Baptists from their northern counterparts and from other more "independent" Baptists in the Southland. Indeed, the first one hundred years of the convention's history, give evidence of the steady growth of a powerful denominationalism.

The seeds of that denominationalism were present from the beginning. Southerners rejected the Northern Baptist "society" approach to denominational endeavors in favor of a more centralized order in which agencies and boards were linked by an over-arching convention system. Each body retained an independent board of trustees, but appointments to those boards were made at the yearly meeting of the convention.

The convention constituted itself in 1845 for "directing the energies of the whole denomination in one sacred effort, for the propagation of the Gospel."[22] The denomination was seen as the means to accomplish that evangelical end. It was never to supersede the local congregation as the basic source of ecclesiastical authority. Nonetheless, the developing denominational program was a common denominator which united the diverse congregations across the South in a common endeavor, evangelism and missions. Churches which guarded their autonomy tenaciously were willing to participate in denominational cooperation in order to accomplish broader evangelical and missionary tasks which their limited resources could not provide. The denomination thus created a catholicity among certain Baptist churches in the South.

By the early twentieth century Baptist churches were increasingly characterized by distinct denominational programs accepted in varying degrees by local churches. Bible study literature, written by Southern Baptists, printed and circulated by the Southern Baptists Sunday School Board, created a "uniform lesson" for use in all the churches. This literature further served to separate Southern Baptists from independents who eschewed extra- Biblical commentaries. Mission boards which used funds collectively to send out and support missionaries were distinguished from non-Southern Baptist congregations which directly sponsored individual missionaries and frequently attacked boards as unbiblical.

Successful programs evident in local churches and in other denominations were "integrated into the organization and functions of the general body."[23] For example, the inter-denominational Laymen's Missionary Movement became a prototype for the Baptist Men's Movement in the South. While participating in the broader movement early on, Southern Baptists soon pulled away and began their own laymen's work which, by 1950, had evolved into the Brotherhood Commission of the SBC.

This mood was characteristic of Southern Baptist attitudes toward other groups - too much outside influence might weaken denominational consciousness. Early leaders of the denomination reflect this concern. J.B. Gambrell, Texas Baptist teacher and editor, warned in 1917 that "our most cherished beliefs, our deep sense of duty will not permit us to enter into any federation, or what not that would, in any way, obscure the position set out above, or hinder us in the full and fill preaching of the whole counsel of God to all the people of the world."[24]

Gambrell's own pilgrimage as pastor, teacher, and editor demonstrated another aspect of Southern Baptist denominational consciousness, the appearance of a group of professional organizers committed to denominational programs. These individuals played a major role in expanding organizational methods throughout local, state, and regional groups.[25] By the mid twentieth century Southern Baptist identity was increasingly "programmatic." In that way Baptists defined themselves in terms of institutional organization and stability.[26] Committed denominationalists sought to retain unity, to encourage compromise, and to keep the organization spiritually alert, financially solvent, and statistically successful.

Samuel Hill notes that by the 1950's and 60's, three "types" of leaders kept this unity alive. "Organizational men" kept programs updated and optional. Others stressed "spiritual" unity in common mission and discipleship. "Charismatic personages" utilized their powerful personalities to turn the convention from "potentially divisive issues" to unified endeavors.[27]

Denominational stability and uniformity combined with Southern culture to create a sense of "Southern-Baptistness" which held in balance theological and local diversity. Even with this organizational uniformity, however, there was a diversity in Southern Baptist life, historically, practically and to some extent theologically. Historical distinctives are evident in the presence of numerous traditions in the South, each legitimately Baptist, sharing common doctrines and dramatic differences. Early Baptist presence in the South has frequently been characterized in terms of the so-called Regular and Separate and Landmark Baptist traditions.

The Regulars were Calvinists who came from New England in the 1690s to found the First Baptist Church of Charleston and other churches in the deep South. Their congregations were warmly evangelical, though somewhat suspicious of the emotional excesses of revivalistic technique. Their worship services were simple but ordered, in the traditional Calvinistic pattern. They sang the psalms, preached the scripture, called for conversion and subscribed to the basic doctrines of the Westminster Confession. Their ministers were educated and erudite, many even numbered among the "gentlemen theologians" of the old South. The Regular Baptist tradition characterized numerous churches in the major population centers of the South.[28]

The Separate Baptist tradition was brought to the South in the 1750's, also to the Carolinas, in the establishment of the Sandy Creek Baptist Church. Founded by two revivalistic New Englanders, Shubal Stearns and Daniel Marshall, this church became the parent of over forty other congregations. Converted in the Congregational revivals of the First Great Awakening, Stearns and Marshall accepted Baptist views and revivalistic methods which were not acceptable to the more cautious Regulars. They separated from the Regulars and brought their brand of revivalistic religion onto the American frontier. Their church life was characterized by bold, enthusiastic preaching, spontaneity in worship, the use of simple gospel hymns, and an increasingly modified Calvinism with greater stress on the role of free will. Suspicious of education as inhibiting spiritual religion, these churches called preachers whose gifts of proclamation often excelled their educational qualifications. The Separate Baptist tradition flourished on the American frontier. Its activistic evangelicalism spread throughout Kentucky, Tennessee, Arkansas, and Texas, moving West with the population until by 1917, 13.49 per cent of all Southern Baptists were in Texas. This southwestern explosion is a continuing trend in the SBC, a trend more reflective of the Separate than the Regular Baptist orientation.[29]

Landmark Baptists suggested that Baptist churches stood in a line of succession throughout history to John the Baptist and Jesus in the Jordan River. This form of primitivism provided a history for a people who rejected traditions and desperately needed an identity

in the churches to complement the wasteland of frontier denominationalism. Baptists alone believed they possessed the qualities of
the New Testament Church - all other groups were mere "Societies."

In addition to this historical diversity, Southern Baptists have
increasingly demonstrated theological division over the individual
and social implications of the gospel. John Lee Eighmy showed that
the Social Gospel movement did have a limited impact on segments of
the convention and frequently came in conflict with the individualistic approach. The latter groups stressed the church's primary call
as evangelizing individuals and, in Eighmy's view, "usually upheld
the values of the existing social order."[30] The former emphasized the
church's responsibility to address corporate issues of sin. As such,
Eighmy believed, it destroyed the theological "uniformity" of Southern
Baptist social thought.[31]

These differing, often opposing traditions, were held in check, I
would suggest, by a powerful union of Southern culture and Southern
Baptist denominationalism. As the culture and the denomination
became more pluralistic, the scene was set for a theological
confrontation between factions of the convention.

Historians have documented the decline and fall of the Solid
South since the end of the Civil War. Most of them were correct in
their assessment of the powerful social pressures confronting Southern
culture. They were less astute in tracing the chronology of this
decline.[32] A new generation of historians and sociologists have found
increasing evidence for the dissolution of Southern culture during the
last two decades.

C. Vann Woodward wrote in 1960, "the time is coming, if indeed
it is not already arrived, when the Southerner will begin to ask
himself whether there is really any longer much point in calling
himself a Southerner."[33] Woodward described the South in terms of a
cultural revolution which would affect all of its major institutions.
As regional distinctives disappeared, a cultural vacuum was created.
Typically Southern "faults" - share cropper agriculture, one party
politics, Jim Crow laws - were being replaced with less distinctive
faults common to other regions of the American nation.[34] Likewise,

typically Southern values were confronting the values of a more pluralistic nation. Thus Woodward wrote of the Southerner: "Bereft of his myths, his peculiar institutions, even his familiar regional vices, he may well reject or forget his regional identification as completely as the immigrant."[35]

Southern Baptists, so closely identified with southernness, could not escape the cultural crisis of the region. Many of the pluralistic influences which created a crisis in regional identity had a similar impact on denominational self-consciousness.

In 1960, Samuel Hill noted that the forces of the "Southern regional faith and culture" had long influenced each other, but new cultural disruptions were driving a "formidable wedge" between the two. Thus Hill concluded that "the future may well seem ominous to a conservative and culturally pampered institution as its confronts a new social order and climate of opinion."[36]

Hill was correct, and disruptions in the SBC during the last twenty years illustrate the truth of his analysis. Increasingly, the denomination as a source of unity and stability has been called into question.

Southern Baptists have maintained a lovers' quarrel with their denomination almost from the beginning. Given their fierce individualism and local church autonomy, it is amazing that denominational loyalty has prevailed at all. Disputes over mission boards, cooperative financial programs, socio/political positions taken by denominational agencies, and the bureaucratic nature of the convention organization have evoked criticism from all segments of denominational life. Yet throughout its history the convention has avoided a major schism. Why? Because, says historian Walter B. Shurden, Southern Baptists were willing to live with compromise, even contradiction, since "denominational unity is more important to most Southern Baptists than theological arguments ..."[37]

The early denomination-builders did their work well. They communicated a sense of "programmatic" denominational identity as the means by which a diverse people accomplished the gospel goals of evangelism and mission. Indeed, most Southern Baptists came to believe the claim that they represented "the last hope, the fairest hope, the only hope for evangelizing this world on New Testament principles ..."[38]

This sense of loyalty has disturbed ideologists on the right and the left who insist that Southern Baptists seem less concerned for Truth than for denominational unity. Rather, Shurden suggests, such unity permitted a broader search for truth beyond the confines or narrow ideologies and creedalistic dogmatism.[39] Increasing assaults from the right and the left, coupled with growing pluralism in the denominational programs, have served to weaken the fragile consensus of the convention.

During the civil rights movement of the 1960's and 70's, for example, those Baptists influenced by the social gospel dimension of Christianity frequently criticized the convention's failure to respond with prophetic indignation to the battle for human rights. They saw the denomination as equivocating on issues of racial justice as it had on slavery years before. In order to protect its assets, its programs, and its corporate life, the SBC thus gave minimal or indifferent response to crises which were dividing the nation.

By the 1970's and 80's fundamentalists in Southern Baptist ranks were singing the same song over different issues. The convention, its boards and bureaucrats, was compromising theological truth - namely biblical inerrancy - for the sake of denominational solidarity. So an increasing number of charismatic and articulate preachers denounced any denominational unity which obscured theological orthodoxy. As one recent leader insisted, the denomination was merely the "net" used for catching fish (converts) and when the net is dirty with liberalism it must be cleaned and liberals purged.[40] Compromise necessary to maintain denominational diversity was denounced as equivocation from orthodox truth. Thus knowingly or unknowingly, the fragile nature of denominational unity was threatened by the need for ideological uniformity or social responsibility.

At the same time, denominational programs became more pluralistic in an effort to appeal to an increasingly diverse constituency. Programmatic uniformity was less regimented as churches exercised broader options for incorporating Southern Baptist organization to local concerns and ideological positions.

Such flexibility was always present but denominational loyalty was long fostered by efforts at defining the true Southern Baptist church as one which manifested the total denominational program. Special recognition was given to those churches which maintained the most "standardized" programs. Recent trends, however, indicate the gradual but steady decline of many classic programs and organizations - Church Training, Brotherhood, Woman's Missionary Union, and even Sunday School.[41] Likewise, certain large mega-churches, many displeased with the "liberalism" of denominational literature and programs, have opted for their own literature, methods and ministries apart from convention related programs and materials.

Pluralism of programs has raised questions as to what actually constitutes a Southern Baptist Church. Currently a congregation which gives a minimum of $ 250.00 to the Cooperative Program, that collective method for funding convention institutions, is entitled to a maximum of ten messengers at the annual meeting. Some churches give only the minimum money, withholding funds often as protest against the policies of agencies and institutions. This has led to efforts, hitherto unsuccessful, to require that a certain percentage of the church's budget be given to the Cooperative Program. Fundamentalists demand the right to designate funds to those programs they deem orthodox. Such efforts clearly serve to weaken denominational identity and loyalty from within.

The pluralism of American life tends to weaken denominational loyalties from without. As the South loses its traditional identity, as it is invaded by outsiders, and as Southern Baptists expand outside the South, pluralism of belief and experience is bound to occur. Since the 1950's Southern Baptists have taken their faith to so-called "pioneer" areas beyond the South. Often these efforts were begun by transplanted Southerners who wanted a little piece of Alabama or Texas to provide security in the backside of the American desert (Chicago, New York, or Boston). As these churches evangelized the "natives," however, persons became Southern Baptist who had never been south of the George Washington Bridge. They did not, many denominationalists lamented, understand the need to do things the way they were done in the "Baptist Zion" of the South. Southernness in outlook and program again confronted pluralism.

Likewise, Southern Baptist youth in increasing numbers disregarded the warnings of their elders and married persons "outside the faith." (That did not mean Moslems, it meant Methodists.) This serious sociological phenomenon brought persons into the denomination who had not been raised Southern Baptist, or even Southern. Many were not pleased when re-baptism was required of them. Others questioned the rationale behind organizational practices which many of the faithful accepted as both Baptist and biblical. Pluralism again created a crisis in Baptist denominational identity.

With the breakdown of cultural and denominational restraints, theological tensions long present in Southern Baptist life have become increasingly pronounced. In response to denominational and cultural pluralism, many church leaders urge the convention to unite around "historic Baptist doctrines." Given the diversity of Baptist theological traditions, precise doctrinal definitions are difficult to construct. In many debates, both sides can claim to represent the historic Baptist position with some validity. Even the briefest survey illustrates the dilemma.

Confessionalism and Soul Liberty

Southern Baptist utilize a Confession of Faith, approved in 1963, as a basic statement of doctrine. It reflects the modified Calvinism of the earlier New Hampshire Confession of 1833. Within its broad framework, however, there has been room for diverse theories of scripture, atonement, eschatology and conversion. Likewise, the preamble to the confession contains that historic Baptist creedal disclaimer, the ultimate authority of Scripture and conscience over "man made" confessions. As Southern Baptists divide over confessional/creedal uniformity and soul liberty they often may claim history on either side.

Conversionism and Christian Nurture

The need for individual regeneration has long been a hallmark of Southern Baptist evangelical concerns. The church is to be composed of believers who have made the appropriate profession of faith at an age when moral judgments can be recognized. Southern Baptists demand that decision of all who would belong to a Baptist church. Yet as a nurturing people, Baptists have also stressed the importance of training children in the faith. This means that the baptismal age has been lowered considerably over the years and that conversion has frequently been seen as process as well as dramatic event. Some see no contradiction in these two ideas since nurtured children will eventually have a conversion experience. Others, however, note the tendency of more Baptist youth to profess faith in pre-teen, even pre-school years, as indicative of some confusion over the nature of conversion, the appropriate time and candidate. Conversionists and nurturers can both claim to represent the classic doctrine of the convention.

Biblical Literalism and Pietistic Spirituality

Southern Baptists have always described themselves as "people of the Book," bound together by the teaching of Holy Scripture. Bible study, Bible preaching and Bible living were essential elements of their faith. In their ethical teaching and doctrinal pronouncements they sound like biblical literalists on the order of the slogan "the Bible says it, I believe it, and that settles it." At the same time, they were also pietists, concerned with heart religion and personal spirituality. So they could say with traditional pietists that the issue is less what you believe about Scripture, than whether the truths of Scripture are at work in you. This pietistic spirituality often makes Baptists sound more concerned for experiential uniformity than doctrinal uniformity. Literalists and pietists may appeal equally to Baptist heritage.

Calvinism and Arminianism

We have already noted that the Calvinistic tradition of the Regulars and the more Arminian tradition of the Separates were both present among early Baptists in the American South. Southern Baptists have tended to use the language of Calvinism - election, purification, foreknowledge, depravity, Sovereignty, etc. - but to define those terms from a decidedly Arminian perspective - free will, repentance and faith, general atonement, prevenient grace. In reality most Southern Baptists tend to be Arminian on every major doctrine except perseverance of the saints. Nonetheless, this modified Calvinism/Arminianism has meant that ideologues of both theological perspectives could claim Baptist doctrine as consistent with their own.

Church and Sect

This brief survey of theological tensions, indeed inconsistencies, among Southern Baptists illustrates the difficulty of trying to retain denominational unity by means of doctrinal uniformity. In a sense, the SBC is a denomination which preaches like a sect but acts like a church. Over the years it has moved to a via media, a middle way between the sectarian effort to escape the cultural and the churchly effort to dominate it. If the denomination and the culture can no longer hold those forces in check, there seems little way to avoid schism as factions divide over sectarian and churchly expressions of the gospel.

Thus the contemporary dilemma. Southern Baptists are confronting a dual identity crisis. They are living in a day when it is increasingly difficult to determine what it means to be Southern and what it means to be Baptist. Both elements which have given uneasy but powerful unity to a collection of diverse and autonomous congregations are being called into question. It is no wonder that Southern Baptists are searching for new ways to define themselves and their movement. What, the historian asks, might be the alternatives?

First, convention leaders may continue to act as if cultural and denominational forces are still intact, naively believing that current controversies can be neutralized by that compromise and inertia inherent in denominational machinery. They may attempt traditional methods for uniting the faithful with nebulous slogans and watchwords, refusing to confront the reality of denominational identity crisis and impending schism.

Second, the denomination may experience schism - more probably fragmentation. As ideologists on the right gain increasing control of convention agencies and seek to impose varying degrees of theological uniformity, fragmentation becomes increasingly inevitable. If they fail in their efforts, they may be forced to withdraw from the SBC. As existing pluralism of doctrine and practice becomes less acceptable, there may be less room for those individuals, churches and agencies which refuse to conform. Given the fragile unity of the denomination and the diverse polity of the churches, there is no way to predict the course which schism might take. Clearly, any schism would mean the loss and/or reorganization of existing institutions, missionary efforts and other benevolent concerns.

Third, given enough time, and thus the defusing of present tensions is imperative, the convention might seek to develop a new denominationalism which allows for that classic unity in diversity characteristic of Southern Baptists. It might seek to "remythologize" its traditions as a denomination of theological integrity but doctrinal diversity responding to cultural transitions while retaining the best of its Southern heritage. It might then re-evaluate its motives for evangelism and mission, its current captivity to aspects of American culture, and the significance of its "evangelical catholicity" for the entire Body of Christ. It would also pursue a "new pluralism" by which a people bound by certain biblical imperatives might allow for diverse practical, even theological, approaches to the evangelical and communal calling of the Church of Jesus Christ.

NOTES

[1] Martin E. Marty, "The Protestant Experience and Perspectives," in American Religious Values and the Future of America (Philadelphia: Fortress Press, 1978), p. 40.

[2] Ibid., p. 46.

[3] Ibid., p. 47.

[4] Richard Maurius, "The War Between the Baptists," Esquire (December 1981), pp. 46-55; Missouri Word and Way (October 2, 1980); and Virginia Religious Herald (September 18, 1980).

[5] Clifford Geertz, The Interpretation of Cultures (New York: Basic Books, Inc., 1973), p. 89. Such studies include Samuel S. Hill, Jr., Religion and the Solid South (Nashville: Abingdon, 1972); Hill, Southern Churches in Crisis (Boston: Beacon Press, 1966); John Lee Eighmy, Churches in Cultural Captivity (Knoxville: University of Tennessee Press, 1976); and Charles R. Wilson, Baptized in Blood, The Religion of the Lost Cause, 1865-1920 (Athens, GA: University of Georgia Press, 1980).

[6] Marty, "The Protestant Experience and Perspective," p. 33, citing Philip Bagby, Culture and History: Prolegomena to the Comparative Study of Civilizations (Berkeley: University of California, 1963), pp. 84, 104-5.

[7] Mark Shorer, "The Necessity for Myth," in Henry A. Murray (ed.) Myth to Matchmakers (New York: 1960), p. 355, cited in Patrick Gerster and Nicholas Cord, Myth and Southern History: The Old South (Chicago: Rand McNally, 1974), p. 2.

[8] Paul M. Gaston, The New South Creed: A Study in Southern Mythmaking (New York: 1970), p. 8, cited in Gerster and Cord, Myth and Southern History, p. xv.

[9] Charles R. Wilson, Baptized in Blood, The Religion of the Lost Cause, 1865-1920 (Athens, GA: University of Georgia Press, 1980), p. 11.

[10] W.J. Cash, The Mind of the South (New York: Vintage Books, 1941); and C. Vann Woodward, "W.J. Cash Reconsidered," The New York Review of Books (December 4, 1969), pp. 28-34.

[11] Donald G. Mathews, Religion in the Old South (Chicago: University of Chicago Press, 1977), p. xiii.

[12] Ibid., p. xv.

[13] Ibid., p. 249; and Samuel S. Hill, Jr., The South and the North in American Religion (Athens, GA: The University of Georgia Press, 1980), p. 7.

[14] Liston Pope, _Millhands and Preachers_ (New Haven: Yale University Press), p. 34.

[15] Samuel S. Hill, Jr., _Religion and the Solid South_ (Nashville: Abingdon, 1972), p. 36; and Wilson, _Baptized in Blood_, p. 7.

[16] John Lee Eighmy, _Churches in Cultural Captivity_ (Knoxville: University of Tennessee Press, 1976), p. x.

[17] _Ibid._, pp. 75, 94, and Wilson, _Baptized in Blood_, p. 10.

[18] _Ibid._, p. 202.

[19] _Ibid._, pp. x-xi.

[20] Rufus Spain, _At Ease in Zion_ (Nashville: Vanderbilt University Press, 1961), p. 211.

[21] _Ibid._, p. 214.

[22] Robert A. Baker, _A Baptist Source Book_ (Nashville: Broadman Press, 1966), p. 116.

[23] Robert A. Baker, _The Southern Baptist Convention and Its People, 1607-1972_ (Nashville: Broadman Press, 1974), p. 345.

[24] J.B. Gambrell, "Christian Union," in _Parable and Precept_ (New York: Fleming H. Revell, 1917), p. 176.

[25] Baker, _The SBC and Its People_, pp. 346-7.

[26] _Ibid._, p. 357, citing Blake Smith, "The Southern Baptist 'Invasion': Right or Wrong?" _Foundations_ (October 1959), pp. 324-25.

[27] Eighmy, _Churches in Cultural Captivity_, p. 206.

[28] Walter B. Shurden, "The Southern Baptist Synthesis: Is it Cracking?," in the 1980-81 Carver Barnes Lectures, published by Southeastern Baptist Theological Seminary, 1981, pp. 5-6. Shurden notes the presence of other regional traditions in SBC life. The two I mention merely illustrate the broad diversity of Baptist beginnings in the South.

[29] _Ibid._, and Baker, _The SBC and its People_, pp. 316-18, 320-26.

[30] Eighmy, _Churches in Cultural Captivity_, p. x.

[31] _Ibid._, pp. x-xi.

[32] Charles P. Roland, "The Ever-Vanishing South," _The Journal of Southern History_ (February 1982), pp. 3-20.

[33]C. Vann Woodward, _The Burden of Southern History_ (Baton Rouge: Louisiana State University Press, 1960), p. 3.

[34]_Ibid._, p. 5.

[35]_Ibid._, p. 15.

[36]Samuel S. Hill, Jr., _Southern Churches in Crisis_ (Boston: Beacon Press, 1966), p. xiii.

[37]Walter B. Shurden, "The Problem of Authority in the SBC," _Review and Expositor_ (Spring 1978), p. 225.

[38]Kenneth K. Bailey, _Southern White Protestantism in the Twentieth Century_ (New York: Harper & Row, 1964), pp. 153-54, citing _Birmingham Alabama Christian Advocate_ (June 29, 1948).

[39]Shurden, "The Problem of Authority in the SBC," pp. 226ff.

[40]Memphis, _Commercial Appeal_ (July 3, 1982), p. A10.

[41]_The Quarterly Review_ (July-September, 1980), pp. 8ff. These statistics are for the period 1970-1979.

John E. Martin

The Religious Spirit in the Poetry of Emily Dickinson and Theodore Roethke

Emily Dickinson and Theodore Roethke make strange bedfellows. What could a shy and retiring 19th century woman poet have in common with a blustering male poet of the 20th century? Dickinson withdrew from society to confine herself to the lonely task of a poet who, after an initial effort, refused to publish. Roethke sought the communication of the classroom and lecture circuit and was intent on achieving recognition for his poetic efforts. To choose religion as a unifying element seems hardly likely. Emily Dickinson was incapable of professing the formal religion of her environment and spent the rest of her life unaffiliated with the church.[1] Roethke's biographer provides no evidence of a connection between Roethke and organized religion.[2] Even Neal Bowers, in his intuitive study of mystical elements in Roethke's poetry, admits that "... Roethke was not a religious man, at least not in any orthodox sense."[3]

Nevertheless, the purpose of this paper is to show that "a religious spirit" pervades the poetry of both writers and can be seen as a common bond linking the unlikely pair. This religious spirit comprises a search for a deeper meaning in nature and self involving a mysterious opening to a transcendental Other. I will begin with Dickinson, then take up Roethke and finally add a brief conclusion.

Emily Dickinson

This section is concerned with a study of the religious spirit in a small number of Emily Dickinson's poems. At first sight this may appear quite strange, since the more standard approaches to Dickinson have been in terms of her cultural context, or her psychological difficulties or more recently from a feminist point of view.

Richard Chase in his fine, differentiated biography, insists: "We must begin, at least, with New England if we hope to gain a true perspective of the myth, the poet, and the poems."[4] He then studies her life and poetry against this cultural background. John Cody takes a psychoanalytic approach to Dickinson's life and poetry explaining the known phenomena of her life, such as her long seclusion in her father's house, or the non-publication of the vast majority of her poems, in terms of serious psychological disturbance.[5] Adrienne Rich, countering the psychoanalytic view, presents Dickinson's life and work as the only viable and healthy response of a remarkable, creative woman artist to a male dominant culture incapable of understanding and accepting her art.[6]

In reading a large number of the more than 1700 poems now available to us I began to feel that another perspective would add depth and unity to the approaches mentioned above. In spite of Dickinson's rejection of traditional Puritan Christianity, there pervades in her work an attitude toward nature, herself, and the world that can be seen as an opening to the other, to the uncanny, to the transcendent. It is this attitude that I call religious in the broadest sense.

Inder Nath Kher has taken a similar approach in The Landscape of Absence: Emily Dickinson's Poetry. He stresses the fact that Dickinson's poetry taken as a whole focuses on the human predicament and destiny and describes one of her unique gifts as follows. "She shows a remarkable ability to pierce the material world and discover in it the symbols of a spiritual reality."[7] Quoting Dickinson, Kher points out that the creative I in the poems is not primarily the actual biological, historical person but the creation of her poetic imagination.[8] It is not just Emily the woman, recluse, love-lorn, 19th century inheritor of a Puritan past, but the poetic genius shining through and transcending her own personal life who has such a brilliant insight into the nature of the universe and the extraordinary talent to impress this on the minds and hearts of her reading public through the uniqueness of her diction and imagery.

The poems to be analyzed have been chosen to bring out the various aspects of the religious approach mentioned above. The first poem illustrates her intense perception of nature in all its concreteness and her unique selection of details.

> The morns are meeker than they were -
> The nuts are getting brown -
> The berry's cheek is plumper -
> The Rose is out of town.
>
> The Maple wears a gayer scarf -
> The field a scarlet gown -
> Lest I sh'd be old fashioned
> I'll put a trinket on. 9 (12)

This quaint description of autumn first reflects the atmosphere of that time of year by the personification of the morning. "The morns are meeker than they were," reminding one of Keats' 'mellow fruitfulness,' not only describes the softness of an autumn morning in contrast to the brightness of summer, but suggests autumn's almost biblical acceptance of the gradual demise of power. The commonplace of the second line is followed by the remarkably imaginative picture of berries ripening. The unusual combination of the rose and out of town emphasizes the personification and completes the initial picture. An early poem, the first two lines of the second stanza do not come up to the creative uniqueness of those in the first, but the last two lines show at least that the lyrical narrator is herself involved in the natural progressions of the season. The poem is, of course, light in tone, but still mirrors Dickinson's sense of the concrete, uniqueness of vision and expression, and human involvement with nature.

The next poem introduces the reader to the cognitive power most essential for coming to grips with the transcendent: wonder.

> Wonder - is not precisely Knowing
> And not precisely Knowing not -
> A beautiful but bleak condition
> He has not lived who has not felt -
>
> Suspense - is his maturer Sister -
> Whether Adult Delight is Pain
> Or of itself a new misgiving -
> This is the Gnat that mangles man - (1331)

The sense of wonder at the existential condition man finds himself in is a "beautiful but bleak condition": beautiful because it opens man up to the possibility of going beyond his limited natural powers to understand the universe - he has not lived who has not felt this -, bleak, because one is left in the terror of standing before the mystery of life without complete understanding or assurance. Being in suspense about the ultimate meaning of life is "the Gnat that mangles man -."

Nevertheless to stand in wonder leads to vision, even if that vision is not perfect, or as St. Paul puts it: "... now we see in a mirror dimly."[10]

The following poem expresses the condition and quality of such vision.

> Our lives are Swiss -
> So still - so Cool -
> Till some odd afternoon
> The Alps neglect their Curtains
> And we look farther on!
>
> I t a l y stands the other side!
> While like a guard between -
> The solemn Alps -
> The siren Alps
> Forever intervene! (80)

The economy of this poem increases its impact. A compressed allegory, the poem makes use of three symbols, the Swiss, the alps and Italy. Into the calm unemotional routine of everyday life - the Swiss - comes a vision. It is unusual - some odd afternoon - and depends on something outside ourselves - the alps' neglect. We have caught a glimpse of Italy - the promised land, of warmth and love and fruitfulness. But our vision is incomplete. The alps' neglect is only partial. They stand solemnly, if temptingly, to prevent total vision and ultimate fulfillment.

A poem similar to the one above in some respects intensifies the moment of vision.

> The Soul's distinct connection
> With immortality
> Is best disclosed by Danger
> Or quick Calamity -

As Lightning on a Landscape
Exhibits Sheets of Place -
Not yet suspected - but for Flash -
And Click - and Suddenness. (974)

Most striking about this poem is the emphasis placed on the soul's present connection with immortality. Immortality in this poem is not viewed primarily as a state of eternal life in the future, but as an actual condition of the person here and now. It is only necessary to have the experience which can trigger this awareness, such as those of danger or calamity. The disclosure of the soul's connection with immortality - a state supremely transcending the normal course of life burdened with the seeds of death - is revealed most graphically by the simile of lightning. The flash and click and suddenness of lightning illuminates the unnoticed aspects of a landscape. The lightning opens reality unseen to vision in a moment of intensity. The lightning simile could also be applied to the function of Emily Dickinson's poems. Her best reveal insights into the depth of human experience with sudden simpleness - an image, symbol, simile or metaphor reenacts the profound human experience of insight into the meaning of human life as going beyond the ordinary, earth-bound routines, exposing the true nature of man caught between the temporal movement of his social role in history and his permanent spiritual self, transcending society and history - relating to immortality. The exact nature of that relationship and its ultimate meaning for man is never revealed completely in Dickinson's poems, but the existence of such a condition is brilliantly illuminated.

In poem 1001 Dickinson distinguishes between the form of life and life, between life unexamined and untried and life lived to fulfill ecstatic need. That life is more than limited, earthbound, self-bound immanence is brought out most clearly in the next poem.

I heard, as if I had no Ear
Until a Vital Word
Came all the way from Life to me
And then I knew I heard.

I saw, as if my Eye were on
Another, till a Thing
And now I know 'twas Light, because
It fitted them, came in.

I dwelt, as if Myself were out,
My Body but within
Until a Might detected me
And set my kernel in.

And Spirit turned unto the Dust
"Old Friend, thou knowest me,"
And Time went out to tell the News
And met Eternity (1039)

The poem needs little explanation. The difference between illusion and reality has not even by Plato been captured more accurately. Only when the Vital Word from without, the Light from beyond, the Might of the other make their impact on the human person can he or she really see the interconnection between time and eternity, between immanence and transcendence.

The interpretation of the preceding poems leads to one of Dickinson's most mature artistic creations. "What mystery pervades a well."

What mystery pervades a well!
The water lives so far -
A neighbor from another world
Residing in a jar

Whose limit none have ever seen,
But just his lid of glass -
Like looking every time you please
In an abyss's face!

The grass does not appear afraid,
I often wonder he
Can stand so close and look so bold
At what is awe to me.

Related somehow they may be,
The sedge stands next the sea -
Where he is floorless
And does no timidity betray

But nature is a stranger yet;
The ones that cite her most
Have never passed her haunted house,
Nor simplified her ghost.

To pity those that know her not
Is helped by the regret
That those who know her, know her less
The nearer her they get. (1400)

Kher considers the central feeling or idea of the poem to be "the human dilemma of being surrounded and engulfed by a sense of reality which is at once so close and so remote."[11] Emily Dickinson's attitude towards nature, so pertinent for understanding this poem, is complex and ambivalent, arousing fear but also providing happiness, peace and harmony. One has only to compare "I dreaded that first robin so" (348) with "Nature is what we see" (668) to find an excellent example of Emily Dickinson's reflections on nature. A closer reading of the present poem can illuminate the main theme expressed by Kher and an ambivalent attitude towards nature that provides considerable evidence of Dickinson's poetic embodiment of an opening to the transcendent.

The well, symbolic of nature as a whole, is first and foremost a mystery, pervaded through and through by the mysterious. The mystery involves the dialectic of familiarity and distance in one. "The water lives so far - residing in a jar" speaks of remoteness and limitation. "A neighbor from another world" involves the familiar and the strange.

In the second stanza it is just this dialectic between familiarity and strangeness, the unbounded and the bound that makes the well so difficult to grasp. The limits are obscured by "his lid of glass" reflecting illusion rather than the reality of its depth. But the face of the well conjures up threat and danger, the bottomless, unlimited abyss. Other elements of nature, the grass and the sedge, seem capable of risking danger with ease and familiarity. But the persona of the poem stands in awe - the emotion felt by the religious man in the face of a God wrapped in the veil of darkness and the unknown. The situation is familiar to the believer, mystic or not: Without the leap of faith, the plunge into the dark mystery of being - so adequately symbolized by the sea - the mystery remains. The poet demands that the reader become humble and free and bold like grass and sedge in order to understand the mystery. But awe - that mixture of dread and reverence - prohibits the unconscious familiarity nature itself has in the face of its own mystery. In the last two stanzas man's predicament is beautifully summarized. Those who claim an easy understanding of nature, of life, have clearly missed the interior reality, the haunted house, the ghost - terms connoting not only danger but attraction and intimacy. Those who know nature become, like Socrates, more and more convinced of their own ignorance of her.

The poem, somewhat light in tone, at times matter-of-fact, shows deep insight into the profoundest mystery of life. The well, nature, Being are at once near and far, welcoming and awe-inspiring, familiar in one dimension, strange, foreign, threatening and mysterious at a deeper level. Here Dickinson most brilliantly captures in symbol and imagery the problem of immanence and transcendence at the heart of being. To understand that the immanent aspect of our being in nature, in the world of society and history is at its deepest level a call to a meaning beyond, strange, unlimited, mysterious is as challenging as the perception of the reality of the well. It demands risk and humility and attains to a knowledge that is dark, dim and incomplete. To a bureaucratic, technological society this kind of knowledge is neither meaningful nor available. Possibly only the poet or the madman can make us aware that the search for and openness to the mystery of life aiming at a transcendental meaning is ultimately the crowning of human potentiality.

I would like to interpret two more poems which deal with this same basic problem within a more overt religious framework.

> Some keep the Sabbath going to Church -
> I keep it, staying at home -
> With a Bobolink for a Chorister -
> And an Orchard, for a Dome -
>
> Some keep the Sabbath in Surplice -
> Ijust wear my Wings -
> And instead of tolling the Bell, for Church,
> Our little Sexton - sings.
>
> God preaches, a noted Clergyman,
> And the sermon is never long,
> So instead of getting to Heaven, at last -
> I'm going, all along. (324)

In the poem quoted above, Dickinson contrasts traditional religious practice with that characteristic of a religion of nature, unique and subjective. The first two stanzas demand little interpretation. They are a straight-forward statement in light poetic terms of a religious feeling coming from nature as opposed to that at church - the private, natural religion of home, of bird singing and orchard providing a chapel of nature instead of the formality of the building of organized religion with surplice and bell. When Dickinson contrasts surplice with wings she suggests, in my opinion, the power of the person herself/himself in touch with nature to soar into the transcendent world of God without the constrictions of traditional ritual.

In the last stanza Dickinson states in her typically cryptic manner, with touches of light irony, the ultimate meaning of this contrast. The implied comparison between God and a clergyman is, of course, ironical and arouses in the reader at least a smile, if not a soft chuckle, as if God's word would only be listened to when he appears in the guise of an institutional minister. But God's preaching, unlike the traditional Puritan sermon, is concise, to the heart of the matter. And the heart of the matter for Dickinson is not that religious practice should end up being the mechanical performance of rites that promise to "get us to heaven," the pay-load at the end of a drab and uneventful religious life. For Dickinson religion is the experience of consciously being in touch with the mystery of heaven - "I'm going, all along."

The last poem to be discussed is similar in theme to the previous one, but involves a change in tone that brings out the ultimate nature of Dickinson's religious feeling most dramatically.

> My period had come for Prayer -
> No other Art - would do -
> My Tactics missed a rudiment -
> Creator - Was it you?
>
> God grows above - so those who pray
> Horizons - must ascend -
> And so I stepped upon the North
> To see this Curious Friend -

> His House was not - no sign had He -
> By Chimney - nor by Door
> Could I infer his Residence -
> Vast Prairies of Air
>
> Unbroken by a Settler -
> Were all that I could see -
> Infinitude - Had'st Thou no Face
> That I might look on Thee?
>
> The Silence condescended -
> Creation stopped - for Me -
> But awed beyond my errand -
> I worshipped - did not "pray" - (564)

In an interpretation stressing the typical Americanness of this poem, Giles Gunn points out that there is a radical change in attitude from the ironical stanzas at the beginning to the seriousness at the end caused by the intrusion of the American landscape.[12] Though Gunn focuses on this element he also sums up nicely the quality of the awe-inspiring religious experience called worship.

> Having originally set out to comment upon the termination of what is regarded as an odious kind of spiritual exercise, in this case prayer, the speaker is suddenly left at the end of the poem recalling the inexplicable commencement of a different and wholly unforeseen and unmanageable kind of spiritual experience called worship. [13]

What Emily Dickinson has done in this poem is to move the speaker from the mechanical exercise of routine prayer, which she ridicules by questioning whether God was in fact left out of the process, to the radical confrontation with the Other. This experience takes her out of herself, transports her into a world indefinite, beyond and, above all, demanding a response of awe and worship.

One of the most fascinating aspects of Emily Dickinson's poetry is its penetration of surface reality, be it natural, social or historical, to reveal Being as profound, mysterious and transcendent. Her special gift is the ability to communicate this vision to her readers through simple forms, unique diction and evocative imagery. This section has attempted to show that a religious approach to her poetry provides the reader an entry to a level of meaning not completely captured by cultural, psychological or feminist readings.

Though the poems analyzed are few and some of them relatively unknown, I suggest that the pattern of a unique use of nature to arouse wonder, instil vision and awaken a sense of awe is applicable to a wider reading of Dickinson's poetry. This would, in turn, reveal in broader scope and greater depth the intense religious spirit of a poetic imagination that sees in the world of man and nature the mystery of the transcendent.

Theodore Roethke

The religious spirit in the poetry of Theodore Roethke is both more obvious and more complex. Much Roethke criticism has taken a religious approach to his poetry. Nathan Scott emphasizes the sacramental nature of Roethke's art. Commenting on Roethke's contemplation of the concrete, he says:

> ... as the concrete particular is confronted with such intensity, it takes on the lustre of a "something more" and is felt to be an outward and visible expression of something "else" which is wonderful and has value. In short, it is conceived in some sort to be a sign or token of "numinous" reality, of the tremendous mystery of the Holy. 14

The complexity involved here is the exact meaning of the "something more," the "something else," the "numinous," the "mystery of being." Is this "something" - to be sure, below the surface of the obvious phenomenality of reality - immanent or transcendent? The answer to this question is anything but obvious.

Approaching Roethke not so much from the nature of what is contemplated but the kind of vision involved, Neal Bowers insists on the mystical quality of Roethke's poetic insight.[15] In an enlightening study Bowers demonstrates Roethke's knowledge of Evelyn Underhill's treatise on mysticism and interprets the poetry as a development in keeping with Underhill's five steps: 1) the awakening to a sense of divine reality, 2) the purgation of self, 3) illumination, 4) the dark night of the soul, 5) unity.[16] However, on finishing Bowers' study, the reader is still not sure of the exact nature of the relationship between immanent and transcendent reality as the object of Roethke's poetic mystical vision.[17]

The aim of this section of the paper is to examine Roethke's developing attitudes towards nature and the self in reference to immanence and transcendence. Unlike Gerard Manley Hopkins, whose insight into the divine penetration of nature and the self is guided by a Christian (Scotist) philosophical and theological system enabling him to perceive the way in which "The world is charged with the grandeur of God,"[18] Roethke was forced to open himself to his own experience of nature and self to achieve a vision of reality in all its depth.

The poems that most characteristically reflect the initial experience are to be found in the greenhouse sequence contained in The Lost Son and Other Poems.[19] Lynn Ross-Bryant asserts: "In these poems Roethke establishes the primary world of his poetry."[20] She, then, focuses on the fact that Roethke's experience of growing things began in his father's greenhouse where man and nature combine in the process of growth, a source of mystery and wonder.[21] The initial contact of a sensitive youth with nature created at the hands of an overbearing father opens a wealth of possibilities. Roethke, in touch with the vegetable world of nature as created, may sense a meaning in the natural world leading beyond it. But the inhibitions imposed on his sensibilities by a fear-inspiring father will clearly make the journey to the interior of nature and self, and possibly beyond, fraught with danger and obstruction.[22]

"Cuttings" and "Cuttings (later)," the first two poems of the greenhouse sequence, provide an appropriate starting place. In "Cuttings (later)" Roethke describes the poetic persona's subjective response to the intense contemplation of growth displayed in "Cuttings."

Cuttings
(later)

This urge, wrestle, resurrection of dry sticks,
Cut stems struggling to put down feet,
What saint strained so much,
Rose on such lopped limbs to a new life?

I can hear, underground, that sucking and sobbing,
In my veins, in my bones I feel it, –
The small waters seeping upwards,
The tight grains parting at last.

When sprouts break out,
Slippery as fish,
I quail, lean to beginnings, sheath-wet. (37)

The transplants ("Cut stems") or, as in "Cuttings," "Sticks-in-a-drowse," planted in "sugary loam," depend first on a gardener's care, the proper cut, the essential nutrients of water and earth. At this point the life-struggle is immanent, an urge, a wrestling to develop and come to fulfillment. The persona in the poem participates in this effort, intuits the parallel between himself and nature. He senses in himself the surge of life, but "quails," flinches, cowers at the challenge faced by leaving the womb, "sheath-wet." The religious symbolism of "resurrection," "saint strained" and "new life" should not be ignored. Just as the cutting moves from the natural life it shared with its mother plant to a life of its own transcending its original condition, so the poetic persona is faced with the task of transcending the natural life in the womb to become an independent person, whatever that may involve.

The nature and difficulty of this struggle is brought out most intensely in the "Weed Puller" (39). The weed puller is forced to live with the "grubs and snails and sharp sticks," with the "fetor of weeds," though aware of the beauty of lilies, roses and cyclamen above. "Crawling on all fours, alive, in a slippery grave," he senses the perversity of the human condition caught in the dirt of self and environment with an urge to transcend it towards the beauty above.

In a poem dealing more directly with nature itself, elements of both awe and anguish are present. "Moss-Gathering" describes in exact detail the process of loosening moss from the earth. Then the poet recounts his subjective response.

But something always went out of me when I dug loose those carpets

of green, or plunged to my elbows in the spongy yellowish moss of the marshes:

And afterwards I always felt mean, jogging back over the
logging road,

As if I had broken the natural order of things in that
swampland;

Disturbed some rhythm, old and of vast importance,

By pulling off flesh from the living planet;

As if I had committed, against the whole scheme of life, a
desecration. (40)

The poet is filled with a sense of his own meanness, a feeling of
anguish at having desecrated "the natural order of things," a
"rhythm, old and of vast importance." He feels the sacramental
significance of nature, which he has violated and from which he is
separated, and has lost some essential elements of himself in the
process. In "The Waking" (51), however, he is in tune with nature.
He hears the wren's voice and the stone's song, is at one with a
grove of apples, listens to the river running with the result that

... all the waters
Of all the streams
Sang in my veins
That summer day.

Nathan Scott makes much of the role of song in Roethke's poetry.[23]
He presents extensive evidence of Roethke's urge to sing but insists
that his jubilation "is also always, finally, a response to a music
which is heard ..."[24] His interpretation suggests an answer to the
question of immanence and transcendence posed as central to this
study. Roethke's "... imagination of reality as a vast antiphony
rests ... upon a lively intuition that both the human and nonhuman
modes of existence are animated and empowered by some primal
reality, which may be denominated as Being itself."[25] This absolute
being is "the 'otherness' in which the creatures of earth
participate" and makes possible "the world's great choral fugue."[26]
Scott's position that Roethke's poetry contains an insight into the
sacramental presence of an Other in the self and in nature – a
penetration of transcendence into immanence – is based on the whole
of Roethke's work and goes considerably beyond what can be
affirmed of the greenhouse and early nature poems. Here we have
seen a surge of life, a mixture of good and evil, the poetic

persona's intense contemplation of nature as greenhouse artifact, a reverence for nature leading to guilt at its violation and a union with it bringing great joy. The road toward a deeper realization of a possible transcendence is one of pain and purgation, of hope and despair, of submersion into the slimy depths of self in the hope of discovering the ultimate meaning of self in relation to the Other.

This struggle is illustrated remarkably well in "The Lost Son" and other longer sequences in that volume. Though time and space confine me to but limited comment I would like to give a brief description of this struggle and its outcome. A poem of considerable structural freedom filled with the pre-rational language and imagery of the unconscious, "The Lost Son" portrays a flight from father and self into the pit of the womb from which a return and a new beginning become possible. The journey begins at a cemetery and involves a dramatic appeal for help in the face of intense uncertainty.

> Voice, come out of silence,
> Say something.
> Appear in the form of a spider
> Or a moth beating the curtain.
>
> Tell me:
> Which is the way I take;
> Out of what door do I go,
> Where and to whom? (54)

But the poem ends in hope. Though

> It was beginning Winter,
> An in-between time ... (58),

a light of indefinite quality appears. The response is as follows:

> A lively understandable spirit
> Once entertained you.
> It will come again.
> Be still.
> Wait. (58)

The experience of the spirit seems to be a reference to Roethke's strange encounter in the woods while teaching at Michigan State.[27] Whether mystical or manic, self-induced, as Roethke asserts, or the result of overwork and a psychological breakdown, it opened the poet to a reality closed to rational endeavor. "Be still and wait" is the proper disposition to await a possible return of the spirit capable of revealing the truth of the meaning and goal of human life.

For Roethke to grasp the spirit is not a matter of analytical reason. In "I cry, Love! Love!" he rejects reason as "That dreary shed, that hutch for grubby school boys!" (92) And in "The Waking" he says: "We think by feeling. What is there to know?" (108) This putting aside of reason in favor of intuition is a central theme right from the beginning of Roethke's poetry. Open House, his first volume published, is filled with poems focusing on this topic.[28] "The Signals" is a typical example of this.

> Often I meet, on walking from a door,
> A flash of objects never seen before.
>
> As known particulars come wheeling by,
> They dart across a corner of the eye.
>
> They flicker faster than a blue-tailed swift,
> Or when dark follows dark in lightning rift.
>
> They slip between the fingers of my sight.
> I cannot put my glance upon them tight.
>
> Sometimes the blood is privileged to guess
> The things the eye or hand cannot possess. (8)

The flash and lightning rift, similar to Dickinson's "Lightning on a Landscape,"[29] reveal to the blood what the fingers of sight, the eye or hand cannot grasp. The blood symbolizes the direct, emotionally involved, experience of reality not open to the manipulations of reason referred to in fingers, eye and hand.

"A Walk in Late Summer" in Words for the Wind (1958) relates this type of experiential knowledge to the problem of transcendence. Uniting himself to a gull and small creatures with midnight eyes, the poet again rejects rational understanding, "What is there for the soul to understand?" (149) Still, "God's in that stone" and "Body and soul transcend appearances." "A late rose" is "a blaze of being." If the rational process is incapable of penetrating to the core of reality, how does Roethke achieve his insight into the interrelation between stone and God, immanence and transcendence.

In the conclusion of the poem Roethke suggests a solution.

> The long day dies; I walked the woods alone;
> Beyond the ridge two wood thrush sing as one.
> Being delights in being, and in time.
> The evening wraps me steady as a flame. (150)

By accepting the dying day (symbolic of his approaching death noted in the third stanza), placing himself in a setting (the woods alone) conducive to contemplation, the persona of the poem allows himself to be taken up in the embrace of enlightening nature and perceives the being delighting in being and in time. The possibility of being as transcendent, penetrating time is at least hinted at here.

From the greenhouse poetry through "The Lost Son" to "The Waking" and Words for the Wind Roethke has plunged the poetic persona of his "Song of Myself" into ever deeper circles of darkness and light in preparation for the experiences expressed in The Far Field, his last and posthumous volume. I would like to sketch the end of this journey as revealed in three longer poems in that book, "Meditation at Oyster River," "The Abyss" and "In a Dark Time."

Referring to "North American Sequence" as a whole, Rosemary Sullivan disagrees with Karl Malkoff's feeling that here "Roethke aspired to a mystical transcendence of the phenomenal world."[30] She insists that "far from rejecting it, Roethke sought to immerse himself in nature in order to find his personal regeneration there."[31] A profound immersion in the world of nature does not, of itself, contradict a union with the transcendent. The question is to what extent Roethke grasped this and expressed it in his poetry.

"Meditation at Oyster River" is, as Sullivan points out, an attempt to escape the falseness of the self-centered self to achieve peace and integrity by merging with nature, especially as symbolized by water.[32] In a long and lovely lyrical passage Roethke establishes the setting of the poet at the sea, dabbling his toes in brackish foam, then retiring to a rock higher up on the cliff-side. The scene is ideal for meditation. Silence dominates: no sound, no violence, the gulls no longer engage in "their cat-mewing, their child-whimpering." "The wind slackens, light as a moth fanning a stone." (190) Attuned to nature, the poet becomes aware of the difficulty of shrugging off the false self - "The self persists like a dying star." (190) But his wish to be with water despite the danger of destabilizing the self leads to the flesh taking on the pure poise of the spirit. He enters into the "hummingbird's surety, the kingfisher's cunning" and shares the freedom of a childhood river delivered from its wintry constriction by the spring thaw. The poem concludes with the poet rocking "with the motion of morning" submitting himself to ways of water, of nature and being rewarded with the vision of a world shining in the first of the moon. It is the conclusion that allows for an interpretation somewhere between Malkoff and Sullivan. If Roethke is clearly not attempting to escape the world of nature through mystical transcendence, his immersion in nature may have the effect of providing a vision, "a shining" of something both in nature but leading beyond it, of Scott's sacramental presence.

This interpretation is, granted, somewhat tenuous, but the conclusions of both "The Abyss" and "In a Dark Time" shed more light on the matter. William Heyen, in an article interpreting "The Abyss" as a compact expression of Underhill's five stages of mysticism, towards the middle of his argument, states: "If, to this point, there have been insights into the falseness of the individual self, subsequent insights will reveal the transcendent reality in the world."[33] In the last two sections of the poem, Roethke makes this relatively clear.

> In this, my half-rest,
> Knowing slows for a moment,
> And not-knowing enters, silent,
> Bearing being itself,
> And the fire dances
> To the stream's
> Flowing. (221)

The result of restraining the active operations of the rational mind in favor of opening oneself to "not-knowing," to the movement from without immerses one in being itself. The symbols of fire, dancing and flowing water, used constantly throughout the complete works, refer to illumination and true life.

If Roethke's first response is to question the meaning of this experience ("Do we move toward God, or merely another condition?"), at the end of the poem union with nature and the transcendent is achieved.

> I am most immoderately married:
> The Lord God has taken my heaviness away;
> I have merged, like the bird, with the bright air,
> And my thought flies to the place by the bo-tree.
> Being, not doing, is my first joy. (222)

Through a surrender of self, a false self concerned with security based on selfishness and the superficiality of finite rational activity, a state of union with nature and a power inflaming nature with Being can be arrived at.

The last stanza of "In a Dark Time" only substantiates this interpretation.

> Dark, dark my light, and darker my desire.
> My soul, like some heat-maddened summer fly,
> Keeps buzzing at the sill. Which I is I?
> A fallen man, I climb out of my fear.
> The mind enters itself, and God the mind,
> And one is One, free in the tearing wind. (239)

This is a profound statement of the end of a journey Roethke's poetic persona has been engaged in from the greenhouse until now.[34]

Conclusion

In a culture that, at least on the surface, has moved from the Puritan's "city on a hill" to "the secular city," it is encouraging to find two unlikely American poets revealing a truly religious spirit in their poetry. Though, or possibly because, neither Dickinson nor Roethke were affiliated with formal religion, both in their own way have plunged to the depths of their experience of self and nature to show an opening to a transcendence as the possible meaning of life. I have approached Dickinson more through a very limited selection of poems that flash out partial insights of her profound religious vision and Roethke more from a systematic development of the journey of his poetic persona towards an immersion in nature and true self leading to transcendence. Both Dickinson and Roethke in their unique and beautiful poems have presented us with keen insights into the true

religious nature of man – a being confined by time, history, and
society, subjected to the ravages of uncontrolled sensuality and
imperfect reason, but also open to the spirit who "over the bent
World broods with warm breast and with ah! bright wings."

NOTES

[1] See J. Burbick, "One Unbroken Company: Religion and Emily
Dickinson," New England Quarterly, 53 (1980), pp. 62-75, for a
more differentiated view. Though Burbick argues for a closer
connection to organized religion, I find the evidence unconvincing
at least with respect to the poetry.

[2] Allan Seager, The Glass House: The Life of Theodore Roethke (New
York: McGraw-Hill Book Company, 1968).

[3] Neal Bowers, Theodore Roethke: The Journey from I to Otherwise
(Columbia: University of Missouri Press, 1982), p. 13.

[4] Richard Chase, Emily Dickinson (London: Methuen & Co. LTD.,
1952), p. 8.

[5] John Cody, After Great Pain: The Inner Life of Emily Dickinson
(Cambridge, Mass.: The Belknap Press of Harvard University
Press, 1971).

[6] Adrienne Rich, "Vesuvius at Home: The Power of Emily Dickinson,"
Shakespeare's Sisters, eds. Sandra Gilbert and Susan Gubar
(Bloomington: Indiana University Press, 1979), pp. 99-121.
For a more extensive feminist literary critical treatment of
Dickinson, see Sandra Gilbert and Susan Gubar, The Madwoman in
the Attic (New Haven: Yale University Press, 1979).

[7] Inder Nath Kher, The Landscape of Absence: Emily Dickinson's
Poetry (New Haven & London: Yale University Press, 1974) p. 2.

[8] Ibid.

[9] All references to Dickinson's poems are taken from The Poems of
Emily Dickinson, ed. Thomas H. Johnson, 3 vols. (Cambridge,
Mass.: The Belknap Press of Harvard University Press, 1955). The
parenthetical numbers refer to the chronological numbering in this
work.

[10] 1 Corinthians 13.12.

[11] Kher, p. 40.

[12] Giles Gunn, The Interpretation of Otherness (New York: Oxford

University Press, 1979), pp. 192-195.

[13] Ibid., p. 194.

[14] Nathan Scott, The Wild Prayer of Longing (New Haven: Yale University Press, 1971), p. 78.

[15] Bowers, Theodore Roethke.

[16] Ibid., pp. 26-27.

[17] A number of critics have written on religious aspects of Roethke's poetry. See, among others, Lynn Ross-Bryant, Theodore Roethke (Port Washington, N.Y.: Kennikat Press, 1981), for an overall view. For more specific studies, see Richard A. Blessing, "Theodore Roethke's Sometime Metaphysical Motion," Texas Studies in Literature and Language, XIV (1973), 731-49; William Heyen, "The Divine Abyss: Theodore Roethke's Mysticism," Texas Studies in Literature and Language, XI (1969), 1051-1068; and Rosemary Sullivan, "A Still Center: A Reading of Theodore Roethke's 'North American Sequence,'" Texas Studies in Literature and Language, XVI (1975), 765-83.

[18] The Poems of Gerard Manley Hopkins, eds. W.H. Gardner and N.H. Mackenzie (fourth edition), (Oxford: Oxford University Press, 1982), p. 66. Hopkins had available the scholastic notion of the analogy of being, God as Absolute Being sharing himself in a contingent way with limited, transient, created being. His presence in the world of nature and self can be seen as real but partial and leading to his own absolute Transcendence.

[19] All references to Roethke's poetry will be to The Collected Poems of Theodore Roethke (New York: Doubleday and Company, Inc., 1966). The page references will be found in parenthesis in the text.

[20] Ross-Bryant, Theodore Roethke, p. 27.

[21] Ibid., p. 28.

[22] Though my main intention is to focus on religious aspects, Roethke has a history of manic-depressive mental illness partially caused by his relationship to his father.

[23] Scott, pp. 80-85.

[24] Ibid., p. 80.

[25] Ibid., p. 85.

[26] Ibid.

[27] For an extended account and interpretation of this event, see Seager, The Glass House, pp. 88-89; Bowers, pp. 8-10.

[28] See Bowers, Theodore Roethke, chapters 4 and 5 for an excellent treatment of this problem in Open House.

[29] See above, p. 5.

[30] Sullivan, "A Still Center," p. 765.

[31] Ibid., p. 766.

[32] Ibid., pp. 768, 771, 772.

[33] Heyen, "The Divine Abyss," p. 1059.

[34] For an incisive, comprehensive interpretation of this poem and the "Sequence, Sometimes Metaphysical" as a whole, see Blessing, "Theodore Roethke's Sometime Metaphysical Motion," pp. 731-49.

John G. McGraw

Loneliness and Religion in America

This presentation focuses on loneliness from an experiential -conceptual perspective[1] with reference to American loneliness and religion. It is claimed that loneliness is both "the experience most common to all" and yet "the most misunderstood."[2] As happens a phenomenon may be disguised or hidden by its sheer evidentiality; thus it becomes misunderstood or, more likely, simply unnoticed. Loneliness, as a non-esoteric and non-exotic experience (and for that reason, among others, not a subject of widespread systematic study until recently), has been compared to the "common cold ... easy to catch, hard to cure, rarely fatal but always unpleasant and sometimes wretched beyond bearing."[3]

The claim that loneliness is "<u>the</u> experience most common to all" would render it the most universal of universals, the most distinctively human experience. Whether it is such or whether it is <u>a</u> universal in the sense of "each, always, and everywhere" are issues largely beyond the scope of this paper. Perhaps, at the very least, loneliness is applicable to mankind as a "common human pattern," that is, as a "set of cross-cultural uniformities."[4]

Surely another factor in its misunderstanding has been the tendency to confound loneliness with "family" phenomena including alienation, isolation, nostalgia, homesickness, and homelessness in its literal, cultural, or metaphysical/ontological types; or with cognate phenomena such as boredom and depression. These considerations are also beyond the limits of this presentation. What then is loneliness?

Loneliness is generally regarded, at least by its American investigators, as a kind of aloneness; hence, an analysis of the latter is in order.

It has been said that humans are:

> So alone in birth.
> So alone in life.
> So alone in love.
> So alone in death. 5

Each of the above assertions could be factually false or true (save
that of death since no attribution, strictly speaking, can be made
about it because it is the end of experience and not the experience
of the end) depending, for example, on the definition of the word
"alone." Similarly, the poignant and haunting lamentation below:

> Alone! that worn-out word,
> So idly spoken, and so coldly heard;
> Yet all that poets sing and grief hath known
> Of hopes laid waste knells in that word ALONE! 6

While attempting to sort out the more pertinent meanings of the word
"alone" (and aloneness), it is worth remembering that two
formidable, if not insurmountable, obstacles hamper this analysis.
One consists in the fact that all experiences are, arguably,
partially one's alone (only). The other, and perhaps the less trivial
claim, resides in the reality that not only are one's experiences
partially one's alone but one's experience of his or her aloneness is
alone, that is, different from others. Thus the aloneness of
experience is not the same as the experience of aloneness.
Analogously, the same can be said of aloneness with respect to
loneliness and of the experience of loneliness relative to the
loneliness of the experience.

Granted these obstacles, one can still hope to discuss profitably
four foundational meanings of aloneness which will be thence passim
related to loneliness and to American meanings of these terms.
Firstly, and etymologically considered, the word "alone" is from the
Middle English "allone," which is comprised of the words "all" +
"one." It emphasized oneness, permanent or temporary, in the sense
of one's being all by oneself; that is, when used literally and
unqualifiedly, one was physically at a distance from others, other
companions.[7] Thus "all of one" was apart from others whereas before
this distancing one was, in some sense, a part of others, especially
of significant others such as companions.

However, the etymological meaning does not indicate whether aloneness is a negative and/or positive condition. The American usage of the term still retains the original usage as to the first meaning and it also refrains from prescribing the condition. In any event, studies of those Americans who are chronically lonely (henceforth called the lonely), that is, those whose "world" involves loneliness as a life-style, tend to regard being physically alone as a decidedly negative condition. The tendency to reduce loneliness to or to equate it with aloneness, or vice-versa, will be called "aloneliness" for the purposes of brevity and clarity. Aloneliness is obviously a combination of the words "alone" and "loneliness." It is recalled that "lonely" and in turn "loneliness" are actually derived from the word "alone."

In principle being alone is neither a necessary nor sufficient condition for loneliness, or vice-versa. As is well known, one can be alone and not be lonely, or lonely and not be alone. Indeed loneliness can be more intense in the presence of others, especially others from whom one normally expects meaningful intimacy and intimate meaning which are the two inseparable ingredients lacking in all forms of loneliness. For being and living alone (and never before have so many, absolutely and proportionally speaking, lived alone in the history of humanity as now, especially in America, but in general in the more affluent countries), Americans have a colloquialism: "all by one's lonesome." Lonesome means to cause or have lonely feelings, especially with respect to lacking past or present relationships and/or ambiences. This colloquialism is illustrative, perhaps, of American aloneliness.

Being alone, therefore, is not generally considered being lonely. However, being alone when one does not wish to be alone is a condition of being lonely (being lonely is essentially feeling lonely). It is claimed that for Americans being alone is lonely when aloneness is recognized by others as inappropriate.[8] In general, being alone, freely and constructively, is designated as solitude; loneliness, on the other hand and in itself, is considered a destructive (emotionally, mentally, and often physically) way of being alone.

The second meaning of aloneness pertains to what western philosophy has traditionally called the problem of individualization (the _principium individuationis_, more precisely), which concerns the ontological status of individuals with respect to their fundamental, individual, entitative constitution and the principle(s) by which this is effected. The American philosopher, R. M. Zaner, has characterized this individualization and awareness of aloneness in the following manner: there is "for every self that by which it is itself and is utterly alone ... a self which can only be discovered _to_ the self."[9] Furthermore, this is the self which antedates all choosing and creating and whatever screens it erects to conceal itself from itself and to mask itself from others.[10] In what can be labeled "structural loneliness," there is a desire to overcome the aloneness and separateness of self from the other (other selves, the universe, God, and the like) by being integrated into or integrating the other by means of a structural and entitative unity so as to constitute a duality or _tertium quid_ (both of which are a oneness, numerically considered).

An example of the above type of aloneliness is that furnished by the American psychologist, James Howard, according to whom humans are entrapped in their bodies, that is, their "flesh-colored cages." Because they cannot overcome this solitary confinement, they are condemned to endless loneliness. Each person exists in his or her "unique epidermal envelope as a separate thing."[11] No one can leave or enter this cage into which one is born, lives and dies, and which one wears as a "funeral shroud."[12] Consciousness appears to be reducible to physical and physiological sensations and the being of the self is totally material. Material beings are incommunicable in terms of their identities and all communication, for Howard, ultimately fails because language is essentially, if not purely, private.

In order to overcome what can be called "functional loneliness," the parties in their respective aloneness form not a unity of structure and identity but a union through function, identification, or communication. An example of the above and of aloneliness is given by the American philosopher, B.L. Mijuskovic, who defends both the Cartesian reflexive-ego view of consciousness as well as the Leibnizean self-conscious monadic type.

While his account of loneliness embraces various lines of argumentation, his central thesis is that the structure of consciousness is such that it makes loneliness not only possible but, in Kantian terms, necessary and universal, that is, a priori.[13] Not only is it universal in this sense, but it appears that he regards loneliness as the "universal of universals" in that the avoidance of it is the fundamental force in consciousness and conduct.[14]

In this version of functional loneliness, the reflexive immaterial ego or self-conscious monad can never reach the other in any permanently satisfactory way, because it will ultimately be thrown back upon itself in a manner from which there is no exit. While humans are not, he says, always aware of their lonely aloneness in the sense of their actually thinking about or feeling it, still they remain "psychologically alone and metaphysically isolated."[15] For this philosopher one can conclude that communication fails because of the egocentric bind the self (especially if it reflects on its reflexiveness, so to speak) discovers to and in itself. Indeed he maintains solipsism is not false metaphysically but only repugnant and terrifying psychologically.[16] Mijuskovic, seemingly, would require, as a necessary condition for escaping loneliness, a human consciousness endowed with total transparency of self to self and self to other and vice-versa.

The third meaning of aloneness also involves consciousness and awareness of separateness but the intentional model of consciousness is now considered. Before proceeding it is noteworthy that the lonely are frequently absorbed in preoccupation with self which behaviorally manifests itself in timidity and shyness. These traits of the lonely are principally due to insufficient self-esteem which in itself is considered to be the most consistent feature of loneliness and is an effect and, more generally, a cause of it. The timidly or shyly self-conscious are often deeply defensive; significantly, the original meaning of awareness was a cautious, guarded vigilance.

The central concern of the analysis of this meaning of aloneness is not the psychological but the epistemological and metaphysical. In the intentional model consciousness of aloneness is necessarily mediated by the other (self) since consciousness is viewed as outer and other directed. If consciousness were not so structured, awareness of aloneness and loneliness would be experientially and conceptually inexplicable. Linguistically it would be nonsensical. This has already been seen in the etymology of the word "alone," because to be "allone" signified that one was separate from a previous union with others (companions). In fact the etymology would suggest that consciousness of aloneness is based on a separateness from significant others (companions). In other words consciousness is primarily directed towards others in terms of affective meaning or intimate meaning, more precisely.

Be that as it may, consciousness of aloneness requires that the other is prior to awareness of self or, at least, co-given with it. Loneliness is, therefore, an instantiation of the radical sociality of mankind. Indeed the notion of a finite person, absolutely alone in the universe, seems not only horrendous but selfcontradictory, that is contradictory to the nature and notion of a self.

The fourth meaning of aloneness consists in the emergence and awakening of the self not to its being alone and single but to its being singular and unique. Uniqueness as distinctive separateness (versus separation as in the estrangement of alienation and self-alienation) includes the "I-am-me" experience (Herbert Spiegelberg)[17] which, in my view, contains the following elements. Firstly, there is the dawning upon the self that it is a self and that it is precisely this unique self. This apparition is a pre-reflective intuition of the self that is never fixed and final. Secondly, there is the realization that the self belongs to itself and to itself alone. This feeling of self-possession should not be equated with self-possessiveness, which, if habitual, isolates the self from others. Self-possession is a necessary condition for belonging to others in a union of freedom, integrity, and dignity. It is relevant to underscore the fact that the lonely do not feel unique but rather painfully redundant and totally replacable. What singularity and distinctiveness are theirs are felt by them as being impediments to their attainment of any relationships which might relieve or remove their loneliness.

Moreover, insofar as the lonely are neurotic, they may be said to have little or no viable true self in lieu of which, according to K. Horney, they fabricate an ideal but false self.[18] To compensate for the resultant feelings of not belonging to a real self or to others, the lonely are prone to substitute addictions and addictive relationships. The self-deprecation of the lonely goes far in explaining the reports and self-reports of their anger, guilt, aggressiveness and, sometimes, violence.

The notion of the self as alone, unique, and therefore belonging to itself, is, according to P. L. Berger, the root element in the appearance and evolution of the Western "autonomous individual," the idea of which commenced within the Hellenic and Israelite traditions.[19] These traditions were synthesized by Christianity and the latter's Renaissance and Reformation revolutions produced the modern world with its "modern drama of liberation and loneliness."[20] For Berger the "autonomous individual" views itself as unique in the traits beyond those it has in common with others, even those to whom it most fully belongs. Ontologically, this means that uniqueness is the essential reality of the self; ethically, it implies that such uniqueness ought to be recognized by all others; as such, it constitutes the basis of "every (Western) assertion of the rights of the individual as against his community."[21]

At this point one might well recall A. Angyal's widely shared position that humans necessarily exhibit two fundamental inclinations: one towards independent self-rule and law (autonomy) and the other towards interdependent self-rule and law (homonomy).[22] These tendencies are existential correlates and a failure to harmonize them synergistically leads invariably not only to the failure of both self-rule and joint rule but also eventually to rule by third forces or factors (heteronomy). The logical outcome of excessive autonomy is atomism; that of extreme homonomy is monism. The lonely illustrate a failure to blend these tendencies. The atomistic "loner" and the monistic "joiner" are replicated in groups and societies. The excessively autonomous individual, group, or society will generate its own negation in the conformist, "groupie," or collectivist. The ideal relationship is one of "interindependence," which recognizes the ultimacy of the self but also the necessity of authentic communication and dependence among selves.

Uniqueness itself involves two elemental notions of aloneness: that of privacy and that of freedom. Autonomy, the governance of self according to the laws of a presumed and primordial real and true self, is the ground for the respect of persons and the right to that aloneness known as privacy. Privacy is the natural right of the person to be alone and to be left alone, upon one's volition, by all others. Belonging to oneself and not to others, especially the state, is what the word "privacy" means in one of its original significations.

In democratic societies and groups, there is an acknowledgment and defence of the right to privacy which "protects the individual's interest in becoming, being, and remaining a person."[23] By privacy is meant a "social ritual by means of which an individual's moral title to his existence is conferred."[24] It is conferred socially but it stems from being a person and it is upon that basis that it is bestowed.

Privacy as exercised can be in private or in public, alone or with others. It includes non-intervention by others when one is all by oneself (e.g., physical seclusion); or with oneself in self-communication (e.g., solitude); or when one is alone in the midst of others (anonymity); or with others in private seclusion; or with others in public (e.g., an outdoor cafe).

Privacy can be examined from the perspective of the control and management of the personal and private information revealed by the individual. Following A. Westin one can distinguish four types of privacy: anonymity, solitude, reserve, and intimacy.[25] In anonymity one can disclose personal information without one's identity being revealed. The lonely, for example, may avail themselves of "anonymous" phone-in radio programs to make themselves heard and understood. The lonely feel anonymous in the sense that whatever identity they might have is indistinguishable and nameless. They feel that their presence is unnoticed and their absence not missed. Moreover they tend to believe that they alone are lonely and all others are content, if not happy, alone or together. In the extreme they feel they are non-existent or, more colloquially, nobodies or "zeroes." This conviction of their anonymity, to the point of inexistence, is symbolized by walls, doors, fences and the like. These barriers and boundaries separate other beings from their nothingness.

Feeling anonymous may take the opposite direction. Instead of feeling like no one in particular or just anyone, there is the greater fear by the lonely of being the only one who exists, a fear occurring in acute loneliness and psychotic episodes (H. Guntrip maintains that the "core of all serious mental disorders" is loneliness).[26] Symbolically this is portrayed by the spaceless, timeless, solitary existence on the sea or desert. An endless solitary existence devoid of others would be the ultimate void.

Whether they do not exist or whether it is the others who do not, the lonely feel their anonymity as a falling away, a falling apart, or as being lost. Without the presence of significant others and sometimes any others, they feel not only that these others are missing but that they are missing. Consequently the lonely are terrified by anonymity because if others do not see them, they feel that they will cease to be. For the lonely esse est percipi. For example, shyness is essentially the fear of having others see the worthlessness one feels about oneself.

The second type of privacy is solitude which may occur in the midst of others but generally occurs at a chosen distance. As mentioned above the lonely tend to fear such distancing. They also tend to fear solitude because it can entail meditation, contemplation, reflection, and silence, all of which require a certain mental aloneness. The lonely fear being alone in solitude because they feel they might discover their total emptiness. Hence the lonely keep busy in boredom to kill time and fill their empty self-space. Solitude is perhaps the greatest prohibitor of loneliness and the chief means to cope with it or cure it. The ability to be creative in solitude is the other side of the ability to communicate. The lonely lack the ethical traits and/or social skills to be constructively alone or with others.

Reserve is the withholding of personal information which is judged to be too private and privileged to divulge. As opposed to anonymity the identity of the self is known. Anonymity refers ordinarily to the desire of the self for physical and psychological separation from others and the public at large. Reserve generally implies seeking psychological separation from another self or from a small group of others when in their presence. The reserved person is taken to be one who is in control of "input" and "output" whereas the lonely tend to feel they are not in control of either self-disclosure or input from others. The lonely feel that what they have to disclose is, at any rate, menial or demeaning. Generally the lonely disclose less than the non-lonely (lacking confidence, they lack confidants) or they disclose more but inappropriately.[27]

The fourth type of privacy is intimacy and since the latter is one of the two essential elements lacking in loneliness, it would be useful to delineate the notion of loneliness more fully. Loneliness entails a breakdown in the basic self-network of meaningfully intimate and intimately meaningful relationships. Intimacy refers to the revelation of that which is inmost to the self, its most privileged meanings: cognitive, volitional, and affective, be they in relation to body, mind or spirit. The various types of meanings interpenetrate one another but intimacy pertains chiefly to the affective aspects of meaning which include love, friendship, affection, devotion, care, and attentiveness, to name some of the primary components. But intimacy also requires cognitive and volitional meanings which lend it vision and resoluteness. Intimacy without meaning reinforces the guilt and self-deprecation of the lonely. Intimacy intensifies and enlivens meaning. Intimacy is significance signatured and personalized. Meaning without the warmth, openness, honesty, sympathy, and the "positive regard" of intimacy becomes cold, objectivistic, objectifying and ultimately meaningless. The self in its privacy is a sanctuary both in the sense of a sacred treasury of intimacy and meaning and as a refuge from the mundanely exterior and public.

The lonely seem to be unable or unwilling to open this sanctuary and asylum sufficiently to meet their needs for significant relationships. As in all vicious circles, the lonely have ever-increasing desires for intimacy and meaning but insufficient characterological resources and communication skills to attain them. In summary intimacy is that form of privacy which necessitates others and hence is social in nature whereas anonymity, reserve and solitude are non-social forms of privacy.[28]

At this point it is possible to present a more complete picture of loneliness, especially of the chronic type. As noted previously it is a destructive way of being or feeling alone in which there is a rupturing or rending of one's habitual world due to a lack of intimacy and meaning in one's relationships, whether these last take the form of interpersonal, social, cultural or cosmic dimensions (the last form includes ultimate realities such as divinity, ultimate purpose or concern, the meaning of the universe and such).[29] Loneliness primarily pertains to future relationships for which one yearns or longs; secondarily, to present relationships which one misses; and lastly, to past relationships which one mourns. Of course, it is not the relationship as such which is crucial but the who or what which constitutes the relationship. "Having relationships" or "networking" or "interfacing" and like phrases themselves seem to suggest the language of loneliness, if not alienation.

The identities of the mourned and missed are known whereas the identity of the other who is longingly desired is not usually known. The desired other assumes for the lonely a special and ideal status. It is special because loneliness is invariably a question of the quality of the relationship rather than the quantity as such. The unknown, moreover, has the status of an abstract ideality which may or may not be derived from the real others of past or present relationships. Loneliness is a felt discrepancy between the desired and the unachieved qualitative relationship(s); this gap is often affected when comparisons are made, consciously or otherwise, to past or present others. On the other hand, the gap may contain no comparison of the imagined ideality of the desired other to the mourned or missed. Also this ideality may or may not be compared to a real other who forms the new and desired relationship.

Despite the special and ideal standing of the unknown other, the desperation of the lonely may condition or cause one to seek mere "quantitative" relationships or to settle for "just anyone." Another strategy is to endow a real other with fictional or exaggerated qualities of specialness and ideality (à la the crystallization theory of Stendahl) as when the lonely fall "desperately in love" with a real yet imagined other.

Another manner of coping with the malaise and malady which chronic loneliness often engenders is to lower expectations of self and/or other. In the case of the lonely perfectionistic personality, this adjustment is particularly painful since this person anxiously seeks certitude in knowing whether the "compromise" is a step up or down in self-worth or a step to or away from the ideal intimacy and meaning it seeks.

While chronic loneliness is in itself a destructive condition, due in great part to the negative emotions it entails with their accompanying pain and suffering, it may contribute to greater self-knowledge and eventually to enhanced self-esteem and social skills. Still, the pain and suffering of chronic loneliness often desensitize the lonely to the needs of the others for whom they search. This has a tendency to turn others away from what the latter regard as lonely egocentricity. Additionally, chronic loneliness seems to paralyze or, contrariwise, panic consciousness to its detriment and sometimes to its disintegration. The suffering of loneliness (Gabriel Marcel calls it the only suffering) may effect a "metanoia" but it is doubtful that for the mass of humanity it has this positive effect.

The intense desperation of loneliness furnishes it with its venturous character. This is exemplified in the anxious but eager risks the chronically lonely undertake to satisfy their need to meet the other. But any meeting and especially its prolongation are hazardous to those with minimal self-esteem since rejection and acceptance of self both promote apprehensiveness. All this assumes, however, that one can meet the other. It has been said, and perhaps rightly, that happiness is finding without looking; unhappiness is looking without finding but loneliness is not knowing where to begin to look.[30]

Besides, the lonely often believe, as stated above, that only they are lonely; hence, they feel, no one is looking for them and when there is a meeting it is often an exercise of calculation and estimation rather than a genuine encounter. The desperately lonely persist in their endeavors despite their frustrations and despite their beliefs that their efforts will continue to be abortive. This tenacity indicates that intimacy and meaning are basic needs as well as meta-needs (A. Maslow) and from an ontological perspective seem to be like the transcendentals of Aristotle. In America in recent years loneliness has become a matter of big business or the "loneliness industry," as it is called,[31] or the "industrialization of affectivity" (Ralph Keyes) or "agapurgy" (Henry Burger). It is impossible to investigate here the progress of such "business" but it indicates the national seriousness of the problem (or more cynically the use of this affliction for profit).

Loneliness has, "perhaps more than any other word in the English language, a mournful, if not eerie sound to it."[32] If mournful is taken to mean not only the grief for those relationships permanently lost but also those possible for which one awaits in sorrow and dejection, then the word surely describes loneliness. The despondency and depressiveness which literally engulf the lonely, and which in the extreme collapse them into both despair and depression, are surely mournful. As to the eeriness of its sound, it is known that originally the term signified terror and timidity. The latter's relationship to loneliness has already been marked.

As to the terror of loneliness, its "naked horror," (L. Binswanger) Frieda Fromm-Reichmann observed that her mental patients were so terrified of their own experience of loneliness that they could not dare even mention the word "loneliness." Most people, she believed, attempt to hide their loneliness, not only because of the fear it instills or awakens in them, but also because "loneliness is a most unpopular phenomenon in this group-conscious culture."[33] One should add that not being one of the group is not to be popular, and if one is not popular, one is lonely.

Studies indicate that Americans are not very sympathetic to the chronically lonely; they consider them to be weak, dependent, and often unsuccessful "losers." Americans are supposed to be independent, "cheerful, competent, successful, and happy"; being lonely is, according to David Reisman, a "kind of un-American activity,"[34] even though Americans seem to make a career of loneliness. In the "Bradburn" 1969 national survey, 26 per cent reported feeling "very lonely or remote" from others during the "past few weeks." In the "Maisel" national poll of the same year, about 11 per cent reported feeling "severely lonely" during the past week. Since 1969 some experts believe loneliness has greatly increased and is now a national epidemic.

In terms of other types of privacy, Americans have customarily considered those who have sought solitude for prolonged periods as being odd, eccentric, weird or, worse, isolates and anti-social loners. As to reserve Americans generally regard it as unsociable, secretive, pretentious, even "foreign" behavior. Americans usually consider reserve as being non-friendly whereas they prefer open, outgoing, sociable and friendly behavior. The psychological barriers reserve imposes in one-to-one or small group associations are generally unapproved by Americans.

With respect to anonymity, while Americans dislike being unknown (recognition and fame being signs of success) and dislike not having the opportunity to know and be known by one another, they want such knowledge on their own terms and conditions. They crave anonymity in this sense and generally resent any invasion of anonymity.[35] The lack of anonymity, for example, in small-town America is not something Americans generally relish although they may be nostalgic for the life it represents. Americans can be entirely open to complete strangers whom they have just met but often consider the perfect neighbor to be one who has lived next door for ten years yet all remain completely unknown to one another. Because Americans have so much space and the money to purchase it, "the ideal of the unfettered individual, rugged, free, and secluded, has reached its zenith. Howard Hughes is the only logical conclusion."[36]

As for intimacy Americans have through the loneliness industry developed "temporary love systems" with hit and run or hit and miss intimacy. However, since instant intimacy, or the desire for it, does not necessarily lead to commitment and permanence, there is the need for sustaining communities many of which are "disposible." Americans, 20 per cent of whom move yearly (almost always they are the affluent and educated), want communities but those especially in which they need not be known intimately.[37] Americans want community; they are perhaps obsessed with it. However, they want individuality and individualism more.[38] It can be safely assumed that the present capacity for all forms of privacy, loneliness, as well as community to a degree and kind unimaginable previously is due in great part to contemporary technology. For example, the communications and transportations industries can isolate or unify those in today's "global village."

As to the eerie sound of loneliness, it is recalled that the word "eerie" comes from the Middle English word "eri" and means "filled with dread."[39] What is most dreaded is perhaps the cosmic types of aloneness and loneliness, for example, dying and death. But the dreadful has, in some philosophical circles, come to suggest the anguish about or before one's own sense of nothingness which is felt both everywhere and nowhere. The eerie as dreadful in this sense would seem to be quite applicable to loneliness in that its nothingness is experienced as hollowness and emptiness and is felt as nowhere; yet it is experienced as everywhere in the depressing and despondent emotions inherent in loneliness.

Having considered uniqueness as aloneness in terms of that aloneness called privacy with its various types, it remains to consider uniqueness as that kind of aloneness experienced in freedom. The notion of privacy itself is most useful in connecting uniqueness to freedom, because privacy entails the moral right to self-determinism (freedom) and is "a condition of the original and continuing creation of the person."[40] Consequently, the singularity and uniqueness of the person require privacy (and the proper admixture of anonymity, reserve, solitude and intimacy) for the freedom necessary for the creation of self (a creation that is not, of course, ex nihilo).

What is often referred to as the right to self-realization necessitates freedom. The latter, according to Berger, implies that the self is solely responsible for itself alone, at least as the autonomous self views its freedom. This right is the most radical aspect of such autonomism and is symbolized par excellence by America.[41]

Freedom is the supreme value for America (and the highest honor its citizens can obtain is the "Medal of Freedom"). Historically freedom was liberation from various tyrannies and authoritarianisms as well as a liberty to do what the individual chose through self-determination, self-reliance, and self-expression, all values Americans revere. The "self-made man," the traditional American hero, the successful man, was ultimately the "lone" man (women traditionally could be lonely and express their loneliness but seldom could be "lone"). Colloquially stated, the "self-made man" was he who could "go it alone" or "make it alone"; more recently it was "doing it my way" or, in counter-culture language, "doing one's own thing." In any case "being me is being free" and vice-versa.

The rights to life, liberty and the pursuit of happiness (and perhaps nowhere else but in America is there a right to happiness) are ideally, for Americans, one and the same entity: individual success. Whether success as wealth, fame, rank and the like brings happiness is problematic. What is more certain is that being unsuccessful means loneliness in America. Perhaps Americans have, with their liberation from constraints and restraints and their excessive competitive individualism, produced a freedom which is at the expense of equality (that is, justice, which is the objective foundation of meaning) and of fraternity (that is, community, whose life blood is intimacy). The American way of life has perhaps been both excessively autonomous and homonomous, which together or separately spells loneliness. Of course, one and the same individual can be both excessively independent with respect to out-groups and excessively dependent with respect to in-groups.

But if loneliness looms large for many Americans, so do belief in God and religion, which, as noted below, help to alleviate American loneliness. At one time (1968) according to a Gallup Poll, 98% of Americans believed in God. The New York Times reported (June 22, 1986) that the combined church membership of some 224 denominations was 142,172,138 of whom approximately 125 million were Christian. In a 1981 survey investigating the extent to which traditional American values have endured in contemporary society, it was discovered that the one factor which consistently and dramatically affected the values and behavior of Americans was religious belief, which proved more significant than gender, age, status, and political persuasion.[42] In 1977 and 1978 Gallup Polls, it was reported that 86% of Americans regarded religious belief "to be fairly or very important" in their lives and that 50 million Americans considered themselves "born again" believers.[43]

For American Christians God is the foundation of all meaning and value (for American believers, in general, ethical values are religious values). The Christian God is, moreover, the Absolute Other, the Ultimate Person of intimacy both in the sense of the supreme "lover" and beloved and also in the sense that God intimately knows us all and all of us in our deepest being. Thus belief in God is the continual source of stability, safety, and security; and of being accepted, understood and cared for in all one's folly and frailty, and forgiven for one's sins. Through belief (faith) one can be victorious over the ultimate aloneness, and perhaps loneliness, of dying and death and ultimately enjoy everlasting happiness in a perfect community. The meaning of life and death are thus assured. When human communication fails one can always resort to an ever present infinitely personal companion through prayer and worship. When God seems absent or hidden, this can be interpreted as the believer's making spiritual progress. After the "test" or "trial," God will return in even greater intimacy and life will assume deeper meaning.

Of course it has been frequently argued that God is but the loneliness of man (e.g., J.-P. Sartre). However, whether religious belief is a projection based on the need for comfort and consolation (and thus consists in a sacrifice of truth in the process), the fact of the matter is that religious belief reduces or relieves not only American spiritual loneliness but it also "works" in the case of other forms of loneliness, especially those of an interpersonal and cosmic nature.

In one survey of mainly American Christians, it was found that those who regarded Jesus as a personal lord and savior were less lonely than those whose commitment to him was essentially to his ethical teachings. However, both groups, who may be said to live their faith, were less lonely than those who merely used their faith for self-serving or purely expedient purposes.[44] Additionally, the survey found that all three types of believers were significantly less lonely than non-believers.[45] Whether, however, the believers were less lonely because of the greater "personalness" of the commitment itself or were so because of their involvement in religious groups was unknown.[46] For many American believers their congregation is a vital part of their social and communal life, and so to some extent their social and cultural loneliness are diminished thereby.

Some religions not only assuage the loneliness of Americans but induce it and even prey upon it. Using Erich Fromm's distinction between humanistic and authoritarian religions, it can be said that the latter profit from the low esteem of the lonely (and give them a new but inauthentic identity) for their own business. Because loneliness generally correlates inversely with self and other acceptance, "just world beliefs, and belief in the trustworthiness, altruism and favorability of human nature,"[47] authoritarian religious leaders can exploit and reinforce this pessimism for their own gains. An example of the above is the Reverend Sun Myung Moon and his Unification Church whose "recruits" are socially and physically isolated from family and friends, are never left alone, and are "love-bombed" (the last being the perversion of intimacy through mental violence).

Americans are undoubtedly genuinely grateful for the extensiveness of their liberty and perhaps especially for their freedom of religion and the liberty to choose their own faith. Indeed they seem to cherish liberty as the supreme value and this is mirrored in mainstream American religions. In fact liberty itself seems to have been a kind of original religion of Americans and so it has remained. Because of the traditionally rigid separation of church and state, mainstream American religions are reluctant to criticize the excessively autonomous individualism which pervades the "American dream" epitomized in the saying, "only in America," which means essentially that in America alone can one come from "nowhere and nothing" to be successfully rich and richly successful.

It is true that such self-made and religious American millionaires abound in the United States (of course it is preposterous that in reality such wealth is in any real sense "self-made"). Should one conclude that the 34 million Americans who live below the poverty line (ABC News, May 25, 1986) are also self-made? Liv Ullmann recently said at my university that loneliness is the illness of the rich nations and poverty is the illness of the poor nations. But poor Americans living in the richest nation in history get a double dosage of loneliness. Moreover, they are frequently made to feel ashamed and guilty for their poverty and loneliness. Perhaps a theology of liberation and a religion that services all the oppressed is the one most needed in the United States. Poverty and its attendant loneliness is but one area which should be the active concern of American religions. The awesome power at the disposal of American religion would, of course, only be effective if its members would practice what their leaders preach.

The autonomy which has pinnacled in America can of course be positive or negative. The sense of aloneness which invariably accompanies autonomy is, to repeat, neither a necessary nor a sufficient condition of loneliness. Much of American loneliness could be alleviated by a liberty devoted to a more responsible and equitable distribution of economic, social, and political power. The social and cultural loneliness which results from irresponsible and inequitable distribution is not only inhumane but also dangerous, for where intimacy and meaning end, destructiveness and violence begin.

NOTES

[1]L.A. Peplau and D. Perlman discuss eight approaches to loneliness, namely, the psychodynamic, phenomenological, existential, sociological, interactionist, cognitive, privacy model, and the general systems theory in their article, "Eight Approaches to Loneliness," in L.A. Peplau and D. Perlman, eds., Loneliness: A Sourcebook of Current Theory, Research and Therapy (New York: John Wiley & Sons, 1980), pp. 123-134. The approach of this paper is a preliminary attempt at integralism.

[2]I.J. Tanner, Loneliness: The Fear of Love (New York: Harper & Row, 1973), p. xi.

[3]H. Fromme, The Ability to Love (New York: Simon & Schuster, 1966), p. 158.

[4]P.L. Berger, "Western Individuality: Liberation and Loneliness," Partisan Review 52, no. 4 (1985), 324.

[5]Aubier and de Lara's Spain, cited in A. Burton, "On the Nature of Loneliness," American Journal of Psychoanalysis 21, no. 1 (1961), 34.

[6]E. Bulwer-Lytton's The New Timon, Part II, cited in W.L. Dusenburg, The Theme of Loneliness in Modern American Drama (Gainesville: University of Florida Press, 1960), p. 8.

[7]Webster's New World Dictionary of the American Language, 2nd college edition, s.v. "alone."

[8]M. Mead, "Loneliness, Autonomy and Interdependence in Cultural Context," in J. Hartog et al., eds., The Anatomy of Loneliness (New York: International Universities Press, 1980), p. 403.

[9] R.M. Zaner, _The Context of the Self: A Phenomenological Inquiry Using Medicine as a Clue_ (Athens, Ohio: Ohio University Press, 1981), p. 151.

[10] Ibid.

[11] J.A. Howard, _The Flesh-Colored Cage_ (New York: E.P. Dutton & Co., Hawthorn Books, 1975), p. 3.

[12] Ibid.

[13] B.L. Misjuskovic, _Loneliness in Philosophy, Psychology and Literature_ (Assen, The Netherlands: Van Gorcum, 1979), p. 99.

[14] Ibid., p. 11.

[15] Ibid., pp. 9, 49.

[16] Ibid., p. 27.

[17] Zaner, p. 154.

[18] K. Horney, _Neurosis and Human Growth_ (London: Routledge & Kegan Paul, 1951).

[19] Berger, p. 326.

[20] Ibid.

[21] Ibid.

[22] A. Angyal, _Foundations for a Science of Personality_ (Cambridge, Mass.: Harvard University Press, 1985).

[23] J.H. Reiman, "Privacy, Intimacy and Personhood," in F.D. Schoeman, ed., _Philosophical Dimensions of Privacy: An Anthology_ (Cambridge: at the University Press, 1984), p. 314.

[24] Ibid., p. 310.

[25] A. Westin, _Privacy and Freedom_ (New York: Atheneum, 1970), cited in V.J. Derlega & S.T. Margulis, "Why Loneliness Occurs: The Interrelationship of Social-Psychological and Privacy Concepts," in Peplau and Perlman's _Loneliness_, p. 158. I am indebted to Derlega and Margulis for their insights regarding Westin's classification of privacy.

[26] H. Guntrip, "Sigmund Freud and Bertrand Russell," _Contemporary Psychology_ 9, no. 35 (1973), 263-281, cited in G. Satran, "Notes on Loneliness," _Journal of The American Academy of Psychoanalysis_ 6, no. 3 (1978), 285.

[27] Derlega and Margulis, p. 160.

[28] Ibid., p. 157.

[29] A. Sadler and T.B. Johnson, "From Loneliness to Anomia," in Hartog et al.'s The Anatomy of Loneliness, pp. 42-58.

[30] Attributed to José Ortega y Gasset.

[31] S. Gordon, Lonely in America (New York: Simon & Schuster, 1976).

[32] Tanner, p. 2.

[33] F. Fromm-Reichmann, "Loneliness," in Hartog et al.'s The Anatomy of Loneliness, p. 346.

[34] D. Reisman in Foreword to R. Weiss, Loneliness: The Experience of Emotional and Social Isolation (Cambridge, Mass.: The Massachusetts Institute of Technology Press, 1973), pp. xvii-xviii.

[35] R. Keyes, "We the Lonely People," in Hartog et al.'s The Anatomy of Loneliness, p. 408.

[36] Ibid., p. 409.

[37] Ibid., pp. 416-419.

[38] Ibid., p. 407.

[39] Webster's New World Dictionary of the American Language, 2nd college ed., s.v. "eerie."

[40] Reiman, p. 310.

[41] Berger, p. 327.

[42] J. Pollack and P. Finn, The Connecticut Mutual Life Report on American Values in the '80s: The Impact of Belief (Lanham, Maryland: University Press of America, 1984).

[43] R.F. Paloutzian and C.W. Ellison, "Loneliness, Spiritual Well-Being and the Quality of Life," in Peplau and Perlman's Loneliness, p. 231.

[44] Ibid., p. 234.

[45] Ibid.

[46] Ibid., p. 233.

[47] W.H. Jones, "Loneliness and Social Behavior," in Peplau and Perlman's Loneliness, p. 239.

Thomas J. S. Mikelson

Cosmic Companionship in Martin Luther King, Jr.'s Theology of Social Change

Prologue

I want to begin with a brief tableau, a description of a typical situation in the life of Martin Luther King, Jr. We are in a black church somewhere in the old South of the United States.

Before adjourning, the people cross their arms in front of them, joining their hands to the hands of their neighbors on either side, while they sing:

> God is on our side,
> God is on our side,
> God is on our side, today,
> Oh, deep in my heart I do believe,
> We shall overcome, someday. 1

The hour is late. The sanctuary is packed with people, singing, clapping, and swaying. These people marched today. There were ugly confrontations with angry crowds of whites, brutality from law enforcement officers, and many arrests. They were afraid today, but here, singing together in the church, they are radiant.

The young preacher in the pulpit has spoken to them about the significance of today's activities, the objectives of the present campaign, and about their discouragement. "We have moved all these months," he said, "in the daring faith that God is with us in our struggle."[2] He has reminded them, in familiar terms, of their commitment to love and nonviolence.

> ... the nonviolent approach does something to the hearts and souls of those committed to it. It gives ... new self respect. It calls up resources of strength and courage ... Finally, it so stirs the conscience of the opponent that reconciliation becomes a reality. 3

At the end, he shared with them his dream of a beloved community in which all persons are free to become what God intended them to be, where none are constrained by oppressive racism, poverty, militarism, or materialism.

In recent days, he has traveled thousands of miles, given many speeches, attended strategy meetings in New York and Atlanta, and worried about funds for the campaign. In spite of his weariness, his words have lifted the people here and their singing now lifts him. He is Martin Luther King, Jr., and these people are part of the Civil Rights Movement in the United States.

The date could be any year from the beginning of the bus boycott in Montgomery, Alabama (December 5, 1955), until the murder of Martin Luther King, Jr., in Memphis, Tennessee (April 4, 1968). This church could be any one of hundreds in which such gatherings are held. This town could be Birmingham, Alabama, St. Augustine, Florida, Philadelphia, Mississippi, or any one of scores in the deep south of the United States where civil rights campaigns are conducted.

Many of the leaders here are ministers of black churches and many of the people are members of black churches. The spontaneous harmonies and stirring rhythms of the music resemble black gospel hymns and the spirit of the meeting is unmistakably suggestive of worship. The singing, the speaking, the invocations, the themes and values, and the meeting house itself, are suggestive of black church life.

The movement under King's leadership has a spirituality of love, courage, the redemptive value of unmerited suffering, the infinite worth of every person, reconciliation, and confidence. This spirituality is an inclusive construct with roots in the black integrationist tradition of Frederick Douglass, W.E.B. DuBois, and the National Association for the Advancement of Colored People (N.A.A.C.P.); in the nonviolent protest tradition of Gandhi and Thoreau; in Protestant liberal theology; and in the gospel of the black church.[4] Its primary roots are in his family, his church, and his theological education. That explains why the targets of most terrorist bombings by the Ku Klux Klan and white citizens councils are black churches or the homes of black preachers.

King's Religious and Intellectual Background[5]

There were three formative influences in King's religious and intellectual development: his family, his church, and his education for the ministry. Because his father, grandfather, and great grandfather were ministers before him, the influences of family and church were intertwined and both led naturally to the ministry.

From the beginning of his life, the church was "a second home" to him, a world of association and values.[6] He understood himself most deeply as a preacher.

> I am many things to many people; Civil Rights leader, agitator, trouble-maker and orator, but in the quiet resources of my heart, I am fundamentally a clergyman, a Baptist preacher. This is my being and my heritage for I am also the son of a Baptist preacher, the grandson of a Baptist preacher, and the great grandson of a Baptist preacher. The Church is my life and I have given my life to the Church ... 7

King remembered his parents as loving and intimate and he was close to his "saintly grandmother, [his mother's mother]." In his family, he writes, "love was central" and "lovely relationships were ever present." As a graduate student, King wrote that this family background had prepared him to think of "God as loving" and the "universe as friendly." It was easy, as he said, for him "to lean more toward optimism than pessimism about human nature mainly because of my childhood experiences." As he wrote of his own religious development:

> Conversion for me was never an abrupt something. I have never experienced the so-called crises [sic] moment. Religion has just been something I grew up in. Conversion for me has been the gradual in-taking of the noble ideals set forth in my family and my environment, and I must admit that this in-taking has been largely unconscious. 8

King's birthplace and longtime home city was Atlanta, "the capital of the state of Georgia and the so-called 'gateway to the south.'" In his neighborhood, most people were "of average income" and were "deeply religious." All of his regular playmates were "regular sunday [sic] school goers."[9] In Atlanta, his grandfather and father before him were part of the core of elite black leaders who actively represented the interests of their people. Between 1906 and 1910,

Reverend Adam Daniel Williams had led marches and economic boycotts against an Atlanta newspaper, The Georgian, because of its insults to people of color. Reverend Williams was also an early member of the N.A.A.C.P., which was founded in Atlanta in 1909 under the leadership of W.E.B. DuBois and others. In the 1930's, Reverend King, Sr., led a voting rights and voter registration movement for black people in Atlanta. He led an effort to increase the compensation of Atlanta's black school teachers. And he helped to establish a coalition of black and white leaders to encourage "excellent" race relations in the city. Planning sessions for some of those activities took place in the King home during the years when Martin Luther King, Jr. was a child and a youth.[10] He saw with his own eyes the intimate side of an effectively organized black religious and civic leadership network.

King's father was a Christian fundamentalist preacher. At an early age, his son began to question the concepts of fundamentalism.

> ... at the age of 13 I shocked my sunday [sic] school class by denying the bodily resurrection of Jesus. 11

At Morehouse College, where he matriculated at age 15, he was exposed to the ideas of liberal theology.[12] His major field of study was sociology, but he also studied religion with Professor George Kelsey and attended regularly the chapel sermons of Dr. Benjamin E. Mays, President of Morehouse College and a friend of the King family. Both men were trained in modern liberal theology and King responded with curiosity.[13] In that setting, he decided to follow the path of his father into the ministry and selected Crozer Seminary in Chester, Pennsylvania, for his theological education.

> It was in my senior year of college that I entered the ministry ... My call to the ministry was not a miracukous [sic] something, on the contrary it was an inner urge calling me to serve humanity. I guess the influence of my father also had a great deal to do with my going in the ministry ... my admiration for him was the great motivating factor; he set forth a noble example that I didn't mine(sp?) [sic] following. Today I differ a great deal with my father theologically but that admiration for a real father still remains. 14

At Crozer Seminary, King was exposed more fully to the world of modern, liberal Christian theology. He was influenced especially by the teaching and writing of Professor George A. Davis, an "evangelical liberal" in his views. King took 34 of his required 110 course hours with Davis and the influence was significant. Zepp and Smith have analyzed the Davis-King connection and compared the major emphases of Davis' theology with the emphases of King's later published writings.

> Most of the major themes of Martin Luther King were the themes of evangelical liberalism. His stress upon the fatherhood of God and the brotherhood of man, the centrality of religious experience, the concern of God for all life, the rights of man and moral feeling, the humanity of Jesus and his emphasis on love, the dynamic nature of history and God's actions therein, his essential optimism about human nature and history, the tolerance and openness of the liberal spirit, his tolerance toward pluralism of world religions - all of these were key themes of evangelical liberalism embraced early in his intellectual pilgrimage. 15

Also at Crozer, King read some writings of Mohandas K. Gandhi, Reinhold Niebuhr, and Walter Rauschenbusch with interest. He was influenced from that time on by Niebuhr's view of human sinfulness and Rauschenbusch's emphases on prophetic Christianity, on the church as an agent of active social change, and on the Kingdom of God as an attainable ideal.[16] Gandhi's work made its strongest impact on King later in his career, as we will see below. He read and considered the work of Barth, but preferred the general approach of liberal theology.[17] His teacher, George Davis, provided for King a first serious exposure to the writings of the Boston "personalists," especially Edgar Sheffield Brightman and L. Harold DeWolf.

King graduated as valedictorian of his seminary class and entered a program at Boston University for a Ph.D. degree in systematic theology. At Boston University, in seminars with Brightman, DeWolf, and Peter Bertocci, King studied closely the writings of personalist thinkers and those others, especially Hegel, upon whose work personalism depends. King's later work reflects a definite influence of Hegel's dialectical approach.[18] At Boston University, he became a personal idealist in his theology. As he later wrote,

I studied philosophy and theology at Boston University under Edgar S. Brightman and L. Harold DeWolf ... It was mainly under these teachers that I studied personalistic philosophy - the theory that the clue to the meaning of ultimate reality is found in personality. This personal idealism remains today my basic philosophical position. 19

As a dissertation, King chose to analyze, compare, and evaluate the conceptions of God in the theologies of Paul Tillich and Henry Nelson Wieman.[20] His critique of Tillich's and Wieman's thinking is based largely in the philosophy of personalism.[21]

As we turn to the next part of our discussion, we are going to see how these factors - family, church, and education for ministry - were integrated by King into a coherent theological position which provided effective legitimation for social change.

Cosmic Companionship

Two approaches have dominated the study of King's theology up to the present. Scholars such as Zepp, Smith, and Ansbro have tried to identify the intellectual figures who influenced King's thinking.[22] On the other hand, James H. Cone, Paul R. Garber, and William D. Watley have attempted to show that King's theology is influenced more by his black church heritage than by his theological education in predominantly white institutions, and certainly more than earlier interpreters of King recognized.[23]

To my knowledge, no one yet has presented a holistic interpretation of King's theology which shows that, in his growth and development as a theologian, there is an intimate relating and blending of sources that occurs over a period of time. In most instances, it is difficult to identify and extract single sources of influence in King's writings. In his recent essay, "The Theology of Martin Luther King, Jr.," Cone sees more clearly than before, and more clearly than most other interpreters, the importance of considering together, and as a whole, multiple sources of influence on King's theology.

A third approach, the approach of this discussion, is to concentrate primarily on King's theological ideas with secondary attention to textual and biographical influences on his thought.

In this section, we will examine King's conception of God in his dissertation, in his book, Strength to Love, and in some unpublished King manuscripts, mostly prepared texts of speeches and transcriptions of recorded speeches. Strength to Love is a collection of sermons, all of which were written for King's "former parishioners in the Dexter Avenue Baptist Church of Montgomery, Alabama, and [his] ... parishioners in the Ebenezer Baptist Church of Atlanta, Georgia."[24] I am not using King's better known books, articles, and speeches because some scholars believe they were edited (by King and his editorial assistants) in a way to make them more acceptable to supporters of the civil rights movement, especially white liberals. As we analyze some of these lesser known writings, we will see some differences between them and the better known writings.[25]

King struggled throughout his life to understand God, experientially and theologically. During his seminary years, as we have seen, King reflected on factors that had shaped his understanding of God - his family, his church, and his neighborhood associations. Then, in his doctoral dissertation at Boston University, he examined the conceptions of God in the theologies of Paul Tillich and Henry Nelson Wieman. His choice of the dissertation topic and his handling of it show King's growing concern for the question of God. And after his theological education, the question of God is a focal concern in many of King's sermons.

If we examine King's writing and preaching, we find four major emphases in his conception of God. God is omnipotent, good (both moral and benign), personal, and active in human events. This does not describe the God of either Tillich or Wieman. It comes close, however, to describing the God of evangelical liberalism, personalism, and the black church.

A. God's Power

In his dissertation, King applauds Tillich for preserving the omnipotence of God and criticizes Wieman, and even Brightman, for sacrificing it in order to preserve God's goodness.

> Wieman is right in emphasizing the goodness of God, but wrong in minimizing his power. Likewise Tillich is right in

emphasizing the power of God, but wrong in minimizing his goodness ... God is not _either_ powerful _or_ good; he is _both_ powerful _and_ good. 26

In a later sermon he writes:

At the center of the Christian faith is the conviction that in the universe there is a God of power who is able to do exceedingly abundant things in nature and in history ... The God whom we worship is not a weak and incompetent God. He is able to beat back gigantic waves of opposition and to bring low prodigious mountains of evil. 27

B. God's Goodness

It is not enough for King, however, that God is powerful. King's Christian God is both benign and moral. We wish to know, King says in his dissertation, whether God "is good, bad, or indifferent."[28] Again and again during the movement years, King said and wrote that the universe "is on the side of right," "the universe is on the side of justice," and "the moral arc of the universe is long but it bends toward justice." This prominent theme is more than encouragement to discouraged followers. In a brief journal article in 1958 he wrote, it was this "faith in the future" that could enable the nonviolent resister "to accept suffering without retaliation."[29] And to his congregation, he preached:

Beneath and above the shifting sands of time, the uncertainties that darken our days, and the vicissitudes that cloud our nights is a wise and loving God ... Above the manyness of time stands the one eternal God, with wisdom to guide us, strength to protect us, and love to keep us. His boundless love supports and contains us as a mighty ocean contains and supports the tiny drops of every wave. 30

C. God as Personal

King's God, as we would expect from his church background and his study with personalist thinkers, is personal. For King, that means that God possesses, in some transcending sense, the qualities of personality - intelligence and freedom, with primary emphasis on freedom and will.

To say that this God is personal is not to make him a finite object besides other objects or attribute to him the limitations of human personality; it is to take what is finest and noblest in our consciousness and affirm its perfect existence in him. 31

King argues against both Tillich and Wieman in his dissertation.

> The religious man has always recognized two fundamental religious values. One is fellowship with God. The other is trust in his goodness ... True fellowship and communion can exist only between beings who know each other and take a volitional attitude toward each other ... Fellowship requires an outgoing of will and feeling ... Life as applied to God means that in God there is feeling and will, responsive to the deepest yearnings of the human heart; this God both evokes and answers prayer. 32

In his later preaching, the same theme is accented.

> Christianity affirms that, at the heart of reality is a Heart, a loving Father who works through history for the salvation of his children. 33

King's experience of God as personal became increasingly real during the years of the movement. His suffering and the suffering of movement workers deepened his faith in God's personalness and clarified his theological expression of it.[34] In the context of discussing suffering and the agonizing moments of the movement, he writes:

> In the past the idea of a personal God was little more than a metaphysical category that I found theologically and philosophically satisfying. Now it is a living reality that has been validated in the experiences of everyday life. God has become profoundly real to me in recent years. 35

D. God's "Cosmic Companionship"

This powerful, good, and personal God means "cosmic companionship" to those who struggle for justice. This God, whose very character is the moral law of the universe, is engaged in the struggle against evil. Whoever struggles against evil and for justice will experience God's cosmic companionship. This idea is substantially present in King's speech at Holt Street Church in Montgomery, on December 5, 1955.

> We must keep God in the forefront ... Justice is love correcting that which would work against love. The Almighty God himself is ... not the God just standing out saying, 'Behold Thee, I love you Negro.' He's also the God that standeth before the nations and says: 'Be still and know that I am God, that if you don't obey me I'm gonna break the backbone of your power, and cast you out of your international and national relationships.' Standing beside love is always just. And we are only using the tools of justice. 36

Six months after the beginning of the Montgomery boycott, in June of 1956, King addressed the Annual Convention of the N.A.A.C.P. in San Francisco.

> We have the strong feeling that in our struggle we have cosmic companionship. This is why our movement is often referred to as a spiritual movement. We feel that the universe is on the side of right. 37

In April of 1961, at Southern Baptist Theological Seminary, King said, switching his style near the conclusion of his speech,

> But if you will allow the preacher in me to come out now ... we must have faith in the future, the faith to believe that we can solve this problem, the faith to believe that as we struggle to solve this problem we do not struggle alone. But we have cosmic companionship ... The God we worship is not merely a self-knowing God, but he is an ever-loving God, working through history for the salvation of man. So with this faith we can move on. 38

In September of 1963, a few weeks after the conclusion of the Birmingham campaign, a few days after the most famous March on Washington and King's "I Have a Dream" speech at the Lincoln Memorial, four young black girls were killed by a Sunday morning bomb blast at the Sixteenth Street Baptist Church in Birmingham. In King's eulogy at the funeral, he said:

> At times, life is as hard as crucible steel. It has its bleak and painful moments. Like the ever-flowing waters of a river, life has its moments of drought and its moments of flood. Like the everchanging cycle of the seasons, life has the soothing warmth of the summers and the piercing chill of its winters. But through it all, God walks with us. Never forget that God is able to life [sic] you from fatigue of despair to the buoyancy of hope, and transform dark and desolate valleys into sunlit paths of inner peace. 39

King's theology consistently expresses his faith that God is powerful, good (benign and moral), and personal; to express these notions together, God is a source of "cosmic companionship" in the struggle for justice. Those same themes are corroborated in the better known books and articles which we have omitted from this study. These themes are indigenous to King's black church tradition and they are central in the formal theologies which he preferred and in which he was academically trained. This theology, especially as expressed by King, was the spirituality of the civil rights movement. As people

550

suffered in the struggle to change an evil system, their religion reminded them of a powerful, friendly, moral, personal God who walks and struggles with them, and who is able to transform their "dark and desolate valleys into sunlit paths of inner peace."

For King, personality (freedom and intelligence) is God's primary quality. It is God's nature to create processes and structures which produce and sustain personality. Personality presupposes and depends upon a community of love, "beloved community," as King called it; hate destroys community. God is committed to "beloved community" in all of its ramifications. To speak of God's power and God's moral nature means that God has the capability to sustain personality against any and all opposition. Therefore, a person who struggles for personhood and person-producing community, has the promise of God's "cosmic companionship." In his book, Where Do We Go From Here, King wrote,

> Every human being has etched in his personality the indelible stamp of the creator ... The essence of man is found in freedom ... Nothing can be more diabolical than a deliberate attempt to destroy in any man his will to be a man and to withhold from him that something which constitutes his true essence. 40

Nonviolence

Until quite recently, largely due to somewhat misleading accounts of the Montgomery boycott in King's books and articles, scholars believed that King, during his academic training, was deeply impressed by and influenced by Gandhi's satyagraha campaigns and his writings. Then, because of that early influence, scholars believed that King introduced nonviolent values and tactics into the Montgomery boycott from the beginning. We now know this is not a true account. [41]

The civil rights movement, and the churches' involvement in it, should be dated from immediately following the opinion of the United States Supreme Court in their decision, Plessy v. Ferguson, 1892, which legalized and legitimated "separate but equal," the despised principle of Jim Crow. [42] Black nationalism (Bishop Henry McNeal

Turner and Marcus Garvey especially), the Niagara Movement (1905), N.A.A.C.P. (1910), black unions, the attempts to desegregate the United States defense industry (1941) and the United States military forces (1946), attempts to desegregate public schools (1950-54), and attempts to desegregate interstate transportation carriers (1947) – these were all civil rights efforts, frequently supported by black church people, employing methods that were nonviolent. In that entire picture, there is, in fact, no evidence of violent methods.

We must note one other thing. Many black leaders in the United States had been observing Gandhi's work carefully and comparing the plight of untouchables in India with the situation of black people in the United States. Several well known black persons had visited Gandhi in India and interviewed him. Others had been trained in Gandhian methods. Benjamin Mays, Morehouse College president and friend of the King family, was one;[43] Howard Thurman, Chaplain at Boston University and a friend of King all during the civil rights movement was another. Bayard Rustin, who would play a key role in Montgomery, was another.[44] And black union leader, A. Philip Randolph, who had a close, long-time relation to E.D. Nixon, President of the N.A.A.C.P. in Montgomery during the bus boycott, was yet another.[45]

When we talk about nonviolent values and methods in Montgomery and the civil rights movement that followed, therefore, we are dealing with an established tradition – a blend of the black integrationist tradition, the Gandhian nonviolent movement, and the tradition of the black churches.[46] At the beginning of the Montgomery boycott, however, King's leadership was couched in terms of Christian love and a kind of tough justice. In his Holt Street Baptist Church speech, he said:

> Mrs. Parks is a fine Christian Person ... we are a Christian people. We believe in the Christian religion. We believe in the teachings of Jesus. The only weapon that we have in our hands this evening is the weapon of protest ... we're going to work with grim and firm determination to gain justice ... If we are wrong, God Almighty is wrong. If we are wrong Jesus of Nazareth was merely a utopian dreamer and never came down to earth. If we are wrong justice is a lie. 47

In that original speech, King said, "we've got to use the tools of coercion." But in the published version, three years later, the speech reads, "Our method will be that of persuasion, not coercion."[48] Something had changed.

Within a few weeks after the beginning of the boycott, Bayard Rustin and Glenn Smiley, two veterans of Gandhian nonviolent resistance who worked with the Fellowship of Reconciliation, came to Montgomery and remained to play important roles as close advisers to King and trainers in the philosophy and method of nonviolence. In the fall of 1956, James Lawson, another F.O.R. staff person, also joined King as a trainer in nonviolence.[49] Although King, during his years as a student, had listened to inspiring lectures on Gandhi by A.J. Muste and Mordecai Johnson, had read Gandhi, and had written a paper on Gandhi, it was in the movement that he learned most about Gandhi and about nonviolent method. Lawson recalls that King came frequently to training sessions, sitting on the front row with his notebook in hand.[50]

Nonviolence as King writes about it and satyagraha as Gandhi writes about it have many elements in common. Gandhi understood how close ahimsa is to the Christian understanding of love. Self suffering, tapasya, is close to King's understanding of the redemptiveness of "unmerited suffering." King's God, the moral power who is on the side of justice, is near to Gandhi's concept of Truth, sat. The goal of the ideal community, ram rajya, in Gandhi's view, is close to the goal of "beloved community" in King's dream. The agreement of ends and means, the reconciliation of the enemy, and the willingness to "pocket insults" in order to promote the ultimate end of community – all of these factors are shared in common by Gandhi and King.[51]

It would not be accurate to say that King learned all of these things from Gandhi. As has been pointed out earlier, the practice of nonviolence, in many forms (strike, march, boycott, freedom ride, confrontive negotiation, civil disobedience and going to jail) already pervaded the black civil rights movement before King. We can say that King found in Gandhi a compelling synthesis of philosophy and method compatible with the value of Christian love.

> I came to see for the first time that the Christian doctrine of love, operating through the Gandhian method of nonviolence, is one of the most potent weapons available to an oppressed people in their struggle for freedom. 52

This insight almost surely rests on the Montgomery experience with the training in nonviolence by Smiley and Lawson and King's ongoing experience with nonviolence in the movement.

King's nonviolence undoubtedly was reinforced and expanded through his engagement with Gandhian concepts and methods. All evidence indicates, however, that we must look more closely at the black community in the United States and its career with nonviolence, both Christian nonviolence and Gandhian nonviolence, if we are to understand the fertile soil in which the greatest nonviolent leader of the United States put down his roots.

Conclusion

Clearly, King's nonviolence was reinforced and expanded through his engagement with Gandhian concepts and methods, and that influence was already present in the black community in the United States. King was a Christian theologian, however, before his serious engagement with Gandhian satyagraha, and his nonviolence is an expression of his Christian theology. His God is a personal God of power and goodness who is committed to the sustenance of personality and its communal ground. That God is served through love which reconciles and builds beloved community. Nonviolence seemed to King the only means of social transformation adequate to his understanding of God. His God was the God of his family and his church tradition; and it was the God he had struggled to comprehend through the long process of his intellectual development.

As those traditions merged in his thought during his years of public leadership, God's "cosmic companionship" became experientially more real and intellectually more compelling to him. This illumines his firm opposition to the hateful elements in the black power movement and his widening concerns about poverty and the Vietnam War.

NOTES

[1]One of the most famous of the civil rights songs. Other verses are: "We are not afraid," "We shall all be free," "We'll walk hand in hand."

[2]Martin Luther King, Jr., Strength to Love (New York: Harper & Row, 1963), p. 50.

[3]Ibid., p. 139.

[4]James H. Cone, "The Theology of Martin Luther King, Jr.," Union Seminary Quarterly Review, Vol. XL, No. 4, 1986, p. 22. See also, Aldon D. Morris, The Origins of the Civil Rights Movement: Black Communities Organizing for Change (New York: Free Press, 1984). Morris describes the extensive organizational network upon which the movement was based and the central role of black churches and black ministers in that network.

[5]There are several biographies of King. At present, the best one available is by Stephen B. Oates, Let the Trumpet Sound (New York: Harper & Row, 1982). A detailed, two-volume biography will be published in October of this year by David J. Garrow, Bearing the Cross: Martin Luther King and the Southern Christian Leadership Conference (New York: William Morrow and Company, 1986). The author has briefly examined uncorrected galley proofs of Garrow's new book. Valuable biographical information about King is found in Martin Luther King, Sr., Daddy King (New York: William Morrow and Company, Inc., 1980). See the bibliography for other sources.

[6]Martin Luther King, Jr., "An Autobiography of Religious Development." This seven page, unpublished document is found in the Martin Luther King, Jr. Special Collection, Mugar Library, Boston University. It was written by King during his graduate school years.

[7]Martin Luther King, Jr., "The Un-Christian Christian," Ebony, August 1965, p. 77.

[8]"An Autobiography of Religious Development."

[9]Ibid.

[10]Daddy King, pp. 98–111.

[11]"An Autobiography of Religious Development."

[12]The best sources for learning about the formal theological education of King are: Kenneth L. Smith and Ira G. Zepp, Search for the Beloved Community (Valley Forge, Pennsylvania: Judson Press, 1974), and John J. Ansbro, Martin Luther King, Jr.: The

Making of a Mind (Maryknoll, New York: Orbis Books, 1982). King's thought is discussed by Ansbro without adequate regard for the sequence of his development. For an excellent discussion of the scholarly interpretation of King's education and thought, see David J. Garrow, "The Intellectual Development of Martin Luther King, Jr.: Influences and Commentary," Union Seminary Quarterly Review, Vol. XL, No. 4, 1986, pp. 5-20. Stephen Oates, in the first long chapter of Let the Trumpet Sound, entitled "Odyssey," has dealt with these issues but somewhat unreliably. See also James H. Cone, "Martin Luther King, Jr., Black Theology - Black Church," Theology Today, Vol. XL, No. 4 (January 1984), p. 409; and "The Theology of Martin Luther King, Jr.," p. 21. In his 1984 article, Cone rightly argues that the black church must be considered as an important source of influence on King's theology. He fails, however, to see the dynamic blend of sources in King's thinking as an authentic synthesis. In his 1986 article, his presentation is more balanced. See also William D. Watley, Roots of Resistance: The Nonviolent Ethic of Martin Luther King, Jr. (Valley Forge, Pennsylvania: Judson Press, 1985).

[13]Dr. Mays related to the author that King, as a college student, often came to his office after chapel services for a discussion of the ideas in the sermon. (Interview, Atlanta, February 25, 1982).

[14]"An Autobiography of Religious Development."

[15]Smith and Zepp, Search for the Beloved Community: The Thinking of Martin Luther King, Jr., p. 29. See also David J. Garrow, "The Intellectual Development of Martin Luther King, Jr.," p. 7.

[16]Garrow, "The Intellectual Development of Martin Luther King, Jr.," p. 8.

[17]Cone, "The Theology of Martin Luther King, Jr.," pp. 23-24.

[18]For discussions of the influence of Hegel see Ansbro, Martin Luther King, Jr.: The Making of a Mind, many locations; and Garrow, "The Intellectual Development of Martin Luther King, Jr.," pp. 13-14.

[19]Martin Luther King, Jr., Stride Toward Freedom (New York: Harper & Row, 1958), p. 100.

[20]Martin Luther King, Jr., A Comparison of the Conceptions of God in the Thinking of Paul Tillich and Henry Nelson Wieman (Boston University, 1955, unpublished).

[21]The author disagrees with Garrow about the worth of the dissertation as a source for understanding King's thought. Garrow believes it contains "many repeated bows toward personalism," but little of "King's own thinking." I find the dissertation more revealing of King's concerns than does Garrow. It reflects a growing influence

of personalism on King, an influence that lasted throughout his life and even deepened in his later years. There is little doubt, as Garrow writes, that personalist scholars have tended to inflate their own importance for King's mature thought. That should not blind us concerning the contribution of personalism to King's developing thought, either at the time of his dissertation or later, as a subsequent section of this essay will show. There is, in fact, need for further scholarly examination of King's personalism. See Garrow, "The Intellectual Development of Martin Luther King, Jr.," p. 19, note *23.

[22] Kenneth L. Smith and Ira G. Zepp, Search for the Beloved Community, and John J. Ansbro, Martin Luther King, Jr.: The Making of a Mind. Having identified sources of influence on King, e.g., Reinhold Niebuhr, George A. Davis, Walter Rauschenbusch, and the personalists, these interpreters attempt to explicate and extend King's ideas by showing how the others developed their ideas. The great danger of this approach is to overvalue accessible written sources of influence on King's thinking and to undervalue King's creative intellect as well as the unwritten and/or less accessible sources of influence upon his thinking.

[23] James H. Cone, "Martin Luther King, Jr., Black Theology – Black Church," and "The Theology of Martin Luther King, Jr."; Paul R. Garber, "King Was a Black Theologian," Journal of Religious Thought, Vol. 31 (Fall and Winter 1974-75), pp. 16ff., and "Black Theology: The Latter Day Legacy of Martin Luther King, Jr.," Journal of the Interdenominational Theological Center, Vol. 2 (Fall 1980), pp. 29ff.; William D. Watley, Roots of Resistance. The difficulty of this approach, especially in Cone's essays, has been knowing how to value those aspects of King's thought which rather obviously are products of his formal education. A second problem is that evidence for influence of the black church on King's thinking is sometimes indirect, inferential, and difficult to establish.

[24] King, Strength to Love, Preface, p. xi.

[25] Some scholars hold that King's published writings, especially his books and key articles, were influenced by editors such as Bayard Rustin, Stanley Levison, and Harris Wofford. See Garrow, "The Intellectual Development of Martin Luther King, Jr.," p. 5. A second argument is that King spoke and wrote one way to black audiences (King's authentic self) and another way to white audiences (an assumed intellectual posture). See James H. Cone, "The Theology of Martin Luther King, Jr.," p. 28, and "Martin Luther King, Jr.: Black Theology – Black Church," see the entire article but especially, p. 411. There are two issues here. The first is whether writings under King's name represent King's thought or an editorial point of view. The second issue is whether King's writings were slanted for particular audiences, especially for white liberal audiences from whom King (and/or his editors) wanted to

garner financial support for the civil rights movement. These scholars believe that we are more likely to discover King's mind either in writings and recordings of speeches composed and delivered before King became famous (before he depended heavily upon editorial assistance) or in unpublished texts and recordings of speeches which were prepared for and delivered to predominantly black audiences.

On the other hand, one can take the position that writings which bear King's name, certainly his books and major articles, were closely inspected by King after any editing and before their release to publishers. They can, therefore, be taken as expressions of his thought. Preston N. Williams has taken this position in lectures at Harvard University and in personal conversation with the author.

The scholarly question is about the extent of editorial assistance, the range of editorial freedom, and the aims of the editors as well as King's own aims in different settings. There are justifiable questions of editorship concerning King's writings but present evidence does not support a firm scholarly resolution.

One example of an editorial problem is King's speech at Holt Street Baptist Church on December 5, 1955. This was his first speech as President of the Montgomery Improvement Association on the first day of the Montgomery bus boycott. The speech is reported in one version in <u>Stride Toward Freedom</u> and in a somewhat different version on an audio tape of the actual occasion three years earlier. The audio tape and a typescript of it are found in the King Archives in Atlanta. David J. Garrow discusses this issue in "The Intellectual Development of Martin Luther King, Jr.," p. 5. In the unpublished original (1955), King spoke of justice and justifiable coerciveness. He was optimistic, and expressed his values in straightforward Christian terms. In the published version (1958), justice themes are supplanted by emphasis on love, there is mention of "persuasion" rather than "coercion," and there is more "abstract intellectual content." Garrow suggests that this indicates editorial influence. Garrow does not seem to consider that some of the differences between the two texts may indicate authentic changes in King. It is possible that King, reflecting and writing in 1958, conflated the beginning and the end of the Montgomery boycott. As I shall discuss below, King's thinking about love and nonviolence changed significantly during the period of the year-long boycott. As King's thinking about and practice of love sharpened, his thinking became more radical, not less. When Garrow says that the early, unedited King "gave voice to the same heritage the common people of black Montgomery had grown up in," he overlooks the fact that King, at that time, was a trained theologian with a Ph.D. It is far too simple to overlook the problem of the intellectual in leading mass social movements. The King who went to Montgomery was a different King from the one who left home to attend Morehouse College ten years earlier. His theological education and his intellectual growth played no small part in that change.

The extensive congruence of the bulk of King's published writings with the bulk of his unpublished writings will, in the long run, make us reasonably confident that we can discover in them an authentic Martin Luther King, Jr.

[26] King, Dissertation, pp. 297-8.

[27] King, Strength to Love, p. 101.

[28] King, Dissertation, p. 299.

[29] Martin Luther King, Jr., "Out of the Long Night of Segregation," Advance, February 28, 1958.

[30] King, Strength to Love, p. 115.

[31] Ibid., p. 141.

[32] King, Dissertation, p. 272.

[33] King, Strength to Love, p. 94.

[34] See Garrow, "The Intellectual Development of Martin Luther King, Jr.," p. 16. Garrow recognizes the importance of King's faith experience for his theological understanding and calls attention to an experience in King's home in the early weeks of the Montgomery boycott, on January 27, 1956 (see Stride Toward Freedom, pp. 134-35). Many other critical moments in King's life and faith experience could be cited to support this point of view. E.g., the night of the bombing of King's home in Montgomery (see Stride Toward Freedom, pp. 135-37), and King's experience at the Gaston Motel in Birmingham when the movement appeared to be at an impasse and King had to decide whether to go to jail or to go on a speaking tour to raise money (see Why We Can't Wait, pp. 70-72).

[35] King, Strength to Love, p. 141. This chapter of the book is reproduced from his earlier book of 1958, Stride Toward Freedom.

[36] King, Speech at Holt Street Church, December 5, 1955. Unpublished. The speech was extemporaneous. A recording and transcript of the recording are in the King Archives, Atlanta.

[37] Martin Luther King, Jr., "Address to the Annual Convention of the N.A.A.C.P.," Civic Auditorium, San Francisco, June 27, 1956, 8. Unpublished. King Archive, Atlanta.

[38] Martin Luther King, Jr., "Address" at Southern Baptist Theological Seminary, April 19, 1961. Unpublished, King Archives, Atlanta.

[39] Martin Luther King, Jr., "Eulogy For the Four Girls Who Were Murdered in the Church in Birmingham-1963." Unpublished. King Archives in Atlanta.

[40] Martin Luther King, Jr., _Where Do We Go From Here_ (New York: Harper & Row, 1967), pp. 97-99.

[41] Aldon Morris, in _The Origins of the Civil Rights Movement_, provides the best account of how nonviolent values and tactics were introduced into the Montgomery boycott by Bayard Rustin and Glenn Smiley. David Garrow also stresses this later interpretation of nonviolence in Montgomery in his, "The Intellectual Development of Martin Luther King, Jr.," and we can anticipate a full treatment of the matter in his forthcoming book, _Bearing the Cross_. The author has discussed this aspect of the early months of the Montgomery boycott with Bayard Rustin in an interview in New York City.

[42] In speaking here of the beginning of the civil rights movement, I am not speaking of the whole long struggle of black people in the United States for justice and freedom. That struggle is nearly four centuries old and the civil rights movement can be seen as a recent period in the overall struggle. My point here is that the civil rights movement began much earlier than is often recognized and the black churches were involved in it. For understanding the close link between black religion and the black struggle for justice and freedom, see Vincent Harding, _There is a River: The Black Struggle for Freedom in America_ (New York: Harcourt, Brace, and Jovanovich, 1981). See also, Gayraud S. Wilmore, _Black Religion and Black Radicalism: An Interpretation of the Religious History of Afro-American People_ (Maryknoll, New York: Orbis Books, Revised edition, 1984).

[43] The author interviewed Mays about his trip, in 1936, to visit Gandhi. (Interview in Atlanta, 2/25/1982).

[44] Interview of Bayard Rustin by the author, New York City.

[45] Aldon Morris, _The Origins of the Civil Rights Movement_, pp. 157-58.

[46] See James H. Cone, footnote 6 above.

[47] King, "Holt Street Baptist Church Address," December 5, 1955. Unpublished. King Archives, Atlanta.

[48] King, _Stride Toward Freedom_, p. 62.

[49] See Aldon Morris, pp. 157-166.

[50] Interview of James Lawson by the author, University of Southern

California, May, 1984.

[51]For an excellent presentation of Gandhi's religious thought, see Margaret Chatterjee, Gandhi's Religious Thought (Notre Dame, Indiana: University of Notre Dame Press, 1983).

[52]King, Strength to Love, p. 138.

David Lee Miller

On William James' Contributions to the Enduring Themes in American Philosophy

Preface

A gathering perspective has been taking shape in the western world for well over one hundred years, and central to its larger development is what Max H. Fisch has termed "The Classic Period in American Philosophy," a period Fisch fixes "... beginning just after the Civil War and continuing to the eve of the Second World War."[1] As editor of <u>Classic</u> <u>American</u> <u>Philosophers</u>, he cites Charles Peirce, Josiah Royce, William James, George Santayana, John Dewey, and Alfred North Whitehead as the major figures in this "Classic Period." There is now some doubt as to whether Santayana is a bona fide member of this group of philosophers, for neither his sensibility nor his explicit philosophical writings are particularly sympathetic and supportive of either the letter or the spirit of the major American thinkers of this period.[2]

More important, however, is the fact that the central themes of "The Classic Period in American Philosophy" have been pursued with great vigor and commitment well beyond "the eve of the Second World War." Two of the most important and influential thinkers who have continued the main lines of inquiry of this period are Henry Nelson Wieman (1884–1975), and Charles Hartshorne. Hartshorne is yet living, and is extremely active philosophically. In no way then is the focus of thought for "The Classic American Philosophers" moribund or dead. In fact, a number of philosophers in the United States and elsewhere around the world are working with utmost seriousness on the enduring themes from this "Classic Age."

The enduring vitality of this classic philosophical tradition has, to be sure, been obscured by other rising philosophical interests during the last fifty years or so. No question, "The Analytic

Emphasis" is alive and very influential in the United States, and in other parts of the world. This "Analytic Emphasis," however, has tended in definite ways to hide the enormous philosophical pluralism to be found amongst philosophers everywhere, including those philosophers presently working directly with the great themes formulated and explored for us initially by our seminal thinkers of "The Classic Age of American Philosophy" - Peirce, Royce, James, Dewey, and Whitehead.

In other words, what makes the headlines in the newspapers is not inclusive of everything that is happening in the world, and what is up front in the headlines may or may not give an account of the most important events. To extend this analogy, it is quite plausible to believe that much of what never makes the newspapers, not even on the middle or back pages, constitutes the most important happenings of all. In this regard, let us remember that as we focus and concentrate, we exclude, and sometimes what we exclude is clearly important for life and meaning. So it is that exclusion is often expressed by the variously dominant philosophical orientations. Such exclusion is radically ironic, and is a great hindrance to the philosophic quest in its many forms and developments. It is very important then for us to understand and appreciate the fact that the rich and profound heritage of the American philosophical tradition is very much alive in the hearts and minds of philosophers today, and therefore that this continuing tradition has an important and complex "cutting edge" in the present writings of many thinkers working out of this tradition.

The central focus of this essay will be to emphasize topics of basic and enduring importance in "The Classic American Philos-ophers." These are the topics that have stood the test of time, and are at the center of current efforts of the most serious thinkers working on behalf of this perspective. In this connection, the main emphasis will be upon the enduring themes of process, creativity, and relatedness in the thought of William James. It is these three ideas that emerge as crucial later on in the work of Wieman, Hartshorne, and others who have continued this point of view. It is from process, creativity, and relatedness that we have our best clues for better understanding these very same themes in the Oriental tradition, especially in the philosophy and religion of Buddhism.

Process

Process philosophy means essentially a departure from substance philosophy, and James along with the other major American philosophers contributes a great deal to the development of this notion. The western tradition in philosophy, from Aristotle to Berkeley and beyond, is rooted in a fundamental way in the idea of substance. Substance is "the substratum," the unchanging support for the changing and perceivable realities that we experience. Historically, substance is the extremely important non-process view that is the backbone of our various philosophical insights and systems. It dies slowly and with great difficulty. It is in the empiricism of David Hume that it receives its most devastating death blow. Now in this last quarter of the twentieth century, substance is utterly implausible to those thinkers who are continuing work in the American philosophical tradition. Following the lead of James and others, process has replaced substance as the key for explaining reality.

John Dewey was persuaded that Charles Darwin's work The Origin of Species was perhaps the single most important intellectual event in helping us to decisively embrace a process orientation, leaving behind the outmoded and injurious substance view. With this publication, the fixity, finality, and permanency of the western philosophical tradition, including the fixity, finality, and permanency of the notion of substance, is no longer possible as a philosophical perspective. Dewey stresses the point:

> The conceptions that had reigned in the philosophy of nature and knowledge for two thousand years, the conceptions that had become the familiar furniture of the mind, rested on the assumption of the superiority of the fixed and the final; they rested upon treating change and origin as signs of defect and unreality. In laying hands upon the sacred ark of absolute permanency, in treating the forms that had been regarded as

types of fixity and perfection as originating and passing away, the "Origin of Species" introduced a mode of thinking that in the end was bound to transform the logic of knowledge, and hence the treatment of morals, politics, and religion. 3

Clearly, the effects of Darwin's work have been enormous, and the effects upon philosophy likewise have been deep and enduring. In summary, Dewey declares that "The influence of Darwin upon philosophy resides in his having conquered the phenomena of life for the principle of transition, and thereby freed the new logic for application to mind and morals and life."[4] James was impressed with the work of Darwin through early contacts with Louis Agassiz, and through his training as a medical student. James was, of course, thoroughly interested in the emerging experimental sciences of his day, and spent a considerable amount of time both contributing to and following their developments. For James, the process of evolution was an experiential fact, and was taken by him as foundational for lines of inquiry in theory of knowledge, metaphysics, and in the basic questions of morality and religion.

A great deal more was going on to encourage James' formulation of the process orientation. The nineteenth century was aflame with intellectual unrest that suggested a process rather than a substantive view of reality. John Stuart Mill wrote his important essays on the unfinished nature of the relationship of the individual and society in this century, and Karl Marx set forth his dynamic conception of human beings as they attempt to develop a creatively productive place for themselves amid the ongoing processes of history. Moreover, this century bloomed with world- transforming inventions highly suggestive of processive reality, such as the telephone in 1875-1876, and the automobile in 1885. It was only a very short time later, in 1903, that the first successful heavier-than-air airplane flight occurred.

James' focus in articulating his view of process is the individual, human self. It is this self as it flows in the concrete that is the chief object of James' attention and energies. In all of his writings, we find a process view of the self. His <u>Principles of Psychology</u>, far from being merely a contribution to the burgeoning science of the day, offers an extremely detailed account of the individual human self as a concrete phenomenon in process, with reason and logic utilized appropriately for the benefit of the flowing phenomenon. Reason and logic do not serve primarily to predicate, draw conceptual distinctions, and make judgments. Instead, reason and logic serve primarily as windows, so that we might see what is going on in moving, concrete experience. For James, logic and reason emerge out of experience, should always honor the twists and turns of that experience, and should never impose themselves upon concrete and living experience willy nilly, as structures in the interest of clarity and order, with disregard for the inherently unpredictable and vital flow of experience itself.

James labors against the traditional idea of mental or spiritual substance in developing his own ideas of the self as a perpetual process. René Descartes' notion of consciousness as a separate and permanent spiritual substance capable of discovering an indubitable set of clear and distinct ideas about reality is the classic case of what James regards as entirely unacceptable as a perspective on the individual, human self. With this emphasis, James sinks a root into different soil. He is here developing his process view of the self as a dramatic contrast to the substance view of Descartes and others. In his essay "Does Consciousness Exist," he writes that

> For twenty years past I have mistrusted 'consciousness' as an entity; for seven or eight years past I have suggested its non-existence to my students, and tried to give them its pragmatic equivalent in realities of experience. It seems to me that the hour is ripe for it to be openly and universally discarded. 5

James stands sensitively and knowingly within the western tradition with its dominant emphasis upon substance, and therefore feels the need to tell his readers forthrightly that they should bear with him as he attempts to explain that the apparent absurdity of the denial of 'consciousness' as private and permanent is in reality not an absurdity at all, but rather is novel insight into the self as an ongoing process, wherein thoughts and material things are finally indistinguishable from one another, and that any kind of postulated 'substratum' as the enduring receptacle for our thoughts, feelings, and bodily sensations is in fact the absurdity.

He will continue to use the word 'consciousness,' but with a fundamentally different meaning. He writes: "Let me then immediately explain that I mean only to deny that the word stands for an entity, but to insist most emphatically that it does stand for a function."[6]

For James, consciousness is indeed a function, an in-the-making reality which is human experience living forward. As he puts this point in his chapter on "The Stream of Thought" in The Principles of Psychology, "... we must simply say that thought goes on."[7] And later in the same chapter he writes that

> Consciousness, then, does not appear to itself chopped up in bits. Such words as 'chain' or 'train' do not describe it fitly as it presents itself in the first instance. It is nothing jointed: it flows. A 'river' or a 'stream' are the metaphors by which it is most naturally described. 8

When James is describing consciousness, he is always describing a kind of lived experience that moves forward continuously. His description is of the coming into expression of a vivid present that moves unstably beyond to yet another vivid present and so on and on. As such, consciousness is the unending expression of fluency, and intellectual analysis is quite capable of disrupting the natural flow with distinctly negative consequences. James describes the flow of experience, as pre-flective and undifferentiated, in the following:

> Experience in its immediacy seems perfectly fluent. The active sense of living which we all enjoy, before reflection shatters our instinctive world for us, is self-luminous and suggests no paradoxes. Its difficulties are disappointments and uncertainties. They are not intellectual contradictions. 9

Consciousness as human experience living forward through countless varieties of configurations encountered in the encompassing environment suggests very strongly one of the distinguishing marks of the process orientation as first introduced by Charles Hartshorne. Hartshorne, in setting forth Whitehead's Concept of Prehension, explains that according to Whitehead the past influences the present, but that the present does not influence the past. Hartshorne calls this relation one of "asymmetrical dependence."[10] While James was unaware of both process as a philosophical orientation, and asymmetrical dependence as a crucial distinguishing mark of the process perspective, he nevertheless clearly has what we now term a process perspective, and his enormous emphasis upon consciousness, and all of experience as living forward, is pregnant with possibilities for being interpreted in terms of Hartshorne's concept of asymmetrical dependence.

Creativity

In reading seriously the important American philosophers of the nineteenth and twentieth centuries, one gets the distinct feeling that the process they are trying to articulate is the process of creativity. Such process of creativity is explored in numerous ways through the use of different terminologies by Peirce, Royce, James, and Dewey. The remaining member of Fisch's designated "Classic Period" (excluding Santayana), Whitehead, makes explicit use of the term creativity throughout his writings. For Whitehead, creativity is the most fundamental feature of process. Wieman focuses exclusively upon creativity as that process that sustains and transforms in a way that nothing else can do.

Hartshorne confirms the central place of creativity for the American philosophers in the following:

> The word refers ... to a major theme in our philosophical tradition, creativity itself as a philosophical category of cosmic significance. True enough, Bergson, Cournot, and Berdyaev in France, Varisco in Italy, and Fechner in Germany have had versions of the idea; but nowhere has the topic been more persistently and searchingly investigated than in this country [the United States] (Peirce, James, W.P. Montague, Dewey, Whitehead). I am convinced that this concept is an unsurpassed, though long neglected, key to many philosophical problems and their history. 11

Clearly, many other philosophers working in this tradition and other traditions as well share Hartshorne's enthusiasm for the concept of creativity which has been neglected because of its complex ramifications, and its divergence from our received philosophical traditions. Therefore, we need an initial formulation of what creativity is, so that we will be able to see in what sense James is a philosopher of creativity. This procedure is important, for James rarely uses the word creativity, even though it is generally granted that he does make significant contributions to the concept.

Once again, let Hartshorne provide the needed clarity of thought so we might explore the concept of creativity in William James. Hartshorne says that "Creativity is the production of new definiteness. It is the ultimate or universal form of emergence."[12] What this means is that "Process philosophy takes becoming as creative in precisely that sense in which classical determinism denies creativity."[13] Hartshorne continues, saying that "For strict determinism, the definiteness of the world throughout all time is already settled and the future seems indefinite only because of ignorance."[14]

In his essay, "The Dilemma of Determinism," James attempts to persuade us that classical determinism is not an acceptable point of view. He proceeds with his task without trying to convince with theoretical arguments or formal proofs. As usual, James has no pretensions that we can demonstrate or prove anything concerning this issue of indeterminism and determinism. Instead, he appeals undogmatically to our concrete sensibilities and to our capacities for rational inquiry. In this essay, he painstakingly tries to point out the futility, the unacceptability of determinism for our lives as active organisms in the world.

Although he does not use the word anyplace in the essay, James' alternative to classical determinism is creativity in Hartshorne's meaning of the "production of new definiteness." For James, "the production of new definiteness" is possible because the universe has a fundamental element of indeterminism. Such a universe is open, incomplete, and filled with unrealized possibilities. According to James, "Indeterminism ... says that the parts have a certain amount of loose play on one another, so that the laying down of one of them does not necessarily determine what the others shall be."[15] Determinism stands in stark contrast to indeterminism according to James' analysis, and essentially maintains that "Possibilities that fail to get realized are ... pure illusions: they never were possibilities at all. There is nothing inchoate ... about this universe of ours, all that was or is or shall be actual in it having been from eternity there."[16]

It is the "certain amount of loose play," the plethora of "real possibilities," and the existence of "inchoateness" that suggest creativity as a key concept in James' thought, for it is the exercise of creativity as the "production of new definiteness" that naturally emerges from these realities. This indeterminacy which obviously calls for creativity is what James prefers to call the chance dimension of human life and the universe. He jettisons the term freedom in favor of the term chance, thinking that freedom is a term far too eulogistic, and that thereby the use of it instead of chance would play upon the emotions of people in a way that might possibly gain their approval for an indeterministic view of the universe before they have properly felt and reflected upon the issues at stake.

Thus James centers his attention upon explicating the word chance, hoping to deepen the insight amongst his listeners and readers concerning the sharp conflict between the deterministic and indeterministic view of human life and the universe, and finally help them, if they are so inclined, to appreciate more fully that "The great point is that the possibilities are really here."[17] Creativity means then for James acting in terms of these possibilities that are inescapably before us here and now. Our life situations are shot through and through with the ambiguity of chance. We are beset with "maybe," "what if," "ought I," "maybe not," and the like. These chance words refer, for James, to the chance elements that are inextricably connected to all of life.

The "production of new definiteness" is decided here and now as the stream of experience living forward, experience that is asymmetrically dependent, and experience once past that has no opportunity to repeat itself in duplicate form. James' analysis and explication of the merits of indeterminism or chance amounts to a call to creativity, and this call places tremendous responsibility upon individual people to take very seriously the fact that each person makes a real, a very significant difference concerning what emerges as the forms of reality. The world we have, and the world we inherit, are in important ways what people do or fail to do to make them as they are. This call to creativity in James vivifies the fact that living is a risky affair, from which there is no real reprieve from assuming personal and collective responsibility for what happens. Giving that responsibility over to a determinism with its presumption of the necessity of actuality past, present, and future, and its denial of creative response in the midst of real possibilities, clearly in James' view is the giving up of the excitement, the power, and the meaning of life itself.

The opportunity of people to make significant differences in the "production of new definiteness" is at the heart of much that he says about the most basic human issues. In other words, this metaphysical creativity in James' thinking is the fundamental matrix in which creativity in all forms of human experience is best understood. Instances are plentiful in his writings of the call to creativity. For example, in "The Moral Philosopher and the Moral Life," the opening sentence says that "The main purpose of this paper is to show that there is no such thing possible as an ethical philosophy dogmatically made up in advance."[18] As we shape our lives individually and collectively, there inevitably is risk, failure, strenuous effort, and at times disaster; but this, James insists, is the authentic way, the only way to live faithfully in the creative depths that gladly and soberly acknowledge the chance elements that literally pervade all our lives at all times and in all places.

Rational arguments and empirical evidence frequently fall short in providing sufficient grounds for our most important decisions in life. In these cases, the responsibility for choosing falls within our creative powers, that is, within our powers to help share what forms of meaning and values emerge in given situations for ourselves, and for others. In "The Will To Believe," James writes:

> Our passional nature not only lawfully may, but must decide an option between propositions, whenever it is a genuine option that cannot by its nature be decided on intellectual grounds; for to say, under such circumstances, "Do not decide, but leave the question open," is itself a passional decision – just like deciding yes or no – and is attended with the same risk of losing the truth. 19

As others have pointed out, James' Will to Believe is in an important way the right to believe, and this right to believe is fruitfully understood as both the right and the responsibility to respond to the continuing call of creativity, that call that requires the assumption of the obligation to shape oneself and the world through creative choice and action. The Earth is awash with the "production of new definiteness." Is it the type of emergent form that meets with our approval? Is it the kind that is life sustaining and life enhancing? Is it the kind that is a genuine tribute to our response to the call to a creativity that makes us increasingly more fully human in countless forms of challenging and stimulating cooperation and compassion? Very painfully, we are reluctant to answer these questions, and very sadly we note the failure to respond sufficiently with our deepest creative powers in a universe and world described many times by James as filled with real openness, real chance, and real challenge.

Relatedness

A third most important and enduring theme that emerges out of the "Classic Age of American Philosophy" is the theme of relatedness. Writing very recently on "The Future of Process Philosophy," Bernard Loomer believes in fact that Process Philosophy should be understood and referred to as Process-Relational Philosophy.[20] Paul E. Rasmussen in a recent conversation on aesthetic experience in the American philosophers[21] remarked poignantly at a critical juncture that "the parts considered without the whole are truly meaningless." In some ways, the theme of relatedness is the most pervasive of all themes in "The Classic American Philosophers." So true is this, that it is difficult to know who and what to cite first in setting forth this idea. Dualisms, dichotomies, and all other separations are abandoned, as philosophical inquiry is deeply committed to searching out the fullest meanings of relatedness. Despite varied emphases and qualifications, Peirce, Royce, James, Dewey, and Whitehead would assent to Loomer's statement that "Our interdependence is a primordial condition."[22]

The celebrated issues in "The Classic American Philosophers" turn in a fundamental way about the idea of relatedness: Peirce with his emphasis upon the inseparability of doubt, inquiry, belief, habit, and action; Dewey with his voluminous account of the dynamic relatedness of organism and environment; and Whitehead with his compelling description of the relatedness of all of the basic features of reality, expressing most fundamentally the creative advances of the universe at every level. Royce as well places primary emphasis upon this theme of relatedness. For Royce, all selves come to have consciousness and meaning through the process of extended and complex learning from other selves. Through our interchange with others, we develop our attitudes, thoughts, and plans for life. He summarizes:

> Love says to the individual: "So extend yourself in ideal, that you aim, with all your heart and your soul and your mind and your strength at that life of perfectly definite deeds which never can come to pass unless all the members, despite their variety and their natural narrowness, are in perfect coopera- tion. Let this life be your art and also the life of all your fellow members. Let your community be as a chorus, and not as a company who forget themselves in a common trance ..." 23

James' famous notion of radical empiricism is the obvious starting point in order to understand his contribution to the idea of relatedness in the American philosophical tradition. Here again, in radical empiricism we see the departure of James' thinking from the great philosophical contributors in the western tradition. This time the critical reaction is to David Hume. Hume's empiricism is atomistic, not radical. It is an empiricism that says particular and unrelated impressions constantly stream in upon our five senses, and are subsequently unified by the mind. White, granular, hard, and pungent are the unrelated atoms of sense experience that come to be related through the activity of the mind into the experience of tasting salt. James insists that Hume's atomistic empiricism is an abstraction. Experience for James never initially comes in separate bits and pieces. He thinks that Hume made a fine contribution in moving away from traditional Rationalisms and Absolutisms, and is pleased to partially identify his type of empiricism with that of

Hume. He says that his empiricism "... is essentially a mosaic philosophy, a philosophy of plural facts like that of Hume and his descendants, who refer these facts neither to substances in which they inhere nor to an absolute mind that creates them as its objects."[24] James continues: "But it differs from the Humian type of empiricism in one particular which makes me add the epithet radical."[25] At this point James explains the heart of his radical empiricism.

> To be radical, an empiricism must neither admit into its constructions any element that is not directly experienced, nor exclude from them any element that is directly experienced. For such a philosophy, the relations that connect experiences must themselves be experienced relations, and any kind of relation experienced must be accounted as 'real' as anything else in the system. 26

The context for further understanding of James' radical empiricism, and therefore of his idea of relatedness, is his conception of the "World of Pure Experience."[27] For James, pure experience is essentially the notion that marks his most decisive departure from some of the most central philosophical themes of the western philosophical tradition, most notably Descartes' dualism of mind and body, and Hume's atomistic empiricism. Pure experience is the undifferentiated, pre-reflective continuum of life. In it, there are no separate atoms of experience; there are no divisions between minds and bodies; and it has no static elements to qualify it. Rather, pure experience is the process of becoming, the stream of life that carries creativity within its bosom, the fullness of experience out of which other things emerge. It is vivid immediacy prior to sensory, emotional, and intellectual discriminations and qualifications. It is in James' words "The instant field of the present (and) is always experience in its 'pure' state, plain unqualified actuality, a simple that, as yet undifferentiated into thing and thought, and only virtually classifiable as objective fact or as someone's opinion about fact."[28]

The main lines of pure experience are developed fully by James in his essay, "Does Consciousness Exist?" After reading this essay, one is left with the distinct impression that what James is trying to express is a profoundly new version of human experience and reality, a version that in a significant way is forged out of a deeply thought and felt opposition to the great philosophical perspectives of the past. Moreover, it has to be noted that James' contribution of pure experience is also in part generated by the innovative theoretical insights being produced around him during the time in which he lived. In the second half of the nineteenth century, theoretical creations and discoveries as well as the upsurge of world-transforming practical changes brought about chiefly by the new science and technology, cried out for a drastically new philosophical orientation. To all of this, James responded in the effort to present a philosophical view bereft of the main themes of the western philosophical tradition, such themes, that is, of Being, Substance, Dualism, Atomism, and the deep faith that reality is basically available to our cognitive powers of understanding.

James' conception of pure experience is a call for us to return to the concreteness of the undivided stream of life itself. Here, he believed that we have a proper starting point for understanding ourselves and the world in which we live, and here we have a reliable and productive way to anchor our conceptual thinking, perceptual discriminations, and value judgments. Here we have, he believed, a way of living forward, creatively, with a sense of genuine connectedness and belongingness. Pure experience refers to nothing residing underneath, supportive of, and generative of the pure experience. Pure experience is the reality, contains the creative possibilities, and appears as inseparability. For James, there is no going behind it to find anything more real. Such a paradigm of pure experience, the undifferentiated pre-reflective continuum is a distinguishing mark of James' philosophy, and an enduring theme taking many forms in the American philosophers, past and present.

Although relatedness is a pervasive theme in the thinking of James, it is significant that it is a kind of relatedness that is qualified, one might say, as a somewhat weaker type of relatedness compared with the notion as found in most of the other American philosophers. It is not at all difficult to conjecture as to one of the important reasons why James so qualifies his meanings of relatedness. Throughout his writings, there is an obvious and large concern that absolutistic systems of reality eliminate the free, creative process of experience. He is concerned that a kind of closed system of monism reduces and distorts the pluralistic, concrete, and emerging realities as irreplacable droplets of the universe. James puts the gist of his qualification forward when he writes that "My experiences and your experiences are 'with' each other in various external ways, but mine pass into mine, and yours pass into yours in a way in which yours and mine never pass into one another."[29] James describes the type of relatedness that he finds acceptable and what it stands over against in the following:

> Such determinately various hanging-together may be called concatenated union, to distinguish it from the 'through-and-through' type of union, 'each in all and all in each' (union of total conflux, as one might call it), which monistic systems hold to obtain when things are taken in their absolute reality. 30

James feels keenly that he must rescue his radical empiricism and pure experience from his contemporary absolutists, and likewise demonstrate its greater acceptability and relevance for life in contrast to the absolutistic systems in the history of western philosophy. A Jamesian reference to Hegel makes this point most forcibly. He writes:

> In the universe of Hegel - the absolute block whose parts have no loose play, the pure plethora of necessary being with the oxygen of possibility all suffocated out of its lungs - there can be neither good or bad, but one dead level of mere fate. 31

James makes an enormous contribution to the theme of relatedness in American philosophy, helping Dewey, Peirce, Royce, Whitehead, and others to move more deeply into this enduring theme. Yet in some ways James' significant influence seems even greater as we become absorbed in the themes of process, creativity, and relatedness in the important thinkers in the American philosophical tradition in the second half of the twentieth century.

Conclusion: The Living Tradition

James died in 1910, leaving behind him a living legacy of rich insights to inform the thoughts and lives of many other thinkers who followed. Many people working within this tradition of American philosophy have continued to work on these enduring themes of process, creativity, and relatedness that James helped to develop in their early forms of expression. The philosophers who are carrying forward our "Classic American Tradition" in the second half of this twentieth century are literally far too numerous to list, but in the United States, two stand out as especially significant in making major contributions to the three themes of process, creativity, and relatedness. They have been referred to in the preface of this paper, and are Henry Nelson Wieman, just recently deceased, and Charles Hartshorne, living presently in Austin, Texas, USA.

It is not possible here to give an account of the basic views in their respective philosophies. That would require another essay or so. The reasons for re-introducing their names at this point are: 1) To emphasize the point that they are self-consciously continuing the central themes first formulated and explored by James and his colleagues who comprise "The Classic Age of American Philosophy;" and 2) Wieman and Hartshorne best provide the bridge to the Philosophy and Religion of Buddhism, which itself, particularly in certain of its forms, is rooted in the living tradition of process, creativity, and relatedness.

Recognized as major thinkers in the American philosophical tradition, Hartshorne and Wieman appear to have more in common than has generally been conceded, and it is specifically in terms of the two points mentioned above that their greatest commonality is to be found. In the introduction to a recently reprinted monograph devoted to Wieman and Hartshorne, William S. Minor points out that "Charles Hartshorne and Henry Nelson Wieman, for many years, have given their lives as philosophers to further understanding of creativity as its operates in (humans) and (their) world."[32] Minor continues: "Both are process philosophers, stimulated and significantly influenced by their study of the works of Alfred North

Whitehead."[33] As their many students and others working with their contributions know very well, relatedness is a key concept for both Wieman and Hartshorne.[34] Their distinct emphases notwithstanding, Wieman and Hartshorne have taken the lead in the second half of the twentieth century in the United States as philosophers of process, creativity and relatedness.

In rather different ways, Wieman and Hartshorne provide crucial links to Buddhism, the living tradition of the Orient that is deeply expressive of process, creativity, and relatedness.[35] Wieman had little knowledge of Buddhism, but nonetheless develops a point of view strikingly similar to Buddhism. This similarity is receiving increasing documentation in recent years.[36] Hartshorne, on the other hand, has taken Buddhism seriously in the development of his own philosophy. His writings contain numerous references to Buddhism, indicating an appreciative understanding of its major emphases of process, creativity, and relatedness.[37]

The work of Wieman and Hartshorne as well as the work of many other philosophers who are struggling with the insights provided by them, acquires new and important relevance as a living tradition when perceived in confluence with the living tradition of Buddhism. This confluence is providing us with essential resources for living as parts of an Earth that has truly exploded in process, creativity, and relatedness during the last one hundred years. The ages of separateness are gone forever. The Earth and the human parts of it express themselves primarily through process, creativity, and relatedness. Such expressions continually outrun our efforts to understand, appreciate, and honor them. Our chief task is to find commitment and meaning in the midst of them.

As many hundreds of writers and thinkers have been pointing out for decades, we are in the midst of an enormous transformation throughout the Earth, one unprecedented in its depth and scope for good and evil. With this awareness, we need every help that we can get, including both Buddhism and the American philosophical tradition, past and present. These two traditions in their historical resources and present expressions offer truly rich possibilities for the entire life of the Earth. Together, they intimate an almost completely unfound redemptive mode of thinking, feeling, and living, a mode that is fundamentally consonant with the functioning and development of the whole Earth. William James would have understood well this growing together of the fundamental and vital insights and values of Buddhism and the American thinkers on behalf of an Earth that is in continual process of creative synthesis.

NOTES

[1] Max H. Fisch, editor, Classic American Philosophers (New York: Appleton-Century-Crofts, Inc., 1951), p. 1.

[2] John E. Smith, The Spirit of American Philosophy (Albany: State University of New York Press, 1983), p. xii.

[3] John Dewey, "The Influence of Darwinism on Philosophy," Classic American Philosophers, Max H. Fisch, editor, p. 336.

[4] Ibid., p. 339.

[5] William James, Essays in Radical Empiricism (New York: Longmans, Green and Co., 1912), p. 3.

[6] Ibid., p. 3.

[7] William James, The Principles of Psychology (New York: Henry Holt and Co., Volume One, 1950), p. 225.

[8] Ibid., p. 239.

[9] James, Essays in Radical Empiricism, p. 92.

[10] Charles Hartshorne, Creativity in American Philosophy (Albany: State University of New York Press, 1984), p. 110.

[11] Ibid., p. xii.

[12] Ibid., p. 104.

[13] Ibid., p. 104.

[14] Ibid., p. 104.

[15] William James, "The Dilemma of Determinism," Essays in Pragmatism, Alburey Castell, editor (New York: Hafner Publishing Company, 1948), p. 41.

[16]Ibid., p. 41.

[17]Ibid., p. 64.

[18]Ibid., p. 65.

[19]Ibid., p. 95.

[20]Bernard Loomer, "The Future of Process Philosophy," Process Philosophy: Basic Writings, Jack R. Sibley and Pete A.Y. Gunter, editors (Washington, D.C.: University Press of America, 1978), p. 534.

[21]Conversation with Paul E. Rasmussen, Chairperson, Department of Philosophy, University of Wisconsin - La Crosse, La Crosse, Wisconsin, USA.

[22]Loomer, "The Future of Process Philosophy," Process Philosophy: Basic Writings, p. 534.

[23]Fisch, Classic American Philosphers, pp. 211-212.

[24]James, Essays in Radical Empiricism, p. 42.

[25]Ibid., p. 42.

[26]Ibid., p. 42.

[27]Cf., pp. 39-99 in Essays in Radical Empiricism.

[28]James, Essays in Radical Empiricism, p. 74.

[29]Ibid., pp. 47-48.

[30]Ibid., p. 108.

[31]William James, The Will To Believe and Other Essays (New York: Dover Publications, 1956), p. 292.

[32]William S. Minor, editor, Charles Hartshorne and Henry Nelson Wieman (Lanham, MD: University Press of America, Inc., 1969), p. xi.

[33]Ibid., p. xi.

[34]Cf. Hartshorne's "The Social Conception of the Universe," in his Reality as Social Process, 1953, and "A Philosophy of Shared Creative Experience," in Creative Synthesis and Philosophic Method, 1970. For Wieman, "Creative Good," in The Source of Human Good, 1946, and "The Problem of Religious Faith," in Man's Ultimate Commitment, 1958.

[35]Cf. Buddhism and American Thinkers, 1984, edited by Kenneth K. Inada and Nolan P. Jacobson (Albany, New York: State University of New York Press).

[36]Cf. the soon to be published Proceedings of the Henry Nelson Wieman Centennial Congress. S.S. Rama Rao Pappu's essay is "Creativity in Buddhism and Wieman," and my essay is "Creative Interchange as the Bodhisattva Ideal."

[37]Cf. Nolan P. Jacobson's dedication and prefatory remarks in Buddhism and the Contemporary World (Carbondale, Illinois: Southern Illinois University Press, 1983).

Charles S. Milligan

The Pantheistic Motif in American Religious Thought

Pantheism has appeared in many places, times, and forms. It is not distinctively American. However, it has been a persistent view, albeit always a minority position, and although there have been tendencies toward it in institutionalized religion, primarily it is to be found elsewhere in American religious thought. It is my contention that it is among poets, novelists, and essayists that it has been notable. These writers have a considerable influence on the religious thinking of people, sometimes more than theologians and philosophers and ecclesiastics. In any case, they represent an important dimension of the religious thought of a people.

A further contention which I put forward is that Pantheism has undergone some significant developments in the twentieth century in the expressions we find among American writers. The purpose of this paper is to lift up examples of Pantheistic thought and to single out the changes which I believe characterize views in this century.

I define Pantheism as the view which identifies God with the All - everything whatever. I choose the term "All," because to say "world" or "universe" is often thought of primarily in physical terms. If I say, "reality," that is apt to be understood in spiritual or non-material terms. If by "universe" you understand that to include qualities and patterned structures, potentiality and thoughts (of such beings as are capable of thinking), in a word everything whatever - omnitudo realitatis, to borrow the scholastics' term -, then the identification of God with that is what I mean by Pantheism.

It is necessary to explain why I am by-passing discussion of Panentheism. It is, I agree, different from Pantheism, although many avowals would be common to both. I will explain some of the differences in the discussion of de-anthropocentrism, but wish to acknowledge here that I have found Hartshorne and Reese's

<u>Philosophers</u> <u>Speak</u> <u>of</u> <u>God</u> useful and informative. However, their scheme of analysis is not applicable to literature with the precision appropriate to philosophy.

There is an important difference in terminology. Hartshorne says:

> ... pantheism, properly so called, supposes that, although God includes all within himself, still, since he cannot be really complex, or mutable, such categories can only express human ignorance or illusion. Thus, common to theism and pantheism is the doctrine of the invidious nature of categorical contrasts. 1

That is certainly correct as regards classical Pantheism, but, I claim, not as regards recent Pantheism which is emphatically naturalistic in its metaphysics and empirical in methodology. My contention is that a typological label ought to represent a clear designation of a basic claim, but not be tied to a list of particular doctrines explicating the views attached to that claim. Just as Theism has had many developments and varieties, so Pantheism. Pantheism need not be tied to the particular doctrines of its classical versions. It is not built-in to its fundamental claim - God is the All - that it must reject categorical contrasts or di-polarity. In fact, the outstanding feature of contemporary Pantheism is that the All is dynamic, variegated, mutable and individuating. Such themes are characteristic of modernism and it is not surprising to find them emphasized in Neo-pantheism.

There are divergent opinions about the nature of nature, but in all which can be labeled Pantheistic there would be an emphasis on God as not merely in nature, but God as Nature, and Nature - in the richest, fullest, comprehensive sense - as God. Some versions are simplistic and naive; others are refined, complex and profound.

Walt Whitman's Pantheism

John Dewey said, "artists have always been the real purveyors of news."[2] Poets, as artists, have often anticipated trends in thought. The poet's characteristic task is to express in the music of words <u>particular</u> instances of the significance of life. That is not necessarily optimistic, but it must be penetrating and illuminating. Themes drawn from nature often are used for this and consequently there is always the risk that Pantheism will be mistakenly attributed to a poem. For example, Robert P. Tristram Coffin, writing about a fox and a fish, concludes with these lines: "There is a strange holiness around / Our common days on common ground." Plainly that is an affirmation which could be made from many different theological positions. It illustrates the fact that it is a tricky business to discern from poetry what the poet's theological position, if any, is. But in some cases the connection is clear.

The theologian has a similar task, namely to explicate the significance of life, but to do so <u>systematically</u> in its deepest and widest context, usually with the vocabulary and by means of the symbolism of a particular religious heritage. Sometimes a thinker manages to be both poet and theologian, but in the main the task of vivid particularism and that of coherent systematizing diverge. In view of that, it strikes me that turning to the poets is worthwhile for understanding the religious thought of a people. They may well emphasize views not conspicuously present in the voices of establishment professionals.

Walt Whitman is the obvious place to begin with American Pantheism. He was thoroughly American, for good and ill. As Whitehead recognized, "Whitman brought something into poetry which was never there before. Much of what he says is so new that he even had to invent a form for saying it. Whitman seems to me to have been one of the few very great poets that have ever lived."[3] As for Whitman's Pantheism, "We are Nature - long have we been absent, but now we return ... We are snow, rain, cold, darkness - we are each product and influence of the globe."[4] Notice that already with him we have a dynamic Pantheism. "All is a procession; / The universe is a procession, with measured and beautiful motion."[5] Excerpts from a few poems will serve to establish Whitman's unequivocal Pantheism.

Thought of the Infinite - the All!
Be thou my God ...
Or Time and Space!
Or shape of Earth, divine and wondrous!
Or shape in I myself - or some fair shape, I, viewing,
    worship
Or lustrous orb of Sun, or star by night:
Be ye my Gods. 6

All must have reference to the ensemble of the world, and
    the compact truth of the world;
There shall be no subject too pronounced - All works shall
    illustrate the divine law of indirections. 7

I hear and behold God in every object, yet understand God
    not in the least,
Nor do I understand who there can be more wonderful than
    myself.
Why should I wish to see God better than this day?
I see something of God each hour of the twenty-four, and
    each moment then ... 8

The line which for me most perfectly depicts Whitman is, "I sound my barbaric yawp over the roofs of the world."[9] There you get the unadorned affirmation, the Americanism, if you will, pure and unalloyed. While it is egotistical, it implies the interconnectedness of existence, "the ensemble of the world." In contrast with classical Pantheism, Whitman's dynamic Pantheism affirms these characteristics:

1. Particularization: the authentic significance of particular, individual entities, and that they are not less significant for being temporal.

2. Interdependence: the reality of societal or configurational groupings is recognized and celebrated. Individuality is not isolated but social. He sings his land and people as well as "Songs of Myself."

3. Urbanization: thus Whitman celebrates the city with its noise and confusion, and not merely the serene pastoral scene. The bustle, hustle, and hassle of Manhattan was no less natural than that the beaver builds a dam and the bird a nest.

4. Tragedy: although extravagantly optimistic at times, he nevertheless dealt poignantly with death, irretrievable loss, oppression and waste, and he did not cover over these stark realities with concluding lines of saccharine piety.

Whitman went through a period of spiritualizing his worldview with New England Transcendentalism, but the major part of his writing by far was in the vein of naturalistic Pantheism.[10] It was, however, quite different from the classical versions.

Kindred Voices

Sidney Lanier (1842-81) was of a different temperament and style, closer to a romantic type of Pantheism, but he, too, recognized evil as real.

> And all outrageous ugliness of time,
> Excess and Blasphemy and squinting Crime
> Beset me, but I kept my calm sublime:
> I hate them not, Nirvâna. 11

While it is true that he saw evils (and precious values) ultimately absorbed into the All, the comfort of that was not supernal bliss, but relief from the sorrows in life. It is debatable whether Lanier was a Pantheist[12] - that depends on which poems you regard as expressing his own deepest convictions -, but he certainly stressed many of its themes. His sanctuary of worship was the Marshes of Glynn.

Emerson was not a Pantheist in the designation adopted here, but I want to call attention to his di-polarity and to suggest that at times he seems to have ventured into Pantheistic modes of thought, straying from his more usual Idealism with its Oversoul. Observing that we meet "polarity, or action and reaction" in every part of nature, he wrote in his remarkable essay, "Compensation:"

> The entire system of things gets represented in every particle. There is somewhat that resembles the ebb and flow of the sea, day and night, man and woman, in a single needle of the pine, in a kernel of corn, in each individual of every animal tribe. The reaction, so grand in the elements, is repeated within these small boundaries ... 13

Later he says:

> Under all this running sea of circumstance, whose waters ebb and flow with perfect balance, lies the aboriginal abyss of real Being. Existence, or God, is not a relation or a part, but the whole. (Ital. added) 14

It appears to me that "the aboriginal abyss" and "existence" as synonymous with God are rather different from his more characteristic Idealism.

Henry David Thoreau presented a forthright Pantheism. The earth is a living organism, not the emanation from an Oversoul or Cosmic Mind. The particular living entities are not less real than the global organism nor less significant because they are not immortal.

> There is nothing inorganic ... not a fossil earth, but a living earth; compared with whose great central life all animal life and vegetable life is merely parasitic. 15

He meditates on the patterns in the sand by the water's edge and sees it as the leaf-form carried out in all things, inanimate as well as animate.

> The very globe continually transcends and translates itself, and becomes winged in its orbit. Even ice begins with delicate crystal leaves ... The whole tree itself is but one leaf, and rivers are still vaster leaves whose pulp is intervening earth, and towns and cities are the ova of insects in their axils. 16

Thoreau was averse to anything resembling systematic theologizing, yet we do find passages where his religio-metaphysical position is stated.

> I see, smell, taste, hear, feel, that everlasting Something to which we are allied, at once our maker, our abode, our destiny, our very Selves; the one historic truth, the most remarkable fact which can become the distinct and uninvited subject of our thought, the actual glory of the universe; the only fact which a human being cannot avoid recognizing, or in some way forget or dispense with. 17

There is no hint of a spirit or self hidden within nature. There is simply this given matrix, the everlasting Something, the actual glory of the universe. Some years later, when he was deeply depressed over the slavery issue and northern temporizing with it, it is not surprising that he was restored in hope by finding a white water lily. It was by virtue of the powers of nature that he found it possible not to "despair of the world."[18]

My point by way of these examples has been not merely to show that there have been Pantheistic writers, but, as the particular writers cited indicate, that these were very significant and influential on the shape of American culture. They were not primarily interested in defending a theological position or institutionalized religion. Yet many people who were involved in institutionalized religion resonated to their thought. It was a remarkable shift, in less than a century, for the liberal American religious view to move from Deism toward Pantheism. The Deists viewed God as virtually removed from nature, being its Author or Architect. Their spiritual descendants emphasized God as thoroughly indwelling. The reason is not obscure. It was due to the transition from the last stages of a mechanistic, Newtonian cosmology, which required an external Designer, to a biologically oriented, evolutionary view of nature, in which God would be more akin to growth and experimentation. It was the shift in the understanding of nature which required a shift in the conception of God. The epistemological predilection which undergirded this shift was for naturalistic methodology, as contrasted with supernaturalistic, authoritarian, or spiritual modes of explanation and justification.

As a historical note it may be added that there were many other nineteenth century poets and writers who affirmed Pantheistic views, some of whom were competent, if not great, poets, and whose works were widely loved, including many regular church people. The outstanding example would be William Cullen Bryant's "Thanatopsis," and earlier in this century a typical one, William H. Carruth's "Each in His own Tongue," with the line, "Some call it Evolution, / And others call it God;" or Elizabeth York Case's "There Is no Unbelief."

De-Anthropocentrism

By de-anthropocentrism is meant the rejection of human qualities as applicable to God (or the Cosmos), or as Spinoza said, "human attributes have no place in God."[19] It does not necessarily follow from that that human qualities of value lack significance, rather that humans hold no place of special privilege in the scheme of things. The classic statement, so often quoted, comes from Stephen Crane (1871-1900).

> A man said to the universe:
> "Sir, I exist!"
> "However," replied the universe,
> "The fact has not created in me
> A sense of obligation." 20

It is in denying that there is any special providence given human beings, either as a whole or for some special portion of individuals, that Pantheism is sharply set apart from most other theistic positions, i.e. positions in which a conception of God is intellectually important and held to be enriching to the psyche or devotionally significant. Contemporary American Pantheism also differs from the classical in that in the classical versions it was usually taught that the individual is insignificant, unreal or deficient in actuality, and often that the correct religious practice is to obliterate the sense of individuality and personhood.[21] In the present version, meaningful personhood is emphasized, but alongside that is the requirement of humility and the danger of hubris. Humility is called for not because all individuality will be absorbed into some magnificent Ocean of Being, but because it depends upon humanity – or those humans who possess power – whether the race will survive. The All, or God, is not going to guarantee that.

It is understandable that it disturbed Christian authorities when the Copernican revolution presented the claim that the earth was not the center of the physical universe. But Christendom eventually adjusted to that. Equally – perhaps more profoundly – it now challenges Christianity, Judaism, and other religions to confront the hypothesis that God has no special providence for humanity and is not going to save us from ourselves. Pantheists have not been the only ones of religious persuasion to come to that view. God as The–Great–Puller–of–Chestnuts–out–of–the–Fire is dead for many devout people. Pantheists by and large never did believe in such a God. Many Personal Theists have come to this view, but retain a concept of God as a Person in some sense and some eschatological privilege for humans, or for some humans. De–anthropocentrism is the rejection of any such claim, at least as the term is meant here.

Individual entities, including human beings and their cultures, are of value: that is asserted by modern Pantheism. But that does not mean they will be preserved or their value perpetuated. The cosmic reality has come to fruition in such entities, but can go on with its destiny whether or not such flowerings endure or perish.

However, that is no reason to reject the cosmic reality, rather to praise or at least affirm its marvelousness. God, as the All, is not to be faulted because its character does not have human welfare and destiny at its center. The ancient warning against hubris remains valid and, to the surprise of some, applies to theology.

Lynn White, Jr. charged that "Especially in its Western form, Christianity is the most anthropocentric religion the world has seen."[22] Whether it is the most such or not, it has been emphatically anthropocentric. Surely the biblical view, with some excepted passages, overwhelmingly presumes a special concern on God's part for human beings. It is not to be wondered at that the new, realistic skepticism about anthropocentrism causes a deep wrenching within organized religion.

It is exacerbated by a shift in the form which the problem of evil takes. In classical form it addressed the question, "Why does evil exist?" It has shifted to the question, "How is it, if God is just and has a special providential care for humans, that evil falls upon some people in such flagrant disproportion to their deserving?" Any theodicy which resolves that question in such a way that all individual life conditions are really as they should be is simply offensive to the modern mind. The theory (as in Kant) that a future estate will compensate is unsatisfactory if one believes that this earthly existence is of genuine importance in its own right. The theory, as in Hartshorne,[23] that God holds in eternal memory all meaningful achievement and goodness is meaningful for those who have had opportunity to actualize such things, but not for the millions who had but little possibility for survival, let alone realization of such values. They are twice cheated. What I have attempted to do in the foregoing critique is to articulate in prosaic terms the mood and convictions which I think are typical of the Pantheistic poets.

Sidney Lanier described finding solace in an aspect of nature following his extreme distress over petty religious quarrels. Notice in particular what he views as being the word of God.

> I fled in tears to the woods, and laid me down on the earth.
> Then somewhat like the beating of many hearts came up to me

out of the ground; and I looked and my cheek lay close to a violet. Then my heart took courage, and I said: "I know that thou art the word of my God, dear Violet" ... 24

That was nineteenth century romantic Pantheism. Compare that with a poet of this century, Harriet Monroe (1860-1936), editor for many years of what was the most important journal of poetry, Poetry: A Magazine of Verse.

> I gained also a realization of the heroic audacity of the "thousand creeds" in imposing a name and a more or less human personality upon the Creative Force animating the universe, an audacity which amazes me but does not persuade me. Call the Force God and worship it at a million shrines, and it is no less sublime; call it Nature, and worship it in scientific gropings and discoveries, and it is no less divine. It goes its own way, asking no homage, answering no questions. (Ital. added) 25

That is Pantheism; it is not Panentheism. It is not romantic; it has excised sentimentality, which is a lingering vestige of anthropoid projection upon nature. Thoreau had made this transition:

> I love Nature partly because she is not man, but a retreat from him. None of his institutions control or pervade her. There a different kind of right prevails. In her midst I can be glad with an entire gladness. If this world were all man, I could not stretch myself. I should lose all hope. 26

But in doing so, Thoreau often disparaged humans and culture. It is more characteristic of the newer Pantheism to accept and affirm humanity, but again without maudlin sentimentality or the extravagant praise of Whitman.

Einstein represented the later view. Speaking of scientific discipline and discovery as moving one "by a profound reverence for the rationality made manifest in existence," he went on to say:

> This attitude, however, appears to me to be religious, in the highest sense of the word. And so it seems to me that science not only purifies the religious impulse of the dross of its anthropomorphism, but also contributes to a religious spiritualization of our understanding of life ... In their struggle for the ethical good, teachers of religion must have the stature to give up the doctrine of a personal God, that is, give up that source of fear and hope which in the past placed such vast power in the hands of the priests. 27

These views were not received by religious professionals with joy. I think it necessary to understand that a goodly number of sensitive and thoughtful people have come to adopt these Pantheistic views, as well as to see the clear distinction made with reference to radical de-anthropocentrism.

As an example of partial de-anthropocentrism, I select a book which is far more sympathetic to quasi-pantheistic views than most: In Christian Identity and Theological Education, Professors Hough and Cobb give attention to "the anthropocentric fallacy." However, by that term they mean the idea of human salvation apart from the natural environment. "In Paul's vision the whole creation will share in the final salvation; there is no dualism of the human and natural worlds."[28] That is plainly preferable to the doctrine of human domination over, and exploitation of, nature. That may be correct as regards Paul's soteriology, but whether it avoids the centrality given to human beings is debatable, and is aggravated when we read: "Although it is true that only human beings participate in the imago dei ..."[29] Surely, however that is interpreted, it carries the presupposition that God, whatever God is, is to be conceived in some very important way in terms drawn exclusively from human qualities. It is just such partial de-anthropocentrism that Pantheists reject. For it cannot be reconciled with the understanding of life experience and values in the context of our comprehensive matrix of existence. It does not ring true to life.

Tensions Between Pantheism and Religious Tradition

In explicating Pantheistic views it is my intention that the issues be sharpened and the antagonism made understandable which has generally characterized Judaic, Christian, and Muslim responses to it. In time the mystic Pantheists were accomodated, but only after a time and then selectively, often because they spiritualized the All. I cite al-Ghazali, Bruno, and Spinoza as examples. Modern Pantheism presents a continuation and intensification of this tension with traditional forms of religious understanding. It is important also to emphasize that Pantheism as here interpreted is quite different from contemporary American religions where the All is conceived as Spirit, Mind, the Absolute, Soul, or such. For in the New Thought Movement and others where "Religious or Metaphysical Science" is paramount, you have a very different orientational perspective. Anthropocentrism there is as pronounced as in any orthodox position. Pantheism is typically naturalistic and empirical, at least as I am using the term. That it can be used in other ways, of course, is readily admitted.

However, given the usage meant here, it is not surprising that far more Pantheists are to be found among poets, dramatists, essayists and novelists than among theologians and philosophers. We find these people referring to deity as It by way of intimating the inappropriateness of projecting human attributes upon the cosmos. At times they use the metaphor of the Cosmic Mother to suggest the birthing nature of reality. In recent years this has also been done due to the influence of feminism, but often that is a different matter in which the supernatural God idea as a being is retained, but with the objection to that being's being regarded as male. We find the birthing concept in earlier writers, as in Thoreau, where earth's fecundity "suggests at least that Nature has some bowels, and there again is mother of humanity."[30] It is not unusual, then, to find an incidental phrase in a contemporary novel, where the feminist view is conjoined with the birthing one, as in these words: "... the great brooding mother of all the seas and stars, all the leaves of trees, all the gestures of men, Venus Genetrix ..."[31]

In The Color Purple Celie becomes disillusioned with the personalized Christian God. In the latter part of the novel Shug refers to God as "it," and Celie is puzzled.

> It? I ast.
> Yeah, It. God ain't a he or a she, but a It.
> But what do it look like? I ast.
> Don't look like nothing, she say. It ain't a picture show. It ain't something you can look at apart from anything else, including yourself. I believe God is everything, say Shug. Everything that is or ever will be. And when you can feel that, and be happy to feel that, you've found It. 32

Of course writers have long since found criticism of conventional religion to be grist for their mill, but it seems to me that their way of returning to nature as the alternative is significantly different from that of earlier Romanticism. E. E. Cummings, for example, rejects the way philosophers and scientists have treated "sweet spontaneous earth," and the way religions have buffetted earth "that thou mightest conceive gods," concluding about the earth "thou answerest them only with spring."[33] He draws no lessons from spring, nor moralizes about it, simply names it and, as it were, points to it.

Again, how sparse is Richard Eberhart's conclusion after visiting a familiar graveyard:

> I went away,
> Slowly, tingling, elated, saying saying
> Mother, Great Being, O Source of Life
> To whom in wisdom we return,
> Accept this humble servant evermore. 34

There is no need there of some sacrament intervening as the channel of grace, for the place and the experience are the sacrament.

Robinson Jeffers (1887-1962) provides a particularly interesting case, because he commented on his religious views quite explicitly. They are unequivocally Pantheistic.

> I believe that the universe is all one being, all its parts are different expressions of the same energy, and they are all in communication with each other, influencing each other, therefore parts of one organic whole ... This whole is in all its parts so beautiful, and is felt by me to be so intensely in earnest, that I am compelled to love it, and to think of it as divine. 35

Turning now to the first stanza of his "Shine Perishing Republic," in the light of that statement of his lifeview, we catch his worshipful response.

> While this America settles in the mould of its vulgarity,
>   heavily thickening to empire,
> And protest, only a bubble in the molten mass, pops and
>   sighs out, and the mass hardens,
> I sadly smiling remember that the flower fades to make
>   fruit, the fruit rots to make earth
> Out of the mother; and through the spring exultances,
>   ripeness and decadence; and home to the mother.
> You making haste haste on decay: not blameworthy; life
>   is good, be it stubbornly long or suddenly
> A mortal splendor: meteors are not needed less than moun-
>   tains: shine perishing republic. 36

There you have the given earth with its ways for humans as well as plants, and an affirmation of human experience, precious although momentary. The older response of wonder, love and praise is there, but exorcised of anthropocentrism and disguised hubris.

One other poet must certainly be mentioned, Robert Penn Warren, recently appointed as our first Poet Laureate. His importance as a novelist would be reason enough for our attention, but his selection by the Congress – especially at this time – is remarkable, for he has with all candor disavowed a religious perspective. Yet he is obviously a person of religious sensitivity, insight and intellectual integrity.

> Warren espouses no formal religion and maintains he descended from a family of unbelievers. He protests too much. Warren's writing is enmeshed in the theme of Original Sin, and one is haunted by his remark in an interview, "I wish I were religious." 37

Many of his lines of thought are congruent with modern Pantheism, if not explicitly announcing that view. There is nothing of the perfect beneficence of the eternal ocean of being. Individual characters are treated with recognition of their particular uniqueness, but it is not the older individualism. Above all, these things are not romanticized. He conceives "the purely private self as incomplete and of the community as analogue or projection of the individual." "Time," Warren has said, "is the dimension in which God strives to define His own being."[38] It is not only an expanding universe, it is an intensifying one in which precious actualities emerge and where the tragic dimension is also real and to be acknowledged.

That there is tension, to say the least, between Warren's view and conventional religion is plain enough in "Summer Storm (circa 1916), and God's Grace." After vivid description of the destruction brought by a violent storm, we have this:

> And darkness rides in on the wind.
> The pitchfork lightning tosses the trees,
> And God gets down on hands and knees
> To peer and cackle and commend
> His own sadistic idiocies.

But you also have a kind of acceptance of the way things are and an affirmation of the human will to survive.

> Raw-eyed, men watched. They did not speak.
> Till one shrugged, said he guessed he's make out.
> Then turned, took the woods-path up the creek. 39

Finitude and Affirmation

The problem with the language which speaks of God as "the soul of the universe" and the world as "the body of God" is that it suggests a dualism between mind (or soul) and body, with the soul being the real part of this assemblage. Theologians in recent times have stressed the wholeness of humans, not a soul in a body, but a being with differentiable parts, such as mind and body, whose reality is in its wholeness. There has been some reluctance to apply that reasoning to God, where the physical is as truly part of the reality of God no less than character or the subsistent, patterning, ordering functions. Thus when Melville, for example, wrote: "There is, one knows not what sweet mystery about this sea, whose gently awful stirrings seem to speak of some hidden soul beneath," nature was seen as the mask of God and the hidden soul as the ultimate reality.[40] The shift in thought may be subtle, but it is definite when the holistic mode of understanding is applied to the cosmos as one reality with di-polar functions. Of course this Whiteheadean view is to be found in diverse philosophies. My point is merely that it has been utilized in contemporary Pantheism.

There is also a shift in ethical philosophy. Romantic Pantheism held that nature provided both the ground for human ethics and instruction for its rules. Live in accord with nature. Existentialism - at least in some versions of it - held that there is no available ground for value or sound ethical guidance. Each individual must choose norms and commitments, recognizing with anguish that there is no basis for the choice. The characteristic Pantheistic position, as I read it, combined these opposing views to an extent. On the one hand there are certain ethical principles in nature in its non-human manifestations which are instructive for human survival and significance, such as cooperation, nurture of the young, consideration of future consequences, and the like. On the other hand, there are other ethical norms and concerns for which the ways of nature provide no sanction, such as justice, personal integrity, and compassion. These principles are the human contribution. They are as "natural" as the instincts of other forms of life. They are the contribution (when followed) that humans contribute to the rest of nature, to the living earth, and indeed to God.

In a way the Existentialists were right: this is an uncomfortable position to be in, so much so that the appeal is strong to attribute our moral judgments - and especially the ones which do not have strong sanction exhibited in the jungle or even in the nearby quiet pond - to a Heavenly Father Authority. The fact is, so Pantheists would have it, that the human species is one of earth's experiments among many, and it is largely up to us to see how it will turn out. "We are," Thoreau said, "the subjects of an experiment which is not a little interesting to me."[41] Here, again, we see the difference between modern Pantheism and Idealism, including the Neo-Platonic form. Idealism usually holds that ethical principles pertaining to human relations can be confidently derived from the nature of the deity. Pantheism finds no reliable basis for that either in nature or in history.

In closing I must acknowledge that inadequate attention has been given to essayists who write from a scientific background with a commitment to ecology. The subject could have been approached through that route, although I think the poets anticipated them to an extent. To give but one example, Lewis Thomas illumines the radical interrelatedness and interdependency of all life forms, yet with insight into the uniqueness of human beings and the significance of language in culture and values. He avoids religious vocabulary, but I find his writing profoundly religious and highly instructive for a Pantheistic position. In common with many others he affirms cooperation to be far more basic in nature than early evolutionists appreciated with their emphasis on the competitive struggle to survive. In connection with Gaia (the earth as a living organism), he says:

> This world seems to me an even stranger one than the world of very small things in biology: it looks like the biggest organism I've ever heard of, and at the same time the most delicate and fragile ... 42

Pantheism is a theism, not in the sense of Personal Theism, Absolute Idealism or Gnosticism, but in the sense that it beholds reality in a worshipful as well as analytic mood, and expresses that in gratitude and devotion. With respect for the persistent human hunger that finds gratification in such diverse ways within as well as among the religions of the world, it nevertheless characteristically criticizes vigorously the forms in which any religion claims divine sanction for hostility and inhumane practices. Pantheism is not likely to become a popular, dominating faith, yet as I have tried to show, it has been widely influential in American religious thought. And that, in my view, is sufficient. It is like leaven hidden in the communal loaf.

NOTES

[1] Charles Hartshorne and William L. Reese, Philosophers Speak of God (Chicago: University of Chicago Press, 1953), p. 2. Cf. Hartshorne, Man's Vision of God (New York: Harper and Row, 1941); The Logic of Perfection (LaSalle: Open Court, 1962); The Divine Relativity (New Haven: Yale University Press, 1948).

[2] Intelligence in the Modern World, ed. Joseph Ratner (New York: Modern Library, 1939), p. 399. Originally in The Public and its Problems.

[3] Lucien Price, Dialogues of Alfred North Whitehead (Boston: Little, Brown, 1954), p. 22.

[4] Walt Whitman, Leaves of Grass. I am following the definitive edition of David McKay (Philadelphia, 1900). However, since there are so many editions, titles of poems will be cited. These lines are from "We Two - How Long we Were Fool'd."

[5] "I Sing the Body Electric," sec. 7.

[6] "Gods," 1, 7.

[7] "Laws for Creations."

[8] "Walt Whitman" [I Celebrate Myself], sec. 48.

[9] Ibid., sec. 52.

[10] Cf. Richard Chase, Walt Whitman – Reconsidered (New York: W. Sloane, 1955), pp. 64, 148ff. The social character of reality was richly developed by G.H. Mead, Dewey, Whitehead, Hartshorne et al.

[11] "Nirvâna," stanza 12.

[12] William Hayes Ward interpreted Lanier differently on this point, Poems of Sidney Lanier (New York: Scribner's, 1894), p. xxxviii.

[13] The essay is no. III in Emerson's Essays, First Series (1841), par. 7.

[14] Ibid., eighth paragraph from the end.

[15] Thoreau, Walden (1854), sec. "Spring."

[16] Ibid.

[17] Thoreau, A Week on the Concord and Merrimack Rivers (1849). The quotation occurs just prior to his poem, "Rumors from an Aeolian Harp." Although this was his first book, it is the most remarkable for our subject.

[18] "Slavery in Massachusetts," The Liberator (July 21, 1854). The reference is to the next to last paragraph.

[19] Letter number 23 in the conventional listing.

[20] The Collected Poems of Stephen Crane (New York: Knopf).

[21] To emphasize this point I refer to a letter Melville wrote to Hawthorne, commenting on Goethe. It is quoted by Richard Chase, cit. sup., p. 148. Melville wrote:
In reading some of Goethe's sayings, so worshiped by his votaries, I come across this, Live in the All. That is to say, your separate identity is but a wretched one, – good; but get out of yourself, spread and expand yourself, and bring to yourself the tinglings of life that are felt in the planets Saturn and Venus, and the Fixed Stars. What nonsense! Here is a fellow with a raging toothache. My dear boy, Goethe says to him, you are sorely afflicted with that tooth; but you must live in the all, and then you will be happy! As with all great genius, there is an immense deal of flummery in Goethe.
Whether or not that is fair to Goethe, as an expression of this stream of Americana, it captures the quintessence. Of course throughout history there have been deeply religious people who

have denied that God has a special or privileged destiny for humans or that ethical claims can be derived from a conception of deity, e.g. W.H. Bernhardt. On the latter point see Frederick Ferré's comments on Gustafson's ethics in the essay on "Boston Personalism."

[22] Lynn White, Jr., "The Roots of our Ecologic Crisis," Science, 1967. Reprinted in Paul Shepard and Daniel McKinley, eds., The Subversive Science (Boston: Houghton, Mifflin, 1969), p. 347.

[23] The Logic of Perfection, chap. 10.

[24] Quoted in The Poems of Sidney Lanier, p. xxxix.

[25] Harriet Monroe, A Poet's Life (New York: Macmillan, 1938), p. 454, see p. 450.

[26] Winter, vol. VIII, p. 106 in the Riverside edition of Thoreau's works (Boston: Houghton, Mifflin, 1893).

[27] Science, Philosophy and Religion: A Symposium (New York, published by that symposium, 1941).

[28] Joseph C. Hough, Jr. and John B. Cobb, Jr., op. cit. (Chico, CA: Scholars Press, 1985), p. 57.

[29] Ibid., p. 56. There are repeated references to the "works of God," an expression I find dubious and based on highly selective use of history, where what one approves of is retroactively baptized as a work of God. I have dealt with this view in "The Modes of God's Causal Activity," The Iliff Review, XXXVIII (Winter 1981), no. 1.

[30] Walden, "Spring." Whitman was even more emphatic on this.

[31] Ursula K. LeGuin, The Word for World Is Forest (New York: Berkley Books, 1976), p. 95.

[32] Alice Walker, The Color Purple (New York: Washington Square, 1983), pp. 177f. It must be added that Walker is not a Pantheist in the usage adopted here, however she stresses the claim that God is not a scopic entity, but heteroscopic.

[33] "O Sweet Spontaneous Spring."

[34] "The Soul Longs to Return Whence it Came," closing lines.

[35] This is from an interview with Jeffers, quoted by Robert Ian Scott, "The Great Net - The World as God in Robinson Jeffers' Poetry," The Humanist, vol. 46 (January, 1986), no. 1, p. 29.

[36] Op. cit., first stanza.

[37] Thomas L. Connelly, "Robert Penn Warren as Historian," in *A Southern Renascence Man* (Baton Rouge, LA: Louisiana State University Press, 1984), p. 11.

[38] Harold Bloom, "Sunset Hawk: Warren's Poetry and Tradition," *ibid.*, p. 78.

[39] Op. cit. See Robert Penn Warren, *Selected Poems: New and Old, 1923-1966* (New York: Random House, 1960).

[40] This concept of nature as the mask of God is quite evident in *Moby-Dick*. E.g., note the conclusion of chaps. XXXV and XCIX, where "some certain significance lurks in all things," and CXIX and CXXXII where "what cozening, hidden lord and master, and cruel, remorseless emperor commands me; that against all natural lovings and longings." See also, Newton Arvin, *Herman Melville* (New York: W. Sloane, 1950), pp. 172ff.

[41] *Walden*, "Solitude." Although similar to Wieman's views, his stress on "trust in God" tends to be the exclusive religious requirement, and unfaith being rebellion against God. In Neo-Pantheism, as I understand it, unfaith would be rebellion against – or denial of – one's human responsibility and humane responsiveness. The human assignment is to be and become oneself in authentic relationships. Unfaith, then, has several attributes, including to affirm given finitude, enact justice, and to delight in the bonds of relatedness. See Charles Hardwick's essay, "'Faith' in a Naturalist Theology."

[42] Cf. Lewis Thomas, *The Medusa and the Snail* (New York: Viking, 1979); *The Lives of a Cell* (New York: Viking, 1974); *Late Night Thoughts on Listening to Mahler's Ninth Symphony* (New York: Viking, 1983). The quotation is from the last book, p. 75. See also pp. 152, 102ff., 128f.

[43] As a closing note I will repeat acknowledgment that on many points my position is consonant with Hartshorne's and that I am greatly indebted to him. Where I part company is in such language as "the divine memory" and his insistence that "nothing is lost." His doctrine of dual transcendence has been helpful and clarifying, although I interpret it somewhat differently. See Gene Reeves, "To Be Is to Be for Others," and Hartshorne, "Reeves and Stearns on my Idealism," *American Journal of Theology and Philosophy*, vol. 7 (January, 1986), no. 1.

Creighton Peden

F. E. Abbot: The Prophet of Free Religion

Introduction

Our story focuses on the most significant intellectual revolution in American history, which occurred between 1859–1917. Several key facets flamed the fires of this revolution. Protestant theology was being transformed in the spirit of democracy which, acting on the principle of growth, required adaptation to a changing society and its needs. In a society flush with the democratic ideal, the principle that Atonement was limited to an elected few was increasingly viewed as unjust. Under the impact of technological breakthroughs, an industrial metamorphosis occurred in the United States which generated a breath-taking rate of social change. Following the Civil War, the average American citizen began to develop a new attitude toward the central government as a powerful instrument for saving and giving direction to society. Another key facet was the philosophical and theological impact of the scientific method. Darwin's theory of evolution hit at the core issue of whether humans were a special creation of God. Comte's positivistic philosophy welcomed the end of rationalistic philosophies and theologies and proclaimed that in the new intellectual age humans were to be the masters of their own destinies. An aggressive humanism, a new religion of humanity, emerged as part of the foundation of this intellectual revolution. This religion of humanity sought to secure and protect a larger human freedom and responsibility. The prophets of this new religion were devotees of science, viewing science as a tool for more properly understanding the nature of reality and for building a new society. One of the most outspoken speakers for this humanism was Francis E. Abbot. The purpose of these comments is to explore his life and philosophy of religion to understand better his contribution to modern religious thought.

Biographical

Francis Ellingwood Abbot (November 6, 1836 - October 23, 1903) was born into an academic family with a strong Puritan orientation. From his father he gained a life-long interest in scientific and philosophical concerns. Abbot was head of his class at the Boston Latin School, received his undergraduate degree (1859) and finished his first year of theological studies at Harvard University, graduated from Meadville Theological School (1863), and received one of the earliest Doctor of Philosophy degrees in the Department of Philosophy conferred by Harvard (1881).

In June, 1864, he became pastor of the "First Unitarian Society of Christians" in Dover, New Hampshire. At this point the Unitarians had no common creed. In 1865 the Unitarians held for the first time a national organizational meeting and adopted the following Preamble which effectively established a creed for the denomination:

> Whereas, The great opportunities and demands of Christian labor and consecration at this time increase our sense of the obligation of all disciples of the Lord Jesus Christ to prove their faith by self-denial, and by the devotion of their lives and possessions to the service of God and the building-up of the Kingdom of his Son: -

> Article I. - Therefore, the Christian churches of the Unitarian faith here assembled united themselves in a common body to be known as the National Conference of Unitarian Churches to the end of energizing and stimulating the denomination with which they are connected to the large exertions in the cause of Christian faith and work. 1

Abbot, and many others, objected to the Preamble because it failed to emphasize the old Unitarian principle of the right of "free inquiry." Therefore, at the National meeting in 1866 Abbot unsuccessfully proposed a reformed Preamble which stressed the need for free inquiry and the need for Christianity to be reconciled in light of understandings afforded by modern science. By taking this position, Abbot effectively terminated any opportunity for professional advancement as a Unitarian minister. He also found academic appointments, for which he had been nominated, closed at Cornell University because he was not "a broad Churchman" and at Harvard University because of his "radicalism."

Abbot was a person who held and stood for deep convictions. Realizing that he could not confess "discipleship to the Lord Jesus Christ," he preached his farewell sermon at Dover on March 15, 1868, stressing that his purpose had been to preach the pursuit of truth and not to support dogmatic opinions. At the completion of the service, Abbot found himself drafted by a majority of the congregation into becoming the minister of a "to-be organized First Independent Society of Dover." A lawsuit emerged over the control of the old church building by the new Society; and when the Supreme Court of New Hampshire ruled that Abbot could not continue to preach in that building, he immediately resigned on October 1, 1868.

The Unitarian Society of Toledo, Ohio, issued several unsuccessful invitations to Abbot to become their minister following his resignation at Dover. Due to the persistence of the Toledo congregation, he agreed to a two month trial ministry in July and August, 1869, with the understanding that at its conclusion his future ministry would be determined by the congregation's voting whether to continue as Unitarians or to become a free fellowship. The vote was in favor of Abbot and withdrawal from Unitarianism, so for the next four years he served as minister of the "First Independent Society of Toledo."

While Abbot had been developing his professional life as a minister of free inquiry during the 1860's, he also was beginning a career as a writer and editor. In 1861 he wrote "The Phenomena of Time and Space," a paper which was published in 1864 as two articles in the North American Review. These articles established Abbot at home and abroad as a very promising young thinker.

Professor Charles Elliott Norton, one of the most noted scholars at Harvard, praised Abbot for displaying qualities "of a very rare and high order," and being as well "also an exact and original thinker."[2] Chauncey Wright complimented him even more highly: "I know of no philosophic writer in this country who surpasses him in vigor and clearness of style or in earnestness of devotion to the pursuit of true opinions in the abstruser matters of thought."[3]

Having failed in his attempt to get Unitarianism committed to free inquiry and the modernization of Christianity in light of knowledge gained by the scientific method, Abbot joined with Emerson and others in establishing the Free Religious Association. The aim of the Association is expressed essentially in the first two articles of the Constitution which reads:

   I. This Organization shall be called the Free Religious Association. - its object being to promote the practical interest of pure religion, to increase fellowship in the spirit, and to encourage the scientific study of man's religious nature and history; and to this end, all persons interested in these objects are cordially invited to its membership.

   II. Membership in this Association shall leave each individual responsible for his opinions alone, and affect in no degree his relations to other associations; and nothing in the name or constitution of the Association shall ever be construed as limiting membership by any test of speculative opinion or belief, - or as defining the position of the Association, collectively considered, with reference to any such opinion or belief, - or as interfering in any other way with that absolute freedom of thought and expression which is a natural right of every rational being. 4

In his article entitled "Positivism in Theology,"[5] Abbot was careful to establish that the intellectual foundation for the Free Religious movement was expressed seven months before his 1866 defeat at the meeting of the Unitarian Conference at Syracuse. Abbot applauded the intellectual reform which had been gradually developing through the employment of the scientific method. He explained that this reform relied on "the principle, that all human knowledge must be built on the basis of experience, according to laws which experience itself reveals, but cannot originate; that facts duly certified and comprehended, must yield all knowledge that shall stand the test of scientific criticism; that these facts must, at the outset, be assumed to harmonize and to conform to subtle, all-pervasive, all-comprehensive law."[6] While some desired to limit the scientific method to purely physical phenomena, Abbot contended that science, properly interpreted, includes also spiritual phenomena. Religious knowledge is but one area of science. Opinions about God are subject to the same laws of thought and to the general principles which regulate the opinions concerning the physical universe. He contended that the great religious problem of the age was whether Theism or Atheism will prevail as the faith of the future. He borrowed from Dr. Hedge a popular phrasing of this issue: "the Bible or the Mathematics as the basis of preaching, - in the long-run it must come to that."[7] He believed that in the future science will expand beyond its present materialistic limitations to include also human religious experiences. The task, as Abbot viewed it prior to the 1866 Syracuse meeting, is for liberal Christianity to take the leadership in placing religion and theology within the proper domain of science. Accomplishing this task implies three things:

> 1. Liberal Christianity must unequivocally and emphatically distinguish between religion and theology. It must inculcate the one as simply living in God and for man; it must relegate the other to the domain of pure science, as perhaps auxilliary, but not essentially, to the highest spiritual development. In other words, as a religion, it must regard personal righteousness and genuine devoutness as alone important; while as a theology, it must regard unlimited freedom of thought as both a right and a duty, and build entirely on the basis of Positive Science ....

> 2. Liberal Christianity must adopt the general method of all true science, - analysis of verified facts, and synthesis of the results deductible from them. At present, it pretends to discard the infallibility of "Scripture," yet rests all its doctrines on a "Scriptural" basis ...

> 3. Liberal Christianity must, then, after relinquishing the pretense of being "Scriptural" or "Evangelical," concentrate its energies on the different task of working out a coherent theological system - a rational, yet religious, philosophy of the Universe ... The time has come to attempt scientific systemization, or the organization of Theism as theological science. 8

Although the intellectual foundation for free religion had been indicated by Abbot in "Positivism in Theology," the idea for the Free Religious Association originated with William James Potter. On the way back to Boston from their defeat over the Preamble at the "Battle of Syracuse" in 1866, Potter revealed to Abbot and Edward C. Towne his plan for a spiritual anti-slavery society. After several developmental meetings, there appeared in the Spring of 1867 a notice in religious and secular newspapers in New York and Boston that a "Public Meeting, to consider the conditions, wants and prospects of Free Religion in America, will be held on Thursday, May 30 at 10 a.m., in Horticultural Hall, Boston. The following persons have been asked to address the meeting, and addresses may be expected from most of them: R.W. Emerson, John Weiss, Robert Dale Owen, William H. Furness, Lucretia Mott, Henry Blanchard, T.W. Higginson, D.A. Wasson, Isaac M. Wise, Oliver Johnson, F.E. Abbot, and Max Lilienthal."[9] When the appointed hour arrived, the very large hall was packed. When Abbot's time to speak came, he proclaimed the new religion of humanity:

> Brothers and sisters, we want to work for humanity. We have a new gospel to proclaim, - the gospel of religion and science, two in one, - the goal of faith in man carried out to its extremest consequences, - the gospel of repose in the infinite Love which works through Universal law ... a radical gospel, the gospel of the "Enthusiasm of Humanity." 10

In the afternoon a formal constitution was adopted for the purpose of promoting the interest of pure religion and the scientific study of theology. However, people were to be responsible for their own opinions and were free to join any other organization. The first person to sign as a member was Ralph Waldo Emerson. The main effort of the Association was to spread through tracts and lectures the basic principles of free religion. Abbot participated actively in these endeavors. For example, a Horticultural Hall Lecture series was sponsored from 1870 through 1878, with Abbot presenting a lecture entitled "The Scientific Method in Religion." While the Free Religious Association served as a platform for liberal religious voices, it was never able to weld these voices into a liberal movement of national importance because the spirit of radical individualism remained dominant.[11]

Abbot's most noted contribution to the free religious movement came in his establishing and then editing The Index from 1870 to 1880. Although it was not at first an official publication of the Free Religious Association, leading members of this group incorporated as the Index Association for the purpose of publishing The Index. Abbot explained the policy of the journal as accepting "every result of science and sound learning, without seeking to harmonize it with the Bible. It recognizes no authority but that of reason and right. It believes in Truth, Freedom, Progress, Equal Rights, and Brotherly Love."[12] According to Abbot, "The great purpose of The Index - the purpose which gave its birth and continued to give it life - is to show how, out of decaying Christianity, a deeper and broader and higher faith is developing slowly in the heart of Christendom, and to do what it can in the way of fostering this better faith. Its work is therefore both destructive and constructive - destructive so far as it would hasten decay of the old, constructive so far as it would promote the growth of the new."[13] Abbot, who consistently antagonized his associates, was removed as business manager of The Index by the Board of Directors in 1873 over a dispute with the printer and advertising agent. He immediately resigned the editorship but was quickly reinstated at the annual meeting of the stockholders. The "Index Troubles" were given much press by Abbot's enemies and affected the financial stability of the publication. Following reinstatement, Abbot moved The Index in 1873 to Boston, where he could be in closer association with his stronger supporters.

Although the 1870's were busy years for Abbot in publishing the first periodical in America that championed free religion, he also gave of himself in opposition to the determined effort by Christians to amend the U.S. Constitution in the interest of Christianity. In 1872, a national convention was held in Cincinnati for the stated purpose of committing the American people constitutionally to proclaiming God "as the author of its existence and the source of its authority, of Jesus Christ as its ruler, and of the Bible as the foundation of its laws and the supreme rule of its conduct."[14] The only person at the meeting who opposed the object of the convention was Abbot. He arose and addressed the delegates from carefully prepared remarks, informing them of the dangers inherent in their effort. While the majority might have the power to affect the proposed Constitutional change, Abbot pointed out that freedom-lovers will never submit "to any such outrageous oppression, whether in the name of God or man. I make no threat whatever, but I state a truth fixed as the hills when I say that before you can carry this measure and trample on the freedom of the people, you will have to wade through seas of blood. Every man who favors it votes to precipitate the most frightful war of modern times."[15]

Following the meeting in Cincinnati, Abbot began a movement to organize liberal minded people throughout the country to protect their threatened liberties. Of course, Abbot used The Index as a vehicle through which he challenged freedom-lovers to band together against the obvious threat to their liberties. Liberal leagues began to organize in small and large communities until in 1876 enough societies existed to sponsor an organizational meeting of a National Liberal League. This meeting was held in conjunction with the Centennial celebration in Philadelphia. Abbot was elected President of the National Liberal League, which had as its sole purpose accomplishing the total separation of church and state. In order to accomplish this purpose, Abbot proclaimed at the meeting the following practical objectives for the League:

1. The adoption of a "Religious Freedom Amendment," to the Constitution of the United States.

2. The comprehensive reform of the various abuses which prevent the total separation of church and state.

3. The formation of local Liberal Leagues everywhere to agitate for these measures an affiliation with the National League.

4. The legal vindication of the religious rights of all oppressed persons regardless of opinion. Individuals are continually oppressed on account of religious opinion all over this country, and nothing is done about it by anyone.

5. The establishment of a Liberal Lecture Bureau for the same general objections; namely, to propagate the general principles on which alone the separation of Church and State can ever be established or maintained.

6. The application of the same principles to any case or cases not previously enumerated or contemplated, under that general purpose which constitutes the whole function of the association. 16

On October 26, 1877, the second convention of the National Liberal League was held at Rochester, N.Y. Many resolutions were passed, generally arguing that the U.S. government is secular and not Christian. The treaty with Tripoli, approved by George Washington in 1797, was sighted as clear proof supporting the secular nature of the United States. The treaty declared that "The government of the United States is not in any sense founded on the Christian religion."[17] The Convention adopted a three point platform for bringing about a completely secular government and society.

1. <u>Total</u> <u>separation</u> <u>of</u> <u>Church</u> <u>and</u> <u>State</u>, to be guaranteed by an <u>Amendment of the United</u> States Constitution: including the equitable taxation of church property, secularization of the public schools, abrogation of Sabratarian laws, abolition of chaplaincies, prohibition of public appropriations for religious purposes, and all other measures necessary to the same general end.

2. <u>National</u> <u>Protection</u> <u>for</u> <u>National</u> <u>Citizens</u>, in their equal civil, political, religious rights: to be guaranteed by the Amendment of the United States Constitution, and afforded through the United States Courts.

3. <u>Universal</u> Education – <u>The</u> <u>Basis</u> <u>of</u> <u>Universal</u> <u>Suffrage</u> in <u>This</u> <u>Secular</u> <u>Republic</u>: To <u>be</u> guaranteed of amendment of the <u>United States</u> Constitution, requiring every State to maintain a thoroughly secularized public school system, and to permit no child within its limits to grow up without a good elementary education. 18

Unfortunately, the purpose of the National League became side-tracked in 1878 over the issue of the circulation of obscene literature through the mail. The majority of the League felt that the principle of a free press protected the circulation of even obscene literature. Abbot held such a resolute position that he was unable to make concessions and compromises. Since he held the position that all liberties must be limited by the laws of truth, justice and moral purity, Abbot could not in any way support obscene literature. Therefore, he resigned as President and as a member of the National Liberal League.

The move to Boston in 1873 was extremely difficult for Abbot and his family. He had no money saved, all pulpits were closed to one so radical, and he had a family of four to support. In addition the move precipitated a breakdown of his wife's health, resulting in an increasing invalidism until her death in 1893. At the suggestion of a friend, he opened a "classical School for Boys" in New York City, but after a year of struggle, he returned to Cambridge and turned his home into a boarding school for boys. Although this effort provided income for the Abbots, he found the work a drudgery which limited his philosophical past. Fortunately, Abbot received a legacy in 1892 which enabled him to devote the remainder of his life to philosophical work.

Philosophy of Religion

By 1881, Abbot's life took a different direction with his efforts to secure a doctoral degree at Harvard University. He had given up the editorship of The Index and was no longer active as a leader in the Free Religious Association or the National Liberal League. Now Abbot began the process of organizing his thoughts in book length manuscripts, but it should be noted that his philosophy showed little change from his previously expressed views. His major publications during these later years are Scientific Theism (1885), The Way Out of Agnosticism (1890), and The Syllogistic Philosophy (1906). During this period Abbot also participated as an occasional member of Charles Peirce's Metaphysical Club.[19]

Abbot's major philosophical contribution is more prophetic than substantive. As Herbert Schneider indicated, "Abbot began with the usual criticism of Spencer, but he added to it a very significant and penetrating critique of Kant and of transcendental idealism."[20] Abbot came of age with the beginning of the evolutionary controversy and viewed this intellectual struggle as a manifestation of a deeper philosophical clash between those interpreting reality from the various traditions of Idealism and those following the new Realism based on the scientific method:

> The theory of Phenomenism versus the theory of Noumenism; the theory of Idealistic Evolution versus the theory of Realistic Evolution; and the Mechanical theory of Realistic Evolution versus the Organic theory of Realistic Evolution, – there are the vital philosophical problems of our century, and their solution must determine and decide that of the vital religious problem of Theism, Atheism, and Pantheism. 21

Abbot focused on the theory of Universals. He attacked Kant for having neutralized the profound insight of the independent, immanent, and determinant constitution of the object as a known thing-in-itself by "declaring the thing-in-itself unknowable."[22] The problem can be solved employing the principle that the essential intelligible constitution of the Universe, which is itself the absolute unity, is manifest in miniature in the constitution of each concrete kind. For Abbot, the "great principle of the Infinite Intelligibility of the Universe is the corner-stone of Scientific Theism."[23] Humans can gain real knowledge of the constitution of the Universe and, thus, form a scientific world view based on a progressive knowledge of the kinds. He rejected as inadmissible in scientific philosophy "anything arbitrary, miraculous, or supernatural, anything beyond or contrary to experience, anything inconsistent with known fact or known law, anything incapable of verification by ascertained congruity with the already ascertained order of Nature."[24] The kinds or concrete forms of existence known by humans fall under three categorical types - the Machine, the Organism and the Person. Abbot contended that the discovery of supreme importance is "that the constitutions of the Machine and of the Organism involve each the other, and therefore are intelligible each through the other alone."[25] From this point he argued, "that the Infinite Universe is at once a Real Machine, a Real Organism and a Real Person."[26] He further contended that the immanent relational constitution of the Real Universe as Absolute Divine Person is based on the scientific method and serves as the ultimate ground of all Art, Science, Philosophy, Ethics and Religion.

Abbot's Scientific Theism received careful European attention and was translated into German. Josiah Royce attacked Abbot in his review of The Way Out of Agnosticism. Royce, among others, noted the marked similarity between Hegel's and Abbot's theory of universals.[27] He further indicated a close relationship between Abbot's position, as previously outlined, and the traditional design argument.[28] While it is true that Abbot failed to realize adequately the influences upon his thought and the problems inherent in his position, he made a significant contribution with his prophetic call for a philosophy grounded on the scientific method. As Herbert Schneider indicates, Abbot "softened the ground for much of the most important work in recent American philosophy."[29]

According to Abbot, the philosophical clash between Idealism and Realism had left the modern person without an adequate view of the universe. Christianity was so tied mythologically and metaphysically to idealism that it was unable to provide constructive thought demanded by the scientific approach to reality. Agnosticism, which is the "denial of the possibility of any comprehensive theory of the universe," had become "the prevalent philosophy of liberalism in the nineteenth century."[30] Abbot realized that if religion was to function adequately, it needed to develop a theory of the universe based on a synthesis of "the facts and laws which modern science has established beyond reasonable doubt."[31] Without an adequate religion, modern persons find themselves in intolerable anguish with the only escape being a stoical suppression of the power to feel. Therefore, "the supreme duty of modern liberalism [is] to press resolutely forward, away from agnosticism, to a positive, scientific, all-comprehensive theory of the universe."[32] This approach will foster the free movement of thought by rejecting a special faculty of faith which "hampers the mind with arbitrary restrictions."[33] The result will be a theory of the universe which enables religion and philosophy to be in creative tension, for these two stand or fall together, or, as Abbot said, "Philosophy is religion comprehended; religion is philosophy felt."[34]

According to Abbot, humans express a "natural religion," which is the universal spiritual aspiration of the race. This natural religion is the underlying oneness of all religions, with individual religions being diverse historical forms of the one. In order to survive, every religion must adapt "to the spirit and circumstances of the times."[35] Christianity reached its zenith in the Catholic Church, with the first stage of decay becoming evident in The Protestant Reformation. Huss, Luther and Calvin, displaying the modern spirit of self-consciousness, were the first apostles of Free Religion. The eighteenth and nineteenth centuries saw an increasing demand of humanity for spiritual freedom. Abbot contended that "the grounds of human hope, the motives of human action, the objects of human aspiration, are slowly changing; and because change in these respects involves corresponding change in all the relations of public and private life, the great visible movements of the age are but indices of the greater invisible movements in the spiritual consciousness of mankind."[36] "Liberal Christianity" has been the most noted modern form of changing religious expression, and it has "reduced the Messianic idea to its minimum dimensions and its minimum power."[37] The next step is to move outside of Christianity which is a dying religion due to its being confined within the limits of the Messianic idea:

> Let me repeat, with emphasis, that while Christianity is the perishing form, religion is the eternal substance, - that the universal truths, the inspiring hopes, the tender consolations, the quickening impulses, the divinely beautiful spirit, which have made and still make the name of Christianity so dear to the undistinguishing many, belong to the eternal substance and not to the perishing form. Religion must endure; but as Christianity came into history, so it must go out from history. 38

The form of religion most compatible with the philosophy of realism, based on the scientific method, is "Free Religion." Unlike the other religions, Free Religion has no history except the history of the human spirit. It has no doctrines, no rites, no church, no scriptures, and no Savior. In their absence, Abbot believed, "it is the soul's deep resolve to love the truth, to learn the truth, and to live the truth, uncoerced and free."[39]

Abbot's Free Religion was based on his previously discussed principle of the essential intelligible constitution of the Universe. Free Religion emphasizes the unity of the Universe. Nature is viewed as an organic, living whole whose laws and forces function to keep all things in harmony and provide a perfect cosmos based on the unity of a perfect order. The human race is a part of this harmony, as are individual persons. What is needed is for individuals and societies to develop their unity of character. Societies will move slowly toward an international cooperative union which will provide "Progress towards a universal and perfect civilization ... based on the principle that the liberty of the individual is absolute except as limited by the equal rights of all individuals."[40] The unity of character for the individual is based on "the principle that the liberty of every faculty is absolute in the exercise of its natural function."[41] Such unity is derived epistemologically from making experience its point of departure and by seeking all answers through a patient study of universal Nature based on the scientific method. Conscience shall govern the unity of individual character based on absolute and universal ideas - "truthfulness, justice, benevolence, purity, honor, integrity, self-respect."[42] By the will of the individual serving the conscience and reason, the animal and spiritual aspects will be in balance enabling each person to be in harmony with the Laws of Nature. The goal of Free Religion and the great endeavor of the nineteenth century is to reproduce the eternal harmony of Nature in the life of societies and in the life of the individual - creating "a civilization grounded on universal reverence for freedom, truth, and the equal rights of all mankind."[43] Abbot's optimism is based on his belief that "the Unity of the Universe is repeated in miniature in the ideal Unity of Mankind; and the ideal Unity of Mankind is repeated in miniature in the ideal Unity of the Person. The macrocosm is mirrored in the microcosm."[44]

What are the differences between Christianity and Free Religion? Abbot saw the cornerstone of Christianity as the false conviction that Jesus was the "Christ of God," while the "cornerstone of Free Religion is the universal soul of man, the common nature of humanity, as the source and origin of the world's religious life."[45] One puts faith in the individual Jesus, but the other puts faith in the spontaneous energies of human nature. Because of its narrow focus on Jesus, the fellowship of Christianity is limited in scope, but the fellowship of Free Religion is inclusive of all humanity. The open character of this fellowship forbids the despising of another's earnest faith and, thus, supports the profound sentiment of human equality. While Christianity undertakes the supreme task to Christianize the world, the supreme goal of Free Religion is to humanize the world. Abbot contended that this difference is clearly manifest in the social ideals of each. He looked forward to a time when the Christian social ideal of a "kingdom of heaven" on earth would be replaced by "a Commonwealth of Man, in which there is neither king nor Lord, but all are free and equal citizens."[46] Christianity calls all to sacrifice their individuality by reproducing the character of Jesus, but Free Religion supports the law of endless variety in natural temperaments and urges all to be themselves. The sharpest contrast between the two is found in their fundamental unlikeness of spirit and tone. By stressing utter submission to the authoritative will of Jesus, Christianity ennobles weakness, patience, submission, resignation, passivity, and absence of self-will. The spirit of Free Religion is essentially different. Because it asserts the divineness of universal nature and a deep trust in human nature, Free Religion produces the free soul which manifests self-reliance and self-respect. As Abbot explained, a deep spiritual antagonism exists between them.

> The one must wane as the other waxes. The one must die that the other may live. God in Christ is the spiritual center of Christianity; hence in Christ himself must Christianity ever have its bond and limit of fellowship, - in the universal extention of the Christian Church it must ever have its social ideal, - in the suppression of self, and utter submission to the will of Jesus, it must ever manifest its essential spirit. But God in Humanity is the spiritual and central faith of free religion; which has thus its cornerstone in universal human nature, its fellowship in the great brotherhood of man, its social ideal in a free republican commonwealth, its spiritual ideal in the highest development of each individual soul, its essential spirit in a self-respect which is at once profound reverence for human nature, and profound repose in universal Nature. 47

Having graduated from Harvard in 1859, Abbot entered the intellectual ferment of the Darwinian era as one who offered a prophetic direction for philosophy and theology, while providing a practical direction for the religious movement which sought to respond to the new scientific approach to reality. In Scientific Theism he made a "major contribution to American philosophical realism,"[48] clearly indicating that philosophy and theology could only be intellectually viable for the new era by adapting its theories and understanding of the nature of reality through employing the scientific method. For religion, this process of adaption required a philosophy of religion which focused on evolving humanity instead of some supernatural savior figure coming from a particular historical religion. Just as philosophy must reject reliance on the historical idealistic approach, religion must cease being limited by the narrow undertaking of historical religions and foster instead an unleashing, through the use of the scientific method, of the energies in nature which will result in humanizing the world. If philosophy and theology can adapt methodologically to the empirical orientation, "natural religion," building upon this adaption, can free humans from a misdirected supernatural idealism and offer instead a faith in nature and trust in human nature.

NOTES

[1]F.E. Abbot, "The Scientific Method in Religion" ("Abbot Papers": Harvard University Library Archives), p. 119.

[2]"The Abbot Memorial," Universal Religion, Vol. XI, No. 9, p. 152.

[3]Ibid., p. 152.

[4]F.E. Abbot, "The Scientific Method in Religion," p. 120.

[5]F.E. Abbot, "Positivism in Theology," Christian Examiner, March, 1866, pp. 234-267.

[6]Ibid., pp. 237-8.

[7]Ibid., p. 257.

[8]Ibid., pp. 263-4.

[9]Stow Persons, Free Religion (New Haven: Yale University Press, 1946), p. 45.

[10]Report of Addresses at a Meeting Held in Boston, May 30, 1867, to Consider the Conditions, Wants, and Prospects of Free Religion in America. Together with the Constitution of the Free Religious Association There Organized (Boston, 1867), pp. 37-9.

[11]Stow Persons, Free Religion, pp. 51f.

[12]F.E. Abbot, "The Index," "Abbot Papers," "Free Religion," Vol. IV, p. 10.

[13]Ibid., p. 877.

[14]Universal Religion, Vol. XI, No. 9, p. 160.

[15]Ibid., pp. 160-1.

[16]"Centennial Congress of Liberals," "Abbot Papers," p. 42.

[17]"Resolutions Adopted By The National Liberal League at Rochester, Oct. 26, 1877," "Abbot Papers," p. 8.

[18]"Platform of the National Liberal League, Adopted At Rochester, New York, October 26, 1877," Abbot Papers."

[19]Cf. Daniel D. O'Connor, "Peirce's Debt to F.E. Abbot," Journal of the History of Ideas, Vol. 25, pp. 543-64.

[20]H.W. Schneider, "The Influence of Darwin and Spencer on American Philosophical Theology," Journal of the History of Ideas, Vol. VI, No. 1, pp. 15-16.

[21]F.E. Abbot, Scientific Theism (London: Macmillan, 1885), p. viii.

[22]F.E. Abbot, The Way Out of Agnosticism (London: Macmillan, 1890), p. 33.

[23]Ibid., p. 125.

[24]Ibid., p. 44.

[25]Ibid., p. 53.

[26]Ibid., p. 65.

[27]Cf. Josiah Royce, "Dr. Abbot's 'Way Out of Agnosticism,'" International Journal of Ethics, Vol. 1, No. 1, p. 106.

[28]Ibid., p. 111.

[29]H.W. Schneider, "The Influence of Darwin and Spencer on American Philosophical Theology," p. 16.

[30]F.E. Abbot, The Way Out of Agnosticism, p. viii.

[31]Ibid., p. x.

[32]Ibid., p. xi.

[33]F.E. Abbot, "The Conditioned and the Unconditioned," North American Review, Vol. 99, p. 402.

[34]Ibid., p. 402.

[35]F.E. Abbot, "The Genius of Christianity and Free Religion," American Philosophic Addresses, 1700-1900, Joseph L. Blau ed. (New York: Columbia University Press, 1946), p. 689.

[36]Ibid., p. 634.

[37]Ibid., p. 690.

[38] Ibid., p. 690.

[39] Ibid., p. 701.

[40] F.E. Abbot, Truths for the Times, 2nd edition (Toledo, Ohio: Index Association, 1872), p. 11.

[41] Ibid., p. 12.

[42] Ibid., p. 13.

[43] Ibid., p. 15.

[44] Ibid., p. 14.

[45] F.E. Abbot, "The Genius of Christianity and Free Religion," p. 703.

[46] Ibid., p. 705.

[47] Ibid., p. 707.

[48] H.W. Schneider, "The Influence of Darwin and Spencer on American Philosophical Theology," p. 326.

Manfred Pütz

Emerson and Kant Once Again: Is Emerson's Thought a Philosophy Before, After, Beside, or Beyond Kant?

On July 19, 1837, Emerson wrote in his <u>Journal</u>: "by knowing the systems of philosophy that have flourished under the names of Heraclitus, Zoroaster, Plato, Kant ... I get thereby a vocabulary for my ideas."[1] He came back to the topic of philosophical nomenclature in his lecture "The Transcendentalist" when he stated: "The extraordinary profoundness and precision of that man's [Kant's] thinking have given vogue to his nomenclature, in Europe and America ..."[2] We may assume, then, that part of the fascination Kant's philosophy held for Emerson lay in its specific and artfully constructed nomenclature, and that Emerson's own thinking took shape under the influence of and in constant interaction with it.

However, it can also be shown that Emerson spoke much but knew little of Kant; that he repeatedly misapplied the terminology of Kantian philosophy; and that almost any term from Critical Idealism that found its way into Emerson's writings did so as an integral part of an idiosyncratic Emersonian discourse which by no means can be called Kantian.[3] This essay is not a belated attempt to pursue once more the complex history of philosophical influences on Emerson, nor is it meant as a final reckoning of his shortcomings in philosophical terminology and thought.[4] Rather it is addressed to the problem of how Emerson, through a specific reception and application of philosophical nomenclature, fashioned a view of Critical Idealism suited to his own purposes. It entails the further problem of whether it is conceivable that one thinker can absorb and build upon the conceptual groundwork of another thinker whom he has imperfectly understood, and yet manage to forge a convincing philosophy of his own in the process. What interests me specifically is whether it can be claimed at all that Emerson built on the fundaments of Kantian thought and, in doing so, went <u>beyond</u> Kant by constructing something new out of the transformed elements of a philosophy which he allegedly left behind.

Henry A. Pochmann, who has held that there is a distinctive Kantian phase in Emerson's thinking (from 1830 to 1838), has also stressed that Emerson displayed more than one single attitude towards Kant and German Idealism.[5] I do not think it necessary to identify such a dubious phase in Emerson's development, or to deal exhaustively with all of his wavering considerations and echoes of Kantian thought. In contrast to Pochmann, I would rather maintain that certain basic concepts of Kantian origin as much as their specific application are a pervasive feature of Emerson's discourse almost throughout all stages and that it is these concepts which give a considerable part of Emerson's thinking its peculiar twist. In order to demonstrate this point, I have singled out three passages from widely different Emersonian texts spread over a considerable period of time. These texts are a letter of 1834 to his brother Edward, the 1842 lecture "The Transcendentalist," and the essay "Experience" (1845) which is commonly considered to be one of the deeper works of the mature Emerson.

II

On May 31, 1834, Emerson wrote a letter to his brother Edward in which he stated his convictions on Reason and Understanding as cornerstones of a philosophical edifice under construction:

> Now that I have used the words, let me ask you do you draw the distinction of Milton Coleridge & the Germans between Reason & Understanding. I think it a philosophy itself. & like all truth very practical. So now lay away the letter & take up the following dissertation on Sunday. Reason is the highest faculty of the soul - what we mean often by the soul itself; it never <u>reasons</u>, never proves, it simply perceives; it is vision. The Understanding toils all the time, compares, contrives, adds, argues, near sighted but strong-sighted, dwelling in the present the expedient the customary. Beasts have some understanding but no Reason. Reason is potentially perfect in every man - Understanding in very different degrees of strength. The thoughts of youth, & 'first thoughts,' are the revelations of Reason. The love of the beautiful & of Goodness

> as the highest beauty the belief in the absolute & universal superiority of the Right & the True. But understanding that wrinkled calculator the steward of our house to whom is committed the support of our animal life contradicts evermore these affirmations of Reason & points at Custom & Interest & persuades one man that the declarations of Reason are false & another that they are at least impracticable. Yet by & by after having denied our Master we come back to see at the end of years or of life that he was the Truth. 6

We should be aware that Emerson wrote this letter at a time when he was under the influence, concomitantly, of Carlyle's views on the subject; of Coleridge's dealings with it in The Friend, in Biographia Literaria, and in Aids to Reflection; of various sketches of what Emerson believed to be "German" philosophy; and, of course, under the influence of the Scottish School of Reid, Stewart, and others. However, I consider it a moot point to determine, as so many scholars have tried, who the leading voice in this concert of influences was. It is more illuminating, I think, to see the passage in the light of a functional relationship which had been established by Kant and which had served as the background foil for almost all further attempts of the time to deal with Reason and Understanding as philosophical principles.

In Kant, pure Reason (reine Vernunft) is a theoretical and speculative faculty which applies pure concepts (reine Begriffe) to alleged objects beyond experience. As such it falls into the circumference of a theoretical philosophy and epistemology which deals with questions of the possibility of experience and forms of knowledge. Practical Reason, in contrast, is the faculty to reflect upon the maxims of the will and the principles of action regulated by the moral law. As such it does not pursue theoretical knowledge, but rather the question of what should be done according to the laws of a world of intelligible beings. Understanding (Verstand), on the other hand, is the faculty of applying concepts (pure or empirical) to the phenomenal world of experience. As can be seen, the three faculties under scrutiny have their distinct realms and inherent limitations, and cannot be regarded as giving contradictory views of one and the same matter under the same aspect.

In the above passage, Emerson juggles these faculties around until almost all distinctions are purged out of them and, consequently, until their functions (whether Kantian or not) are invalidated. He claims an inherent opposition, even contradiction, between Reason and Understanding, declares Reason the higher faculty, enthrones it as a reliable means of access to the noumenal world beyond appearances, and thus opens the floodgates of a speculative metaphysics which Kant had closed by demonstrating that pure Reason made an illegitimate and hence a deceptive use of the pure concepts of understanding. It has been argued that Emerson's confusion goes back to a somewhat cavalier use of the term Reason which could be set right. It appears that Emerson means practical Reason whenever he says Reason and that many of his above statements make better sense when we take this shift into consideration. And indeed, Emerson's emphasis on such terms as practical, impractical, Interest, Goodness, and Right suggests a strong orientation towards practical philosophy and a centering upon practical Reason as the epitome of Reason as such.[7] Moreover, passages from other works signal that Emerson was aware of the "two worlds" of Kantian philosophy, the phenomenal and the noumenal, and of the concomitant proposition that practical Reason was the only possible path into the realm of the intelligible. Thus he opens his essay on Montaigne with the sentence: "Every fact is related on one side to sensation, and on the other to morals."[8] And in the same essay he equates Reason with "the Law," a formula which in a similar wording can be found in many other Emersonian works.[9] Yet, even if we concede that Emerson generally meant practical Reason when he said Reason, the internal obfuscations of his views and what was to follow from them cannot be explained away. For what Emerson really does in the given passage, as in many later contexts, is to suggest that practical Reason is the central principle of his philosophy while at the same time he makes it perform the work of pure or speculative Reason. As the terms perceive, vision, thought, and truth document, Emerson concentrates on modes of cognition or forms of knowledge which, under an epistemological aspect, have to legitimize themselves as to their fields of application and range. But practical Reason, which, in the given passage, is constantly associated with forms of cognition, is not a principle of cognition at all but rather the faculty of grasping the moral law, in conjunction with which certain postulates (different from cognitive knowledge) can be established. In short, pure Reason in its speculative function is concerned with questions of theoretical truth and with objects of cognition beyond the confines of experience, whereas practical Reason is concerned with questions of right or wrong and with postulates that arise from man's nature as a moral being and an entity of the intelligible world.

What, then, happens when Emerson adopts "the distinction of Milton Coleridge & the Germans between Reason & Understanding" and fits it into his own philosophical scheme? Beside the fact that he concentrates exclusively on two faculties and thereby neglects others such as imagination (Einbildungskraft) and judgement (Urteilskraft) which could have proved useful in tackling the philosophical problems he encountered, the following picture can be drawn. First, where Kant sees a dichotomy between Reason and Understanding – each with its complementary functions and limitations – Emerson insists on an artificial opposition between the two faculties, bringing them into a false hierarchy, and saddling Reason with more responsibilities than it can bear. Second, where Kant makes a clear distinction between theoretical and practical Reason, Emerson intermixes both and then confuses their capacities and achievements. And third, if for Kant the one form of Reason offered a potential access to the realm of the noumenal, for Emerson this realm is paradoxically barred since he seeks access to it through the speculative use of a form of Reason which cannot negotiate such an access. Thus Emerson's thinking even at an early stage begins to take shape not as a new philosophy beyond Kant, but rather as a step backwards to the traditional metaphysical speculations before Kant. It documents that he did not grasp the full significance of Kant's programmatic dictum (which should have been particularly dear to Emerson) that he wanted to limit the claims of Reason in

625

order to make room for faith.[10] And it documents another persistent feature: Emerson clearly longed for an instrument that guaranteed his unconditional access to the realm of the noumenal and to the apprehension of eternal truth – preferably moral truth – beyond phenomenal experience. Whatever instrument or faculty of the mind seemed to offer itself for this purpose, Emerson would attempt to convert it, even against explicit warnings, into a vehicle for his moral-metaphysical ventures. In this respect, Emerson's method of claiming Reason as an instrument for the attainment of divine truth resembles a little the strange but entertaining method pursued by the "Lutheran" and the "Popish" doctors of Divinity in their dispute over the stranger's nose in Tristam Shandy: "... it just served as a frigate to launch them into the gulph of school-divinity, – and then they all sailed before the wind."[11]

III

With Emerson's lecture "The Transcendentalist" we are beyond his early gropings for a "vocabulary for my ideas,"[12] beyond the stage where he relied almost exclusively on Coleridge, Carlyle, and others to tell him what German philosophy and the Kantian system in particular meant, beyond the first statement of his own philosophy in Nature, and well into a phase where he confidently undertook to sketch the gist of Kantian philosophy as he understood it.[13] In an extended passage dealing with the origin of the term transcendental Emerson states:

> It is well known to most of my audience that the Idealism of the present day acquired the name of Transcendental from the use of that term by Immanuel Kant, of Konigsberg, who replied to the skeptical philosophy of Locke, which insisted that there was nothing in the intellect which was not previously in the experience of the senses, by showing that there was a very important class of ideas or imperative forms, which did not come by experience, but through which experience was acquired; that these were intuitions of the mind itself; and he denominated them Transcendental forms. The extraordinary profoundness and precision of that man's thinking have given vogue to his nomenclature, in Europe and America, to that extent that whatever belongs to the class of intuitive thought is popularly called at the present day Transcendental. [14]

Beyond the fact that Emerson seems to understand the connection between Locke and Kant, several key terms of Kantian philosophy catch our attention: idea, imperative, intuition, and transcendental. Emerson's application of these terms can be taken as a measure of his penetration of Kant's epistemology and, I think, as an indication of his own deviant orientation evolving in interrelation with such terms. In the passage quoted, Emerson says ideas but he means concepts (Begriffe), disregarding the decisive Kantian distinction between concept as constitutive for the understanding of experience, and idea as the regulative principle of Reason for the application of pure concepts beyond the realm of experience. In doing so, Emerson re-introduces the possibility of a speculative metaphysics into the confines of an epistemology that had meant to curb the non-legitimate application of pure concepts beyond experience, and thus to make a speculative metaphysics of pure Reason a fruitless venture once and forever.

Concomitantly, the use of imperative forms as synonymous for ideas by which are truly meant concepts, and, furthermore, suggestive of the imperatives of practical Reason, not only inter-mixes the distinct realms of Understanding and pure Reason of the first Critique, but also establishes a confusion between Kant's theoretical and practical philosophy much in the same way pure or speculative Reason and practical Reason had been intermingled earlier by Emerson. It should be noted that the confusions involved here do not pertain to terminological quibbles but rather touch the center of transcendental idealism: for they unwittingly destruct both the internal workings of Kant's philosophy and the relational structure of the second Critique as a complement to the first Critique.

Such distinctions gain an added dimension when we observe Emerson's reading of the terms intuition and transcendental in the foregoing passage. To claim that the forms "through which experience was acquired ... were intuitions of the mind" implies a telling confusion between intuitions and concepts, and transforms Kant's philosophy into an unbounded intuitionism which it was clearly not.

Intuition generally means "sinnliche Anschauung" in Kant, that is to say the immediate apprehension of an object by the senses under the pure forms of intuition, space and time. Intuitions are presented to the mind to be synthesized and generalized with the help of unitary concepts (a function of Understanding) so that they can be thought. It is obvious in the foregoing passage that Emerson is not at all talking about intuitions in the Kantian sense, but, most likely, about pure concepts or categories as the a priori forms of Understanding which make knowledge related to experience possible. The crucial distinction of Kant's epistemology, namely that between intuition, the pure forms of intuition (space and time), the concepts (categories) of Understanding, and the ideas of Reason is now in shambles. This confusion will not even be avoided if we refrain from taking Kant's narrow sense of intuition as the only sense, but rather refer to a more general and traditional, non-Kantian usage of the term in English. In modern philosophy, the OED holds, intuition means: "The immediate apprehension of an object by the mind without the intervention of any reasoning process."[15] Even according to this definition intuitions and concepts are essentially different. Intuitions as immediate apprehensions cannot be seen to fulfill the functions of concepts because concepts are precisely not an immediate but a mediate form of cognition. One could even say that concepts are the mediators per se between the world of sensory perception and the world of Understanding in that they are the only instruments of Understanding in the process of apprehending objects of experience as objects of thought. Any cognition of an object, then, is either intuition or concept, but not both in the same respect.[16]

However, one might argue that Emerson, in the given context, uses the term intuition in yet another sense and variation which had been established and held against Kant by Jacobi, Schelling, and other post-Kantian philosophers and which might have entered Emerson's vocabulary via Coleridge, who had dealt with it explicity.[17] I am speaking of the term intellectual intuition which would indeed signify a faculty that transcends experience and is still capable of apprehending truths directly, i.e. without the intervention of a medium. Yet Kant, in his first Critique, had reflected upon the possibilities of intellectual intuition and had explicity denied its existence as far as the human mind was concerned.[18] Hence it would make no sense to claim intellectual intuition as a central faculty of Kant's system unless, of course, this is being done out of ignorance of the philosophy allegedly explained.

Whatever the reason for Emerson's misapplication of the term intuition in the Kantian context, the results of the misapplication are obvious. In using the terms the way he does, Emerson merges the two elements indispensible for the constitution of knowledge, intuition and concept (the transcendental basis of which Kant had analysed separately in his transcendental Aesthetic and his transcendental Analytic), into the false unity of an Emersonian intuition that denies the limitations as much as the necessary interrelation of both elements. If concepts without intuitions are empty, and intuitions without concepts blind, as Kant had held,[19] then one could say of Emerson's intuition that it is blind and empty at the same time.

Intuition in this muddled sense becomes equated in Emerson with that which he believed to be Reason, and Reason with inspiration, and inspiration with instinct or spontaneity, and all of these with a form of vision which carries the human mind far beyond the confines of experience to which Kantian philosophy wanted to restrict it in its pursuit of that which is knowable. In the course of this transition, intuition loses almost all defining features Kant had ascribed to it, though Emerson seems to believe that he is talking about Kant's intuition.

It is one of the consequences of Emerson's unchecked intuitionism that, as he revealingly stated in an earlier passage of the lecture, the Emersonian idealist ends up with the "transfer of the world into the consciousness."[20] In this way Emerson leaves the ground of Critical Idealism and re-establishes a form of unbounded speculative Idealism which sees the phenomenal world as a product of intuitive consciousness - a decisive turn which Kantian philosophy precisely avoids. The transition is directly documented in the following two sentences where Emerson takes the step from an idealism which is still open to a critical analysis of the balance between consciousness and the world as appearance, to an idealism which has tipped the scales in favor of an unchallenged priority of intuitive consciousness:

> The idealist takes his departure from his consciousness, and reckons the world an appearance.
>
> His experience inclines him to behold the procession of facts you call the world, as flowing perpetually outward from an invisible, unsounded centre in himself, centre alike of him and of them, and necessitating him to regard all things as having a subjective or relative existence, relative to that aforesaid Unknown Centre of him. 21

Moreover, just as Emerson missed the distinction between idealism and Critical Idealism, he had difficulties with the distinction between transcendent and transcendental. Admittedly, he had always voiced reservations about the term Transcendentalism when applied to his own philosophy.[22] But in relation to Kant he readily accepted the term and attempted to give it a definite meaning. However, as the foregoing passage shows, Emerson at best caught reverberations of what amounts to the secondary sense of transcendental in Kant, while, by and large, he seems to have missed its primary meaning. Norman Kemp Smith, perhaps the most competent interpreter of Kant in the English speaking world, writes about this differentiation:

> But later in the Critique Kant employs the term transcendental in a second sense, namely, to denote the a priori factors of knowledge. All representations which are a priori and yet are applicable to objects are transcendental. The term is then defined through its distinction from the empirical on the one hand, and from the transcendent on the other. 23

Emerson refers to this sense of transcendental when he says that "the intuitions of the mind" were denominated "transcendental forms" by Kant, and that what belongs to the class of intuitive thought is called transcendental. It has been shown in our foregoing discussion that this statement is wrong since it misrepresents the nature and function of intuition in Kant. However, it should also be noted that Emerson bypasses the primary sense of transcendental and immediately jumps to the secondary sense of the term in his view of Kant's philosophy. "'Transcendental' is primarily employed by

Kant," to quote Norman Kemp Smith again,

> as a name for a certain kind of knowledge. Transcendental knowledge is knowledge not of objects, but of the nature and conditions of our a priori cognition of them ... this title applies only to such knowledge as constitutes a theory or science of the a priori. Transcendental knowledge and transcendental philosophy must therefore be taken as coinciding; and as thus coincident, they signify the science of the possibility, nature, and limits of a priori knowledge. 24

Although this is admirably clear, I want to elaborate a little on the topic. Surpassing knowledge beyond the limits of experience implies an act of going beyond which may be called transcendent. Surpassing knowledge, however, into the direction of the conditions and the possibility of the constitution of knowledge defines the act of transcendental reflection as the only legitimate and epistemologically safe act of transcending. Thus the transcendental turn in Kant indicates something similar to the meta turn in modern parlance. Just as a metalanguage is language that talks about the workings of language, a transcendental reflection transcribes a form of thinking that turns back upon the nature and condition of reflection as such. In short, it is reason (in the widest sense) reflecting upon itself as reason, or, if you wish, the mind turned upon itself as the problem of the mind.[25]

It is doubtful whether Emerson ever understood this basic turn of orientation in Kant's philosophy. But it is safe to say that he made nothing of it in his own philosophical ventures. Emerson's uses of the term transcendental with the corollary of centering on intuition which, in turn, embraces his views on the nature of Reason, rather seem to lead directly to the double misconception of Kantian Transcendentalism characteristic of Emerson. As we have seen before, and as we again have occasion to notice, Emerson believes Reason to be transcendental as a faculty of apprehending truths (moral or other truths) beyond the reach of other faculties such as Understanding. Hence he believes that Reason transcends for higher purposes and with good results. He does not see that any transcendental reflection in the true sense is only transcendental insofar as it establishes the a priori principles and conditions of knowledge by seeking a form of reflective immanence that establishes the basis and the reliability of its own claims.

IV

If Emerson thus leaves us somewhat puzzled by his picture of transcendental Idealism in the lecture on the Transcendentalist, he stimulates new hopes of clarification in his later essay "Experience." And clarification we get from this essay, but mostly to the effect that Emerson is moving away from transcendental Idealism in more ways than before. The title "Experience" suggests that Emerson wants to address one of the central epistemological problems of modern philosophy. It seems to take its opening gambit from familiar questions such as: What is experience? What makes experience possible? What accounts for our trust in experience? However, the opening statements of the essay sound a somewhat different note:

> Where do we find ourselves? In a series of which we do not know the extremes, and believe that it has none. 26

> All things swim and glitter. Our life is not so much threatened as our perception. Ghostlike we glide through nature, and should not know our place again. 27

> Dream delivers us to dream, and there is no end to illusion. Life is a train of moods like a string of beads, and as we pass through them they prove to be many-colored lenses which paint the world their own hue, and each shows only what lies in its focus. 28

As such statements show, the central feature of Emerson's approach to experience is not that of a transcendental analysis trying to decide what the universal elements of experience are and how they work together to constitute reliable knowledge, but rather an attempt to decide how experience _feels_ for the individual, what it means for the person experiencing, and which hopes, doubts, and shifting emotions are connected with it.[29] In line with this orientation the key word of the essay becomes _mood_. This is neither surprising nor illegitimate, but it does underline a philosophical orientation which leads away from anything transcendental Idealism has ever been. Transcendental philosophy can be seen as a systematic reflection on the interrelation between experience and the self. Yet, the focus of this reflection is invariably on an abstract, universal self which, terminological quibbles aside, may be called the transcendental self, the transcendental unity of apperception, etc. Transcendental

Idealism of whatever kind analyses the relation of such a universal self (seen as conditional and constitutive for experience) to highly generalized forms - in contrast to specific contents - of human experience. Emerson's approach, however, is totally different. He radically individualizes the problem of experience in that he pulls emotions, moods, and changing private states of consciousness into the center of his analysis, and then pursues their inherent problematics. Just as the lecture "The Transcendentalist" had started out with general propositions on the nature of Transcendentalism and then turned into a long reflection upon the role of individual Transcendentalists in society, so the overwhelming message of "Experience" becomes that the real epistemological problem of Transcendentalism lies in the individual self and its mysterious moods and private states of consciousness. In the one case, Emerson externalizes the problem of Transcendentalism, while in the other he individualizes it. Consequently, what Emerson offers in the essay is not an epistemology of human knowledge but rather, as Stanley Cavell has put it, an "epistemology of moods."[30] We may add that an "epistemology of moods" by the very nature of its subject is an epistemology of private instead of universal states of consciousness.

Almost everything Emerson pursues and finds in "Experience" takes its coloring from this idiosyncratic approach. Since he individualizes the problem of experience, most questions are now addressed to the problem of changing frames of mind materializing in highly personal states of consciousness. To be sure, there is still a strong belief in something which transcends these states and which does not change as the moods come and go:

> If I have described life as a flux of moods, I must now add that there is that in us which changes not and which ranks all sensations and states of mind ... Fortune, Minerva, Muse, Holy Ghost, - these are quaint names, too narrow to cover this unbounded substance. The baffled intellect must still kneel before this cause, which refuses to be named, - ineffable cause, which every fine genius has essayed to represent by some emphatic symbol ... 31

Moreover, there is still the belief in Emerson that there are lines of communication between the noumenal realm of the "unbounded substance" and the human mind: "Into every intelligence there is a door which is never closed, through which the creator passes."[32]

However, the human faculties or instruments of access to any form of more than private elucidation have fallen victim to moody doubts, or have turned into merely subjective impulses of reaching out for that which cannot be obtained. Quite concretely, the binding interpersonal norms of practical Reason (the "Law" which Emerson held so dear), turn into the merely subjective intimations of the moral sentiment.[33] The perennial though abortive attempts of speculative Reason to reach out for a truth beyond phenomenal experience turn into impulsive private excursions of alternate failure and success. And the categories of Understanding as much as space and time as the pure forms of intuition - both secure and binding within the predefined realms of their application - become "colored lenses" distorting the view of the universe:

> We have learned that we do not see directly, but mediately, and that we have no means of correcting these colored and distorting lenses which we are, or of computing the amount of their errors. Perhaps these subject-lenses have a creative power; perhaps there are no objects. Once we lived in what we saw; now, the rapaciousness of this new power, which threatens to absorb all things, engages us. Nature, art, persons, letters, religions, objects, successively tumble in, and God is but one of its ideas. 34

Small wonder that all that remains for Emerson at the end of "Experience" is his expressive wish to know, coupled with the doubt that he will ever know: "I am very content with knowing, if only I could know."[35] Emerson is unhappy about the results of his investigation, but he does not see that he himself has structured the analysis in such a way that the results were unavoidable. An epistemology of moods and private states of consciousness is hardly possible because as a theory it would imply the very step from the particular to the universal which Emerson so obviously shuns. In contrast, a transcendental epistemology of consciousness is possible, but only on a plane of generalization and differentiation beyond Emerson's aims or reach in "Experience." From the perspective of Kantian epistemology - the nomenclature of which Emerson constantly evokes in his venture - the essay "Experience" at best reaches the level of the popular misinterpretation of the Critique of Pure Reason that, after it, all human knowledge had to be seen as completely subjective. Yet one could say that the first Critique had actually established the opposite of this allegation. If an object is that which appears to a subject, and if - as Kant had demonstrated - the conditions of the cognition of objects define at the same time the conditions of the objects of cognition,[36] then Kant's epistemology makes human knowledge as objective as possible. Emerson, I think, misses this truly transcendental turn as so many others have missed it. As a consequence, he falls into the dual trap of subjectivism and private intuitionism which no longer allows for the escape he so diligently seeks. In his essay "Experience," Emerson predetermines the results of his attempt to reach an absolute, interpersonally binding, more than subjective truth by asking questions which can only be answered in the negative. In this process, experience itself becomes a private world of subjectivism into which a struggling Emerson falls while complaining that he is about to be shut in without reasonable hopes for escape.

V

Thus Emerson proceeds, trusting and distrusting, affirming and doubting, mingling hope and despair. But nothing except the occasional confirmation of a belief held prior to all investigations will come of his endeavors, because he has not learned - as he could have learned from Kant - where he can trust and where he must doubt. Yet, time and again Emerson claims Kantian terminology as the instrument of his analysis and borrows fragments of Kantian thought in support of his own convictions. Are these the makings of a philosophy beyond Kant?[37] Or, rather, telling indications of the perplexities after Kant? Somewhat older forms of criticism have leaned towards the latter reading, whereas more recently there is a wave of criticism tending towards the former interpretation. Such vindications of Emerson usually stress the postenlightenment, the paradoxically probing, the heroically futile dimensions of Emerson's thought. They range from Harold Bloom's allegation that Emerson figured as the "Orphic Poet" of America, personifying a modern form of gnosis beyond systematic philosophy, religion, or logocentric thought,[38] to suggestions that he intentionally remained suspended at the verge of a metaphysical psychology beyond certitude and hope for redemption.[39] They hold, alternatively, that Emerson prefigured Heidegger's stand on the nature of "true thinking,"[40] or that he was a harbinger of the deconstructionist's joyful, painful affirmations of the void.[41] All this may be partly so, but I remain unconvinced that Emerson thereby went <u>beyond</u> Kant – if only for the reason that I cannot imagine a form of thinking which goes beyond the conceptual fundaments of a preceding philosophy by allegedly absorbing but actually misunderstanding it.

There are other reasons for remaining unconvinced. Emerson's relation to Kant can be seen from at least two different angles. From the perspective of Kantian philosophy itself, Emerson's endeavors are a falling behind. He misuses Kantian thought in an externalizing fashion by appropriating particles of its content and terminology which he then integrates into a conglomerate of convictions of his own. Maybe Emerson even had an inkling of what he was doing. For, when he stated in his <u>Journals</u> that by knowing certain systems of philosophy he got a vocabulary for his own ideas, he conspicuously added: "I get no ideas."[42]

From the alternative perspective of Emerson's own predisposition, the picture is somewhat different. Emerson had good reasons to claim Kant as a crown witness for his views, because he felt that he could draw qualified support from him for his most cherished beliefs: that an intuitive and hence irrefutable grasp of truth was possible, and that the moral law was absolute, divine, inside every human being, and beyond the necessity of empirical or rational proof. But Emerson did not comprehend the context and the philosophical architecture of the evidence offered by his crown witness, and thereby pulled the rug from under his own feet. Kant's epistemology, his transcendental analyses, his differentiation between the realms of practical and pure Reason could have shown Emerson a reliable though difficult path to his own goal, namely the achievement of the greatest attainable measure of certainty about the noumenal sources and the divine sanctifications of human existence. But in his eagerness to find what he wanted and his blindness for what was actually to be found in Kant, Emerson elected to take a short cut and thus, paradoxically, missed the way to the goal he most dearly wanted to reach.

How, then, does Emerson's thought stand in relation to Kant? I think that Emerson meant to place his philosophy of intuitionism somewhere beside or, possibly even, beyond Kant, but that in attempting to do so he fell behind him instead of moving ahead of him. For our own understanding of Emerson's thinking it is important to comprehend this difference between intention and achievement, for I believe that Coleridge was not far off the mark when he wrote: "until you understand a writer's ignorance, presume yourself ignorant of his understanding."[43]

NOTES

[1] The Journals and Miscellaneous Notebooks of Ralph Waldo Emerson, Vol. V, ed. Merton M. Sealts, Jr. (Cambridge, Mass., 1965), p. 343.

[2] "The Transcendentalist," Emerson's Complete Works: Riverside Edition (London: Routledge and Sons, 1903), Vol. I, p. 321.

[3] The several dozen references to Kant in The Journals and Miscellaneous Notebooks alone are ample proof that there is not much depth to Emerson's dealing with Kant and Kantian philosophy. They mostly run the gamut from name dropping to fleeting commentary and/or occasional misrepresentation.

[4] For Emerson's relation to Kant compare among the older contributions: René Wellek, "Emerson and German Philosophy," New England Quarterly, 16, 1 (1943), 41-62 (rpt. in Confrontations, Princeton: Princeton UP, 1965); Henry A. Pochmann, German Culture in America (Madison: University of Wisconsin Press, 1957), pp. 158-92; Joel Porte, "The Moral Law: Emerson's Cosmic Vision," Emerson and Thoreau: Transcendentalists in Conflict (Middletown, Conn.: Wesleyan UP, 1966), pp. 84-90. More recent contributions to the debate will be identified in later references. It should be noted, though, that certain other sources which are frequently quoted in the given context cannot be recommended as reliable. Among them are O.B. Frothingham's Transcendentalism in New England (New York: G.P. Putnam's Sons, 1876) with its dubious sketch of

Kantian philosophy, and Geo Runze's "Emerson und Kant," Kantstudien, 9 (1904), 292-306, with its lack of information on what Emerson wrote and said about Kant (cf. Runze's statement on Emerson: "... über Kant schweigt er sich aus").

[5] Henry Pochmann, German Culture in America, pp. 158ff., 206f.

[6] The Letters of Ralph Waldo Emerson, ed. Ralph L. Rusk (1939; rpt. New York: Columbia UP, 1966), Vol. I, pp. 412-13.

[7] One of the earliest contributions marking the tendency of American philosophical thought, and in particular Emerson's thinking, towards practical philosophy is J.E. Creighton's article "The Philosophy of Kant in America," Kantstudien, 2 (1899), 237-52.

[8] "Montaigne; or, the Skeptic," Emerson's Complete Works: Riverside Edition (London: Routledge and Sons, 1903), Vol. IV, p. 143.

[9] Ibid., p. 170.

[10] Cf. Kant's "Vorrede" to the second edition of his Kritik der reinen Vernunft (B XXX).

[11] Laurence Sterne, The Life and Opinions of Tristam Shandy, Gentleman, ed. Ian Campbell Ross (Oxford: Clarendon Press, 1983), p. 211.

[12] The Journals and Miscellaneous Notebooks, Vol. V, p. 343.

[13] Emerson then had access to the complete translation of Kant's first Critique. See Walter Harding, Emerson's Library (Charlottesville: UP of Virginia, 1967). The edition of Kant's text listed in Harding (p. 156) is Francis Haywood's translation Critick of Pure Reason which first came out in 1838 in London and was followed by a second edition in 1848, which included an appendix "Explanation of Terms, According to Different Commentators" (pp. 591-605).

[14] "The Transcendentalist," pp. 320-21. Cf. also René Wellek's dealing with the passage in his already quoted essay "Emerson and German Philosophy."

[15] Cf. OED, "intuition," sense 5 a.

[16] See Kant's systematic classification and explanation of the terms in B 377 of the Kritik der reinen Vernunft: "Eine Perception, die sich lediglich auf das Subjekt, als Modifikation seines Zustandes bezieht, ist Empfindung (sensatio), eine objektive Perzeption ist Erkenntnis (cognitio). Diese ist entweder Anschauung oder Begriff (intuitus vel conceptus)."

[17] Coleridge deals with Kant's sense of intuition and his denial of intellectual intuition in a note of his Biographia Literaria where

he first explains the Kantian meaning of the term and then indicates that he is going to deviate from this usage. See Biographia Literaria, ed. J. Shawcross (1907; rpt. London: Oxford UP, 1973), Vol. I, p. 190. Coleridge's procedure is legitimate because he knows and says what he is doing, simply claiming the right to deviate from Kant in regard to certain questions. Emerson's way of dealing with the term intuition is different in that he shows no awareness of what precisely he is doing, but rather gives the reader the misleading impression that he is merely transcribing Kant.

[18]Kant addresses the issue of intellectual intuition in B 72 and B 307 of his Kritik der reinen Vernunft. He indicates that intellectual intuition cannot be a property of the human mind, but leaves open the (highly speculative) question of whether it can be regarded as a property of what he calls the "Urwesen."

[19]Kant's actual phrasing is somewhat different: "Gedanken ohne Inhalt sind leer, Anschauungen ohne Begriffe sind blind." (Kritik der reinen Vernunft, B 75).

[20]"The Transcendentalist," p. 315.

[21]Ibid., pp. 314–15.

[22]See Pochmann, German Culture in America, p. 153; and Journals and Miscellaneous Notebooks, Vol. XVI, pp. 21–22.

[23]Norman Kemp Smith, A Commentary to Kant's "Critique of Pure Reason," 2nd ed. (London: Macmillan, 1923), p. 75.

[24]Ibid., p. 74.

[25]Cf. Kant's "Vorrede" to the first edition of his Kritik der reinen Vernunft (A XII). Here he defines the call of Reason in its transcendental aspect as: "... eine Aufforderung an die Vernunft, das beschwerlichste aller ihrer Geschäfte, nämlich das der Selbsterkenntnis aufs neue zu übernehmen und einen Gerichtshof einzusetzen, der sie bei ihren gerechten Ansprüchen sichere, dagegen aber alle grundlosen Anmaßungen, nicht durch Machtsprüche, sondern nach ihren ewigen und unwandelbaren Gesetzen, abfertigen könne, und dieser ist kein anderer als die Kritik der reinen Vernunft selbst."

[26]"Experience," Emerson's Complete Works: Riverside Edition (London: Routledge and Sons, 1903), Vol. III, p. 49.

[27]Ibid., p. 49.

[28]Ibid., pp. 53–4.

[29]Cf. Robert E. Abrams who characterizes Emerson's approach as "metaphysical psychology" in the "form of prayer." See "Emerson at

the Limits of Metaphysical Psychology," <u>Pacific Coast Philology</u>, 18, 1-2 (1983), p. 14.

[30] Cf. Stanley Cavell, "Thinking of Emerson," <u>New Literary History</u>, 11 (1979), pp. 167-76. Cavell's essay starts with the same assumption as mine, namely that "I hear Kant working throughout Emerson's essay on 'Experience' ..." (p. 168). Yet, in his further analysis of Emerson's relation to Kant, Cavell comes to quite different results.

[31] "Experience," pp. 73-4.

[32] Ibid., p. 58.

[33] Ibid., p. 74.

[34] Ibid., p. 77. Again Emerson might have been influenced by Coleridge. See Coleridge's "Dejection, an Ode" for similar misapprehensions. For a discussion of Coleridge's ode under the perspective of Kantian philosophy, compare A.O. Lovejoy, "Coleridge and Kant's Two Worlds," <u>Essays in the History of Ideas</u> (Baltimore: Johns Hopkins UP, 1948), pp. 260ff.

[35] "Experience," p. 85.

[36] See Kant, <u>Kritik der reinen Vernunft</u>, B 197.

[37] Cf. A.J. Cascardi, "Emerson on Nature: Philosophy beyond Kant," <u>ESQ</u>, 30, 4 (1984), pp. 201-10.

[38] Among Harold Bloom's many contributions on Emerson, see in particular his chapter "Emerson: The American Religion" in <u>Agon: Towards a Theory of Revisionism</u> (New York: Oxford UP, 1982), and the chapter "The Native Strain: American Orphism" in <u>Figures of Capable Imagination</u> (New York: Seabury, 1976).

[39] Robert E. Abrams, "Emerson at the Limits of Metaphysical Psychology," <u>Pacific Coast Philology</u>, 18, 1-2 (1983), pp. 14-22.

[40] Stanley Cavell, "Thinking of Emerson," <u>New Literary History</u>, 11 (1979), p. 172. For a more recent treatment of Emerson's relation to Kant, see also Cavell's "Genteel Responses to Kant? In Emerson's 'Fate' and in Coleridge's <u>Biographia Literaria</u>," <u>Raritan</u>, 3, 2 (1983), pp. 34-61.

[41] David L. Smith, "Emerson and Deconstruction: The End(s) of Scholarship," <u>Soundings</u>, 67, 2 (1984), pp. 379-98.

[42] <u>Journals and Miscellaneous Notebooks</u>, Vol. V, p. 343.

[43] Coleridge, <u>Biographia Literaria</u>, ed. J. Shawcross (1907; rpt. London: Oxford UP, 1973), Vol. I, p. 160.

Gregory P. Rich

Jonathan Edwards's View of the Freedom Requisite for Moral Agency

If we are completely predestined to act as we do, then do we have the freedom required for moral agency, i.e., the freedom required for our being fit subjects of praise or blame, reward or punishment? In eighteenth-century New England, this question was a primary source of theological controversy. Lining up on one side of the question were the Calvinists, claiming that predestination would not rule out the freedom requisite for moral agency. Lining up on the other side of the question were the Arminians, claiming that predestination would rule out the freedom required for moral agency. Who was right?

In this paper after describing the theological and historical context of the controversy between Calvinists and Arminians, I shall focus on the way that the leading Calvinist, Jonathan Edwards, defended the view that divine predestination would not rule out the freedom requisite for moral agency. I shall offer two main reasons for believing that Edwards did not show that divine predestination is compatible with the freedom requisite for moral agency. First I shall argue that Edwards did not provide good reason to believe that what he called ordinary freedom is the freedom requisite for moral agency. Second I shall argue that there is good reason to believe that such freedom is not the freedom requisite for moral agency.

Of the four branches of the Protestant Reformation, the Lutheran, the Anglican, the Reformed, and the Radical, the Reformed branch had the strongest influence on the development of Puritan theology (Smith et al. 3; Ahlstrom 78, 125). As a result, New England Puritan theology, from the start, was a form of Calvinist theology (Ahlstrom 130-31; Conklin 4). The key idea within Calvinist theology is the idea of God's sovereignty (Newlin 2; Ahlstrom 79). God, according to Calvin, "governs heaven and earth by his providence, and regulates all things in such a manner that nothing happens but according to his counsel" (qted. in Manschreck 189). Further, according to this idea of sovereignty, God, as supreme authority, is in no way subject to, or limited by, anything outside of himself (J. Edwards 380). God's sovereignty, according to Edwards, amounts to "his ability and authority to do whatever pleases him" (J. Edwards 378).

Three of the more important Calvinist doctrines, the doctrine of original sin or utter depravity, the doctrine of irresistible grace, and the doctrine of unconditional election, reflect this key idea of God's sovereignty (Newlin 2-3; Manschreck 189). According to the doctrine of original sin, due to Adam's sin, God's image in humankind has become so warped that humans cannot avoid sin, except by God's grace. According to the doctrine of irresistible grace, God's grace cannot be resisted. And according to the doctrine of unconditional election, before creation God in his mercy predestined some individuals for salvation and others for damnation, and his doing so did not depend in any way on the faith or the good deeds of these individuals.

Although primarily Calvinists, some of the early New England Puritan divines, such as Thomas Hooker and Thomas Shepard, substituted a doctrine of the covenant for the doctrine of unconditional election (Newlin 4; Ahlstrom 152-53). According to the doctrine of the covenant, God's grace is dependent on, or conditional on, obedience to his commands (Ahlstrom 131; Latourette 814). By making obedience to God's commands necessary for God's grace, the doctrine of the covenant implied that God could not indiscriminately bestow his grace, and so the doctrine of the covenant, in effect, limited God's sovereignty. Not all early New England Puritan divines accepted the doctrine of the covenant, however. Some, notably John Cotton, held to the doctrine of unconditional election, believing that divine grace is a more arbitrary matter (Ahlstrom 152).

Those who did reject the doctrine of unconditional election were in partial agreement with Jacobus Arminius, a theologian of the

Dutch Reformed Church. Around the turn of the seventeenth century before the Puritan migration to New England, Arminius had claimed that God's grace is conditional on his foreknowledge of faith (Ramsey 3). Although Arminius had also made other criticisms of strict Calvinism, few if any early New England Puritan divines agreed with these criticisms (Ahlstrom 131). Arminius had argued that because of Christ's atonement, salvation was possible for all, not just for a fortunate few. He had also "insisted upon the cooperation of the human will" (Leith 46) in receiving grace. Thus besides rejecting the idea of unconditional election, Arminius had rejected the idea that only some can be saved and the idea that grace cannot be resisted.

The Calvinist Synod of Dort in 1619 condemned Arminius for not believing that the will is enslaved, for not believing that the will is predetermined. Thereafter, according to Perry Miller,

> "Arminian" among Protestant nations was a smear word, and any and every effort to augment human responsibility by giving the natural will a power to act in some degree by itself was castigated as Arminianism (105-06).

When 'Arminian' was not used as a smear word, it often had an extremely broad meaning. According to Sydney Ahlstrom, "In America the term often was a synonym for 'liberal' or 'broad and catholic'" (404). Somewhat less broadly, by the eighteenth century in New England, 'Arminian' had come to signify any view expressing moral objections to strict Calvinism (Ramsey 3), and especially any view giving free, unpredetermined human choices a major role in the gaining of salvation (Ahlstrom 404). Deniers of original sin, irresistible grace, unconditional election, or predestination would alike be labeled "Arminians."

In the early eighteenth century, New Englanders began to drift toward Arminianism and away from Calvinism. After the Restoration, by the beginning of the eighteenth century, Arminian theology had become orthodox Anglican theology (Ramsey 82; Ahlstrom 96). In 1722, after careful study of Arminian theology, the rector of the College of Connecticut (now Yale), Timothy Cutler, and the college's only tutor, Thomas Brown, along with five ministers from nearby towns, defected to Arminianism, taking Anglican vows (Ahlstrom 224). By 1734 some of the more conservative New England ministers were writing tracts lamenting the spread of Arminianism among young ministers (Newlin 64). Laymen as well had been shifting to Arminian principles (Ahlstrom 224-25), and increasingly did so during the 1740s. In 1750 Jonathan Edwards said of Arminian principles that

> the progress they have made in the land, within this seven years, seems to have been vastly greater, than at any time in the like space before: and they are still prevailing, and creeping into almost all parts of the land (qted. in Ramsey 5).

Edwards worried that Arminian principles were coming to prevail among non-Anglican and Anglican alike (Miller 108).

Arminian arguments had been persuasive. As early as 1710 the English Anglican Arminian, Daniel Whitby, in his Discourse on Five Points had undertaken a point by point refutation of Calvinist theology as it had been expressed by the Synod of Dort in 1619. Against the doctrine of original sin, the doctrine that we are unable to avoid sin except by God's grace, Whitby objected that "if we be necessitated, neither sins of omission nor sins of commission, would deserve that name" (qted. in J. Edwards 299). In 1738 an English non-Anglican, John Taylor, joined Whitby in criticizing the doctrine of original sin. Whitby and Taylor were extremely popular in New England. Perry Miller says of them that "For New Englanders, these two were the literary spokesmen of the age ..." (110).

American writers also contributed to the drift away from Calvinism and toward Arminianism. By 1745 the American Anglican Arminian, Samuel Johnson, one of the defectors from the College of Connecticut in 1722, had written A Letter from Aristocles to Authades Concerning the Sovereignty and Promises of God, a pamphlet attacking Calvinism. In this pamphlet Johnson argued that the doctrine of unconditional election, as it involves predestination, is inconsistent with human moral agency and divine benevolence. He said that the doctrine

> is contrary to the nature and attributes of God, because it appears plainly inconsistent with the very notion of his being a moral governor of the world: for it represents Him as laying his creatures under a necessity of being what they are,

whether good or bad, and so leaves no room for either virtue or vice, praise or blame, reward or punishment, properly speaking (qted. in Newlin 107-08).

According to Johnson, then, if God foreordains humans to act as they do, then they _must_ act as they do, and in that case they are not moral agents, i.e., not beings who can be virtuous or vicious, praiseworthy or blameworthy. Moreover, Johnson claimed that if humans are not moral agents, then it is not fair for God to condemn any of them to eternal torment. Thus Johnson concluded that the doctrine of unconditional election is inconsistent with both human moral agency and divine benevolence. Johnson's pamphlet generated a pamphlet war between Arminians and Calvinists, pamphlet answering pamphlet for three years (Newlin 135-39).

For both Calvinists and Arminians, no small matter, but salvation itself, was at stake. Of his _Letter_, Johnson claimed that "the eternal interest of the souls of men is very nearly concerned in it" (qted. in Newlin 107). Johnson believed that Calvinist principles "are equally destructive to the right belief of both God and Gospel" (qted. in Newlin 107). Further, according to Johnson, Calvinist principles undermine our efforts to repent, "since, for aught we know, we may be absolutely excluded from all possibility of succeeding by a sovereign and inexorable decree of reprobation" (qted. in Newlin 108). Johnson claimed that Arminian principles, in contrast, encourage efforts to repent, because these principles represent God as loving his creation, as desiring the happiness of his creatures in proportion to their merits, and as willing to help them to be happy (Newlin 108).

On the Calvinist side, Edwards predicted that if Arminian theology came to be widely accepted, it would lead to "spiritual and eternal ruin" (qted. in Ramsey 5). The way Edwards saw it, the Arminian view of freedom, by making humans depend less on God and more on themselves, involves a pernicious misunderstanding of the proper relation between humans and God (Cherry 188). Edwards believed that the Arminian view of freedom, by giving humans, not God, the credit for salvation, would detract from the glory of God (J. Edwards 469). Edwards claimed that when sinners seek redemption, nothing is more important than that they "be properly convinced of their real guilt and sinfulness in the sight of God, and their deserving of his wrath" (J. Edwards 466). According to Edwards, Arminian principles hinder such a conviction by providing excuses, such as 'He can't help not loving his neighbor' (J. Edwards 467). Thus Edwards concluded that Arminian principles, instead of promoting redemption, impede it.

In 1731 in his first published sermon, God Glorified in the Work of Redemption by the Greatness of Man's Dependence upon Him in the Whole of It, Edwards attacked Arminianism (Newlin 65; R. Edwards 22). In the mid-30s in a series of sermons that led to an extremely successful revival at his church, Edwards argued against Arminianism by arguing for "justification by faith alone through grace" (Conklin 54-55; Sweet 129; Ahlstrom 282). By 1747 Edwards had decided that he would write a long work defending Calvinism and refuting Arminianism (Ramsey 2). In this work, Freedom of the Will, which appeared in 1754, Edwards gave a sustained scriptural and philosophical defense of Calvinist principles against Arminian principles.

Edwards wrote on the freedom requisite for moral agency because he believed that most of the key points at issue between Calvinists and Arminians could be settled by determining what kind of freedom is necessary for moral agency (J. Edwards 431). Edwards noted that Arminians rejected the doctrine of total depravity, the doctrine of irresistible grace, and the doctrine of unconditional election on the ground that these doctrines rule out the freedom required for moral agency (J. Edwards 431-434). Thus according to Edwards, one major nub in the dispute between Calvinists and Arminians concerns the kind of freedom that is requisite for moral agency.

According to Arminians, if we are completely predestined in all that we do, we always act of necessity, and so do not have the freedom requisite for moral agency. In contrast, according to Edwards and the strict Calvinists, though we are completely predestined in all what we do (J. Edwards 431, 433), the necessity that this puts us under does not conflict with the freedom requisite for moral agency (J. Edwards 405-06). Arminians claimed that since we have the freedom required for moral agency, we are not necessitated. Edwards and the Calvinists claimed that we have the freedom requisite for moral agency even though we are necessitated.

Edwards believed that by paying close attention to the meanings of 'freedom' and 'necessity,' the key terms in the dispute, he could show the plausibility of Calvinism and the absurdity of Arminianism. Like Thomas Hobbes, John Locke, and David Hume, Edwards believed that a proper understanding of freedom and necessity would result in a belief that there is no conflict between them. Here is a general overview of Edwards's defense of Calvinism.

According to Edwards, "The plain and obvious meaning of the words 'freedom' and 'liberty,' in common speech, is power, opportunity, or advantage, that anyone has, to do as he pleases" (J. Edwards 163). Edwards claimed that this common freedom, a power to do as one pleases, is the freedom requisite for moral agency (J. Edwards 406, 453-54). In contrast, Arminians claimed that the freedom requisite for moral agency essentially involves three features: a self-determining power in the will, indifference, and contingence (J. Edwards 164). According to Edwards, the self-determining power in the will amounts to a "certain sovereignty the will has over itself," (J. Edwards 164) by which it determines its own acts, without being dependent on external causes or anything prior to its acts. Edwards explained indifference as an "equilibrium whereby the will is without all antecedent determination or bias" (J. Edwards 203). Contingence, Edwards believed, amounts to an opposition to all necessity, an opposition to a sure and fixed connection between the act of will and any ground of its existence (J. Edwards 165). Arminians believed that such freedom, a freedom of the will which involves self-determining power, indifference, and contingence, is the freedom required for moral agency.

Edwards rejected Arminian free will for a number of reasons. First, he claimed that talk of freedom of the will does not make good sense, since only agents and not their powers have freedom (J. Edwards 163-64). If it does not make good sense to talk of freedom of the will, then it does not make good sense to claim that such free will is requisite for moral agency. Second, Edwards left aside his first objection and gave two arguments for the impossibility of Arminian free will. He argued that since Arminian free will requires a self-determining power in the will and such a power is impossible, then Arminian free will is impossible (J. Edwards 172-74, 190). He also argued that since Arminian free will requires choice while in a state of indifference and such choice is impossible, then Arminian free will is impossible (J. Edwards 196, 203). If Arminian free will is impossible while moral agency is possible, then Arminian free will is not the freedom requisite for moral agency. Finally, Edwards argued that even if Arminian free will is possible, no one has it, since either universal causation (J. Edwards 180-85, 213) or divine foreknowledge (J. Edwards 239ff., 257-58) rules out the contingence required by Arminian free will. If no one has Arminian free will, then those who believe that we are moral agents should not believe that Arminian free will is the freedom requisite for moral agency.

On the basis of such arguments, Edwards claimed that Arminian free will is not the freedom required for moral agency (J. Edwards 453-55). Edwards seemed to think that because of such arguments, the only thing properly called freedom is a power to do as one pleases. Believing that he had laid to rest the Arminian alternative to what he called ordinary freedom, Edwards seemed to think that since it was commonly believed that a power to do as one pleases is the freedom requisite for moral agency, then such a power is the freedom requisite for moral agency (J. Edwards 406, 358-59, 171).

Edwards went on to argue that such freedom does not conflict with any necessity resulting from divine predestination (J. Edwards 405-06, 431-33). In trying to make his position clear, Edwards clarified the kind of necessity "which especially belongs to controversies about acts of the will" (J. Edwards 152, 154). He defined such necessity, metaphysical necessity, as "the full and fixed connection between the things signified by the subject and predicate of a proposition, which affirms something to be true"

(J. Edwards 152). According to Edwards, future events are necessary "by a connection with ... something that already is, or has been; so that one being supposed, the other certainly follows" (J. Edwards 153-54).

Edwards also distinguished two kinds of metaphysical necessity: moral necessity and natural necessity. By 'moral necessity,' he meant

> that necessity of connection and consequence, which arises from such moral causes, as the strength of inclination, or motives, and the connection which there is in many cases between these, and such certain volitions and actions (J. Edwards 156).

By 'natural necessity' he meant the necessity that humans "are under through the force of natural causes" (J. Edwards 156), as opposed to moral causes. An example of a natural necessity would be the connection between a person's being wounded and his feeling pain. An example of a moral necessity would be the connection between a person's virtue and his choice to tell the truth. Thus for Edwards, what is morally necessary, but not what is naturally necessary, crucially depends on one's motives or inclinations.

Edwards believed that since our choices are always determined by our strongest inclination or motive (J. Edwards 142), our choices are always morally necessary, and never naturally necessary. Edwards claimed that such moral necessity does not conflict with the freedom required for moral agency (J. Edwards 453). He reasoned that if moral necessity is a sure and fixed connection between one's motives and his choices while the freedom requisite for moral agency is a power to do as one chooses, then "the moral necessity which universally takes place is not in the least inconsistent with anything that is properly called liberty" (J. Edwards 453).

Predestination of our wills, according to Edwards, need only put us under a moral necessity (J. Edwards 405-06). He said that God's

> universal, determining providence, infers some kind of necessity of all events; such a necessity as implies an infallible previous fixedness of the futurity of the event: but no other necessity of moral events, or volitions of intelligent agents, is needful in order to this, than moral necessity; which does as much ascertain the futurity of the event, as any other necessity (431).

Thus, according to Edwards, God's universal ordering of the circumstances which determine human choices only implies that those choices are morally necessary. Thus Edwards concluded that the only necessity resulting from divine predestination, moral necessity, is perfectly compatible with the only thing properly called freedom, a power to do as one pleases. In this way Edwards argued that the necessity brought on by divine predestination is no threat to the freedom requisite for moral agency.

Did Edwards show that divine predestination would not rule out the freedom required for moral agency? I do not believe so. Many of his main arguments against Arminian free will rest on mis-interpretations of key phrases. Relying on the idea of freedom as a power to do as one pleases, Edwards claimed that talk of freedom of the will does not make good sense because it amounts to talk of a power of willing which itself has a power of willing (J. Edwards 163, 137). Arminians could easily avoid this criticism by interpreting 'He has freedom of the will' to mean 'He is the sole author of his choices, and he has a power to choose other than he does' (Campbell 160, 162). Edwards's two arguments for the impossibility of Arminian free will also involve important mis-interpretations. In the first argument, he interprets 'The will determines itself' as 'The self determines its acts of will by willing' (J. Edwards 172, 190). This interpretation, however, does not involve contingence, whereas Arminian free will does involve contingence. Arminians could avoid the force of Edwards's argument by interpreting 'The will determines itself' as 'The soul determines its acts of will without being determined to determine them.' In his second argument for the impossibility of Arminian free will, Edwards interpreted 'He chooses while in a state of indifference' to mean 'He has a preference while not having a preference' (J. Edwards 196). Arminians could turn aside this argument by interpreting 'He chooses while in a state of indifference' to mean 'He chooses while being able to go either way, while being able not to choose.'

But even supposing that one of Edwards's arguments against Arminian free will makes its point, that would not show that common freedom, a freedom which is compatible with divine predestination, is the freedom requisite for moral agency. If we cannot or do not have Arminian free will and yet Arminian free will is required for moral agency, then we cannot be or are not moral agents. Therefore, those who believe that we are moral agents should not believe that Arminian free will is the freedom requisite for moral agency. But even if Arminian free will is not the freedom required for moral agency, it does not follow that common freedom is the freedom required for moral agency.

To try to show that common freedom is the required freedom, Edwards appealed to common sense or common beliefs. He claimed that a power to do as one chooses is "the only liberty that common sense teaches to be necessary for moral agency" (J. Edwards 406). He seemed to think that the freedom commonly believed to be required for moral agency _is_ the freedom required for moral agency. But if this is his argument, his argument fails because of its reliance on the authority of common sense or common beliefs (Cf. Kaufman and Frankena xxxv). All sorts of false things have been regarded as common sense. For instance, it was just common sense that the earth was flat and the center of the universe. All sorts of superstitions have been commonly believed. Common sense does not seem to be a reliable authority since what is regarded as common sense varies from one culture to the next and varies within the same culture over time. If one's own view has become part of what is regarded as common sense, then the appeal to common sense is little better than an appeal to one's own view. When common beliefs are due to a lack of reflection or a lack of awareness of problems that have been raised for such beliefs, the appeal to common belief is no better than an appeal to common ignorance.

Edwards seemed to think that if he could answer the Arminian criticisms of the common sense view, then the common sense view would be vindicated. To the objection that common freedom need not be the higher sort of freedom, the freedom requisite for moral agency, Edwards, seemingly thinking of Arminian free will as the only alternative, responded that "it is impossible for anyone to rise higher in his conceptions of liberty than this" (454). The trouble with Edwards's response is that Arminian free will is <u>not</u> the only alternative to common freedom. According to Edwards, common freedom, a power to do as one chooses, does not take into account "anything of the cause or original of that choice" (J. Edwards 164). Another alternative to common freedom is a kind of freedom similar to it, but unlike it in taking into account how the person came to make his volition. Since Edwards did not explain why this freedom would not be higher than common freedom, he did not provide good reason to believe that common freedom is the only freedom requisite for moral agency.

In fact, there is good reason to believe that common freedom is not the freedom requisite for moral agency. If we have the freedom requisite for moral agency, we must have a significant ability to act otherwise. But when we have common freedom, we need not have any significant ability to act otherwise. Therefore, common freedom is not the freedom requisite for moral agency.

Edwards suggested two responses to this type of argument. First, he suggested that when we have common freedom, we always have an ability to act otherwise. And second, he suggested that, in any case, having the freedom requisite for moral agency does not require having an ability to act otherwise. Neither of these responses is convincing.

Edwards said that

> In the strictest propriety of speech, a man has a thing in his power, if he has it in his choice, or at his election: and a man can't be truly said to be unable to do a thing, when he can do it if he will (162).

Edwards added that if it is improper to say that the person cannot do a different external act than the one he does, it is even more improper to say

> that he is unable to exert the acts of will themselves; because it is more evidently false, with respect to these, that he can't if he will: for to say so, is a downright contradiction: it is to say, he <u>can't</u> will, if he <u>does</u> will (J. Edwards 162).

Thus Edwards suggested that when we have common freedom, we must have an ability to act otherwise.

But if this is the only ability to choose otherwise that we have when we have common freedom, then common freedom does not involve any significant ability to choose otherwise. According to Edwards, we _always_ have the ability to choose otherwise, since it is always true that we _can_ choose otherwise if we _do_ choose otherwise. But when we only have this ability to choose otherwise, we need not have any control over the choices we make. Yet if we have any significant ability to choose otherwise, we must have some control over what choices we make. Therefore, since common freedom involves only an Edwardsean ability to choose otherwise, common freedom does not involve any significant ability to choose otherwise.

Perhaps Edwards believed that having the freedom requisite for moral agency does not require having any significant power to choose otherwise. When he claimed that ordinary freedom does not include within its meaning "anything of the cause or original of that choice" (J. Edwards 164), he suggested that even if a cause took away all significant ability to choose otherwise, one could still be free in the required way. Thus Edwards suggested that having the freedom requisite for moral agency does not require having any significant ability to choose otherwise.

But, on the contrary, it seems clear that if we do not have any significant ability to choose otherwise, we do not have the freedom requisite for moral agency. If we are completely predetermined to make our choices _and_ have no significant ability to choose anything else, then we do not have any control over which choices we make; and, without such control, we lack an important kind of freedom. Without this important freedom, which involves a power to choose otherwise, we are not moral agents; for, if it is not up to us what choices we make, then we do not deserve praise or blame for our choices. Thus it seems clear that having the freedom requisite for moral agency requires having a significant ability to choose otherwise. And in that case, since having common freedom does not require having any significant ability to choose otherwise, common freedom is not the freedom requisite for moral agency.

Edwards's defense of Calvinism crucially depends on his claim that common freedom is the freedom requisite for moral agency, for common freedom is the only freedom that Edwards showed to be compatible with divine predestination. But this crucial, linchpin claim, that common freedom is the freedom requisite for moral agency, faces two serious problems: Not only did Edwards not provide good reason to believe that common freedom is the freedom requisite for moral agency, but there is good reason to believe that common freedom is not the freedom requisite for moral agency. Because of these problems, Edwards did not provide good reason to believe that divine predestination is compatible with the freedom requisite for moral agency. And so Edwards did not provide an adequate defense of Calvinism against Arminianism. Anyone who would adequately defend Calvinism against Arminianism must show why divine predestination would not rule out all significant ability to choose otherwise; for, if divine predestination would rule out all significant ability to choose otherwise, the Arminians were right: divine predestination would rule out the freedom requisite for moral agency.

REFERENCES

Ahlstrom, Sydney E. A Religious History of the American People (New Haven: Yale UP, 1972).

Campbell, C.A. On Selfhood and Godhood (New York: Macmillan, 1957).

Cherry, Conrad. The Theology of Jonathan Edwards: A Reappraisal (Garden City: Doubleday, 1966).

Conkin, Paul K. Puritans and Pragmatists: Eight Eminent American Thinkers (New York: Dodd, 1968).

Edwards, Jonathan. Freedom of the Will. Vol. 1 of The Works of Jonathan Edwards. Ed. Paul Ramsey. 5 vols. (New Haven: Yale UP, 1957).

Edwards, Rem B. A Return to Moral and Religious Philosophy in Early America (Washington: UP of America, 1982).

Kaufman, Arnold S., and William K. Frankena. Introduction. Freedom of the Will. By Jonathan Edwards. Ed. Arnold S. Kaufman and William K. Frankena (Indianapolis: Bobbs, 1969), ix–xxxviii.

Latourette, Kenneth Scott. <u>A</u> <u>History</u> <u>of</u> <u>Christianity</u> (New York: Harper, 1953).

Leith, J.H. "Arminius, Jacobus." <u>Abingdon</u> <u>Dictionary</u> <u>of</u> <u>Living</u> <u>Religions</u>. Ed. Keith Crim (Nashville: Abingdon, 1981).

Manschreck, Clyde L. <u>A</u> <u>History</u> <u>of</u> <u>Christianity</u> <u>in</u> <u>the</u> <u>World</u>. 2nd ed. (Englewood Cliffs: Prentice, 1985).

Miller, Perry. <u>Jonathan</u> <u>Edwards</u> (N.p.: William Sloane, 1949).

Newlin, Claude M. <u>Philosophy</u> <u>and</u> <u>Religion</u> <u>in</u> <u>Colonial</u> <u>America</u> (New York: Philosophical Library, 1962).

Ramsey, Paul. Introduction. <u>Freedom</u> <u>of</u> <u>the</u> <u>Will</u>. By Jonathan Edwards. Ed. Paul Ramsey (New Haven: Yale UP, 1957), pp. 1-128.

Smith, H. Shelton, Robert T. Handy, and Lefferts A. Loetscher. <u>American</u> <u>Christianity</u>: <u>An</u> <u>Historical</u> <u>Interpretation</u> <u>with</u> <u>Representative</u> <u>Documents</u>. 2 vols. (New York: Scribner's, 1960), Vol. 1.

Sweet, William Warren. <u>The</u> <u>Story</u> <u>of</u> <u>Religion</u> <u>in</u> <u>America</u> (New York: Harper, 1950).

John K. Roth

American Ground: Philosophy and Religion in the United States

"This land is your land, this land is my land ...
This land was made for you and me."

Woody Guthrie (1956)

Expecting one's nation to last forever reflects wishful thinking more than dispassionate analysis. But even if nationhood and nationality are destined for oblivion, the nature and time of their demise are unknown in advance. Left to make the best of what they have, millions of late twentieth-century persons find that such a goal requires coming to terms with the lives they lead on American ground. How Americans cope with their national identity, in turn, affects the fate of the earth.

Nearly ninety, Robert Frost favored John F. Kennedy's inaugural with verse. But when he was about to read the poem prepared for that 1963 occasion, Washington's January wind gusted the lines from his view. From memory, Frost presented "The Gift Outright" instead, reminding Americans, first, that "the land was ours before we were the land's."[1] American identity is unthinkable without the land, for it has meant, in a word, possibility. Reality may be frustrating, disappointing, even crushing. The lure of possibility, however, seems able to transcend all of that. So restless people packed their bags with hope and went - as Frost put it - "to the land vaguely realizing westward." They took the ground and occupied it, but still it was not theirs. What they found was strange, if not unmapped; the territory was wild, even when it was a wilderness. The new space was so distant from what they left behind, its future as uncertain as it was unknown. Possibility was a fickle friend. So it is and shall remain.

"Unstoried, artless, unenhanced," the land Frost saw would not become their "land of living" until Americans discovered the irony of being in it. That irony consisted of intending one thing and unintentionally producing another, which Americans still do as often as not. The American people would create and tell their stories about the land, enhance it with arts and crafts, and while thinking that the United States was "such as she was," they would discover that she was becoming - sometimes worse than they knew, sometimes better than they thought.

Outside observers often understand Americans better than they do themselves. A salient example is provided by the French statesman and philosopher, Alexis de Tocqueville, whose tour of the country resulted in the classic called Democracy in America. Following up on his early impression that nothing characterized Americans so much as their emphasis on equality, Tocqueville began the second half of his book with a chapter entitled "Concerning the Philosophical Approach of the Americans." "Less attention," he there observed, "is paid to philosophy in the United States than in any other country of the civilized world."[2] Nevertheless, continued Tocqueville, "of all the countries in the world, America is the one in which the precepts of Descartes are ... best followed" (p. 429). Prizing individualism so much, he explained, Americans are Cartesians in their propensity to display "a general distaste for accepting any man's word as proof of anything" (p. 430). Instead they rely on "individual effort and judgment" to determine what they believe (p. 429).

As with most of the American qualities he discussed, Tocqueville found "the philosophical approach of the Americans" possessing both assets and liabilities. Skepticism might nurture a praiseworthy critical attitude; self-reliance could produce desirable innovation. But a cunning consequence of those assets was the undermining of authority and tradition. That result could yield other mischief. For where reliance on authority and tradition are severely undermined people still seek confirmation of their beliefs in the judgments of others. Then the despotism of unthinking conformity, which is a long way from the public spirit that ensures real freedom, will not be far behind.

Tocqueville's uneasiness about American individualism was justified, and the consequences for the country's national well-being are enormous. In sum, while American individualism honed ingenuity and industry that took the nation to positions of economic and political world leadership, the same spirit drew Americans further apart even as they lived closer together in conformity. Now giving self-fulfillment precedence over civic virtue and a publicly responsible patriotism, Americans seem to care more for individual wealth than for their commonwealth.

Abundant evidence for these contentions can be found in the sociological survey of American ground conducted recently by Robert N. Bellah and his associates. Borrowing one of Tocqueville's phrases to title the study, they assayed "habits of the heart" in the powerful American middle class of the 1980s. There, Bellah found, "individualism may have grown cancerous – that it may be destroying those social integuments that Tocqueville saw as moderating its more destructive potentialities, that it may be threatening the survival of freedom itself."[3] In short, many Americans tend to be so obsessed with personal self-fulfillment that their capacity for commitment to the basic institutions of marriage, family, politics, and religion is dangerously impaired. Tocqueville, of course, would have found none of this surprising. His ambivalence toward democracy was considerable just because he feared it would unleash a sense of self-interest so badly understood as to starve senses of civic obligation and wither concern to seek first what is best for the community as a whole.

Sensing that "radical" is more apt than "rugged" to describe America's contemporary individualism, Bellah is skeptical that an adequate social ethic can be built on its foundations. Nor is he very optimistic that different foundations can be dug in American ground. Once more following Tocqueville, however, Bellah and his colleagues think that "biblical religion" might provide a cause for hope. Biblical religion, of course, is not one thing. Thus, it often has had divisive effects in America. What Bellah banks on is religion's capacity to make people concerned for persons and causes beyond the confines of individualistic self-fulfillment. Religion can have this effect, at least in part, because it points to a moral order that stands beyond the vicissitudes of historical relativity and thereby can inspire persons to pursue what is good for the community.

Bellah's hopes for America do not suppose that religion provides a sufficient resource to accomplish all that is needed if American ground is to support the public beliefs and institutions that sustain democracy and freedom. The requirement is to locate and create a variety of resources to drive home the importance of pursuing the common good. Fortunately, the land still contains such possibilities. To identify some of them, consider that among the national treasures of the United States there are notable American philosophers and theologians who can help its people to revision both how a healthy democracy requires obligations that transcend individual interests and how religion has a special part to play in fostering that understanding.

Tocqueville wrote that "the Americans have no school of philosophy peculiar to themselves, and they pay very little attention to the rival European schools. Indeed they hardly know their names."[4] Like many of his judgments, that one was not infallible then and even less would it stand now. For American thinkers have developed a variety of distinctive philosophical perspectives. In one way or another, relations between individualism and community have often been their focal point.

Such relations found an American expression on 20 May 1927. Opening the throttle on the Spirit of St. Louis at 7:52 that Friday morning, Charles A. Lindbergh taxied down a Long Island runway to begin his solo flight across the Atlantic. Nearly thirty-four hours later - it was 10:24 p.m. Paris time on Saturday - "Lucky Lindy" and his plane emerged from the darkness to touch ground again. A world had journeyed with the "Lone Eagle," and his flight's significance was not lost on American ministers who preached to their Christian congregations the next day. A typical example of the sermonic rhetoric that Sunday was to be found in the words of the Reverend Dr. Russell Bowie of Grace Episcopal Church in New York

City. Within his topic, "The Lure of the 'Impossible,'" Bowie remarked that Lindbergh "manifested that indomitable heroism which, whether ... in victory or defeat, has made possible the progress of the human race toward the mastery of its world. ... There is a fund of moral heroism as well as a fund of physical heroism among men, which thrills to the challenge of the impossible."[5]

That same Sunday morning, far to the west of Paris and New York, another Christian pastor preached to his congregation. If the record does not show what Reinhold Niebuhr told those predominantly blue-collar workers in Detroit, it is doubtful that his sermon was as effusive and glowing as Russell Bowie's. For during this period, one of the entries in Niebuhr's diary included these words:

> I wish that some of our romanticists and sentimentalists could sit through a series of meetings where the real social problems of a city are discussed. They would be cured of their optimism. A city which is built around a productive process and which gives only casual thought and incidental attention to human problems is really a kind of hell. Thousands in this town are really living in torment while the rest of us eat, drink and make merry. What a civilization! [6]

The son of German immigrants, Reinhold Niebuhr saw a world that was certainly "this side of paradise," to borrow the title of one of F. Scott Fitzgerald's early novels. Amory Blaine, the leading character in the story, admitted that "'I detest poor people,'" and Fitzgerald's description of that young American included the observation that "it was always the becoming he dreamed of, never the being."[7] Niebuhr's outlook was different. As a young pastor in Detroit, and later as one of the most perceptive thinkers America has yet produced, Niebuhr worked to develop a religious perspective relevant to the broad social and political questions of his day. From 1930-1960, he was to theology in America what John Dewey was to philosophy.

Born in Vermont, that bastion of Yankee individualism, John Dewey spent most of his life in the collective hustle of Chicago and New York. His experience led him to Individualism Old and New (1929-30). Writing in a depression situation, Dewey saw that the long-standing American emphasis on "individualism" provided a pivotal issue for the nation and the world. In the United States, argued Dewey, individualism has a natural history. If the outcome of that history has been problematic, the ideal neither can nor should be excised. American identity depends on it. Therefore, Dewey's effort was to revision individualism so that it would not be a hindrance but a help.

Always somewhat mythological, old-style American individualism, contended Dewey, had been modeled after the image of self-reliant, self-made pioneers. They saw opportunities for personal fortunes and set out to win them on their own. Dewey believed that circumstances were threatening that ideal. A basic reason was that America was increasingly organized in huge corporations. Ironically, that had occurred because the old individualism was once an effective dream. It spurred people to build amazing businesses and industrial plants, but this very success had burst the bubble. Though individuals remained, more and more their lives were becoming cogs in wheels that turned out products collectively. People were becoming incorporated; most lacked the opportunity needed to "make it" on their own.

According to Dewey, a dangerous exception to his analysis did exist. Old individualism could still take the form of measuring success in terms of money. Even within the corporate structure, such individualism could yet find expression in grabs for all-that-one-can-get. Dewey believed, too, that Americans had learned new ways to clutch collectively so that management and labor, even government and people, seated themselves repeatedly at a table of hard bargains. In most cases, though, Dewey sensed that the individual remained the loser. As the old individualism persisted, alienation and frustration rose. Even if the old ideal dissolved in one person, its presence in others took a toll as the rounds of competition spiraled on - right into a crash.

Dewey advocated no return to a pre-industrial, pre-corporate America. Assuming such a reversal had been possible, he would not have favored it. Even in the midst of an economic slump, he saw vast increases in knowledge and technological power as vindicating the potential for good that use of scientific method can bring to life. His point was rather that human intelligence must be used more extensively and rigorously than ever to harness that potential and to channel it so that humanizing benefits accrue. Instead of encouraging the practical rationality of "cost-effectiveness" to become the tail that wags the dog, Dewey thought that Americans must rally ingenuity to discern a revised and renewed understanding of what the initiatives of individualism ought to entail.

Thus, Dewey's "new" individual would be scientifically oriented, at least in terms of an education that would equip him or her with critical methods for tackling life's problems. In addition, this individual's concern would focus on the social utility of action and planning, on the broad range of effects that policies have on national and international life. While recognizing that Americans must build upon and beyond - rather than tear down - their existing industrial, scientific, and technological base, Dewey's individual would have an awareness tempered by understanding that economic concerns are appropriate just to the degree that they serve civic quality. That concern, Dewey believed, argued in favor of a strong role for government in guiding social and economic development. It also suggested that the individual's pursuit of happiness would best find its fulfillment in working for the well-being of society. If those efforts sometimes required persons to oppose established policies, Dewey hoped their attitudes would nonetheless seek to overcome alienation between individuals and society, labor and management, government and people.

Viewing this sketch today, Americans would not be likely to agree on its content. But they might concur with Dewey when he argued that "the problem of constructing a new individuality consonant with the objective conditions under which we live is the deepest problem of our times."[8] The reason for that concurrence, moreover, would not be simply that "the United States has steadily moved from an earlier pioneer individualism to a condition of dominant corporateness" (p. 36). Even if the United States is witnessing a decade in which there have been more small businesses started than at any comparable period in our history, the fact remains that Americans also live in the shadows of multi-national corporations and of unprecedented economic competition from other countries, most notably those of Asia. National destiny, and thus the American's sense of individualism, is influenced and threatened by a web of economic and political forces that move beyond American control.

John Dewey thought "the publicity agent is perhaps the most significant symbol of our present life" (p. 43). That observation still has merit. The only change is that the publicity may be controlled by Arab oil or Japanese productivity. Far from being a nation of the self-employed, Americans find it increasingly difficult to know their real employers face to face. Companies own companies as much as individuals do. Too many Americans live "in a situation which is so incomplete that it cannot be admitted into the affections and yet is so pervasive that it cannot be escaped: a situation which defines an individual divided within himself" (p. 50). That part of Dewey's appraisal still fits the United States.

The basic problem facing Americans, contended Dewey, was that "of forming a new psychological and moral type" (p. 83). Probably that order is more than Americans can handle. Fortunately, it may also be true that such an order is unnecessary to reclaim and act upon the purposes for which America has arisen. For what Dewey talked about was essentially something quite close to the core of an already existing American sensitivity. Indeed, that sensitivity is alive, if muted, even now.

Robert Bellah and his colleagues observed, for example, that the contemporary American does not always practice the radical individualism he or she preaches. Functionally, American lives are given much of their meaning by familial, communal, public ties that transcend the individualistic calculus of self-fulfillment and cost-benefit analysis at which Americans have become so verbally adept. If Americans express yearnings for autonomy and self-reliance better than they acknowledge needs for and experiences of social commitments that sustain them, nevertheless they do sense that those relationships of memory and hope are the substance of their lives.

Those relationships serve Americans well, moreover, just to the extent that people think of them less as the means to personal self-satisfaction and more as essential elements of personhood.[9]

Anticipating what Bellah has confirmed, Reinhold Niebuhr shared Dewey's ethical and pragmatic concerns, but his sense of tragedy in human life was more profound, thus giving him a special perspective for criticizing some of the excesses to which national life, including that of the United States, is prone. Niebuhr and Dewey disagreed on many points. The latter, for example, did not share Niebuhr's fundamental conviction that history involves a personal God. Nevertheless their views on the individual and the community or, as one of Niebuhr's most influential books would call it, on The Nature and Destiny of Man, contained much that can fit together well.

Niebuhr's previously mentioned diary ended in 1928 as he was about to begin his career as a professor and a writer. But it contains many of the notes that Niebuhr would sound repeatedly in the decades ahead as he explored the relations between love, power, and justice. In one of its last entries, for example, he wrote:

> I persevere in the effort to combine the ethic of Jesus with what might be called Greek caution because I see no great gain in ascetic experiments. I might claim for such a strategy the full authority of the gospel except that it seems to me more likely to avoid dishonesty if one admits that the principle of love is not qualified in the gospel and that it must be qualified in other than the most intimate human associations. When one deals with the affairs of a civilization, one is trying to make the principle of love effective as far as possible, but one cannot escape the conclusion that society as such is brutal, and that the Christian principle may never be more than a leaven in it. [10]

Following up on those observations, Moral Man and Immoral Society (1932) remains one of Niebuhr's most significant books. The study owes that status to its investigation of the hypothesis that individuals can be - and even are likely to be - far more moral than human groups, especially as those groups are organized today into modern political states. Thus, if F. Scott Fitzgerald correctly called Amory Blaine a "romantic egotist," Niebuhr argued that the dangers of such individualism were pale by contrast with what emerged when collective egoism came to the fore.[11] It could consume the individual, bring good intentions to naught, and unleash global power struggles that endanger every person. Standing beside such might, the contributions of morally or religiously motivated men and women seemed fragile and weak, and yet Niebuhr also believed they can work like leaven and make all the difference. "Realities are always defeating ideals," Niebuhr had written as early as 1919, "but ideals have a way of taking vengeance upon the facts which momentarily imprison them."[12] Perhaps "vengeance" was overly strong, however, for later Niebuhr would note that all too often moral and religious ideals "can be victorious only by snatching victory out of defeat" (p. 39).

As well as any American ever has, Niebuhr understood the nature of human power and aspiration. He discerned the cunning within reason and the irony within history. Undergirding his interpretation of American experience in particular were at least two premises that are especially important. First, he believed, human beings are infected by original sin. Niebuhr's understanding of that admittedly unpopular notion, however, was very down-to-earth, even common-sensical, for he located its significance in "the obvious fact that all men are persistently inclined to regard themselves more highly and are more assiduously concerned with their own interests that any 'objective' view of their importance would warrant."[13] Second, he found the American version of this original sin to be located in the nation's presumption that its ways not only represent a clean break from a corrupted past but also remain so fundamentally innocent and virtuous that they could rightly be identified with God's will for the world. As Niebuhr saw them, the facts suggested an alternative view. "The irony of our situation," he argued "lies in the fact that we could not be virtuous (in the sense of practicing the virtues which are implicit in meeting our vast world responsibilities) if we were really as innocent as we pretend to be" (p. 23).

American ground spawns power. Such might, Niebuhr affirmed, is never won, used, or even lost innocently. The land, however, is riddled with irony when people persuade themselves differently. To make his case, Niebuhr distinguished irony from pathos and tragedy.

Pathos resides in unmerited suffering that results from events in which none of the agents involved can rightly be held responsible or guilty. Its clearest examples are found in the pain and grief brought on by nature's fury in earthquakes or tornados. Tragedy arises from conflict of another kind. The many claims life makes are not always harmonious. One good must sometimes be sacrificed for another, but even more unfortunate is the fact that life so often involves what Niebuhr called "conscious choices of evil for the sake of good" (p. vii). Such choices are the essence of tragedy. By contrast with both pathos and tragedy, irony dwells in gaps between intention and consequence that yawn neither by accident nor by conscious design alone.

Niebuhr's point was not that American life lacks pathos, tragedy, or even an abundance of blatant wrongdoing. But neither did he think that the United States was the most corrupt nation on earth. Just the opposite struck Niebuhr as closer to the truth, and therefore he anguished over the peculiar degree to which Americans wreak havoc in the world and upon each other because they know themselves insufficiently. Niebuhr tried to show Americans that their virtues contain hidden defects, that the nation's strength is weak just to the extent that it is vain, that its yearnings for security will breed insecurity if they go too far, that America's considerable wisdom may be reduced to folly unless limits are better recognized.

Pretension, grandiose pride, and unwarranted self-righteousness - these perennial idols were the objects of Niebuhr's criticism. He wanted Americans to learn, not to their sorrow but before it became too late, that their reach may exceed their grasp. Yet he recognized one irony more, namely, that such disillusionment has no foregone conclusion. It "either must lead," he warned, "to an abatement of the pretension, which means contrition; or its leads to a desperate accentuation of the vanities to the point where irony turns into pure evil" (p. viii). In a nuclear age, Niebuhr's ultimate "either/or" is especially harsh, for it portends apocalypse if Americans fail to acts wisely. But even if they do, Niebuhr would be the first to admit, such action may not be enough. For the United States is not the only responsible party or even the one most likely to bring about the end. America cannot save the world or even itself singlehandedly. That was one of Niebuhr's fundamental points. Yet his revisioning critique was offered with a hopeful expectation that looked for Americans to do their best.

Recognizing that love untempered by justice becomes sentimental and impotent, Niebuhr believed that justice without mercy retains a harsh edge that will leave people unreconciled in hatred. His study of history, power politics, and a modernized, industrial, economic order led to a realism about human beings somber enough to suit many a dour Puritan. But if he was correct in saying that there is "enough original sin in human nature to create opposition" to the substance of the gospel, Niebuhr also found that "there is enough natural grace in the human heart" to respond to that message as well.[14] As Fitzgerald described Amory Blaine, there was "no God in his heart, ... his ideas were still in riot ..."[15] That description might fit many Americans, then and now, but not Niebuhr. He kept confidence in "a Divine Power, whose resources are greater than those of men, and whose suffering love can overcome the corruptions of man's achievements, without negating the significance of our striving."[16]

Niebuhr never counted on religion to be the unifying element in American life. Not only did he recognize that the varieties of our religious and non-religious experience were too extensive for that outcome to occur. He also harbored skepticism about so-called "civil religion," suspecting that it typically legitimated established ways undeserving of the favor. In that respect, Niebuhr had learned from Karl Marx. But he also drew the line where Marx's influence was concerned. Though Niebuhr agreed that religion could be the opium of the people, he stressed that its role could and must be very different. Religion, he believed, was properly a critic of culture. Within America, he affirmed, one of its tasks was to keep attention focused on the personalism that lies at the core of democratic individualism.[17]

The best insights of Western religious and democratic political theory, attested Niebuhr, converge to affirm the sanctity of individual personhood. The religious sensitivity of Americans could provide a much needed leaven, he added, to make that belief a "resource for the highest forms of social realization."[18] For to the extent that any individual or group takes seriously the individual personhood of another, the recognition that respect is owed them receives a boost. Thus, Niebuhr helps us to see that religion, though it cannot unify us, remains a vital ingredient in any sound understanding of why and for what America exists.

Niebuhr's instinct about America suggested to him a creed that combined competition and cooperation. The energy encouraged by individual freedom, he thought, could result in common purposes. Quarrelsome differences as brothers and sisters might keep driving home the fact that Americans are one people, if not a family. By communally ensuring each other basic rights to go their own ways, Americans could stay together on the same way. Still seeking the covenant so rarely found, Americans need to use the irony within their history as a prod to discover the twists of biblical paradox that Niebuhr also loved to employ: The ones who try to secure their own ways alone are far more likely to lose themselves than those who do their best individually in order to take on the risks of giving their lives for others. A coherent individualism requires caring to understand that interdependence makes independence possible. Personal initiative that does not serve others impoverishes the communal spirit that gives it birth and vitality.

Each in his own way, Dewey and Niebuhr urged that, through ability and effort, individual Americans could achieve success and thereby reveal the depth of their potential for creating and sharing a true commonwealth, one that would extend beyond American ground. Yet, hopeful though they were about the American future, their optimism remained rightly guarded by critical - even skeptical - questions. Dewey pondered whether Americans would use their vast scientific and technological skill for rational moral ends. Niebuhr tried to find the needed ways to make relevant the messages contained in the ancient traditions of Passover and Easter. They both knew that, if American ground is truly made for you and me, that prospect requires special public effort. That effort must revision how the highest forms of social realization depend not only on the sanctity of the individual person's life but also on cooperative dependence. Such a process entails that more than the becoming should occupy Americans. The being, the substance of what the United States has been and is, must be reckoned with equally. For the being informs and even determines what the becoming can possibly be.

NOTES

[1] Robert Frost, "The Gift Outright," in The Poetry of Robert Frost, ed. Edward Connery Lathem (New York: Holt, Rinehart and Winston, 1969), p. 348.

[2] Alexis de Tocqueville, Democracy in America, ed. J.P. Mayer and trans. George Lawrence (Garden City, NY: Doubleday Anchor, 1969), p. 429.

[3] Robert N. Bellah et al., Habits of the Heart: Individualism and Commitment in American Life (Berkeley: University of California Press, 1985), p. vii.

[4] Tocqueville, p. 429.

[5] Quoted from Kenneth S. Davis, The Hero: Charles A. Lindbergh and the American Dream (Garden City, NY: Doubleday & Company, 1959), pp. 213-14.

[6] Reinhold Niebuhr, Leaves from the Notebook of a Tamed Cynic (San Francisco: Harper & Row, 1980), p. 143.

[7] F. Scott Fitzgerald, This Side of Paradise (New York: Charles Scribner's Sons, 1970), pp. 256, 17-18.

[8] John Dewey, Individualism Old and New (New York: Capricorn Books, 1962), p. 32.

[9] On these points, see Bellah, especially pp. 20-22, 50-51, 81-84, 138-41, 150-55, 246-47, 277, 281-96, and 307.

[10] Niebuhr, Leaves, pp. 196-97.

[11]See Fitzgerald, p. 1. See also Reinhold Niebuhr, _Moral Man and Immoral Society_ (New York: Charles Scribner's Sons, 1960), p. xii.

[12]Niebuhr, _Leaves_, p. 23.

[13]Reinhold Niebuhr, _The Irony of American History_ (New York: Charles Scribner's Sons, 1952), p. 17.

[14]Niebuhr, _Leaves_, p. 41.

[15]Fitzgerald, p. 282.

[16]Reinhold Niebuhr, _The Children of Light and the Children of Darkness_ (New York: Charles Scribner's Sons, 1972), p. 190.

[17]Reinhold Niebuhr's writings are filled with references to Karl Marx's philosophy and its subsequent Soviet interpretations. He finds merit in Marx's critical insights about the development of capitalism in the nineteenth century, but there is little sympathy for the versions of Marx's theory and practice that Soviet policy from Lenin onward has carried out. Niebuhr spent much of his life disputing what he regarded as Marxist dogma. At the same time, he urged continuous self-critical analysis of American democracy as well. For further detail about Niebuhr's relation to the religious aspects of Marxist thought, see Reinhold Niebuhr, Introd., _On Religion_ by Karl Marx and Friedrich Engels (New York: Schocken Books, 1971).

[18]Niebuhr, _Children of Light_, p. 81.

Hans Schwarz

The Electronic Church as an Expression of the American Religious Mind

In the February 17, 1986 edition of <u>Time</u> Magazine the cover feature was: "Power, Glory - and Politics. Right-wing Preachers Dominate the Dial." This cover article on the electronic church, plus an interview with the prospective presidential candidate Marion Gordon ("Pat") Robertson, revealed some interesting statistics. The so-called Jesus network "comprises 200 local TV stations that have religious formats (more than double the figure a year ago), 1135 radio stations (up 91 from last year)" and altogether it reaches tens of millions of homes.[1]

The electronic preachers spent $1 billion, possibly even $2 billion to purchase TV and radio time last year. According to a 1984 survey an estimated 13.3 million people of the national TV audience are regular viewers of the electronic church. This nearly equals the combined membership of the United Methodist, Presbyterian, and Episcopal churches. Altogether 61 million Americans have at least a minimal exposure per month to the electronic church. Pat Robertson with his daily TV shows reaches 16.3 million TV households per months, while sixth ranking Jerry Falwell still gets into 5.6 million TV households per months with his weekly shows.[2]

Who are the representatives of the electronic church? The top entrepreneur is Pat Robertson whose 4.000 employees at the Christian Broadcasting Network in Virginia Beach, Virginia, work amid strict security. His 24-hour CBN network reaches 30 million subscribers, making it the largest Christian cable operation, with its own evening news cast and with special emphasis on right-wing issues. According to the February 1986 <u>Time</u> Magazine article "CBN just passed American Airlines as the nation's heaviest user of WATS telephone lines" (i.e., toll free long distance telephone lines for people to call in for requests, comments, prayers, and pledges of support).[3] Yet a couple of months later CBN had to forfeit their WATS line since revenues did not increase as expected. Even some forty workers had to be let go. Yet Pat Robertson is not poverty-striken. He has his own university with 715 graduate students and, when at home, resides on campus in a university-owned $420,000 mansion or crosses the country in the company's jet to build up momentum for his right-wing religious political course.

Jim Bakker, who once worked for Robertson and whose receipts exceed $100 million a year has his own PTL (Praise the Lord or People That Love) show and a Heritage USA park near Ford Mill, South Carolina which enjoyed 5 million visitors last year. While his approach is similar to that of Robertson he too does not abhor the amenities of this world and has a $449,000 retreat in Palm Springs.

Quite different in approach is Robert Schuller with his weekly Hour of Power. Robert H. Schuller was educated in the Dutch Reformed Tradition and from humble beginnings he gradually expanded his ministry and finally built his $18 million Crystal Cathedral largely paid for by viewer donations. On Sundays he gathers there in the neighborhood of Disneyland, California, an indoor congregation of 3000 and an outdoor congregation of 300 car members in a drive-in situation. But his real influence comes with his TV ministry which is also syndicated in Australia, New Zealand, and the Armed Forces Network. In the style of Norman Vincent Peale he portrays an optimistic Christianity of "possibility thinking" with slogans such as "Turn your scars into stars" or "turning stress into strength."

While Schuller is perhaps the best representative of popular middle class religion in the USA today,[4] Jerry Falwell is the foremost representative of the still growing new right. This fundamentalist preacher of genial manners but granite opinions is pastor of the 21,000-member Thomas Road Baptist Church in Lynchburg, Virginia, and his Old-Time Gospel Hour in the style of Dwight L. Moody is seen in the USA, Canada, West Africa and Japan. He has used his TV influence to launch the Moral Majority, an influential conservative political lobby, with which he wants to instill old-time values into a decadent society. In a more direct way he also backs president Reagan's political, economic and moral ideas. Of course he also has his own university, Liberty University with 7000 students.

One could also mention the brash, rafter-ringing Pentecostal preacher and gospel singer Jimmy Swaggart with a 7000-seat worship center just outside Baton Rouge, Louisiana, who takes in $140 million a year. He has mission and charity offices in 53 countries, owns his own printing plant which prints 24 million items a year, and lives comfortably with his wife in a mansion next to their son, the houses being worth a least $1 million.[5] Small surprise that he can say that "the Lord has been good to me." Many more representatives of the electronic church could be mentioned, such as Rex Humbard and his Cathedral of Tomorrow in Akron, Ohio, now bought out by the faith healer Ernest Angley, or Evangelist Billy Graham with his headquarters in Minneapolis. Yet with the exception of Billy Graham, whose use of the electronic media is relatively sparse, their stories would be similar.

For completion's sake, however, one dare not overlook Oral Roberts of Tulsa, Oklahoma, the faith healer, whose TV audience helped to build the 4600-student Oral Roberts University complete with School of Theology and 294-bed City of Faith hospital and research center. Though financially he may have overtaxed himself with his medical school. He even sold his law school. At age 69 he is increasingly looking towards his son Richard to take over his "business," he is still strong in building up his empire of faith healing of the whole person, of spirit, mind, and body. His favorite slogans, "Our God is a good God," "Expect a miracle," and "Something good is going to happen to you," show an interesting blending of fundamentalist faith-healing and the power of positive thinking.[6]

What does this phenomenon of the so-called electronic church amount to and why are the mainline churches so little represented in it? The second question is answered rather quickly. The priorities in terms of finances and ministry are quite different from the mainline churches. Oral Roberts, for instance, spent well over $8 million per year, according to a 1979 publication, to buy TV time, Jerry Falwell $14 million a year for TV and radio time, and Jim Bakker $8 million.[7] Of course, for every dollar spent, they receive four dollars in donations. Though their ministry is widespread, it is focused on one person, the evangelist, and the contact with this person is exclusively through the media. Only rarely and only if one is a potentially high giver is one even allowed to shake the evangelist's hand.

Mainline churches work very differently. They are much more person and clientele centered. For instance, The American Lutheran Church with 2.3 million baptized members has 4600 ordained ministers who serve 4900 congregations all over the USA and in several locations abroad. It instructs 530,000 Sunday School students and spends $65-million outside its own congregations for such things as world hunger, inter-church aid, theological education, aiding its colleges, supporting indigeneous churches throughout the world and maintaining in these churches more than 300 long-term missionaries.[8] The mainline churches, such as The ALC also maintain a modest radio ministry supported separately through voluntary contributions. But TV ministry is usually too expensive and takes the pastor too much away from the ministry to his or her own parishioners to be seriously pursued.

The mainline churches have also discovered that the electronic church does not reach out to the unchurched, unless one talks about a negligible number. According to a 1979 Gallup survey 85 percent of the regular viewers of such programs are professed born-again Christians and, even more surprising, two thirds are regular churchgoers.[9] This means that the electronic church functions primarily as a means of edification for believers, just as in days past only a small fraction of those who attended the big city revival campaigns were unchurched. In typical revivalist fashion one feels a need to surrender to Christ over and over again. But is it really an altar call as it was with Billy Sunday and still is with Billy Graham?

Jerry Sholes, a former close associate with Oral Roberts, writes:

> With the advent of electronic religion ... the church has been artificially extended into our homes. The offering plate that gets passed by televised religion has grown so large that it includes the contributions of millions of dollars by millions of people. When you endeavor to trace the "good" that those contributions do, you begin to run into muddy water. A local church does <u>good</u> in its community. A large television ministry tends to loca<u>lize</u> its funds in and around whatever project the television minister wants to "push." No real good ever finds its way back into the community of those millions who contribute to large television ministries.
>
> What <u>does happen</u> is that television ministers enjoy extremely high standards of living ... million dollar homes, expensive cars, big business deals, computerized mailing lists and cash flow patterns that boggle the mind! You begin to suspect that the entire pattern of large electronic ministries is much more close related to the ego of the television minister than to anything else. 10

Indeed a number of electronic church celebrities founded their own university to add respectability to their name. Seeing that the electronic church personalities do not live poorly and that their personal fortunes are greatly enhanced by their religious business, why do people not rebel and cease supporting such lavish enterprises? The answer cannot just lie in the fact that the electronic church is cleverly using all the psychological and marketing expertise it can get. Unlike with some other products that the electronic media peddle and that nobody really wants but that are so neatly packaged that the producer still makes a sale on them, with the electronic church the viewers get what they want. Or, to say it even more pointedly, the electronic church fills a need in their viewers and this means in the average American.

We may not be far from the truth, when we surmise that the electronic church is deeply related to some significant traits in the American character if not in humanity in general. People who watch a religious TV program do so in the privacy of their homes, free from the social constraints of church attendance and membership and the responsibility that goes with them. "TV ministries tend to contribute to the continued privatization of the Christian faith."[11] Even if an evangelist invites his viewers to bring their own bread and wine in front of the TV to join his communion service, this hardly encourages individuals to get involved with those in need in their own communities. There may also be a parallel between the electronic church in the United States and the People's Church in Germany. Though church attendance in Germany is notoriously low, church members still pay their church tax indicating by this that they want someone else to do their ministry for them.

Through the image on TV in the living room, the presence of a dynamic personality of the evangelist is created. Unwanted traits of the preacher are carefully edited out so that we do not see the other side of the messenger. Computerized correspondence creates the aura of intimacy between this super-evangelist and the viewer. But no personal contact is established. "The pseudo-intimacy of communication and interaction that results fits the anonymity and privatized nature of our age."[12]

The electronic church entertains more than it educates and it seldom addresses theological issues. When we hear from a recent study that "social, moral, and political topics are considered most frequently," we might suspect that the electronic church indeed does some good.[13] But it does so only for the conscience of the viewers in that they feel that someone cares about the ills of society. Thus they send in their donations that the crusade may continue. The viewers themselves, however, do not rise up and go into action. They rest assured that someone else cares. The evangelists make us believe "that they are doing the work of Christ in a way that the organized church is either unable or unwilling to do."[14] This is done by substitution for the viewers. The viewers send in their money so that the evangelists can fulfill the mission of Christ.

This kind of reasoning engendered in the viewers is in subtle or manifest ways rejected by every conscientious pastor. Pastors refuse to do ministry for their people. Instead they encourage their flock to do their ministry together with the pastor. "Equipping the Saints" is a program of The ALC. Equipping the one saint, i.e., the evangelist, is the program of the electronic church. The notion of the church as the body of Christ that witnesses and cares about the community is supplanted by the idea that there is a mighty pseudo-fellowship that supports a person and his program and that individuals are rewarded according to their financial contributions.

Yet what do the electronic evangelists really advocate? When you listen to them they are against liberalism, socialism and communism. "They may lambast anti-poverty and school lunch programs, Medicare, social welfare, and overseas aid. The basic objection seems to be that such government-sponsored initiatives interfere with a free market, laissez faire system, reward the undeserving and nonproductive, and restrict and penalize the industrious."[15]

While all electronic evangelists would oppose theological Darwinism as atheism, they are heirs of the optimistic 19th century in which Herbert Spencer's notion of the survival of the fittest was heralded as opening new opportunities and new vistas. As a theology of the cross is transformed into a theology of glory and as something good is happening today, there is no room for the weak and the sick. The TV personalities with their Hollywood makeup, their expensive clothes, and their carefully rehearsed manners transmit a kind of optimism fitting for the new world and for a new and better society in which we will be blessed and the less fortunate will be promptly forgotten.

Jerry Falwell's Moral Majority which emerged out of the electronic church points into the same direction. Attention is focussed on issues such as homosexuality, pornography, abortion, prayer in public schools, and the need to increase military spending. He proposes that citizens band together and vote for (or against) candidates on the basis of how they stand on those issues. While such action at least arouses the viewers to vote in a certain way, their actions are not informed by scriptural criteria other than the one-sided ones of Jerry Falwell. Yet his notion of what scripture says is pre-decided by his statement: "Americans are sick and tired of the way the godless liberals are running our nation."[16] Falwell adopts the value system of a large segment of society, of the middle-class that has worked hard climbing the ladder and that is naturally unwilling to share with those who do not belong to it by virtue of race, personal calamity, or natural disposition.

Success, positive thinking, and the place of America in God's divine plan, this is a trinity cherished by many U.S. citizens. But it is prone to neglect the less fortunate apart from condescending charities, and it smoothes over the radical nature of the gospel. How the Christian gospel is soft-pedaled becomes evident in Christian talk shows where people talk about having "met the Lord" and having a "personal relationship with Jesus." The title Christ hardly appears since it seems important that one is "on a first-name basis with the Son of Man."[17]

This newly created intimacy diminishes the awe-inspiring and threatening aspect of the divine Lord and the pantokrator. Now the question is no longer how well the Lord governs, but rather whether I like him and whether I can trust him. The relationship to the Savior becomes emotional and egalitarian. One feels happy because one knows Jesus. Yet what happens when relationships established on this basis become strained? Furthermore who initiated the relationship and who sustains it? The conviction of "I have found it" places the emphasis on me and on the rewards I receive in terms of "instant" gratification. When religion becomes a "hit" and God or rather Jesus a "pal" then we can cancel the relationship any time it becomes boring or strained and we can snub the other when he becomes demanding. The electronic church essentially makes us feel good and if this is no longer occurring we can turn it off and tune out. A true conversion, however, to a new allegiance other than our own preference is hardly forthcoming.

While the mainline churches preach the good news of loving and forgiving God who will also grant new eternal life, the electronic church has realized that one must be more concrete and must promise instant gratification. Electronic evangelists no longer preach fire and brimstone sermons but we hear instead: "I pray that as I stretch forth these hands which I've given to God, that a miracle in your finances, in your health, in your marriage, and in your relationships with people will begin to happen now, this very day, at this very moment. Amen and Amen."[18]To which one might add: "And please continue to send in your checks."

Health, wealth, and happiness, the desires of modern humanity, are within one's reach as promised by the TV church. As long as these promises are made and contain what the majority desires, the money continues to come to the producer. This means that the message "must be proclaimed in such a way that it meets with the approval of a large share of one's audience."[19] Popular appreciation and the degree of response to the Christian message are the main criteria of what gets proclaimed. In a materialistic age and in a country which has always emphasized success, and doing one's own thing in terms of individualism, a gospel which "is reduced to the common themes of success, positive thinking, and the place of America in God's divine plan," will easily find open ears.[20]

The electronic church does not induce change but reinforces prevailing tendencies. This is also noticeable by the electronic church in general. It sells a trivialized Christianity as a commodity through a large and continuous advertising campaign in bulk quantity. Yet since even the most enlightened Americans feel somewhat guilty, they can send in their donations, and, going beyond the promises of medieval indulgencies, they are not only assured to have done God's will but they will also – so they are told at least – reap some instantaneous benefits. "God will repay you in a multiplied way." What Richard H. Niebuhr stated nearly 50 years ago about liberal Christianity in America still holds for the electronic church with its soapy message: "A God without wrath brought men without sin into a kingdom without judgment through the ministrations of a Christ without a cross."[21] While the electronic church is a rather recent phenomenon, it is at the same time a genuine expression of the American religious mind.

NOTES

[1] Richard N. Ostling, "Power, Glory and Politics. Right-wing Preachers Dominate the Dial," Time (February 17, 1968), p. 38f.

[2] Ibid., p. 43.

[3]Ibid., p. 41. For this change see "Quick Look," in: The Lutheran Standard (May 2, 1986), p. 23, where we read that 3 TV stations were sold and 41 workers were fired. This seems to indicate that the market for the electronic church is limited and one producer is crowding the other.

[4]So rightly Richard Quebedeaux, By What Authority. The Rise of Personality Cults in American Christianity (New York: Harper, 1982), p. 61.

[5]So Richard N. Ostling, loc. cit., p. 44.

[6]Cf. Richard Quebedeaux, op. cit., p. 98.

[7]According to Jerry Sholes, Give Me That Prime-time Religion. An Insider's Report on the Oral Roberts Evangelistic Association (New York: Hawthorn, 1979), pp. 135f.

[8]Statistics according to the 1986 Yearbook of the Lutheran Church of America.

[9]Figures according to Richard Quebedeaux, op. cit., pp. 64f.

[10]So Jerry Sholes, op. cit., p. xi.

[11]So rightly Mark Mullins, "Prime Time Preachers and Popular Religion in America," Crux (September 1982) 18:17.

[12]Harry H. Miller, "Do TV Evangelists Build the Local Church?" Christianity Today (January 13, 1984), 28:66.

[13]Beth Spring, "A Study Finds Little Evidence That Religious TV Hurts Local Churches. But for Many, Prime-time Television Supplants Religion," Christianity Today (May 18, 1984), 28:71.

[14]Mark R. Sills, "The Docetic Church," The Christian Century (January 21, 1981), 98:37.

[15]Leslie K. Tarr, "Are Some Electronic Preachers Social Darwinists? Christians Who Made An Impact on Society Were of a Radically Different Stripe," Christianity Today (October 21, 1983) 27:50.

[16]Quoted in Richard McAfee Brown, "A Response to 'Listen America!' Listen Jerry Falwell!" Christianity and Crisis (December 22, 1980) 40:363.

[17]For the following cf. the perspective comments by Michael Barton, "What a Friend They Have in Jesus," Christian Century (September 19, 1979) 96:887f.

[18]So Oral Roberts in the ending prayer of his TV programs according to Jerry Sholes, op. cit., p. 57.

[19]Peter G. Horsfield in his comprehensive study, Religious Television. The American Experience (New York: Longman, 1984), p. 29.

[20]Mark Mullins, loc. cit., p. 16.

[21]Richard H. Niebuhr, The Kingdom of God in America (New York: Harper Torchbook 1959 [1937]), p. 193.

Marvin C. Shaw

Critical Naturalism in Classical American Philosophy: The Naturalistic Metaphysics of Dewey and Santayana

Santayana and the "New Naturalism"

Nineteenth century thought was characterized by the impasse of two great rival philosophies, and thus was unable to develop a coherent picture of reality. Materialism took physical science as its primary fact. It developed a picture of nature as a system of force and matter in which there was no place for the uniquely human concerns for artistic creation, ethical choice and religious aspiration. It was believed that mind and culture could be reduced by analysis to material particles which were devoid of meaning or value. In contrast, idealism took human cultural creativity as its primary fact. It erected a picture of reality in which the world of natural science was a mere appearance, a projection of human or divine imagination. Materialism attempted to describe nature while ignoring nature's function in creating and sustaining human life and culture; thus it in fact misunderstood nature. And idealism was likewise one-sided. It developed an appreciative view of the ideal creations of mind but failed to see their basis in natural conditions; thus it misunderstood the ideal.[1]

Clearly, what was required was an integrated vision of human life and culture within nature. George Santayana (1863-1952) was the first in American philosophy to construct a "non-reductive naturalism" which would take seriously the primary concerns of both materialism and idealism. His goal was to interpret the ideal creations of human culture in terms consistent with science, as outgrowths of natural powers and processes, and yet in a fully appreciative and non-reductive way. The guiding principle of this "new naturalism" would be that an acknowledgement of the natural mechanism underlying human ideal achievements does not alter their meaning and value.

685

Santayana's five-volume work The Life of Reason (1905-1906) has been called "the classic document of the new naturalism."[2] It was intended as a philosophy of culture as full and appreciative as those of the idealists (such as Hegel and Lotze), but founded on a thoroughly naturalistic view of the basis of human life. Its aim was "the naturalizing of the imagination,"[3] and its method is stated in Santayana's famous summary of Aristotelean naturalism, "everything ideal has a natural basis and everything natural has an ideal development."[4] Human life and its material conditions were to be portrayed in their relatedness, as diverse parts of a continuous whole; there are not two disparate substances, matter and spirit, but one inclusive whole called nature.

Those who were inspired by Santayana's project worked to extend it; but they came to see his own philosophy as a failure actually to synthesize materialism and idealism. His philosophy has been called a "transitional naturalism" due to the lingering dualism within it, and he himself was labeled as "the Moses of the new naturalism" who saw but did not enter the Promised Land.[5] Thus the contribution of Santayana to American naturalism is not in his success, but in the suggestiveness of his attempt. It was left to John Dewey (1859-1952) to work out the classical statement of American critical naturalism.

Dewey's Empirical Naturalism

The book Experience and Nature (1925, 1929) is the most complete statement of Dewey's non-reductive naturalism. It is a naturalistic philosophy, because human life, including its creative and imaginative aspects, is portrayed as the outcome of natural events. Yet it is a non-reductive philosophy because the creations of imagination are not reduced in interest or significance by being placed within nature. Thus Dewey sought to unite the concerns of nineteenth century idealism and materialism.

The "root metaphor" or fundamental image[6] which underlies all of Dewey's thought is the Darwinian idea of the organism interacting with the environment. The event of interaction is like an ellipse, with two foci or poles representing the contributions of both the organism and the environment; the resulting character of the event includes the contributions of both the subject and the surrounding objective context. This leads Dewey to emphasize the continuity of the human and the non-human. Ideas and values arise from the process of interaction, and thus they are not human impositions on nature, but revelations of its actual character.

This same point can be put in a more technical way. Beginning with William James (1842-1910) American philosophy took as its method "radical empiricism." This is based on the claim that traditional British empiricism was not empirical enough. Empiricism had assumed that thought must begin with "sense data" as given in experience, but James believed that "primary experience" is something even more fundamental. In fact, what the older empiricism called the person's "sense experience" is not actually something given in experience; it is the result of a mental analysis of experience. In primary experience, the subject and the object are not as yet distinguished; primary experience is one indiscriminate whole including elements later known to have been contributed by the objective environment, and by the subject and its reactions. The concept of "sense impressions" as in the subject is derived from reflection on this primary experience; it is not simply found in experience.

Dewey derived from this method the concept of "the intellectualist fallacy," by which he meant the error of taking reflective abstractions derived from primary experience by thought as "the real" and dismissing the rest of primary experience as "mere appearance." For example, materialism selects from primary experience the recurrent, orderly patterns and relations found within it, and calls this "reality." Then it dismisses ideas and values, which are also given in the moment of experience, as unreal. The result is the distorted picture of nature as a dead mechanism devoid of value or meaning. When we recognize that this conclusion is the result of the intellectualist fallacy, we conclude that aesthetic and moral values reveal genuine traits of nature.

This will serve as a statement of Dewey's aim and method. What follows is a brief summary of the leading ideas in his naturalistic metaphysics.

1. Every Existence Is an Event[7]

The basic category of Dewey's metaphysics is the event; to exist is to be an event of interaction. An event exists according to conditions set by surrounding events; if it persists, the supportive aspects of the environment are stronger than the destructive. An event is the outcome of the balancing of environing factors; to be is to be the outcome of a process of interaction.

In Dewey's opinion, most philosophy ignores the dynamic or process character of experience and takes the apparently abiding or static aspects of events as alone constituting "reality"; this is the basis of both idealism and materialism. But for Dewey, the event replaces mind or matter as the concept of the ultimate substance underlying everything. "Mind" and "matter" are abstractions derived from an analysis of events. "Matter" expresses the sequential order of events, and "mind" manifests their meanings and their logical relations.

2. Events Have a Qualitative Aspect

Experiences of enjoyment and satisfaction reveal that events have qualities. Thus they can become ends or goals of human action. Recall that according to the notion of interaction, qualities are the outcome of the interplay of organism and environment; they manifest nature as much as they do the organism. The traditional view which claims that the experiencing subject imposes quality on nature is the result of the intellectualist fallacy which takes relations as "real" and qualities as introduced by the organism. But this view leads eventually to the conclusion (in British empiricism) that since all we experience is qualities and they are introduced by the organism, nature itself remains unknown. (This is the "dualism of knowledge" which we associate with Locke and Hume; it is the aim of neo-naturalism to overcome all dualisms.) Science may selectively ignore the qualitative aspect of experience, but it cannot wholly abolish it; for in order to make quantitative measures, we must note qualities as their "markers."

3. Events Also Have an Instrumental Aspect

Practical action reveals the causal, sequential connection of events. Thus events may not only be sought as ends, but used as means. We notice that the qualities of some events can serve as "signs" of other events. That is, event B may always be preceded by event A, so that when we see A, we expect B to follow. If event A is a sign of event B, then we may reproduce the desired event B through acting on event A; an event which is a sign of an experience of satisfaction can be used as a means of control.

Dewey maintained that if we select the instrumental or causal connections of events for attention for the sake of gaining a measure of control, this does not mean that all events are merely means, or that events have only an instrumental and not a qualitative aspect. This is the error of mechanistic materialism, and is a manifestation of the intellectualist fallacy.

Moments of enjoyed quality contain all value, but they are shifting and ephemeral as compared with the mathematical-mechanical relations of events studied by science. Thus modern philosophy, committing the intellectualist fallacy, either denies reality to the qualitative (materialism), or it sees it as another "realm" above and beyond the natural world (idealism). But in fact, as is revealed through the method of radical empiricism, both qualities and instrumental relations are given together in primary experience; one is primary from the point of view of control, and the other is primary from the point of view of enjoyment, and neither is entitled exclusively to the title "real." In the concept of the event, as having both qualitative and instrumental aspects, Dewey seeks to overcome the dualism of a science which is mechanistic and brutal and a high culture which is genteel and effete.

4. Matter, Life and Mind are Continuous

The dualism of mind and body which characterized philosophy since Descartes was regarded by Dewey as a result of the intellectualist fallacy. This dualism is the result of calling the causal or instrumental aspects of experience "matter" and of regarding the qualitative factors as supplied by another substance called "mind." But in Dewey's view, natural events have a qualitative aspect; in interactions involving living organisms these function to produce "feeling," and in interactions with thinking organisms qualities take on a new character not formerly manifest called "meaning." Here, in the presence of a thinking organism, one event can become a "sign" of another. Thus events are not simply physical; the mental is a characteristic which events have at a certain level of interaction. That is, events take on meaning in interactions which include thinking beings.

We cannot reduce the mental to the physical, for both are characters of natural events. Mind is a special kind of natural interaction which is based upon other kinds of interaction called physical. Mind is present when an organism can experiment with ideas or symbols rather than with objects and behavior. Body and mind are not two separate kinds of substance (whose relations and interactions would then be unintelligible); rather they are two kinds of interaction or event, one of which assumes the presence of the other and introduces a new complexity. Thus Dewey hopes to overcome not only Locke's epistemological dualism, but the Cartesian dualism of mind and body.

5. Communication Is the Natural Basis of Ideas

For Dewey, the bridge between existence and essence, or the natural world and ideas, is communication. In the event of communication between intelligent organisms, bare events become "objects," things with meaning. An idea arises when a gesture is taken as a sign, as when a child's spontaneous cry of hunger is taken by the mother as a call for feeding. What was a mere response has now become a sign, an event with meaning.

An idea or name marks out one part of primary experience from its background; this idea is then a rule for the use or interpretation of the event. When the object is called "table" we know how to use it, how to respond to it. These ideas arise through interactions of humans and their environment. The "ideal realm" is thus for Dewey not mysterious and supernatural at all.

6. The Truth of an Idea Is Discovered in Practice

Now we come to the "pragmatism" which though not always understood is always associated with the name of Dewey. An idea is a hypothesis, a plan of action, a rule for how to relate to some aspect of experience. Its truth depends on the outcome of the action it suggests. If the idea effectively guides action, we say it is true and we integrate it into the system of ideas which is our mind. The idea is thus a tool in the adjustment of the organism and the environment. "Truth" means the ability of an idea to remove obscurity and to guide action to successful adjustment with the environment. Ideas acquire this value through the action which tests them.

I believe that John Smith is correct in claiming that this pragmatism is simply an attempt to give meaning to the term "correspondence."[8] Traditionally, one said an idea is true if it corresponds with reality. But of course we can hardly compare our idea of what is real with the real-in-itself, as Kant made clear. Thus Dewey suggests that successful working as a guide to action is the meaning of "corresponding to reality."

7. The Ideal Has a Natural Basis

Dewey also attempted a naturalistic interpretation of the human act of valuing or prizing. A value or an ideal is a particular kind of idea through which we imagine a desired satisfaction which is suggested to us by the memory of a past experience. Valuing is not the subjective imposition of human desires on dead nature; rather, it is a process which involves both poles in the interaction of organism and environment. In the interaction which gives rise to value, nature's qualitative aspect is the objective pole, and selection based on need is the human pole. Qualities, which are genuine characteristics of natural events, are noted as involved in human satisfaction, and then valued, desired and sought again. Therefore, value is a revelation of nature's qualitative character, even though this character is only realized in interactions with goal-seeking organisms.

An ideal or value is "a possibility capable of realization in the concrete natural world, not a superior reality apart from the world."[9] Values are human visions of satisfactions suggested by nature's qualitative aspect, anticipations of ways we might perfect natural situations.

Notice that this implies a rejection of the Platonic "dualism of ends and means" just as Dewey above rejected the dualisms of Locke and Descartes. Platonic dualism separates the realm of enjoyed value from the sphere of practical knowledge. In Dewey's view, since value is rooted in qualities of natural events, factual knowledge of the cause and consequence of experiences of value is relevant to the moral life. The separation of practical knowledge on one hand, and visions of the ideal on the other, which we inherit from Platonism is simply a reflection of the class divisions within Athenian society in which practical knowledge belonged to artisans and enjoyment and contemplation of the ideal was a privilege reserved for the cultured aristocracy. This dualism leads to a science which is brutal and amoral and to morals which are effete and ineffective. Dewey believed that the ideal is not an object of leisurely contemplation, but a guide to possible satisfaction which is useful in social life. Viewed in this way, our social ideals call for reconstruction, since much that we inherit is irrelevant to the way we live, and the possibilities implied in our new knowledge and new social life have not yet been explored so as to yield new values and ideals.

Since value is rooted in qualities of natural events, knowledge of natural events is relevant to morals. What value is we cannot say; it is simply encountered and enjoyed. But inquiry can be directed to the causes and consequences of value experiences. Whenever a question is raised about the actual good of an object or an action, inquiry must turn to the question of what causes it and what it leads to. Thus in the end, scientific knowledge will contribute to decisions regarding values, and philosophy will be involved in social change.

Conclusion: What Is "American" in the New Naturalism

If we ask, what is characteristically American in the new naturalism, we must mention the characteristics of innovation and practi-
cality.

1. Innovation

The new naturalism which dominated American philosophy in the first
half of this century was developed by thinkers who were self-
consciously concerned with innovation. Dewey and his many followers
had a clear sense of the discontinuity of their thought with that of
the past, a definite desire to begin anew.

We have seen how Dewey intentionally, and perhaps hastily and
with insufficient respect, sets aside the dualisms of Plato, Descartes
and Locke. He perceived the philosophical tradition primarily as a
problem and an encumbrance. Some, including Santayana, who was
often critical of the later direction of the new naturalism, see this
as a reflection of the "adolescent" character of American thought.

Dewey was intensely aware of the newness of the American social
experience. He had a sense of the urgency of the task of clarifying
the new values and ideals which were implied within the experiences
of wilderness and the frontier, invention and industrialization, the
immense tides of immigration and the resulting ethnic diversity, and
especially the experience of democratic government in local communities. He regarded the "high culture" that Americans had inherited
from Europe as, on the whole, inappropriate to the actual lives of
American people. This is the source of his criticism of ideals which
are "effete and ineffectual." He did not mean that European tradition
was lacking in itself, but only that it represented an importation.
What was needed was the formulation of a vision of life which had
grown directly out of the farms and cities of America.[10]

2. Practicality

The new naturalism in its dominant Deweyan form is also typical of
the America of its day in its desire to turn philosophy from
speculation to social usefulness.

Many now feel that Dewey actually provides few intellectual solutions to the perennial problems of philosophy. He does not tell us <u>how</u> mind and body are related, or how fact and value are to be conceived, but merely provides us with an "image" of the dipolar event of interaction. Evidently, he thought that that was sufficient as a "working basis" so that we can get on with the "real" problems of social criticism and the attempt to state the values implied within the new American experience.

For Dewey, the real task of philosophy is "value inquiry," the developing of the values which were emerging from a kind of life quite different from that of classical western civilization. He saw his task as inquiry into the "causes and consequences" of value decisions, the reconstruction of inherited ideas of right and wrong so that they would become relevant to the new way he and his compatriots lived. This involved him directly in educational reform and the labor movement, as ways of implementing democratic values.

Dewey is typical of classical Americanism in his claim that ideas and values are tools of adjustment. What is essential is their working in the improvement of social life. The true idea is the one which successfully guides action. Why it does so is not of much interest to Dewey, for this is merely a speculative question; however we answer it, our practice will be the same. Again, ideals are not objects of contemplation as in the "high culture" of the leisure class, but they are plans of action. That value is worth holding which grows out of democratic social experience and furthers its growth; no transcendent or divine sanction is required, and speculation about such is wasteful since it diverts energy away from social reform.

The Contribution of Critical Naturalism

Since the middle of this century, naturalism has been eclipsed in America by British analytic philosophy. The American practitioners of this method now claim to do it better than its British inventors. The rapid spread of the analytic method may be due to the failure of naturalism and pragmatism to provide genuinely "intellectual" solutions to philosophical problems. But it is now clear that the growth of precision which resulted from the importation of the analytic method was accompanied by a shrinking of the scope of philosophic concern, and the virtual disappearance of the philosophical involvement in social criticism. There has been no philosopher for the last thirty years who has been taken seriously as a social or political commentator, as Dewey was for the previous thirty years. Nevertheless, through Sellars and Rorty, the impact of naturalism and pragmatism, expressed in analytically respectable terms, is contributing to Anglo-American analytic philosophy.

Perhaps the clearest continuing contribution of American naturalism to the present is in the area of religious thought. Dewey's sense of discontinuity with the past, and his rejection of the supernatural have contributed to the growth of a radical and naturalistic strand of religious thought found in the writings of H.N. Wieman, Bernard Loomer, Bernard Meland and others. This religious naturalism, associated with the University of Chicago, is clearly the heir of Dewey's naturalism. It survived the passing dominance of European neo-orthodoxy and Crisis Theology and is now making a contribution to the development of process theology, the liveliest theological movement in American theology at present.

NOTES

[1] John Herman Randall, Jr., "The Nature of Naturalism," in Yervant Krikorian, ed., Naturalism and the Human Spirit (New York: Columbia University Press, 1944), p. 363.

[2] Ibid.

[3] John Herman Randall, Jr., "George Santayana: Naturalizing the Imagination," Journal of Philosophy, Vol. 51 (1954), p. 52.

[4] George Santayana, Reason in Common Sense, Vol. I of The Life of Reason (New York: Charles Scribner's Sons, 1905-1906), p. 21.

[5] Eliseo Vivas, "From The Life of Reason to The Last Puritan," in Paul Arthur Schilpp, ed., The Philosophy of George Santayana (Evanston: Northwestern University Press, 1941), p. 350; John Herman Randall, Jr., in Krikorian, loc. cit.

[6] The idea that every metaphysic is based on a "root metaphor" is in Stephen C. Pepper, _World Hypotheses, a Study in Evidence_ (Berkeley: University of California Press, 1961), but Pepper does not characterize Dewey's root metaphor quite as I do.

[7] The phrase used as a title of this section is from John Dewey, _Experience and Nature_, second edition (New York: W.W. Norton Co., 1929), p. 71.

[8] John E. Smith, _Purpose and Thought, the Meaning of Pragmatism_ (New Haven: Yale University Press, 1978).

[9] John Dewey, _Reconstruction in Philosophy_ (New York: Henry Holt & Co., 1919), p. 120.

[10] For Santayana's development of this theme, see James Ballowe, editor, _George Santayana's America, Essays on Literature and Culture_ (Urbana: University of Illinois Press, 1967), and Richard C. Lyon, editor, _Santayana on America, Essays, Notes, and Letters on American Life, Literature and Philosophy_ (New York: Harcourt, Brace, World, Inc., 1968). Santayana's term for the inappropriate importation of European "high culture" was "the genteel tradition."

David M. Speak

The Renascence of Civil Religion in the U.S.: Weber, Lincoln, Reagan, and the American Polity

This project was born in the recognition of a paradox: Ronald Reagan currently enjoys great success as a "feel-good" idol in a time of cynicism, materialism and selfish individualism. His success as a leader stems not from asking for blood, sweat and tears, but from speaking of an America "on the move again." Recent public opinion polls indicate, however, that distrust of government is at Watergate/Vietnam high levels. How can a student of politics explain this apparent contradiction? A first pass at an explanation might suggest that Reagan panders to our materialism and selfish individualism with the biggest string of "buy-now pay-later" budgets in the history of the country. As candidate Bush said, voodoo economics in which we pay our bills by taxing less and spending more - that is a Laffer, but it plays well in Peoria. A second pass at an explanation might suggest that Reagan is a good actor in an age when that is all that is required for success. His election and re-election were engineered in the same way - and using the same talent - that sells Big Macs to millions of Americans each day.

Robert Kaiser in a 1984 NYR article calls Reagan "the nation's host, our presiding master of ceremonies. Not just any old master of ceremonies, I'd suggest, but a particular model, a more genial and animated version of Ed Sullivan, whose program Reagan must have watched in the 1950's" (Kaiser, 6.28.84). Ronald Reagan's professional acting career makes entertainment analogies seem particularly apt for our current head of state. The notion of President as EmCee is not a new one, though. From the moment of our second founding in the Constitution we chose to combine the head of state job with the chief executive's. Thus we have always encouraged a good deal of good showmanship in the White House, demanding the pomp that we lost with the crown in combination with the management skills of a prime minister. In that regard this President is not unique: all Presidents have been actors.

These first two passes at explanation are in themselves both too cynical and not cynical enough - too cynical in that they fail to catch that positive excitement that Reagan engenders and the righteousness in the tone of his admirers; not cynical enough in that the first explanation - economic pandering - is hard to sustain in light of the real costs levied against large numbers of the Reagan faithful by the Reagan policies. As for the second explanation, based on Reagan's skill in his first career in Hollywood, if his acting skill had been great enough to sustain that career, he might never have embarked upon a second career as a public servant. After all, where do you go after "Death Valley Days?" To be fair, Mr. Reagan was released from hosting that memorable bit of syndicated TV because he was already looking too political for the show's cautious corporate sponsor. But it is clear that the zenith of the Reagan acting career was well in the past by the time he left the 20 Mule Team in 1964.

Hardly anyone would suggest that Reagan has presided in fortunate times. The US and World economies have suffered a severe recession since 1980. Regional hostilities have continued at disturbing levels and terrorism has blossomed in lurid red in all parts of the globe. Earthquakes, hurricanes and volcanoes have trashed the temperate zones of our hemisphere repeatedly in the last five years. Some might suggest that, while governing in trying times, the Reagan administration has managed through good fortune or skill to avoid policy failures and thus responsibility for hardship suffered. Such a claim is refuted by even the most cursory glance at the record. If this administration's policy success rate has not been worse than its recent predecessors, it is not much better, either. No policy failures? This is the administration that promised a balanced budget by 1983 and has created instead more additional debt than all previous Presidents combined. This is the President that promised a sure, swift response to terrorist acts and has (perhaps to his credit) found no acceptable response to the deaths of <u>scores</u> of Americans in embassies, on ships and in airports. After reaching record post-War heights, unemployment in the US has now receded back to the level it held at the beginning of the Reagan administration - a level then deemed "unacceptable" by Reagan himself. Military procurement is in disarray. The shuttle program - even before the recent disaster - was grossly over budget and behind schedule. Bank failures and farm foreclosures are at levels not seen since the Depression. Whether you agree with Reagan's policies or not is not the point. The point is that there have been numerous and significant policy setbacks on Mr. Reagan's watch. Mr. Reagan's success cannot be based on error-free government policy or even particularly good luck. Representative Pat Schroeder's phrase, "the Teflon President," achieved wide currency precisely because Mr. Reagan has presided over some notable policy failures without suffering the negative response which similar failures generated for the Johnson, Nixon, Ford, and Carter Presidencies.

This President does seem different to us - at least different from his immediate predecessors in that august office. In spite of a rash of dire prognostications about presidential failure over the last two decades and a string of foreshortened presidencies, Mr. Reagan enters his sixth year in office with good reason to be optimistic about the successful completion of his second term. Perhaps the most apt image for Reagan's popularity should be drawn not from the field of entertainment, but rather from a field which in these days of media evangelists often seems closely related to entertainment: religion. Reagan's success may be related to the resurgence of civil religion in the United States and to Mr. Reagan's successful exploitation of civil religious themes in the presentation of the work of his administration.

First let me define more carefully what I have called Reagan's success. After five years in office Mr. Reagan enjoys approval ratings in the mid-sixties (quite strong within recorded memory) and the at worst grudging respect of large numbers of political analysts in the media. Mr. Reagan's success consists of his ability to maintain high public prestige over an extended period in office. This success can be and has been overstated, of course. Mr. Nixon, too, was re-elected by a large margin in both popular and electoral college votes. The election which turned Mr. Ford out of office was quite close. Although he presided over a time of enormous civil unrest, Mr. Johnson's record of success with Congress over a period of five years was quite strong. Still, none of that kept us from being increasingly pessimistic about executive leadership in this country. Executive power was held in increasing suspicion, either because it was unmanageable or unchecked. (Reedy, 1971; Schlesinger, 1973; Sorenson, 1975; Cronin, 1980) Nixon sensed the negativity that was waxing during this time, causing him to suggest while campaigning for re-election in 1972 that what the country needed was "the lift of a driving dream." To sense the need was not enough to be able to respond to it, though, and Mr. Nixon's conduct in office vastly increased our concern about executive power. Nor was the antidote in Mr. Ford's frank geniality, nor Mr. Carter's perfervid honesty. Ronald Reagan, at this time at least, is credited with having reversed that tide of pessimism. The perception of success in these circumstances is tantamount to the real thing. What follows is not an explanation of that success, but an attempt to characterize its nature.

While Governor of California, Reagan was fond of referring to himself as "a citizen in temporary service to his government." Repeated re-enlistments have rendered that line less useful, and it has been dropped from the litany. But the stance which Reagan takes vis-a-vis public affairs has not changed. Even after having assumed administrative responsibility, Reagan remains the prophet crying in the wilderness. As a man of the (red, white and blue) cloth, Mr. Reagan represents values, not policies. It is that stance which allows Reagan so successfully to disassociate himself from the failures of public policy which proceed around him. As befits a prophet, he has visions, not plans (notice his current treatment of the deficit). His exhortations are addressed to our souls rather than our rational faculties (how else can you explain the lack of concern about his cavalier treatment of "facts?"). It was this religious stance which elected Reagan in the first place. What I want to address in this paper is not Ronald Reagan and his Ed Sullivan - or teflon - presidency, but rather the phenomenon of which the Reagan style may be a reflection. That phenomenon, which I here label the renascence of civil religion in the U.S., is potentially a much broader event than the Reagan Presidency.

Ironically, a not-dissimilar religious stance worked successfully for Reagan's predecessor as well - at least in his first Presidential bid. Jimmy Carter, in addition to his born-again commitment to traditional religion, campaigned successfully on the money-changers-in-the-temple theme, but was subsequently ensnared in his own rhetoric. Carter became identified with the government - he became a priest, not a prophet. His unsuccessful re-election bid ran aground on his own failure to make a government as good as its people (or at least as good as its people liked to be told they were). The long string of one term presidencies which we have seen since 1960 may reflect the inability of incumbent Presidents to insulate themselves from politics sufficiently to keep the mantle of prophet unsullied with the realities of priest/policy-maker. If Ronald Reagan is the first successful two term President since Eisenhower (and that question may not be decided for years), his success will be based in part at least on his ability to make the Presidency once more a bully pulpit in a profound sense.

This paper is not about Reagan, but about the whole tenor of American politics in the last twenty years. How can we tell if we are witnessing a rebirth of a genuine civil religion in this country? What identifying features distinguish a civil religion from simple nationalism or patriotism? What effects will an active civil religion have upon politics and policies? Is this a cyclical occurrence, and if so, how long is the cycle? None of these questions can be answered precisely. Still, an exploration of the phenomena involved might provide some insight into current events, and an antidote to seeing Reagan only as a successful politician or a successful actor.

The starting point for the further exploration of these questions is Max Weber's categories of legitimate domination. Weber sets out three ideal types of legitimate domination in Economy and Society. Two of these are based upon personal authority, which can be founded upon the sacredness of tradition, custom and convention, or which can be founded upon a surrender to the extraordinary grace of a particular individual's charisma. The third type of legitimate domination rests upon a system of consciously made, rational rules.

> Rationally regulated association within a structure of domination finds its typical expression in bureaucracy. Traditionally prescribed social action is typically represented by patriarchalism. The charismatic structure of domination rests upon individual authority which is based neither upon rational rules nor upon tradition. (Weber, p. 954)

Weber's preference for bureaucracy is both well known and usually overstated. These categories are ideal types, not recognizable in pure form in the world. They are not intended to be chronological phases of the development of civilization. In fact Weber explicitly mentions the fact that charismatic authority, although it generally recedes with the sophistication of society, is liable to pop up even within highly rationalized systems of interaction:

> Since all emotional mass appeals have certain charismatic features, the bureaucratization of the parties and of electioneering may at its very height suddenly be forced into the service of charismatic hero worship. (Weber, p. 1130)

It is the charismatic type of authority which best captures Reagan's appeal. "The bearer of charisma enjoys loyalty and authority by virtue of a mission believed to be embodied in him." (Weber, p. 1117) Reagan's appeal is clearly personal rather than based upon position within a bureaucratic structure. Both his earlier professional career outside politics and the high level at which he initially enters politics point to the fact that his success is based upon personal characteristics rather than those of a dynasty or of the Republican Party itself. Although he now enjoys the "inherited" prestige of the Presidency, his authority has other, deeper roots as well. After all, the prestige of the Oval Office did not bestow a teflon coating on Carter, Ford, Nixon or Johnson. This President has charisma.

But what is unique about Mr. Reagan among recent presidents is not that he has charisma - that must surely attach to a greater or lesser degree to all persons able to run the gauntlet of national electoral politics in this country. What distinguishes Mr. Reagan is that he STILL has charisma after holding office for five years. Charismatic rulership is inherently unstable. "Bureaucracy and patriarchalism are antagonistic in many respects, but they share continuity as one of their most important characteristics." (Weber, p. 1111) Charismatic leadership is always extraordinary and non-routine. "Even though the apostle admonishes the followers to maintain the purity of the spirit, the charismatic message inevitably becomes dogma, doctrine, theory, reglement, law or petrified tradition." (Weber, p. 1122) The prophet as the bearer of charisma is replaced by the priest, whose authority is not charismatic but traditional instead. Mr. Reagan, for whatever reasons, has maintained the prophet's role and managed to avoid the priest's involvement with the operation of the day-to-day business of government. That distance from the routine business of government is evident in the short working days and the long vacations which have characterized this President. Even more telling is the well-known Reagan propensity for getting the facts wrong, or for simply being unaware of the details of his own administration. Rather than liabilities, these have all enhanced Reagan's stature. Conversely, Mr. Carter's fall from grace was precipitated by his identification with the government itself and the details of its operation. The prophet's role insulates while the priest's leaves one open to criticism.

So how has Mr. Reagan managed to remain the prophet while in office? What allows for the maintenance of charisma? Is Ronald Reagan riding a new wave (perhaps of his own making) of civil religion in the US? Just what is civil religion anyway? Before answering that question I need to say what civil religion is not. It is not traditional religion in service of government. Nor is it government in service of religion. It is not Jerry Falwell (as Mr. Mondale fretted) having veto power over Federal judicial nominations. Nor is it the government serving as a cheerleader or recruiter for the Liberty Foundation. If there is a resurgence of civil religion in this country it will not threaten the separation of church and state that we have built into the First Amendment. Civil religion is not religion in a new guise – it is a different form, parallel to traditional religion.

To understand civil religion it is necessary to remember that the structures of government and the structures of traditional religion have much in common. We popularly characterize religion as distinct from government because religion is concerned with morality and government is concerned with legality. We distinguish religion from government by saying that religion is based on salvation while government is based on the threat of coercive enforcement. We make a disjunction between religion and government by saying that religion springs from and is maintained by faith while government springs from and is maintained by reason. Such distinctions fail to capture the essence of religion as much as they fail to understand the nature of government. Organized religion, no matter how intuitivist, or revelationist, is based on law. The promise of salvation is often just the reverse of the threat of damnation. The structure of every church is supported by reasoned claims even if these are only reasoned claims to the elect's inspiration. So religion is very much a matter of legality and coercion and reason. At the same time, government is more than just that. No police force is big enough, or frightening enough to support a government that has absolutely lost the faith of large numbers of its citizens. Most of us obey the law most of the time because we have some commitment to the structure which it supports – not simply because we are worried about being caught and punished. Of course religion needs morality and salvation and faith, but it needs law and threatened enforcement and reason as well. Of course government needs law and coercion and reason, but it needs faith, and a vision of higher truth and some promise of a better future, too. To understand civil religion is to understand this latter side of government. The extent to which government relies upon and self-consciously reinforces this 'higher law' attachment to itself is the extent to which civil religion is present in a particular society. Thus one can speak of a renascence of civil religion under circumstances in which members of a society and its government self-consciously seek, through "higher law" claims, to engender support for the government or the society over which it presides. (Corwin, 1955) Civil religion need not always be conservative of the status quo. On the contrary, because civil religion does base its claim to support upon a higher standard than the government itself, civil religion can and often does play a reformist or even revolutionary role. A stark but not always obvious tension exists within any such claim to authority.

The history of this country, from its earliest visitation by Europeans, has been marked by a strong tradition of civil religion. (Bellah, 1975; Mead, 1975; Nicgorski and Weber, 1976) This land was Eden or the New Jerusalem. John Locke said, "In the beginning all the world was America." (Bellah p. 5; 2d T. 49,1) Two separate strains of traditional religion shared a single vision of this nation's destiny:

> Whether our nation interprets its spiritual heritage through Massachusetts or Virginia, we came into existence with the sense of being a "separated" nation, which God was using to make a new beginning for mankind ... Whether, as in the case of the New England Theocrats, our forefathers thought of our "experiment" as primarily a creation of a new and purer church, or, as in the case of Jefferson and his coterie, they thought primarily of a political community, they believed in either case that we had been called out by God to create a new humanity. (Niebuhr, p. 24)

That vision became the foundation of the civil religion in this land. If civil religion is being born again in the U.S. it is not a new birth but rather the rebirth of an old faith. To see what that particular civil religion encompasses, what values it elevates, and what aspirations it cradles dear, there is no better guide than Abraham Lincoln.

This nation was seen as the recipient of a divine charge to be "as a city upon a hill," a beacon for all of humanity. This mantle of the chosen people forms the foundation for civil religion in the United States and is keenly reflected in Lincoln's political rhetoric.

But almost every nation carries a sense of itself as having a special destiny. There are other features of the American faith which may help us more particularly in deciding whether we are experiencing a renascence of that faith.

First, there is an interesting tension about <u>reason</u> in our national faith. We think of ourselves as a "practical" or "pragmatic" people. We are, paradoxically, attached to reason in a passionate way. There is something superadded to the Enlightenment in this. We argue not just for being guided by reason, but being <u>fervent</u> in seeking its guidance. Consider the following excerpt from Lincoln on persuasion:

> If you would win a man to your cause, first convince him that you are his sincere friend. Therein is a drop of honey that catches his heart; which, say what you will, is the great high road to his reason, and which, when once gained, you will find but little trouble in convincing his judgment of the justice of your cause, if, indeed, that cause really be a just one. On the contrary, assume to dictate to his judgment, or to command his action, or to mark him as one to be shunned and despised, and he will retreat within himself, close all the avenues to his head and his heart, and though your cause be naked truth itself ... you shall be no more able to pierce him, than to penetrate the hard shell of a tortoise with a rye straw. Such is man, and so must he be understood by those who would lead him, even to his own best interests. (Lincoln, 1889, pp. 4-5)

What an interesting tension exists in this vision of persuasion, where truth can be absolutely compelling ("you will find but little trouble ... if ... that cause really be a just one"). And yet reason has no hope without some initial sign of good will. The relationship between reason and passion here is not that of two necessary but not sufficient causes. The posited goal is somehow to achieve a passionate attachment to reason as it is reflected in the law. This tenet of faith is quite clear in Lincoln's widely quoted speech before the Young Men's Lyceum in Springfield in 1838:

> Let reverence for the laws, be breathed by every American mother, to the lisping babe, that prattles on her lap - let it be taught in schools, in seminaries, and in colleges; - let it be written in Primmers, spelling books, and in Almanacs; - let it be preached from the pulpit, proclaimed in legislative halls, and enforced in courts of justice. And, in short, let it become the <u>political religion</u> of the nation; and let the old and the young, the rich and the poor, the grave and the gay, of all

sexes and tongues, and colors and conditions, sacrifice
unceasingly upon its altars. (Lincoln, 1953, Vol. I, p. 112)

The passions of the mob must be subordinated to the rule of law,
but further, the passions of the people must be engaged in support
of the notion of the rule of law.

> [Surviving participants displaying revolutionary fervor] were
> the pillars of the temple of liberty; and now, that they have
> crumbled away, that temple must fall, unless we, their
> descendants, supply their places with other pillars, hewn from
> the solid quarry of sober reason. Passion has helped us; but
> can do so no more. In the future it will be our enemy.
> Reason, cold, calculating, unimpassioned reason, must furnish
> all the materials of our future support and defence. Let those
> be moulded into general intelligence, morality and, in
> particular, a reverence for the constitution and laws (Lincoln,
> 1953, Vol. I, p. 115)

In addition to this passionate attachment to reason, our creed has
always maintained a strong attachment to the expression of reason in
the will of the people. Alongside the Constitution of 1787, with its
careful balances and counterpoised weights, we hold the Declaration
of Independence as a sacred text. That Jeffersonian democracy is
also well reflected in Lincoln's rhetoric:

> Why should there not be a patient confidence in the ultimate
> justice of the people? Is there any better or equal hope in the
> world? In our present differences is either party without faith
> of being in the right? If the Almighty Ruler of Nations, with
> his eternal truth and justice, be on your side of the North, or
> on yours of the South, that truth and that justice will surely
> prevail by the judgment of this great tribunal of the American
> people. (Lincoln, 1940, p. 656)

This democratic spirit is necessarily egalitarian in its implications.
Although a democracy of formal statuses is imaginable, ours has
never been of this stripe. Although classes exist in the U.S., we
have failed to develop any clear public language for the existence
of classes because they did not figure into the Puritanical or
Jeffersonian ideal of democracy.

The final and perhaps most important component of this American
creed which is relevant to the present discussion is better reflected
in Lincoln than anywhere else - a certain humility of judgment
essential to the claim of following a higher law. Mindful of the
executive arrogance of Lincoln, and of his willingness to maintain

the Union at the cost of thousands of human lives, one cannot fail to be struck by the humility which increasingly pervades his wartime statements. Although resolute in his determination to prosecute the war through enormous losses, catastrophic setbacks and consistent failures, Lincoln always publicly maintained the tentativeness of human knowledge and the fallibility of human conviction. His finest moment, the Second Inaugural, is almost wholly characterized by this sense of human fallibility:

> Neither party expected for the war the magnitude or the duration which it has already attained. Neither anticipated that the cause of the conflict might cease with, or even before, the conflict itself would cease. Each looked for an easier triumph, and a result less fundamental and astounding. Both read the same Bible, and pray to the same God; and each invokes His aid against the other. It may seem strange that any men should dare to ask a just God's assistance in wringing their bread from the sweat of other men's faces; but let us judge not, that we be not judged. The prayers of both could not be answered - that of neither has been answered fully.
> The Almighty has His own purposes. "Woe unto the world because of offenses! for it must needs be that offenses come; but woe to that man by whom the offense cometh." If we shall suppose that American Slavery is one of those offenses which, in the providence of God, must needs come, but which, having continued through His appointed time, He now wills to remove, and that He gives to both North and South this terrible war, as the woe due to those by whom the offense came, shall we discern therein any departure from those divine attributes which the believers in a living God always ascribe to Him? Fondly do we hope - fervently do we pray - that this mighty scourge of war may speedily pass away. Yet, if God wills that it continue until all the wealth piled by the bondsman's two hundred and fifty years of unrequited toil shall be sunk, and until every drop of blood drawn with the lash shall be paid with another drawn with the sword, as was said three thousand years ago, so it must still be said, "The judgments of the Lord are true and righteous altogether." (Lincoln, 1940, p. 842)

This broad statement of humility is what launches and grounds the most memorable lines of this address - "With malice toward none; with charity for all; with firmness in the right, as God gives us to see the right, let us strive on to finish the work we are in ..." However much or little Lincoln's actions may have matched these words, this sentiment of humility is what finally binds the best parts of the American civil religion together. Ours is a nation with a sense of a special mission like many others. Ours is additionally a nation that, at its best, finds guidance for carrying out that mission in a passionate attachment to reason as evidenced in the law; a nation that has faith in democratic principles to embody that reason which should guide human endeavor; and finally, a nation mindful of the fallibility of human judgment both individually and collectively.

The years since the second world war - one might argue since the first world war - have been hard on that sense of ourselves embodied in our civil faith. Does Reagan's success in office mark a reversal of the tide? No simple answer is possible. To contribute to whatever answer is possible, it will be useful to look at Reagan's words and Reagan's actions. The messages in the recent State of the Union are useful examples. "Tonight we look out on a rising America - firm of heart, united in spirit, powerful in pride and patriotism. America is on the move." This marks a hopeful beginning, clearly (and as is typical in Reagan speeches) announcing the rebirth of faith in the polity. But as Richard Nixon learned, to issue the call and to raise the troops are two different things. The rest of the message celebrated economic growth, called for lowering taxes, revising welfare, advancing Star Wars, ending abortion, and winning freedom in Afganistan, Angola, Cambodia and Nicaragua. Too often the Reagan rhetoric in each of these areas is non-democratic - ignoring clear majorities in favor of choice in abortion, opposed to increased defense spending, and opposed to U.S. intervention in Nicaragua. In other ways the Reagan rhetoric displays more hubris than humility. Even in the midst of open warfare, Lincoln never characterized the South as an Evil Empire.

And yet Reagan's policy choices have been more responsive to public opinion than his rhetoric would suggest - resulting in his image as a pragmatic politician who talks a hard line but compromises in the end. And Reagan's actions in foreign policy have in many cases at least shown a restraint, a tentativeness that is not inconsistent with humility. Making the best case for Reagan, it is possible to contend that while the substance of his rhetoric (apart from the flourishes) may not match the best parts of our national faith, at least his actions are not inconsistent with it. And while other parts of his rhetoric may give voice to the dark side of our civil creed (the aggressiveness of the sense of mission, the domination of nature), these parts are partial at worst and peripheral at best.

Whether or not you agree with that best case analysis (having underestimated Reagan in the past I am reluctant to repeat the error), the implications for civil religion are the same. If Reagan's success were an indication that we were observing a rebirth in civil religion in this country you would expect the opposite of even the best case. That is, you would expect a public rhetoric tied to the national creed even though governmental actions might deviate from it. Lincoln's hold in the national imagination came from his stirring, yet humble, rhetoric. Lincoln acted with considerable arrogance in carrying out the tasks of executive office. But he is remembered for the Second Inaugural and not the suspension of the writ of habeus corpus. Lincoln's rhetoric addressed and nurtured our civil religion even as his actions deviated from it.

In Reagan's case we have the reverse situation: the main part of the rhetoric moves away from the core values of the civil religion even if one allows that governmental action is not thus deviating from the American civil creed, and may be moving toward these values (a debatable proposition).

If Reagan is successful because of his rhetoric, it is not success tied to the renascence of civil religion in the U.S. He might, of course, be founding a new sect, based on the dark side of the traditional civil creed. Rather than contend that Reagan is rewriting the American tradition, it is easier to contend that Reagan is not successful because of his rhetoric. But this paper began by asserting that he is not successful because of his policies. He is not successful because of his administration's good fortune or skill. His success is apart from all of that, and thus must fall into a residual category - Weber's category of charisma. Charisma is defined by its extraordinary nature. It is a residual category of explanation, the remainder when other possibilities have been excluded.

It may be that a renascence of civil religion is occuring in the U.S. today, but Reagan's success, contrary to popular interpretation, is not a reflection of that possibility. Until the Reagan success is passed from the prophet to the priests successfully (if George Bush is a successful candidate in 1988, will he continue to sound like a Reagan cheerleader?), it is best to treat Reagan's success as the extraordinary, personal authority of a charismatic individual.

REFERENCES

Bellah, Robert N. The Broken Covenant (New York: Seabury Press, 1975).

Berman, Harold J. The Interaction of Law and Religion (Nashville: Abingdon Press, 1974).

Corwin, Edward S. The "Higher Law" Background of American Constitutional Law (Ithaca: Cornell U. Press, 1955).

Cronin, Thomas. The State of the Presidency (Boston: Little Brown, 1980).

Lincoln, Abraham. Address Delivered Before the Springfield Washingtonian Temperance Society (Springfield, IL: O.H. Oldroyd, Publisher, 1889).

Lincoln, Abraham. Collected Works, Roy P. Basler, ed. (New Brunswick, NJ: Rutgers U. Press, 1953).

Lincoln, Abraham. Life and Writings, Philip Van Doren Stern, ed. (New York: Random House, 1940).

Mead, Sidney E. The Nation with the Soul of a Church (New York: Harper & Row, 1975).

Nicgorski, Walter, and Ronald Weber, eds. An Almost Chosen People (Notre Dame: University of Notre Dame Press, 1976).

Niebuhr, Reinhold. The Irony of American History (New York: Charles Scribner's Sons, 1952).

Reedy, George. The Twilight of the Presidency (New York: New American Library, 1971).

Schlesinger, Arthur. The Imperial Presidency (Boston: Houghton Mifflin, 1973).

Sorenson, Theodore C. Watchmen in the Night (Cambridge, Mass.: MIT Press, 1975).

Weber, Max. Economy and Society (Berkeley: UC Press, 1978).

Warren E. Steinkraus

Walter Rauschenbusch and Socially Conscious Religion in America

The effect of the life and teachings of Walter Rauschenbusch (1861-1918), on religious life and thought in the United States is difficult to measure but it has been profound. He is not as well known, of course, as the Nobel Prize winner Martin Luther King, Jr., who acknowledged a great debt to him and whose thought shows markedly the influence of Rauschenbusch's ideas about the nature of Christianity. One of King's own teachers, the late Benjamin Mays, edited a selection of the writings of Rauschenbusch in 1950 at about the time King was studying at Morehouse College in Atlanta. In describing his pilgrimage to non-violence, this is what King wrote about Rauschenbusch in 1955.

> It has been my conviction ever since reading Rauschenbusch that any religion which professes to be concerned about the souls of men and is not concerned about the social and economic conditions that scar the soul, is a spiritually moribund religion only waiting for the day to be buried. 1

Indeed, his reading of Rauschenbusch, he says, led him then to a serious study of the social and ethical theories of the great philosophers.

Another religious thinker influenced by Rauschenbusch, Harry Emerson Fosdick wrote,

> His conscious and unconscious disciples are uncountable, for he opened a new era in the thought and effort of American Christianity, and many who share it now have no idea how deeply indebted they are to Walter Rauschenbusch. 2

Some of those names include Reinhold Niebuhr, A.J. Muste, Kirby Page, F.J. McConnell, John Haynes Holmes, Halford Luccock and Walter G. Muelder, who was one of King's mentors in graduate school. And the great Japanese Christian leader, Toyohiko Kagawa gratefully acknowledged that Rauschenbusch's works "prompted him to promulgate the Kingdom of God movement in Japan."[3]

What is there about the life and thought of Rauschenbusch that had such an effect on King and on so many other religious leaders in North America? I think the answer is to be found in the fact that he made direct connections between his religious views and his actions and he sought in every way to work out practically the implications of religious belief for the world as it is. In short, he took his faith seriously just as a good physician takes discoveries in medicine. When some new medical discovery is reported, some new procedure in medical technology, the alert physician seeks almost at once to apply those findings to sick patients. Medicine is not an intellectual game that is played for the benefit of an elite group of thinkers. It exists to heal the sick and to prevent illness, disease and death where possible. And that was Walter Rauschenbusch's idea of religious truth. What he found to be true and worthwhile in his understanding of Christianity he sought to apply to the daily life of the people who were sick individually and who were oppressed socially and economically. Not very many academic or well paid theologians are willing or ready to view religion in this fashion and the consequence is that they talk to each other in highly sophisticated language but their words mean nothing much to the sorrowing, the social outcaste, the depressed and the oppressed, and the powers that run the world are not in the least bothered. Walter Muelder has pointed out that none has synthesized the gospel of the Kingdom of God, the Christian critique of capitalism, the liberal democratic forces of America and the social ideals of the common man so thoroughly. "No one has made more explicit than he the duty and the power of Christianity both to reform the social order and to redeem the individual. This he did without sentimentality or utopianism."[4]

Walter Rauschenbusch was born in Rochester, New York in 1861, the seventh in a direct line of clergymen which originated in Herford, Westphalia. He was brought up in a religious home "without any social insight or outlook,"[5] spent four years of his childhood in Germany, and returned in 1879 to study at the Evangelical

Gymnasium of Gütersloh in Westphalia. Back in the United States in 1883, he began an active ministry in the slums of New York City in a place called "Hell's Kitchen." There his social vision was awakened. His biographer writes:

> Working among the poor and downtrodden, Rauschenbusch began to formulate a program of social action. He saw the effects of grinding poverty and unemployment. He felt the pang of poverty, the insecurity, the tragedy of malnutrition, especially among the children, and the appalling waste of life through disease and crime in the tenement district. 6

He came to the conclusion that there was something wrong with a socio-economic system which fostered such shocking things and he began to develop a view of social Christianity. He set to work for the renewal and Christianization of the individual and of society. In 1897, he became a professor at the German Baptist Seminary in Rochester, and remained at that post until his death in 1918. With his fine literary talent, he found time to translate such American poets as James Russell Lowell into German, and he helped Ira Sankey compile a book of Evangeliums Lieder, translating 137 out of 344 gospel songs. These reflect his sympathy for simple pietism. His three most important books are: Christianity and the Social Crisis (1907), Christianizing the Social Order (1912), A Theology for the Social Gospel (1917). He published five other volumes, and a sixth, unpublished book, discovered in a vault some twenty years ago, has been published as The Righteousness of the Kingdom (1968). There are 229 articles and reviews including topics like "How Rich Have I a Right to be" and "Revolutionary Religion."

I

Rauschenbusch's sensitivity to human problems, his profound appreciation of the personality of Jesus, and his open-minded attitude towards traditional theology, led him to a reinterpretation of Christianity in primarily ethical terms. He stressed the actual life and moral teachings of Jesus as distinguished from doctrinal theories about his birth, death, atonement and resurrection. While maintaining a respect for individualistic piety, he saw that that emphasis would be a stumbling block to achieving the true Christian ideal of the Kingdom of God.

Accordingly, Rauschenbusch proposed and maintained that the essence of Christianity was to be found in the idea of the Kingdom of God which was so prominent in Jesus' teaching but so overlooked by most of the historic church. In his lengthy treatment of this theme, he demonstrates that the idea of the kingdom was in the heritage of Jesus' past tradition and not newly created by him because the conceptions which ruled the religious life of Israel were the idea of the covenant and theocracy. The Jewish ideal of life was "a righteous community ordered by divine laws, governed by God's ministers, having intercourse with the Most High and being blessed by him with the good things of life."[7] Jesus tried to reawaken that ideal, but his own countrymen had hindered it. He was the successor and heir of the great thoughts of Israel. We read:

> If Jesus had brushed aside the idea of the reign of God on earth, he would have brushed aside the entire Old Testament and the entire past of Israel. 8

This he did not and could not do.

Then Rauschenbusch points out that Jesus took this idea, universalized and spiritualized it. It was not nationality but spiritual fitness that would ensure blessing. The living germ of the Kingdom was to establish a community of spiritual persons "in inward communion with God and in outward obedience to him."[9] The community could not be established by external means, by force or by display. The history of Roman Catholicism and the activities of the Reformers did not accord with that idea for they used torture and the power of princes, consenting to have whole countries change their faith as a monarch directed. Nor do established churches today follow Jesus' ideal when they derive their support from taxes.

> Whenever Christianity shows an inclination to use constraint in its own defense or support, it thereby furnishes presumptive evidence that it has become a thing of this world, for it finds the means of this world adapted to its ends. 10

Rauschenbusch would not have been popular in Europe. Indeed, had his works been translated into German they might have had the two-fold effect of challenging the moribund state-church and the sentimental individualistic piety of the non-establishment sects.

The church elevated and elaborated ceremonies. On this we read: "What need of performing ceremonies to please God, when you can always please him by serving your neighbor?"[11] Ceremonialism is a symptom of spiritual decay. Jesus substituted the idea of God's humanity for the idea of God's favored nation. The traditional slant of the organized church was sound in so far as it preaches the perfection of the individual life. But, he claimed, it is unscriptural and wrong "in not preaching the perfection of the collective life of humanity." And then, with his excellent literary instincts, Rauschenbusch says:

> In place of a church invading the world and wrestling with it, spirit against spirit, we see a church fleeing out of the world and in solitude, with fastings, prayers, and flagellations, guarding the flickering rushlight of personal godliness from the mocking breath of the world .... The Kingdom of God is like unto a burning ship, from which a few escape in a boat and rest on their oars at a distance in helpless contemplation. 12

It is not enough to Christianize individuals, we must, he says, Christianize societies, organizations and nations. They too have a life which may be made better or worse.

But this view was not popular in Rauschenbusch's time, nor is it very prevalent in the Western world today. Individualism still dominates most ordinary religious thinking. It is the major emphasis of the most vocal leaders in North American television evangelism. And their individualism has led to both a tacit and overt support of right wing political ideology, not only because they uniformly have the support of wealth, but because they have an "other-worldly" view of the Kingdom of God which Rauschenbusch spent his life trying to overcome. They cannot see that there are sinful social structures as well as sinful individuals. The emphasis on individual wrong is an easy way to divert the attention from social wrong. Some spokespersons for this viewpoint are not worried about social or economic injustice or even about nuclear annihilation. The latter may bring about the end of civilization, but they see that as nothing more than what they take to be God's plan for the world. They put a theological construction on natural human events. Instead of trying to change the structures in the world which conduce to pain, hardship, disease and misery for the poor, especially in the Third World, they urge the salvation of individual souls and then await heaven. They are doggedly unable to understand Rauschenbusch's dictum: A world of regenerated individuals is not necessarily a regenerated world.

Rauschenbusch went on to show how this conception of the Kingdom of God is really a revolutionary idea. It has application to every area of life. It is revolutionary because "it insists on the sanctification of this life and the victory of the spirit of Christ over the spirit of the world in every form of human society and a corresponding alteration of all the institutions formed by human society."[13] When one thinks of the sanctification of the social order an initial question to confront is the one of economics. Our thinker clearly defended a form of Christian Socialism, while at the same time offering a critique of Marxism.[14] He spent a good deal of time showing up not only the tremendous waste in traditional capitalism but also its inherent structural weaknesses and how by its very nature it injured and oppressed people. He had no illusions that its corrupting influence could be aided by mere reformation.

He spoke also of the revolutionary power inherent in the personality of Jesus noting that his whole life incarnated those principles which contradict the ruling principles of existing human society. "Wherever his personality gains influence over the human soul, the result will be that that soul will go forth to live a revolutionary life."[15] To put it more pointedly: "He has furnished us with the demonstration of a life completely filled with God and absolutely mastered by goodness. Henceforth none of us can be satisfied with anything less."[16] Or again, "The consciousness of God which we derive from Jesus is able to establish centres of spiritual strength and peace which help break the free sweep of evil in social life."[17]

Others too, like E. Stanley Jones[18] and Kirby Page, have come to this realization. In 1950, Page wrote a book called The Creative

Revolution of Jesus: Then and Now, in which he addressed himself to Jesus' revolution in world affairs, race relations, democracy, and economic life. Similarly, in our own time we have thinkers like Dorothy Soelle and Archbishop Dom Helder Camara who echo the revolutionary ideal.

II

A second observation we may make about the contribution of Walter Rauschenbusch to the rise of socially conscious religion in North America is his frank recognition of the role of social causality in human life. His initial appointment was in "Hell's Kitchen" in the slums of New York City. It was during this experience that he realized that the people he ministered to were victims of an unjust social order. They were not isolated individuals who were down on their luck, lazy, or lacking in initiative. They were rather the hapless victims of a socio-economic condition that made it arduous if not impossible for them to grow into wholesome, normal human persons. He saw the results of economic oppression on human lives and he began to assess and analyze the causes.

He noticed not only the difficulties persons in a bad environment had in meeting the ordinary needs of life, he also realized how hard it was for them to appreciate the simple joys of nature. How could God, he asks, "make known his majesty to one who has never seen the Pleiades through the city smoke, or who sees the treasures of snow only in its slush ..."[19] He soon saw that the basal causal factor impinging on human beings was the economic one. It is hard for an individual to improve himself in an essentially debilitating economic situation. He had no abstract faith in the automatic virtues of a rugged capitalism, which, some still claim, will make possible a better life for all if left to itself. Instead, he saw twentieth century capitalism as a ruthless system which ground down personality for the sake of profits, which permitted child labor and sweat shops all for the sake of making more money. "Wealth is made by the suffering of others."[20]

At the same time he harbored no hatred towards those individuals who supported and thrived on the system of exploitation. His purpose, reports his biographer, "was to touch consciences, never to injure the self-respect of individuals."[21] Thus, his approach was essentially ethical. He offered an ethical critique of a system which ruined children, men and women, which made persons into animals, furthered the break-up of the home, furthered prostitution, and the like. Again and again in his writings he points this out.

In 1916, in a widely used booklet for college voluntary study courses called The Social Principles of Jesus, Rauschenbusch tackles in plain language the problem of social causality. One section of this book is called "The Recalcitrant Social Forces" and there he cites, among other things, Jesus' indictment of the governing class (p. 102) and he states that ambition must get its satisfaction by serving humanity. Private property must serve social welfare. One of his study questions reads: "Unlimited acquisition used to be considered immoral and dishonorable. How and when did public opinion change on this?" (p. 118) He then observes that wealth, as Jesus saw it,

> flouted the value of life, dissolved the spiritual solidarity of whole classes, and kept the lowly low ... This is radical teaching. What shall we say of it? ... Has the teaching of Jesus on private property been superseded by a better understanding of the social value of property? Or has his teaching been suppressed and swamped by the universal covetousness of modern life? (p. 126)

In dealing with the social test of religion, Rauschenbusch notes:

> Religion may develop an elaborate social apparatus of its own, wheels within wheels, and instead of being a dynamic of righteousness in the natural social relations of men, its energies may be consumed in driving its own machinery ... It may then become an expensive consumer of social wealth ... a real hindrance of social progress. 22

III

In a view of Christianity which puts the idea of the Kingdom of God as its top priority and which unhesitatingly calls attention to the social causes of human problems, we also find, in the third place, in Rauschenbusch's thought, an unexampled and heightened sensitivity to the issues of human life and the world of nature.

He was sensitized to the fact of human suffering at several levels. He would have had no quarrel with the first Noble Truth of Buddhism, namely that one should come to recognize the pervasiveness of suffering, both obvious and hidden. But instead of finding the cause of that suffering in "attachment" or "clinging," as the Buddhist does, Rauschenbusch found that a major cause of suffering is linked to socio-economic factors. He did not believe in the omnicompetence of the social environment, as Marxists seem to. Rauschenbusch truly believed in the social gospel but also in a gospel for the individual. Those who give a strictly social view of human ills tend to overlook the internal ills of the individual. Rauschenbusch insisted that both areas need redemption. However, since there had been, historically speaking, such undue emphasis on salvation for the individual, he placed most of his stress on the social question. His Christian understanding alerted him to human need at several levels and sensitized him to needs which are still scarcely recognized by the majority of religious persons sixty years later. One of his prayers is for the idle rich "who have vigor of body and mind and yet produce no useful thing," and he asks God, "to forgive them for loading the burden of their support on the bent shoulders of the working world."[23]

He was far-seeing enough to separate the ethical insights of the Master from the eschatological emphasis one also finds commingled with the ethical pronouncements. He took the critical view that some of the utterances attributed to Jesus about the coming Judgment Day and the end of the world were not the central thrust of his teaching but rather reflected the biasses and attitudes of the early church which slipped in to the Gospel narratives. Whenever there was an apparent clash, he judged the teaching by the highest moral insights to be found in the whole message of Jesus. He taught that talk about the end of the world was really diversionary. It is instructive to note, by the way, how Albert Schweitzer dealt with this same dilemma - that is, between the direct ethical teachings of Jesus and assertions about the Judgment Day. Schweitzer did not disentangle the former from the latter. Instead, he proposed that the ethics of Jesus was really an "Interims-Ethik," conceived by Jesus as a way of life for those who envisioned the imminent end of the world. So, for Schweitzer, the radical aspect of Jesus' ethics was set aside, especially that dealing with the wealthy and those they oppressed. Rather, Schweitzer sought to capture the general spirit of compassion found in Jesus. It was that which drove him to Africa as an individualistic medical missionary. He never developed a social gospel. Indeed, Rauschenbusch apparently judged Schweitzer's theology in the way he might judge some contemporary academic theologians of the Tillich type.

> The professional theologians of Europe who all belong by kinship and sympathy to the bourgeois class, and are constitutionally incapacitated for understanding any revolutionary ideas, past and present, have overemphasized the ascetic and eschatological sayings ... [while the sayings] about property and non-resistance seem to them impractical and visionary. 24

Before the feminist movement got under way, Rauschenbusch was speaking and writing about a more Christian view of women and the family. "It is notorious that women are not on an equal footing with men in view of marriage."[25] His sensitivity is revealed in his prayers. One is for women who toil. Another, for mothers, reflects his awareness of "all the women who have yearnings of motherhood but whose lives are barren of its joys." He asks that they may find "an outlet for their thwarted mother love in the wider ministrations of all the lonely and unmothered hearts" in the great family of the earth.[26] Before there was much conscious concern for ecology, Rauschenbusch noted in one of his prayers, "We are wasting the resources of the earth in our headlong greed. We are poisoning the air of land by our lies and uncleanness." His plea is that when our use of the world is over we do not leave "anything ravished by our greed or spoiled by our ignorance."[27] Elsewhere: "In using up the resources of nature faster than we can replace them, we graft on our children for they will have to live in a land of wasted forests, gutted mines, and dried water courses."[28] Moreover, Rauschenbusch reverences animal life and prays, "May we realize that they live not for us alone but for themselves and for Thee, and that they love the sweetness of life even as we and serve Thee in their place better than we in ours."[29]

Of course, Rauschenbusch was a foe of the liquor traffic, something the European bourgeois mind can still scarcely understand. He saw the ruinous effects of alcohol on homes and especially on workingmen. He prayed: "May those who now entrap the feet of the weak and make their living by the degradation of men, thrust away their shameful gains and stand clear."[30] He took an open-eyed and scientific view of alcohol but also wrote: "Alcohol is a spirit born of hell, but he is merely a satellite and tool of a far greater devil, and that is Mammon."[30]

Though there is no straightforward teaching opposing racism, there is a sensitivity to the wrongs of the past. "We are sick at heart when we remember that by the greed of those who enslaved a weaker race [a] curse was fastened upon us all which still lies black and hopeless across our land."[31] His biographer says he never really became familiar with the problem enough to develop a basic position on it. He did, however, notice the dangers of Christianity being imposed by whites on others.[32] Nor do we find Rauschenbusch directly opposing the method of war in his major writings though he did recognize that Jesus "did not answer force by force, nor anger by anger."[33] He expressed the usual general distaste for the military, and recognized in 1917, the tremendous war profits of the corporations.[34] His strongest statement perhaps is this:

> When we comprehend how few wars have ever been fought for the sake of justice or the people; how personal spite, the ambition of military professionals, and the protection of capitalistic ventures are the real moving powers; how the governing classes pour out the blood and wealth of nations for private ends and exude patriotism like a squid secreting ink to hide its retreat - then the mythology of war will no longer bring us to our knees, and we shall fail to get drunk with the rest when martial intoxication sweeps the people off their feet. 35

We do know that Rauschenbusch joined the pacifist organization, The Fellowship of Reconciliation, in the last year of his life.

There is no question that the greatest sensitivity displayed by this noble leader was towards those who suffered under a relentless capitalism. "We cannot stand for poor and laborious people being deprived of physical stature, youth, education, human equality, and justice, in order to enable others to live luxurious lives."[36] If he were living today, he would see readily that the same situation obtains now when the Western nations enjoy luxuries at the expense of those living in misery in the so-called "Third World." With unabashed clarity he says: "If we can trust the Bible, God is against capitalism, its methods, spirits and results."[37] He reminds us of something still valid: "The bourgeois theologians have misrepresented our revolutionary God."[38] And one more quotation of relevance: "Upper class minds have been able to live parasitic lives without any fellow-feeling for the peasants or tenants whom they were draining to pay for their leisure."[39]

There is a deal of strong social criticism in the thought of Walter Rauschenbusch. When one finally awakens to the facts of social causality, the awareness that suffering and oppression are caused by systems and not just unfortunate occurrences, it is hard to retain much optimism or take the view of inevitable progress. Rauschenbusch has sometimes been charged with that latter position himself, but it does not take much reading to find out that Rauschenbusch did not believe that things would get better naturally or automatically. "We have to reckon," he says, "with the fact that there is such a thing as conscious, determined, malicious love of evil." And then on the next page: "The world will not evolve into a Kingdom of God by natural processes. It is uphill work. It is a battle. Every inch will have to be fought for."[40]

What does he offer as a sign of hope? He has taken what he calls a solidaristic view of society, what we would today call a communitarian view. He firmly believed that God was on the side of justice and that his way will ultimately triumph.

> To believe in the triumph of right against all appearances of defeat is the categorical imperative of faith. To deny the former is moral suicide. To surrender the latter is religious suicide. 41

We are told that the coming of World War I virtually broke Rauschenbusch's heart. What would he have said about World War II, the persecution of Jews and others in a mad scheme to promote racial purity? And what might he say in a world where nuclear power could literally lead to the end of all civilization and culture? He would no doubt continue his social analysis, noting imperialistic tendencies in East and West, noting the abject misery and hunger of millions in the Third World and how the wealthy nations exploit and oppress them, incessantly talking about freedom and opportunity. I am sure that he would have favored the work of Mahatma Gandhi and Martin Luther King, Jr., Archbishop Tutu and Archbishop Dom Helder Camara. He would see slight grounds for hope in the United Nations, but not in NATO or the Warsaw Pact. He would still put his trust in the possibility of the church as a redemptive agency in the world and he would welcome the recent work of far-seeing episcopal leaders in both the Roman Catholic and Protestant traditions. He would favor Ecumenism and be thankful for the strides thus far taken. And there is no question that he would oppose with intellectual and spiritual power the resurgence of ignorant individualism of the Fundamentalist type. Had he been alive in the 1950 period, there is no doubt that he would have been called before the Unamerican Activities Committee and/or Senator Joseph McCarthy. And he would have triumphed.

It is probably safe to say that Rauschenbusch's views on social religion are as relevant in broad outline today as they were seventy five years ago. They are still applicable and penetrating in their awareness of what is going on in the world. Indeed, they are necessary if there is to be any real hope for civilization.

NOTES

[1]M.L. King, Jr., Stride Toward Freedom (New York: Harpers, 1955), p. 91.

[2]Dores Sharpe, Walter Rauschenbusch (New York: MacMillan, 1942), p. xiii.

[3]Ibid., p. 13.

[4]W.G. Muelder, Religion and Economic Responsibility (New York: Chas. Scribners, 1953), p. 156.

[5]Sharpe, op. cit., p. 43.

[6]Ibid., p. 61.

[7]Walter Rauschenbusch, The Righteousness of the Kingdom, edited by Max Stackhouse (New York: Abingdon Press, 1968), pp. 80f. Hereafter referred to as ROK.

[8]Ibid., p. 81.

[9]Ibid., p. 87.

[10]Ibid., p. 93.

[11]Ibid., p. 268.

[12]Ibid., p. 100.

[13]Ibid., p. 110.

[14]See Sharpe, op. cit., pp. 203ff.

[15]Rauschenbusch, ROK, p. 129.

[16]Ibid., p. 128.

[17]Rauschenbusch, A Theology for the Social Gospel (New York: MacMillan Co., 1922), p. 154. Hereafter referred to as TSG.

[18]See Jones' Christ's Alternative to Communism (New York: Abingdon, 1935), and Is the Kingdom of God Realism? (New York: Abingdon, 1940).

[19]Rauschenbusch, ROK, p. 230.

[20]Ibid., p. 216.

[21]Sharpe, op. cit., p. 174.

[22]Rauschenbusch, The Social Principles of Jesus (New York: Methodist Book Concern, 1916), p. 142. Page citations in the text are references to this book.

[23]Rauschenbusch, Prayers of the Social Awakening (Boston: Pilgrim Press, 1910), p. 101. Hereafter referred to as PSA.

[24]Rauschenbusch, TSG, p. 158. An example of a contemporary German thinker who knows nothing whatsoever about the view of Rauschenbusch or the idea of ethical applications to society is Joachim Kahl, whose book The Misery of Christianity, trans. N.D. Smith (Harmondsworth: Penguin Books, 1971), is reacting to formal academic theology, not the vital view of Rauschenbusch.

[25]Rauschenbusch, ROK, p. 243.

[26]PSA, p. 93.

[27]Ibid., p. 48.

[28]Rauschenbusch, Christianizing the Social Order (New York: MacMillan, 1912), p. 254. Hereafter referred to as CSO.

[29]PSA, p. 48.

[30]CSO, p. 209.

[31]PSA, p. 114.

[32]TSG, p. 186.

[33]Ibid., p. 263.

[34]Ibid., p. 257 note.

[35]CSO, pp. 349f.

[36]TSG, p. 182.

[37]Ibid., p. 184.

[38]Ibid., p. 184. The only book that has come to my attention dealing with Rauschenbusch's thought from a German point of view is: R. Müller, Walter Rauschenbusch, Ein Beitrag zur Begegnung des deutschen und des amerikanischen Protestantismus (Leiden: E.J. Brill, 1957).

[39]TSG, p. 19.

[40]ROK, pp. 282f.

[41]Ibid., pp. 279f.

Sarah Chappell Trulove and James Woelfel

The Feminist Re-Formation of American Religious Thought

In our paper we have undertaken three tasks: first, to characterize the impact of feminist theological reflection upon contemporary American religious thought and practice; second, to describe major figures and themes in American feminist theology; and third, to locate American feminist theology as an American phenomenon within the historical context of some main emphases in American religious and feminist thought.

The Impact and Challenge of Feminist Theology in Recent American Religious Thought

The revival of feminism in the U.S. beginning in the 1960's has been marked, not only by movements for social and political change on a variety of fronts, but also by the emergence of new approaches to scholarship under the designation of women's studies. The past fifteen years or so have seen a kind of "explosion" of women's studies scholarship throughout the humanities and the social sciences and even in the natural sciences. In various ways women's studies scholarship has raised new critical questions about long-established assumptions, suggested fresh perspectives, and brought to light long-neglected historical resources and other data. Of no field is this more abundantly the case than religious studies.

Feminist religious studies have reflected, accompanied, and influenced institutional changes in American Christianity and Judaism, and many of the leading scholars in the field have been actively involved in those changes. The following are just some of the institutional changes: The number of female clergy and seminarians has increased dramatically over the past ten years, so that now half or more of the students at a number of Protestant theological schools, including some of the most distinguished in the

729

U.S., are women. This development, together with active feminist voices in most of the major Protestant denominations, has resulted in increasing representation by women not only as pastors of churches but also as national and regional denominational executives. The same period has seen the admission of women to ordination in the Episcopal Church and Conservative Judaism, the transformation and the "radicalization" of a number of Roman Catholic women's religious orders, and accompanying activity on behalf of the ordination of women to the Catholic priesthood. In 1984 a commission appointed by the National Council of Churches in the U.S. published the controversial "inclusive language" translation/paraphrase of the ecumenical lectionary of Bible readings for the Christian year. Also under N.C.C. auspices, a commission under the leadership of a distinguished male biblical scholar-translator, Bruce Metzger, has been at work for the past few years on a revised translation of the Christian Bible which eliminates gratuitously gender-exclusive translations of the Hebrew and Greek words used of both human beings and God. Accompanying these and other changes has been a good bit of literature directed to a Christian or Jewish audience, often at a semi-popular level.[1]

Women's studies scholarship in religion generally, and feminist theological criticism and construction specifically, have exerted an increasing and documentable influence upon the wider context of religious studies in the U.S. and the American theological community. In terms of sheer productivity, quite apart from critical and creative challenge, feminist religious scholarship simply cannot be ignored. A 1981 bibliography only of American feminist books and articles in Christian theology from 1970-1980 fills seven pages with single-spaced entries. The visibility and prominence of the "Women and Religion" section in the American Academy of Religion, the largest professional society in North America for scholars of religion, have increased dramatically in its fourteen year history. It numbers among its participants almost all the leading feminist religious thinkers in the U.S. Out of this group has come the recently established Journal of Feminist Studies in Religion, published by

Scholars Press. It is hardly an exaggeration to say that male scholars in religion and theologians who do not by this point take seriously, learn from, and incorporate women's studies scholarship will almost certainly be challenged - and not only by female scholars - regarding elements of bias and incompleteness in their assumptions, sources, methods, and conclusions. There are significant examples of male American philosophers of religion, theologians, and ethicists who have revised their thought and language through the impact of feminist scholarship, and many others whose research, reflection, and writing have been affected in varying degrees. Among male American scholars of religion whose work has been influenced by feminism and women's studies we might mention John B. Cobb, Jr., Tom Driver, William Phipps, J. A. Phillips, Leonard Swidler, Daniel Maguire, and Charles Hartshorne. Of these Phipps, Phillips, and Swidler have specifically made contributions to women's studies scholarship.[2]

Major Themes and Types of American Feminist Theology

Feminist theology may be defined as critical and constructive reflection on the images and ideas of religious traditions in dialectical relationship with women's experience. Judith Plaskow, a Jewish feminist scholar at Manhattan College, usefully characterizes the crucial phrase "women's experience." She uses the expression "women's experience" as the equivalent of Simone de Beauvoir's term "women's situation," which emphasizes the decisive role that socio-cultural circumstances have played in defining what it is to be female and male.[3] According to Plaskow, women's experience is made up of two dialectically interrelated aspects: (a) women's definition by men, who physically and ideologically have controlled human societies at least since very early times; and (b) women's experience of themselves in relation to male definition, which has ranged from passive accommodation to active resistance. Thus women's experience includes both self-alienation as the "Other" by the dominant male definitions of woman, and also struggles for liberation from those external norms. It encompasses both internalization of the myths of "femininity," and also empowerment to overcome them toward greater autonomy and wholeness.

Feminist theologies address both poles of women's experience. Rosemary Radford Ruether, Georgia Harkness Professor of Theology at Garrett-Evangelical Theological Seminary, has described the threefold task of feminist theology in the light of women's experience:

> First, there is a convincing demonstration that the androcentric and misogynist bias of the tradition is serious and constitutes a major flaw. Secondly, one needs to establish alternative norms and sources of tradition to challenge these biases. And, thirdly, one seeks a reconstruction or reenvisioning of the theological themes that will free them from these biases against women. 4

Thus the critical side of the feminist theological task is the documentation and exposure of women's marginalization and dehumanization in the religious traditions. To a very large degree this is directed to the biblical, Jewish, and Christian traditions. The constructive side involves both the historical recovery and the new creation of resources and criteria that affirm and empower the full humanity of women.

Those who engage in the work of feminist theology have shared together in the first task in Ruether's outline. It is with the second and third that they come to a parting of the ways. Thus we can speak of two main groups, each embracing much internal diversity, among feminist theologians: Jewish/Christian or "mainstream," and "post-Christian" or "neo-pagan." In what follows we will briefly characterize a few of the leading thinkers in both groups, focussing on Rosemary Ruether as the single most important figure in American feminist religious thought.

"Mainstream" theological feminism is critical and constructive reflection on the Jewish and Christian traditions carried on by women who themselves continue - however critically and at times tangentially - to be participants in those traditions. Jewish and Christian feminists believe that although the two traditions are heavily weighted by patriarchalism, they also embody in the form of "historical prototypes" experience of the divine as a presence and power in the world calling human beings into greater freedom and justice over against the many powers that oppress and enslave. Contemporary women's experience of empowerment and liberation is affirmed as both confirmation of that historical vision and the norm for interpreting its biblical and traditional manifestations. Jewish and Christian feminists thus see themselves as radical reformers of those religious traditions.

Judith Plaskow is perhaps the most visible and well-known of American feminist theologians who speak out of the Jewish tradition. Her feminist midrash on the ancient rabbinic legend of Lilith, Adam's first wife, has become celebrated and widely used in feminist religious circles. Plaskow retells the story of Lilith and Eve by making Lilith represent the repressed power and autonomy of women, which is feared and driven out by patriarchy and turned into a demonic power. The "return of Lilith" in this new telling is the story of women's reappropriation of their own repressed potential, narrated as a reconciliation and consciousness-raising between Lilith and Eve.[5] In her book Sex, Sin and Grace: Women's Experience and the Theologies of Reinhold Niebuhr and Paul Tillich, Plaskow shows through careful analysis that Niebuhr and Tillich neglect or distort the characteristically "feminine" sins of passivity and self-abnegation.[6]

Letty Russell has been prominent among American feminist and liberation theologians for more than fifteen years. She was ordained to the ministry of the Presbyterian Church in the U.S.A. in 1958, and served for seventeen years as a pastor in the East Harlem Protestant Parish in New York City. She has held a variety of positions with the Y.W.C.A., the National Council of Churches, and the World Council of Churches. Russell is Professor of the Practice of Theology at Yale Divinity School. Among "mainstream" feminist theologians she is one of the most solidly "mainstream," as her autobiographically-oriented essay "Authority and the Challenge of Feminist Interpretation" makes clear."[7] Russell's theology is thoroughly biblical and churchly in its outlook. She has been a leader in discussion and publication of feminist biblical interpretation, most recently in her editorship of the volume Feminist

Interpretation of the Bible, which grew out of a feminist hermeneutics project developed at meetings of the American Academy of Religion and the Society of Biblical Literature.[8] Acutely and critically aware of the patriarchal nature of the biblical texts, Russell nevertheless finds there a "liberating word" for all human beings: "... [The Bible's] authority for my life stems from its story of God's invitation to participation in the restoration of wholeness, peace, and justice in the world .... The particular interpretive key that assists me in continuing to give assent is the witness of scripture to God's promise (for the mending of creation) on its way to fulfillment."[9] Russell has also seen feminist theology as one form of liberation theology, and has stressed the inextricable connections between the liberation of women and the liberation of the poor and ethnic minorities. Her book Human Liberation in a Feminist Perspective - A Theology is perhaps the best example of her general liberationist perspective.[10]

Elisabeth Schüssler Fiorenza established herself as the leading feminist New Testament scholar in the U.S. with her substantial 1983 book In Memory of Her: A Feminist Theological Reconstruction of Christian Origins.[11] Fiorenza is a native of Germany and a Roman Catholic. Formerly on the faculty at the University of Notre Dame, she is currently Talbot Professor of New Testament at the Episcopal Divinity School. In her historical-critical work Fiorenza builds upon the work of form and redaction criticism, but she also brings to her examination of New Testament texts and Christian origins a social-historical perspective focussed on the role of women in the early church. Fiorenza finds in the canonical texts and in non-canonical sources evidences that the earliest Christian communities were characterized by a "discipleship of equals," and that women played important leadership roles. This revolutionary situation grounded in Jesus' own radicalism is only partly visible in the texts because early Christianity quickly lapsed into the patriarchalism characteristic of both Judaism and the surrounding pagan culture. Fiorenza's overarching hermeneutical context is a frankly feminist-theological one, a vantage point from which she exposes both the male bias and the pretense of theological neutrality in much biblical scholarship. In her more recent book, <u>Bread</u> <u>Not</u> <u>Stone:</u> <u>The</u> <u>Challenge</u> <u>of</u> <u>Feminist</u> <u>Biblical</u> <u>Interpretation</u>, Fiorenza elaborates more fully the hermeneutical principles and methodology embodied in <u>In</u> <u>Memory</u> <u>of</u> <u>Her</u>.[12] For Fiorenza the norms for faith and biblical interpretation are not to be found in the Bible itself. Radicalizing the Catholic principle that it is the church that creates and validates scripture, she locates the authority and criteria for biblical interpretation in the "church of women" or "women-church," which she defines as the faith-community of "self-identified women and women-identified men." Fiorenza writes, "The spiritual authority of women-church rests on the experience of God's sustaining grace and liberating presence in the midst of our struggles for justice, freedom, and wholeness of all."[13] Women-church derives its hermeneutical criteria

> <u>not</u> from the biblical writings, but from the contemporary struggle of women against racism, sexism, and poverty as oppressive systems of patriarchy and from its systematic explorations in feminist theory .... It does not understand the Bible as archetype but as historical prototype or as a formative root-model of biblical faith and life. Its vision of liberation and salvation is informed by the biblical prototype but is not derived from it. It places biblical texts under the authority of feminist experience insofar as it maintains that revelation is ongoing and takes place "for the sake of our salvation." 14

The Bible, then, is not a source but "an enabling resource" for women-church. Even the primitive "discipleship of equals" with its pattern of shared male and female leadership, which Fiorenza finds half-buried in the New Testament texts, is not an authority but an "open-ended paradigm." It is a historical example of women's self-affirmation, empowered by the liberating grace of God, which is an aspect of the biblical heritage contemporary women can lay claim to and celebrate.

Like Russell, Fiorenza identifies feminist theology as a critical liberation theology. In her own dialogue with other liberation theologies, she calls them to both a more serious recognition of the particular oppression of women among the poor and ethnic minorities, and a more critical hermeneutics which will spell out in just what senses the Bible is and is not supportive of human liberation.

In our opinion, "towering" over all her contemporaries is Rosemary Radford Ruether, whom we quoted above, Georgia Harkness Professor of Theology at Garrett-Evangelical Theological Seminary in Evanston, Illinois. In sheer productivity alone she outstrips her colleagues, but she is not to be measured by quantity but by her quality and breadth. Raised a pre-Vatican II Catholic, she was one of three sisters. Her mostly absent father died when she was twelve. Her intimate community was comprised mostly of women: her mother, her sisters, aunts, her mother's friends, and nuns. Although her upbringing was more or less traditional, it was a context in which women were strong and knew they had to be and could be. (The one exception to this was an uncle with some Jewish heritage, which may have initially sensitized her to the Jewish-Christian issue.) Educated in Catholic schools, Ruether went on to do her undergraduate work at Scripps College, a women's college in California. There she had a soundly classical and humanistic education. It was in her efforts to reconcile her traditional Catholic faith with the secular and "pagan" orientation of some of her mentors that she became interested in theology.

The summer before completion of her undergraduate degree she married Herman Ruether, a graduate student in Political Science at Claremont Graduate School. They married, she admits, without ever discussing the practicalities of marriage, such as home, children and careers. That the marriage has survived now thirty years is an accomplishment in itself. Herman Ruether is a scholar of Islam, and together they will be doing some collaborative teaching in Israel in the winter of 1987.

It was agreed that Rosemary would go on to complete her education, and in this decision she first encountered both academic and ecclesiastical disparagement of her goals. Ruether did her master's and doctoral degrees at Claremont in classics and patristics. Soon after marriage she was cautioned against the use of birth control methods, told bluntly by a priest that to practice family planning was to be "living in sin." This patriarchal control by the church over a woman's body was one of Ruether's first encounters with the oppression of women by the church, and this has remained an important issue throughout her feminist works. Primary to a holistic theology, she has argued, is the right of a woman to control her reproductive life. The academic world of her professors was more benign. While recognizing Ruether's abilities, they typically took it for granted that she would have children, be a homemaker, and use her education for the promotion of intellectual causes and witty conversation.

Following the completion of their degrees Herman Ruether found employment at an institution in the East, so the family - they now had three children - moved to the Washington, D.C. area where Ruether was hired first as a lecturer and then as a tenure-track faculty member in historical theology at Howard University School of Religion. Ruether remained there for ten years, a period interrupted by leaves to teach at Harvard and Yale.

One is tempted to divide Ruether's career into two periods at this point. The ten years at Howard were marked first by a considerable amount of research into the historical condition of women in Western religious tradition, and secondly by an activist participation in both the civil rights and peace movements. Another significant aspect of her work during this period was her work on Jewish-Christian relations, which is fully articulated in her 1974 book Faith and Fratricide: Theological Roots of Anti-Semitism.[15] In this and in other writings on the issue, Ruether faults the christological orientation of the Christian tradition as being the root cause of anti-semitism. By defining "messiah" over and against inherited Jewish tradition, the church has made scapegoats, enemies of the Jews.

It was also in this period that she wrote Liberation Theology: Human Hope Confronts Christian History and American Power.[16] Published in 1972, this book of essays reveals the range of Ruether's human commitments and scholarly concerns. It includes essays on feminism and the church, anti-semitism, black and Latin American liberation theologies, communitarian socialism, and ecology.

In 1976 Ruether edited and contributed to a book entitled <u>Religion</u> <u>and</u> <u>Sexism</u>: <u>Images</u> <u>of</u> <u>Woman</u> <u>in</u> <u>the</u> <u>Jewish</u> <u>and</u> <u>Christian</u> <u>Traditions</u>.[17] This became one of the early foundational texts in the burgeoning field of women's studies in religion. The book chronicles the historical marginalization and oppression of women in both Judaism and Christianity in all the major periods of their histories to the present time.

Ruether's move to Garrett-Evangelical Seminary in 1976 roughly marks what we believe to be an intensification of her focus on feminist theology, but not to the exclusion of other concerns. Indeed, all these concerns coalesce into a synthesis - a holistic theology which reinstates women as full and equal persons in all respects, but at the same time integrates the liberation from injustices of other oppressed groups and of nature itself. For patriarchal theology is specifically white Western male theology. In a recent article Ruether addresses the question of "The Future of Feminist Theology in the Academy." The question, she says,

> seems to suppose that there is one fixed thought-world called 'theology' and another called 'feminism,' and that one can then ask whether they have a future together. Theology is seen as something which can be defined without reference to feminism and vice versa. But any theology which can be defined without reference to feminism is a particular kind of theology, namely, patriarchal theology. Patriarchal theology is the kind of theology we have had in the past, a theology defined not only without the participation of women, but to exclude the participation of women ... to ask whether patriarchal and feminist theology have a future together is, to say the least, <u>grotesque</u> like asking whether Judaism and anti-semitism have a future together ... 18

Ruether's most systematic statement of her revisionary theology is set forth in her 1983 book <u>Sexism</u> <u>and</u> <u>God</u> <u>Talk</u>: <u>Toward</u> <u>a</u> <u>Feminist</u> <u>Theology</u>.[19] Ruether rejects any theology that presumes to "come from above." God/ess, as Ruether prefers to call deity, is available to us only through finite human imaging and understanding. Theology - whether in Scripture or interpretative tradition - is a product of human experience. As such, theology is validated through experience and codified. What is codified can cease to become meaningful, and when this occurs changes must take place. The protectors of the tradition, the codifiers, will try to protect what is fixed, which is what has occurred repeatedly over the centuries. Patriarchal theology, which is grounded in male experience, has systematically and at times ruthlessly excluded women's experience. Hence the principle on which we must evaluate all scripture and tradition is whether or not it marginalizes or distorts women.

A "first fault" of Christianity was the negation of the earth and all that entails. Straying from the Hebrew affirmation of earthly existence and nature as good, with God and humans in partnership, the early Christians incorporated the dualism reflected in Platonic tradition, including the association of the soul/body division with the difference between male and female. The female was identified with the body, and hence burdened with the logical implications of that association, such as irrationality, carnal propensity to evil, and the need to be subdued or conquered. This negation of the earth and focus on "heaven" has also resulted not only in the rape of women, but in the rape of earth as well. Ruether finds abundant evidence of all this in the Church Fathers, and of course in the Western world it found its most influential theological expression in Augustine, reinforced by the reproductive biology of Aristotle as reaffirmed by Thomas Aquinas and others.

As we have mentioned, Ruether views the early church's christological formation as historically devastating for Jews. She also sees it as destructive to women. To her, the error arises in the interpretation of Jesus as the one and only Christ in human history. Christianity sees Jesus as the true _imago Dei_, the type of authentic human nature, the unique example or model of human existence. Thus specifying Jesus, a male, as the true _imago Dei_ is a problem for women. Women cannot reflect or identify themselves in this divine-human ideal without denying, or attempting to deny (for it can never really be done), their female being. This is clearly seen in the traditional theology of women in the monastic life, in which women must become spiritually "male" in order to attain the monastic ideal. Ruether writes, "Christ as symbol is problematic for feminist theology ... feminist theology can affirm the person of Jesus of

Nazareth as a positive model of redemptive humanity, but only as partial and fragmentary ... other clues and models as well, models drawn from women's experience, from many times and cultures, must be used."[20]

The Virgin Mary has not traditionally been a positive model for women because the church has insisted on "desexing" her. However, Ruether believes that Mary can be favorably recast, basing her view on some positive interpretations in the gospel of Luke. So also can Mary Magdalene, who Fiorenza persuasively argues, on the basis of both biblical and non-canonical evidence, may have been a leader among the apostles in the early church.[21]

Like other feminist theologians, Ruether has also brought to the analysis of moral evil a fresh approach. She locates evil in false naming, projection, and exploitation, which constitute "the fundamental distortion and corruption of human relationality." "Evil comes about," she continues, "precisely by the distortion of the self-other relationship into the good-evil, superior-inferior dualism." "Conversion" from evil, metanoia, is receiving back the gift of community and mutual interdependence - of person with person and with nonhuman nature. Participation in this renewed community of creation is at the same time participation in community with God/ess.[22] Ruether documents the ways in which women have been peculiarly associated with evil in the Jewish and Christian traditions, as a manifestation of the fundamental evil of false naming, projection, and exploitation which distorts and destroys human community. For both women and men, conversion from evil "means a receiving of a grounded self that not only repudiates male group egoism but also overcomes the passivity that acquiesces to the group ego."[23]

Ruether's theological vision has many sources, Christian and non-Christian, and she is concerned to articulate a feminist theology that embraces both Jewish-Christian and neo-pagan themes. Central to her own perspective is the critical appropriation of what she calls the "prophetic principle" from the biblical heritage. She identifies four themes in the prophetic tradition: (a) God's identification with and vindication of the oppressed; (b) the critique of the dominant systems of power; (c) the vision of a new age of peace and justice to come; and (d) the critique of ideology, which historically is primarily religious.[24] But these principles must be universalized by feminism, in which patriarchy itself falls under "the Biblical denunciations of idolatry and blasphemy, the idolizing of the male as representative of divinity."[25]

We can only mention Ruether's most recent work here. She has continued to move more fully into stage three of the feminist theological agenda, the "reconstruction or reenvisioning of the theological themes that will free them from these biases against women." Her 1985 book Womanguides: Readings Toward a Feminist Theology is a collection of readings from the ancient Near East, early Christian sources, religious groups of the recent past, and contemporary writings that lay the groundwork for a new "canonical" foundation for feminist theology.[26] In her latest book, Women-Church: Theology and Practice, Ruether develops an ecclesiology for feminist religious communities that are emerging outside the framework of the institutional church.[27] In addition, she devotes a large portion of the book to bringing together liturgical texts and suggestions for such communities. These include, to cite a few examples, rites of healing for incest and rape victims and battered women, covenanting celebrations for both heterosexual and lesbian couples, a menopausal liturgy, and a "Hallowmas" liturgy in remembrance of the holocaust of women persecuted and killed as witches in late-medieval and Renaissance Europe. With these latest two books Ruether has ably demonstrated that her commitment as a religious feminist is in both range and depth not only a penetrating and original theoretical project but also an active involvement in concretely working to create new forms of faith community.

All feminist theologians, while clearly focussing on feminist issues, view the oppression and liberation of women as inextricably bound up with the oppression and liberation of minority groups and the poor. The approach of feminist theologians to the broader issues of injustice takes its orientation from a perspective articulated historically by Friedrich Engels: that the oppression of women was the original form of human oppression and the prototype for the others.[28] Christian feminist thinkers have perhaps been the most explicit on this score, closely linking Christian feminist activity with the struggles for empowerment of Black, Hispanic, and Native Americans and the poor of the Third World countries – struggles in which churches and religious leaders have of course often played a significant role. As we have seen, Ruether, Russell, and Fiorenza all view feminist theology as a form of liberation theology, and each devotes serious attention to critical dialogue and mutuality of task among liberation theologies.

In this connection it is worth noting that Dorothee Soelle, the German political theologian, has said that it was her experience in the United States that awakened her to feminist issues and their relationship to the issues of social justice and peace with which she had previously been identified. In her more recent writings Soelle has explicitly integrated feminist concerns into her Christian socialist-pacifist theological approach.[29]

Feminist religious thinkers in the "post-Christian" or "neo-pagan" group are persuaded that the Bible, Judaism, and Christianity are inherently and irredeemably patriarchal, and thus do not represent adequate religious alternatives for women who wish to affirm the full integrity of their experience within a context of "ultimate concern." Neo-pagan feminists seek to recover and reclaim ancient religious imagery and myth expressive of goddess worship, using the substantial research done in this area by feminist scholarship in religion, and to reinterpret these myths and symbols as resources for the full psychical affirmation by modern women of their own experience and worth. Let us look briefly at three prominent representatives of neo-pagan feminism.

Carol Christ is best known for her explorations of women's literature as "sacred texts" for the spiritual quest of contemporary women. Christ received her doctorate in religious studies from Yale in the early 1970's. It was she who organized a women's caucus at the 1971 national meeting of the American Academy of Religion, out of which came the Women and Religion section which we mentioned early in the paper. She has taught courses on women's literature and religion at Columbia University and the Pacific School of Religion, and has for several years been on the faculty of California State University at San Jose. Since 1981 Christ has spent her summers teaching about Greek goddesses at the Aegean Women's Studies Institute on the island of Lesbos. In a paper at last year's AAR meeting she told of her own spiritual "initiation" experiences at important goddess sites in Greece.

In her 1980 book Diving Deep and Surfacing: Women Writers on Spiritual Quest, Christ tells of how essential story is to human individual, social, and spiritual identity, and of how historically women have not been able to tell their own stories: "Women live in a world where women's stories rarely have been told from their own perspectives. The stories celebrated in culture are told by men. Thus men have actively shaped their experiences of self and world, and their most profound stories orient them to what they perceive as the great powers of the universe. But since women have not told their own stories, they have not actively shaped their experiences of self and world nor named the great powers from their own perspectives." [30] Christ recognizes that there are many women who are still able to locate themselves in the Jewish and Christian stories, but she is aware of many others (including herself) who cannot. Out of women's particular experiences of "nothingness" - self-abnegation, self-devaluation, and the many negative signals conveyed by family and culture - women can move to self-awakening and self-affirmation through seeing themselves and sharing in stories of other women. Christ describes this awakening as a new expression of mystical experience, in which women experience their grounding in nature and the community of other women. Like other feminist religious thinkers, she deliberately avoids being very specific about the nature of the "powers of being larger than the self" which women must learn to name through their own varied stories. Although Christ asserts that the powers are both without and within the self, she takes a generally functional and pluralistic approach to the nature of the divine. [31]

Likewise functionalist but explicitly reductionistic in her account of the divine in women's experience, Naomi Goldenberg is a kind of feminist Feuerbachian who translates theology into psychology – by which she means a revised version of classical depth psychology as represented, for example, by Carl Jung. Goldenberg did graduate study at Princeton and Yale, and also studied at the C.G. Jung Institute in Zürich. She teaches religious studies at the University of Ottawa in Canada, specializing in the psychology of religion, and is the author of Changing of the Gods: Feminism and the End of Traditional Religions. Believing that it is the psychological power of its images and symbols which constitutes the "reality" of a religious tradition, Goldenberg with characteristic bluntness writes: "Jesus Christ cannot symbolize the liberation of women. A culture that maintains a masculine image for its highest divinity cannot allow its women to experience themselves as the equals of its men. In order to develop a theology of women's liberation, feminists have to leave Christ and the Bible behind them."[32] Goldenberg argues that Christian feminists actually appeal to their own experience as religious authority rather than to Bible or church. With a certain logical sleight of hand she maintains that this "amounts to seeing theology in a more psychological sense, to transforming theology from theorizing about a god 'out there,' to reflecting on forces and values within human senses and feelings."[33] The depth and complexity of the human psyche is fully adequate to account for our gods and goddesses, who are "inner psychic forces" and in no sense external realities.

Goldenberg believes that it is depth psychology that can unify the diverse strands of feminist reflection in religion. While sharing in much of the feminist critique of Freud's theories regarding women, she finds in his studies of religion useful insights into the situation of women. She draws this conclusion: "Religions chiefly concerned with fathers and sons work greater harm on the intellects of women since such religions make resolution of the Oedipal complex even more difficult for women than it would normally be."[34] While Jung's analysis of healthy religion in terms of personal growth, self-affirmation, and non-dogmatism is much more positively useful to women, Goldenberg rejects his theory of archetypes as both intellectually dubious and, as applied to women, a restatement of the myth of the "eternal feminine." Goldenberg has been keenly interested in feminist witchcraft both as a feminist and as a psychologist, and her chapter on forms of contemporary <u>wicca</u>, which center in worship of the Goddess, is a good introduction to this new religious movement. She shows the variety of ways in which the rituals and outlook of feminist witchcraft are designed to express and enhance women's self-esteem and to facilitate their self-development.

Without any question, Mary Daly is the pre-eminent neo-pagan feminist and, with Ruether, the other "genius" of American feminist theology. Among secular feminists and, we understand, outside the U.S. Daly is almost certainly the best known religious feminist. In her relentless global exposure of the oppression of women past and present and her attempt to articulate a new women's culture with a new language, she is a leader and visionary of radical feminism. Daly grew up an Irish-American Roman Catholic, and holds doctorates in both philosophy and theology from the University of Fribourg in Switzerland. She teaches theology at Boston College. Unlike the other thinkers we have considered, Daly stands entirely aloof from the feminist group of the American Academy of Religion. While all the other feminist theologians feel that they must deal with Daly, she feels no need for reciprocity. Her writings, copiously footnoted, reveal a substantial and wide-ranging knowledge of historic and recent feminist literature on the one hand and of the Christian theological tradition on the other; but we look in vain for so much as a mention of any Jewish or Christian feminists. Among contemporary feminists Daly refers only to secular feminists such as Adrienne Rich and to "non-establishment" neo-pagan feminists such as Nelle Morton.

In her first book, <u>The Church and the Second Sex</u> (1968), written out of the creative theological ferment and hope unleashed by the Second Vatican Council, Daly took a reformist position, sharply calling the Catholic Church to account for its subordination and marginalization of women. Becoming increasingly radicalized during the early 1970's, Daly in 1975 wrote a new Preface to a new printing of the book in which she repudiated her position in it and referred to the author as if she were another person.[35]

Daly the radical post-Christian feminist first emerged in her 1973 book _Beyond God the Father: Toward a Philosophy of Women's Liberation_. It was the first in what has become, as of this writing, a trilogy of books each building upon the preceding one and developing more fully Daly's radical-feminist vision. _Beyond God the Father_ is a highly creative critique of Christian misogynism which ranges over just about all the relevant issues. Organized like a systematic theology, the book 'liberates' Christian doctrines by transposing them into fully universal and woman-affirming insights. In all her radical-feminist writings Daly insists that an ontology is essential to a truly whole feminist vision, and as a kind of philosophical "theologian" she has discussed this in terms of an understanding of the divine. Daly's thought in _Beyond God the Father_ is chiefly indebted to Paul Tillich, and her critical appropriation and revision of Tillich's thought continues to influence her later writings. Daly adapted his distinction between technical and ontological reason as basic to her method, and she also made use of his analysis of symbols. Of substantial importance was her creative reworking of Tillich's analyses of existential courage and the idea of God, as developed particularly in his book _The Courage to Be_.[36] As she wrote in _Beyond God the Father_: "The becoming who we really are requires existential courage to confront the experience of nothingness ... at this point in history women are in a unique sense called to be the bearers of existential courage in society .... This confrontation [by women] with the anxiety of nonbeing is revelatory, making possible the relativization of structures that are seen as human products and therefore not absolute and ultimate .... Courage to be is the key to the revelatory power of the feminist revolution."[37] In discussing the idea of God, Daly found in Tillich's characterization of God as "the ground and power of being" a view of God which not only transcends both gender and anthropomorphism but also grounds the empowerment of human beings through existential courage by which the threat of nonbeing is overcome and human potentialities are actualized. God as Being-itself is, according to Daly, God as dynamic intransitive Verb rather than static noun. "Be-ing," as she calls ultimate reality throughout her books, transcends and judges the many gods in whose names women have been oppressed.

With the publication of Gyn/Ecology: The Metaethics of Radical Feminism in 1978, Daly struck out in a more independent and singular direction in developing a feminist world-view.[38] Here she first exhibited her now-celebrated preoccupation with etymological word play and the creation of a revolutionary female language. Although the result can be initially exasperating to read, one is drawn into an enormously imaginative linguistic effort which brings alive old words and stimulates with new ones. Gyn/Ecology is mostly a devastating chronicle of historic and contemporary atrocities against women, including Indian suttee, Chinese footbinding, European witchburning, and modern American gynecological medicine and psychotherapy. In the latter part of the book Daly begins to show, through the metaphors of "spooking," "sparking," and "spinning," how women can, in community with one another, liberate the "wild Goddess" who is the dynamic power of Be-ing in their true Selves. Daly draws substantially on ancient legends of goddesses, and "a-mazes," as she would put it, their patriarchal interpretations. What she is calling for is a feminist revolution of withdrawal from and refusal of oppression by a male-dominated world.

In Daly's most recent book, Pure Lust: Elemental Feminist Philosophy, she "pulls all the stops out." It is an imaginative tour de force which is nevertheless replete with learned sources. Here Daly charts a pilgrimage for "Nag-Gnostic Nags" through three realms of "spheres"; (a) Archespheres, in which women "shrink the alienating archetypes drawn by drones and dangled by flashers to fix/frame women in amnesic oblivion"; (b) Pyrospheres, where with "ontological Passion" women begin a new naming of virtues and

vices, purifying themselves of "the vestiges of demonic domestica-
tion"; and (c) Metamorphospheres, where women explore the three
States of Grace: "Be-Longing, Be-Friending, and Be-Witching."[39]
Characteristically, Daly buries in a long footnote in Pure Lust an
important account of how her view of "Be-ing" or ultimate reality
has developed. She describes how she has moved from the symbol
"God" as Verb to the metaphor "Goddess" as Verb. She has also
moved from speaking in the singular of "power of Be-ing" to the
plural form "powers of Be-ing," which she believes give more
adequate emphasis to the "multiple aspects of transcendence." This
raises the central problem of the one and the many, which Daly
takes quite seriously. She remarks that some feminists speak of
Goddesses. Daly herself opts for an ultimate unity manifesting itself
in multiplicity: "It would be foolish to speak of 'Be-ings.' But
women can and do speak of different Powers and manifestations of
Be-ing, which are sometimes imaged as Goddesses."[40]

American Feminist Theology as an American Phenomenon: Historical Context and Interpretation

The causes of the renascence of American feminism in the 1960's and
1970's are complex, but the immediate background is to be found in
social, political, and economic phenomena of the 1950's and 1960's:
prominent among them the continuing growth of the percentage of
women in the labor force following its dramatic increase during
World War II, medical and social developments making for greater
reproductive freedom for women, and the civil rights and anti-war
movements.[41] What is striking about contemporary American feminism
is the rapidity with which it has affected our laws, institutions,
and public consciousness.[42]

American feminist scholarship in religious studies had its
beginnings in the 1960's, but emerged decisively in the 1970's.[43]
The theological context in which feminist theology arose in the U.S.
was a richly pluralistic one, embodying the legacies of both pre-
and post-World War II developments in American religious thought.
Theology in the U.S. has long been characterized by a wide range of

perspectival and methodological options, paralleling and reflecting somewhat America's sprawling institutional religious pluralism.

We have noted Tillich's influence on Mary Daly's thought. In _Beyond God the Father_ she also acknowledged the significance of Whiteheadian "process" thought for a feminist theology.[44] Some feminist theologians have seen in process thought an ontological analysis which they believe is not only the most generally adequate available but also peculiarly supportive of a feminist vision of God, human beings, and their relationship. Central here is the understanding of God not in the traditional "monopolar" way as omnipotent Creator but as the inherently relational One who "calls" humans and all creatures to the fullest actualizing of potentialities and the greatest enrichment of experience. Among the feminist religious thinkers who work within a process theological framework we might mention Marjorie Suchocki, Dean of Wesley Theological Seminary, and Sheila Devaney of Iliff School of Theology.[45] The "death of God" theologies of the 1960's have influenced feminist religious thought less as a theological framework and methodology than as the announcement of a theme which feminist theologians have reaffirmed in a way that Thomas Altizer and William Hamilton did not envision. The God whose death is now proclaimed is the God of patriarchal power, hierarchy, and natural/supernatural dualism, whose existence is incompatible with the dignity and empowerment of over half the human race.

We have looked briefly at some links between contemporary American feminist religious thought and its immediate theological background. If time and space permitted, it would be illuminating to trace similar connections with dominant trends in both Protestant and Roman Catholic thought in the twentieth century, such as "neo-orthodox" theology, developments in biblical criticism, and post-Vatican II Catholic theology. It is clear, for example, that feminist biblical scholars such as Fiorenza have built significantly upon the work of form and redaction criticism and the more recent social-historical methods; that theologians such as Ruether are indebted to the recovery of the normativity of the prophetic tradition by twentieth century liberal, "neo-orthodox," and biblical theologies; and that Catholic feminist thinkers generally have appealed to the newer official emphases on the church as semper reformanda, the communal process and the essential role of the laity, the modernizing and democratizing of the religious orders, the importance of conscience and personal responsibility in ethics and the religious life, and dialogue both with other religious traditions and with modern secular life and thought. In all these areas feminist theologians have exhibited a sovereign freedom, creatively reshaping and carrying forward even as they build upon previous work. We have noted this also in reporting on the current dialogue between feminist theologies and other liberation theologies.

Finally, and very briefly, we want to call attention to certain aspects of nineteenth-century American feminist and religious thought as historical background to contemporary American feminist theology. The search for connections here becomes more speculative, and we must speak less of direct causal influences and more of intellectual-historical context and tradition. This is particularly the case with nineteenth-century American religious thought, in which "experience" became a distinctive motif and central theological category. In the case of nineteenth-century feminist thought the causal links are more explicitly acknowledged by current feminist religious thinkers. We believe, however, that both phenomena established a distinctively American historical context for the emergence of some of the most characteristic features of American feminist theology.

The feminist movement in nineteenth-century America was rooted in the egalitarian natural rights tradition enshrined in the Declaration of Independence. The early leaders of the women's movement, whose chief opponents were clergymen who quoted the authority of the Bible against them, were also keenly aware that they had to develop a new "liberationist" biblical hermeneutics. Both the extension of natural rights egalitarianism to women and the wresting of biblical interpretation away from their opponents are evident in the Declaration of Rights and Sentiments adopted by the first Women's Rights Convention in Seneca Falls, New York, in 1848.

The Declaration is in part a revision of the Declaration of Independence, and asserts that "woman is man's equal - was intended to be so by the Creator."[46] The preoccupation with a "revisionist" hermeneutics that could find biblical basis for the equality and empowerment of women can also be clearly seen in the writings of the Quaker abolitionist and feminist Sarah Grimke. In her Letters on the Equality of the Sexes and the Condition of Woman, she reinterpreted the Genesis stories of the creation of the first human beings and took on St. Paul, the chief source of the prevailing case for the subordination of women. Grimke frankly wrote that Paul's "mind was under the influence of Jewish prejudices respecting women."[47]

But it was Elizabeth Cady Stanton who was the most radical on the question of women and Scripture. Against the pleas of many of her associates in the women's movement at the end of the nineteenth century, including her long-time friend Susan B. Anthony, Stanton, with the help of a committee of feminists interested in religious issues, published The Woman's Bible in 1895 and 1898.[48] Here she marshalled and commented critically on biblical passages regarding women. We find among contemporary feminist theologians, particularly Christian feminists such as Ruether, Fiorenza, and Russell, clear indications of their appeal to both the liberal-egalitarian American political tradition and the heritage of American feminist biblical hermeneutics.

The historic emphasis on "experience" as theological source and validation in American religious life and thought must also, we believe, be seen as an important tradition in the background of American feminist religious thought even if the links are less explicitly acknowledged. It is instructive in this regard to come to a reading of William Clebsch's book American Religious Thought: A History from an immersion in contemporary feminist theology. Clebsch focusses on the centrality of the category of "experience" in American religious thought as seen particularly in three of America's most creative and influential religious thinkers: Jonathan Edwards, Ralph Waldo Emerson, and William James. Clebsch introduces his subject in this way:

> ... the religious experience of America has been emphatically more voluntary than organic, more diverse than standard, more personal than institutional, more practical than visionary or (in that sense) mystical.
>
> And the thought that has reflected on this American religious experience has typically asked what went on when people acted religiously. It has subordinated strictly theological questions about God to more experiential ones about men and women. Americans like to solve more than they like to concoct problems, and American religious thinkers typically adjusted their ideas of deity to religious experience, not vice versa .... Typically they construed religious experience as really saving men and women (however transitorily or permanently) from otherwise insoluble difficulties, symbolized perhaps by Satan, perhaps by spiritual mediocrity, perhaps by divided selves. Typically they avoided extreme intellectualism and extreme emotionalism, rather conjoining the head and the heart as twin seats of religious experience. ... And typically they interpreted religious experience as coming to terms with, not as escaping from the whole of mankind's environing universe. 49

With little alteration this statement by Clebsch could describe the constructive side of the agenda of contemporary American feminist theologians.

Furthermore, to read through Clebsch's accounts of Emerson and James and then to go back to their own writings is to be reminded that some of our greatest religious thinkers have also been our most radical in terms of breaking through conventions and entirely rethinking the questions of God and faith in connection with human experience. It is specifically to become aware of fascinating parallels between Emerson's and James's methods and conclusions and those of current feminist religious thought. For example, Emerson on God or the "Over-Soul" and self-reliance breathes a spirit very similar in some ways to Mary Daly on Be-ing manifesting itself as the empowering "Background" or "Goddess" in women's Selves.[50] Of course Emerson was attempting to write "generically," which meant obliviously with regard to women's issues; and the parallels in feminist theology must always be seen as creative extensions and "uncoverings." Will James's "radical empiricism," his exploration of the crucial role of belief in shaping the human world, his indissoluble connection of deity with human experience, need, and affirmation, and his testing of religious experience by its fruits, all make contact with presuppositional and methodological aspects of American feminist religious thought.[51]

Twentieth-century developments in empiricist religious thought in the U.S., epitomized in the empirical theology of Henry Nelson Wieman, of course have their roots in the work of Will James and John Dewey along with Whitehead. Fruitful points of contact with feminist theology also exist here, as for example in the understanding of God as what actually operates in human experience to transform individual and social life into greater good. This whole question of the links between the emphasis on the key role of experience in religion and theology in the American theological tradition and contemporary American feminist theology seems to us one that is well worth exploring in much greater depth and detail. But such a task must await another paper ... and perhaps other researchers!

NOTES

[1]See, e.g., Regina Coll, ed., Women and Religion: A Reader for the Clergy (New York: Paulist Press, 1982); Madonna Kolbenschlag, Kiss Sleeping Beauty Good-Bye (New York: Bantam Books, 1981); Letty M. Russell, ed., The Liberating Word: A Guide to Nonsexist Interpretation of the Bible (Philadelphia: Westminster Press, 1976); and Rachel Conrad Wahlber, Jesus According to a Woman (New York: Paulist Press, 1979).

[2]See John A. Phillips, Eve: The History of an Idea (New York: Harper & Row, 1984); William Phipps, Influential Theologians on Wo/man (Washington: University Press of America, 1981); and Leonard Swidler, "Jesus Was a Feminist," The Catholic World, Jan. 1971, 177-183, and Woman in Judaism (Metuchen, N.J.: The Scarecrow Press, 1976).

[3]Plaskow develops her analysis of women's experience as the first chapter of her book Sex, Sin and Grace: Women's Experience and the Theologies of Reinhold Niebuhr and Paul Tillich (Washington: University Press of America, 1980); see also Beauvoir, The Second Sex, trans. and ed. H.M. Parshley (New York: Random House, 1952), esp. ch. XXI.

[4] Ruether, "Feminist Theology," unpublished forthcoming encyclopedia article, typescript p. 2.

[5] Plaskow, "Epilogue: The Coming of Lilith," in Rosemary Radford Ruether, ed., Religion and Sexism: Images of Woman in the Jewish and Christian Traditions (New York: Simon & Schuster, 1974), pp. 341-343.

[6] See, e.g., pp. 62-73 and 109-120.

[7] In Letty M. Russell, ed., Feminist Interpretation of the Bible (Philadelphia: Westminster Press, 1985), pp. 137-146.

[8] In her Foreword to this volume of essays Russell describes the process by which they were produced.

[9] Feminist Interpretation of the Bible, pp. 138-139.

[10] (Philadelphia: Westminster Press, 1974).

[11] (New York: Crossroad Press, 1983).

[12] (Boston: Beacon Press, 1984).

[13] Bread Not Stone, p. xvi.

[14] Bread Not Stone, p. 14.

[15] (New York: Seabury Press, 1974).

[16] (New York: Paulist Press, 1972).

[17] See f.n. 5.

[18] In Journal of the American Academy of Religion 53:4 (Dec. 1985), 703-713.

[19] (Boston: Beacon Press, 1983).

[20] Sexism and God-Talk, p. 115.

[21] Sexism and God-Talk, pp. 139-158. See Fiorenza, In Memory of Her, pp. 304-307, 315-334.

[22] Sexism and God-Talk, p. 163.

[23] Sexism and God-Talk, p. 191.

[24] Sexism and God-Talk, p. 24.

[25] Sexism and God-Talk, p. 23.

[26] (Boston: Beacon Press, 1985).

[27] (New York: Harper & Row, 1985).

[28] Friedrich Engels, The Origin of the Family, Private Property, and the State, trans. Ernest Untermann (Chicago: Charles Carr & Co., 1902).

[29] See, e.g., the following recent books by Soelle: Revolutionary Patience, trans. Rita and Robert Kimber (Maryknoll: Orbis Books, 1977); Choosing Life, trans. Margaret Kohl (Philadelphia: Fortress Press, 1981); The Arms Race Kills: Even Without War, trans. Gerhard A. Elston (Philadelphia: Fortress Press, 1983); Of War and Love, trans. Rita and Robert Kimber (Maryknoll: Orbis Books, 1983); The Strength of the Weak: Toward a Christian Feminist Identity, trans. Rita and Robert Kimber (Philadelphia: The Westminster Press, 1984); and (with Shirley A. Cloyes) To Work and to Love: A Theology of Creation (Philadelphia: Fortress Press, 1984).

[30] (Boston: Beacon Press, 1980), p. 4.

[31] Diving Deep and Surfacing, esp. pp. 9–11.

[32] Changing of the Gods (Boston: Beacon Press, 1979), p. 22.

[33] Changing of the Gods, p. 24.

[34] Changing of the Gods, p. 32.

[35] (Boston: Beacon Press). Yet another edition has appeared, this one in 1985, which includes not only the 1975 "Feminist Postchristian Introduction" but also a new "Archaic Afterwords."

[36] (New Haven: Yale University Press, 1952).

[37] (Boston: Beacon Press, 1973), pp. 23 and 24.

[38] (Boston: Beacon Press, 1978).

[39] (Boston: Beacon Press, 1984), pp. 31–32.

[40] Pure Lust, p. 423.

[41] Although Simone de Beauvoir's The Second Sex was published in 1949, the book which really both signalled and documented the renascence of feminism in the U.S. was Betty Friedan's 1963 book The Feminine Mystique (New York: Dell).

[42] Three examples among many others which might have been cited are (a) the 1973 Supreme Court decision in Roe v. Wade making abortion a Constitutional right; (b) the dramatic growth in the numbers of women entering the professions and active in organized

sports, both strongly encouraged by federal legislation; and (c) the fact that in a recent poll commissioned by Newsweek magazine and published in its March 31, 1986 issue, 54% of all women surveyed considered themselves feminists; the figure was even higher (64%) for non-white women. Of course, people mean different things when they use the term "feminist"; but considering the negative connotations the word has had for many what is noteworthy is that more than half the American women surveyed were willing to identify themselves with it.

[43] An early article by Valerie Saiving Goldstein, "The Human Situation: A Feminine View," appeared in 1960 and has been seen by more recent feminist theological writers as a pioneering essay (Journal of Religion 40 [Apr. 1960], 100–112); Daly's The Church and the Second Sex (1968) was probably the first major work of feminist theology.

[44] Beyond God the Father, p. 188.

[45] See, e.g., Suchocki, God-Christ-Church: A Practical Approach to Process Theology (New York: Crossroad, 1982).

[46] Reprinted in Leslie B. Tanner, ed., Voices from Women's Liberation (New York: New American Library, 1970), pp. 43–47.

[47] Letter XIII, in Letters on the Equality of the Sexes and the Condition of Woman (Boston: Isaac Knapp, 1838); reprinted in Martha Lee Osborne, ed., Woman in Western Thought (New York: Random House, 1979), pp. 98–104.

[48] Elizabeth Cady Stanton et al., The Woman's Bible (New York: European Publishing Co., 1895 and 1898).

[49] American Religious Thought (Chicago: University of Chicago Press, 1973), pp. 3–4.

[50] See Clebsch, pp. 98–99, 108–109.

[51] See Clebsch's discussion of James, esp. pp. 148–170; see also Daly's appreciative reference to and appropriation of James's approach to religion in Beyond God the Father, p. 21. James's legacy can also be seen indirectly in the generally "Kuhnian" epistemology used by feminist theologians. See Fiorenza, Bread Not Stone, pp. 48–49; and Sallie McFague, Metaphorical Theology: Models of God in Religious Language (Philadelphia: Fortress Press, 1982), ch. 3.

Donald L. Turner

The Influence of Some American Religious Groups on Free and Sectarian Religion in Germany

Historical Background

Christianity came to Germany during the third century with the erection of three Catholic episcopal seas, but it did not become dominant until after the conversion of the Frankish king, Clovis, in 496. In the 6th century, Scottish-Irish missionary monks were active. In 722, Boniface became archbishop without a fixed sea, and he dedicated himself to the conversion of the German people. Charlemagne tried to force christianization by the sword, but peaceful means were advocated by his son Louis the Pious. Long term conflicts with the papacy over the mutual responsibilities of church and state were largely resolved by the Concordat of Worms in 1122. Saxony was christianized by the end of the 12th century, and Christianity was extended to the northeast through the military campaigns of the Order of Teutonic Knights.

In 1415, John Huss was burned at the stake because of his critical attitude towards the abuses of the Roman Church, and a century later Martin Luther issued his 95 theses at Wittenberg, marking the start of the Protestant Reformation. Sparked in part by the presence of the Turks in Vienna, the Peace of Augsburg in 1555 provided for an agreement that the faith of a principality would be either Lutheran or Catholic as determined by its leader.

The Thirty Years' War (1618–1648) was fought between Catholic and Protestant princes to determine what religion was to be dominant. The war devastated Germany, reducing the population from 16 to 6 million and virtually destroying commerce and intellectual life. The Peace of Westphalia again accorded the princes the right to determine the religion of their subjects, with the reformed tradition of Calvin and Zwingli also added as an acceptable form of Protestantism.

The religious unity of the German territorial states remained largely unchanged until the time of Napolean when numerous small states were amalgamated into larger political units characterized by greater religious heterogeneity. After World War I and the fall of the monarchy, the Protestant territorial churches lost their political supremacy, although they continued to count as their membership a majority of the population. The Nazis attempted to create a united Protestant church under government control, but the move was unsuccessful.

In the Federal Republic today, without the overwhelming Protestant areas now comprising East Germany, the balance between Protestants and Roman Catholics is nearly equal with Protestants accounting for about 49 per cent of the population and Roman Catholics about 47 per cent. A small fraction of the population belongs to any one of about 260 other religious groups.[1] In recent years, the number of people professing no religion has been increasing because of two reasons: a general slackening of religious loyalties and as a means of avoiding the church tax, a leftover of Bismarckian Germany requiring a citizen to pay a certain surcharge on his income tax to either the territorial Protestant Church or the Roman Catholic Church. In order to avoid the tax, a citizen must renounce his affiliation to the church before a civil authority. There is no evidence to indicate that any significant number of people who leave the established churches to avoid taxation join one of the independent groups whose members are not obligated to pay the church tax.

Roughly speaking, the independent religious groups are divided into free churches (freie Kirchen) and sects (Sekten). Free churches are "churches and associations which have arisen out of an effort to renew the congregational life of the primitive church and to which ecumenical contacts exist or are possible."[2] Examples of free churches are: The Federation of Evangelical-Free Church Congregations (Baptists), The Evangelical-Methodist Church, The Religious Society of Friends, The Pentecostal Societies, The Mennonite Church, and the Churches of Christ. Sects are "societies which mix Christian traditions with sources of revelation which are not biblical, and as a rule, ecumenical contacts are rejected."[3] Examples of sects are: Association of Seventh Day Adventists, Christian Science, The Church of Jesus Christ of Latter-day Saints, Unitarians, Jehova's Witnesses, The World Wide Church of God (Armstrong), and the New Apostolic Church. Some of the independent religious groups in Germany have a long tradition going back to the Reformation, but the majority of them have been imported from America. In this paper, I should like to look at four of those groups in some detail - one free church, The Evangelical-Methodist Church, and three sects, The Seventh-Day Adventists, The Mormons, and The Jehova's Witnesses.

The Evangelical-Methodist Church[4]

Considered historically, Methodism in Germany is largely a repercussion of German emigration to America in the 18th and 19th centuries. Methodism in colonial America not only reached Anglo-Americans but also other immigrants. One group of immigrants, upon whom the movement was to have a profound influence, was the Germans. Francis Asbury and other circuit riders often went through German settlements in Pennsylvania, Maryland, and Virginia, as well as New York. Many Germans heard the Methodist preachers and were converted by them, and they, in turn, became preachers and preached in both German and English. One of them, Heinrich Böhm, reports in his memoirs that great meetings were held on his father's farm in the open-air or in a barn, and one of the pioneers of American Methodism would preach in English and one of the German preachers would continue in the German language.[5]

German Methodist congregations were not formed because Asbury felt that German immigration had reached a climax and that the German language would soon die out in America. Many of the Germans who had been influenced by the Methodist revival preferred to remain in their own Lutheran, Reformed, or Mennonite congregations. Two new denominations were, however, formed by Germans who had been influenced by Methodism: the United Brethren in Christ and the Evangelical Church.

During the 19th century great masses of Germans emigrated to America and settled down in the states of the Midwest. It was soon realized that they needed spiritual guidance and that this guidance should be in the German language. The Methodists chose Wilhelm Nast to start work among the German immigrants, and Nast is considered the father of German Methodism.

Wilhelm Nast was born in 1807 in Stuttgart. As a youth, he was deeply religious, and it was his wish to prepare for missionary service. His family, however, felt he should serve the territorial Lutheran Church in Württemberg and sent him to Tübingen to study theology. While at Tübingen, he experienced a spiritual crisis when he was confronted with rationalistic philosophy. He finished his studies but did not embark on a career as a Lutheran pastor. In 1828, he emigrated to America and took on a position as private tutor in the house of a pious Methodist widow. In the following years, he taught German at West Point Military Academy, and in 1832, he went to Gettysburg, Pennsylvania, where he taught Hebrew at the Lutheran Seminary. Soon thereafter, he joined the faculty of Kenyon College in Ohio. Nast often attended Methodist services, but it was not until 1835 that he had a conversion experience. From then on he dedicated himself to preaching the Gospel among the Germans in Cincinnati, Columbus, and other towns in Ohio.[6]

Until the union in 1897, Methodism in Germany existed in two independent, but closely connected groups: the Wesleyan Association (Wesleyanische Gesellschaft) and the Methodist Episcopal Church (Bischöfliche Methodistenkirche).

The founder of the Wesleyan Association was Christoph Gottlob Müller (b. 1785). In 1806, Müller emigrated to England to avoid being drafted into the army. Homesick and fed up with the superficial hedonistic life of his contemporaries, he one day attended services at the Wesleyan Chapel in Great Queen Street in London and was converted. He joined the congregation and quickly became an exhorter and class leader. Because Württemberg passed an amnesty law in 1815, he was allowed to visit his homeland again. In his father's house, where a group of Herrenhuter met, he told of his own conversion, and his simple testimony led to a number of conversions. The same thing happened the following years when Müller returned to Germany to visit his family. The year 1830 was especially successful because a large number of conversions took place, causing Winninden, a small town near Stuttgart, to become a center of Methodist revival in Germany.

In spite of many requests to stay in Winninden, Müller returned to England, and the local Lutheran pastor took over the care of the group. Müller's friends, however, requested the Wesleyan Missionary Society in London to send him back to Germany as a missionary. After being convinced that this was a divine call, he decided to return to Germany in 1832. His return was the cause of great joy – but also some disappointment, because the relationship to the territorial church became clouded. Like Wesley, Müller never thought of forming a new church, and he always urged his followers to attend the services of the territorial church and to partake of the sacraments there. His work was, however, severely criticized, and sometimes even police force was used against him. The work continued to spread though, and by the year 1848, there were about 1100 Wesleyans in Württemberg. Müller died on the 17th of March 1852.

In the years following Müller's death, while activities remained under the direction of the Wesleyan Missionary Society, Methodism in Württemberg remained in the territorial Protestant Church. In the spring of 1872, however, a law was passed in Württemberg allowing for freedom of religion, thus opening the way for an independent church. On the 17th of June, 1875, eight ministerial candidates, all of whom had served many years as lay preachers were ordained, and the Wesleyan Association became a free church in Württemberg.

The American form of Methodism, episcopal Methodism, was brought to Germany by Ludwig Sigismund Jacoby. Jacoby was born on the 21st of October, 1813, into a Jewish family, but in 1835, he joined the Lutheran Church. He emigrated to America in 1838 and settled down in Cincinnati where he became acquainted with William Nast. He started attending the Methodist Church and underwent a conversion experience on New Year's Eve in 1839. In 1841, he was sent to minister to the German population of St. Louis. Nast had long felt that the Methodists should send missionaries to Germany, and Jacoby was chosen as the first. On the 23rd of December, 1849, he delivered the first Methodist sermon in Bremen to a congregation numbering about 400. The first Sunday school was held in the summer of 1850, and about 80 children were present; a few weeks later the number had grown to over 300.

Jacoby's ill health did not allow him to accept the many invitations he received to preach in other areas of Germany, and it was left to others to spread Methodism to the south and to the east. The brothers Erhard and Friedrich Wunderlich carried on Methodist activities in Saxony. Erhard had become a Methodist in America, and in 1850, he returned to his birthplace, Rüßdorf, to engage in missionary activities. He became disgusted because of the many obstacles placed in his way by the territorial church, however, and returned to America after serving only two years in Germany. His brother Friedrich took up the work, and because of his continued efforts, Saxony became one of the main centers of German Methodism.

In 1897, the Wesleyan Association and the Methodist Episcopal Church in Germany joined together under the latter's name. In spite of resistance by the territorial Protestant churches, it continued to grow, making especially significant gains in the periods following the two world wars. Its relation to the territorial Protestant churches today is very good, and intercommunion exists.

Prior to 1936, the American church sent bishops to Germany, but in that year, the German church won the right to elect its own bishop. He is, however, a member of the American Council of Bishops. The government of the church is very similar to that of the American church with area conferences, annual conferences, and a central conference which meets every four years and is the highest legislative body of the church. The church maintains two theological seminaries, one at Frankfurt which is also owned by the Swiss Methodist Church, and one which was organized in 1950 in Klosterlausnitz in the German Democratic Republic. The church is very interested in social work and has about 1200 deaconesses engaged in social services. In 1968, it joined with the United Brethren Church under the name of the Evangelical Methodist Church and today has about 60,000 members in the Federal Republic and about 30,000 in the German Democratic Republic.

Seventh-Day Adventists[7]

Missionary activity in Germany on the part of the Seventh-Day Adventists began relatively late. Eight persons had become Adventists in 1876 and were baptized by the Swiss preacher Jacques Erzberger, but missionary activities did not begin until after Ellen G. White visited Germany in 1887. In 1888, the Adventists began handing out printed material in Germany, and in the same year, the General Conference in America approved of funds and missionaries for further work in the country. Several missionaries arrived in Hamburg in 1889, and a congregation of about 25 members was formed. Hamburg has remained a center of Seventh-Day Adventist activities, the publishing house being located there in 1895.

Germany was organized as an independent missionary field in 1891, the same year the German Adventists formed the German Union Conference (Deutsche Unionskonferenz) with 2,387 members. By the end of 1913, there were 14,263 Adventists in Germany, and 25 years later, the figure stood at 36,820.

During the period of National Socialism, the Adventists were able to continue their work but only under severely limited conditions. American missionaries were, of course, expelled from the country. Because of the Nazis' desire to purify everything from the "Jewish Spirit," expressions such as "Sabbath," "Sabbath-school," etc. had to be changed. During World War II, over 450 chapels and meeting places as well as the publishing house in Hamburg were destroyed, but they have all been reconstructed. The total membership rose after 1945 to about 40,000 in both parts of Germany, but since then it has been slowly declining. In 1983, there were about 25,000 members in the Federal Republic and about 10,000 in East Germany.

Here in the Federal Republic, the church is organized in the West German Union with headquarters in Hannover and the South German Union with headquarters in Stuttgart. The headquarters of the "Union of the Seventh-Day Adventists in the German Democratic Republic" are located in East Berlin.

Like the American Adventists, those here in Germany are involved in the health-food movement. The "De-Vau-Ge-Gesundkostwerk" was originally located in Hamburg, but, in 1976, it was removed to Lüneburg. The publishing house in Hamburg is still very active. Every two weeks the newsletter, Adventecho appears in more than 10,000 copies, and the missionary paper, The Voice of Hope (Stimme der Hoffnung) appears every month in more than 100,000 copies. Many other publications are produced under the title The Bible Speaks (Die Bibel spricht).

The Church of Jesus Christ of Latter-day Saints[8]

Germany has long been one of the main missionary fields of the Mormons, and a pair of young, clean-cut American men dressed in dark blue suits and approaching passers by in the streets on a busy Saturday morning has become a common sight in this country. Mormonism was first brought to Germany in 1843 by a German traveller who had spent some time in America and while there had become a follower of Joseph Smith. After his return to Germany, he founded a congregation in Darmstadt, but when he returned to America the following year, the little group broke up. In 1851, two missionaries, George P. Dykes and John Taylor, arrived in Germany and started systematic missionary work in Hamburg, where a congregation of twelve members was formed in the same year. Missionary work was hindered, however, when the police took action against the Mormons by forbidding their meetings, confiscating their tracts, and arresting the missionaries.

The Book of Mormon appeared in German in 1852, and by 1853, about 128 Germans had been won over to the faith, about 50 of whom eventually emigrated to Utah.

In 1855, Karl G. Maeser, a school teacher in Dresden, who was to make later important contributions to the intellectual history of the Mormon Church, was baptized. After his baptism, he went to America as the tutor of Brigham Young's children. In 1867, he returned to Germany and for the next three years was the director of the Mormon mission there. He went back to America and was one of the founders of the first Mormon University in Provo, Utah, and from 1888 until his death in 1901, the director of the church's entire school system. During his work in Germany, he founded a magazine called <u>Darsteller</u> (since 1969, <u>Stern</u>), which is still the main publication of German-speaking Mormonism.

Persecution of the Mormons by the police did not stop until the president of the church, Joseph F. Smith, visited Germany in 1906. In the following few years, about 2,500 Germans converted to Mormonism. World War I, of course, proved to be an unfavorable time, but after the war, missionary activities resumed, and by 1925, there were about 11,000 Mormons in the German-speaking countries.

In Nazi Germany, Mormon missions were not forbidden but were, nevertheless, drastically limited. Books and other printed material were confiscated, and many Mormons were arrested on suspicion of treason. At the beginning of World War II, all the foreign missionaries were called back to America, but after 1945, even more money and missionaries were sent back to Germany. The missions were stabilized, and in 1961, the first three "posts" in the Federal Republic were organized in Berlin, Stuttgart, and Hannover. Mormon teachings seem to have found little resonance with the German public, however. In 1983, there were about 21,000 Mormons in the Federal Republic and West Berlin and about 4,500 in the German Democratic Republic. One of the reasons that membership figures are not higher is that since 1945, about 20,000 German-speaking Mormons have emigrated to Utah.

Jehova's Witnesses[9]

While on a tour through various European countries in 1891, the founder of the Jehova's Witnesses, Charles Taze Russell visited

Germany. He felt, however, that there was little use to missionize in this country. Many German-Americans though were translating pamphlets and sending them to their relatives and acquaintances in Germany. In 1897, Zions Wacht-Turm und Verkünder der Gegenwart Christi appeared in the German language. Its editor, the German-American Otto Kötitz, was sent to Germany in 1903, and a few small meetings were established. By 1905, there were about 1,000 subscribers to the Watch Tower in Germany. Russell conducted lecture tours in Germany in 1909, 1910, and 1911, and Joseph Rutherford lectured here in 1913. Their lectures were very well attended, and the movement continued to grow. During World War I, some of Russell's German disciples did military service, but many others refused and were imprisoned. Russell caught the attention of the authorities, and his followers were accused of working with American money in an attempt to destroy the German war effort.

The confusion after Russell's death caused internal conflicts in Europe. In 1920, there was an open split, when Alexandre Freytag, who headed the French-Belgic work in Geneva, left the Serious Bible Researchers, taking a considerable number of his followers with him. Rutherford dissolved the office and set up a new one in Bern. Headed by a former Methodist preacher, Conrad Binkele, the office was responsible for the work in Germany, Switzerland, France, Belgium, the Netherlands, Austria and Italy. The German branch office was under the supervision of a former ship-yard worker, Paul Balzereit from Kiel, and was located in Bremen. From then on, a propaganda campaign with lectures amd printed material was carried out. What drew especially large crowds was the "Photo-Drama of the Creation" that was shown in many German towns and cities. In 1922, Rutherford again visited Germany and his lecture, "Millions now Living Will never Die" was heard by more than 70,000 people in 121 cities and towns. The first German congress was held in Leipzig during the same year. The membership in Germany, which had greatly decreased after 1918, rose again by 1923 to about 3,642, and the work seemed to have taken root. A printing house was set up in Magdeburg in 1923 and in 1926, headquarters were removed to

Magdeburg. Because of the bitter course against the Catholic and Protestant churches, which Rutherford had commanded, there were many conflicts and numerous court cases because of "illegal colportage." The number of Witnesses, however, continued to increase, and by 1933, there were about 35,000 in Germany.

The terrible persecution that the Witnesses suffered under the Nazi-regime drove them underground, but they were in no wise wiped out. In August 1947, there were again 36,526 witnesses in the four occupied zones. The numbers in the Federal Republic grew from 1947 to 1980 from 20,811 to 96,112, in addition to 4,978 in West Berlin.

One of their main areas of activity here in Germany is among the millions of guest workers, since many of these people came from countries where the Jehova's Witnesses are forbidden or extremely hampered in their work. The first Greek group was established in Munich in 1962, and by 1973, there were about 1,560 Greek witnesses in the Federal Republic. There are also Spanish, Italian, Turkish and Yugoslavian groups.

Practically from the beginning the Jehova's Witnesses have been involved in conflict and arguments with their neighbors. Because of many problems with American authorities, the Witnesses opened up a legal office in Brooklyn in 1936 and started publishing a pamphlet containing advice on how to deal with a court of law. Although their conflicts in America were often very bitter and sometimes bloody, it was not until 1933 in Germany that the Witnesses were confronted with a totalitarian dictatorship – the Third Reich. And here it was a matter of life and death. Persecution of the Witnesses started with a futile search of the branch office in Magdeburg in April 1933, severe restriction of their activities by authorities in the German states, and several arrests. On the 25th of June 1933, a quickly called congress adopted a protest that Rutherford and Balzereit had formulated against these attacks, and the protest was sent to all major governing officials. Many Witnesses found it to be very lame, but the directing body was hoping to reach some sort of agreement with the Nazi-government. An accompanying letter to Hitler stressed that the Witnesses had always looked favorably on Germany and that, for this reason, many American Witnesses had had difficulties during WWI. Hitler, however, was not impressed with the letter, and the protest was the reason for further, more severe persecution. On the 28th of June, 1933, the branch office was confiscated and Paul Balzereit was forced to flee to Czechoslovakia. Since Washington intervened, the office was given back to the Watch Tower Society since it had legal deed to the property, but its use was forbidden. Many employed Witnesses, who refused to take part in elections or to join the German Work Front or to say "Heil, Hitler" were fired from their jobs. Many simply withdrew from the limelight and quietly went about their business. Others decided to resist the authorities – as did Paul Balzereit, who, in December 1935 was sentenced to two and a half years in prison and after serving his sentence was sent to the concentration camp in Sachsenhausen and was not released until he renounced the Watch Tower Society.[10]

From the 7th to the 9th of October in 1934 Rutherford held a congress in Basel, in which about 1,000 German Witnesses took part. During the congress, "A Statement to the Government of the Reich" was composed and sent to Hitler. The statement expressed that the Witnesses, "would follow God's commandments at any price, would hold their meetings in order to study God's word, and would pray to God and serve Him as He had commanded." It was further stated that if the Government or governmental officials used force against them because they were obeying the will of God, then their blood would be on Hitler's hands and he would have to answer to the Almighty. This dignified statement shows how decisively the Witnesses were against the Nazi-regime. Other pronouncements followed in which Hitler was warned to leave the Witnesses alone or the wrath of God would destroy him and his Nazi-party. In a fit of anger, Hitler decided that the Witnesses would have to be wiped out of Germany.

Now that the movement was forbidden and despised, the Witnesses decided to go underground and carry on their activities. About 10,000 of them are supposed to have been involved in the underground movement. They met in very small groups, managed to bring literature into Germany from bordering countries, and reproduced the Watch Tower. The country was divided into twelve districts, and the district directors were to visit the groups, to support them, and to supply them with literature. Meetings were held in secret or were disguised. The Gestapo on the other hand, formed a special command that was to trace the Witnesses and their sympathizers, to observe them and search their houses, and to attack whenever the opportunity was present.

The Propaganda of the Witnesses was accused of being a tool of the Jews and the Communists. In a piece of Nazi-propaganda, it was proved, for example, that the political goals of the Watch Tower Society included the establishment of a Jewish world power, that they supported Marxism, and that those countries that treated them in a friendly way – USA, Mexico, Spain, France, Switzerland, etc. – only did so because of Masonic influence.

The persecution of the Witnesses gradually increased and became more brutal, with many of them being sent to concentration camps merely on suspicion and being freed only when they turned in a written renunciation of the Watch Tower Society. Since, however, so many Witnesses were so brave and patient in their sufferings, some Nazis thought that they could be used for the war effort in a positive way. Heinrich Himmler thought they could be used in the east against the Russians "because they could pacify the Russians with their Bible studies." He also felt that they had many positive characteristics, since they are very much against "war, the Jews, the Catholic Church and the Pope." They are "excellent farmers and do not strive for wealth, since they feel that it is a hindrance to eternal life." He considered the religion ideal to re-educate the vanquished according to the will of the vanquisher.

During the Hitler dictatorship, about 1,700 Witnesses lost their jobs, 285 their business, and 860 children were taken away from their parents. Over 6,000 Witnesses were arrested and sentenced to prison and about 2,000 were sent to concentration camps. 635 died in prison, 253 were sentenced to death, and 203 were executed. Some of them renounced their faith, but most of them endured and accepted their persecution.

After the war, the surviving Witnesses in Germany were sent CARE-packages, clothing, and about 1.5 million Watch Tower Society books by their American brethren. At first, they were allowed to work unhindered in the Soviet occupied zone, but they very soon came under the attack of Communists and were accused of being hostile to the state. Again meetings were forbidden, pamphlets and books confiscated, and many arrests made. Where they had once been accused of supporting communism, they were now been accused of supporting American imperialism. In 1956, in East Germany, there was a general amnesty, but it did not apply to the Witnesses. Since 1970, Witnesses in East Germany who are caught attending public meetings are only accused of "creating a public nuisance," and, instead of incarceration, a heavy fine is leavied against them.[11]

Conclusion

It was stated in the introduction to this paper that, of the approximately 260 free churches and sects in the Federal Republic, the majority have been imported from America. At first glance, it would thus seem that American religion has had a rather profound influence on the religious life of Germany. The total membership of the free churches and sects is, however, only a very small percentage of the population, and the membership of the individual groups runs from a few thousand to less than a hundred. Some of the larger ones, especially the Methodists, have had considerable influence in local areas, but generally speaking, the free churches and sects have had little effect on the religious life of the nation as a whole.

NOTES

[1]The standard German reference work on traditional religious groups is Konrad Algermissen, Konfessionskunde, ed. Heinrich Fries, et. al., 8th ed. (Paderborn: Verlag Bonifacius-Druckerei, 1969). For religious groups outside the main stream, the standard is Kurt Hutten, Seher, Grübler, Enthusiasten: Das Buch der traditionellen Sekten und religiösen Sonderbewegungen, 12th rev. ed. (Stuttgart:

Quell Verlag, 1982). This paper is heavily indebted to those two works. Other shorter, but very useful reference works include: Hans-Diether Reimer, Stichwort "Sekten": Glaubensgemeinschaften ausserhalb der Kirchen (Stuttgart: Quell Verlag, 1977); Friedrich-Wilhelm Haack, Grossmarkt der Wahrheiten: Ausschnitte aus dem religiösen Angebot unserer Zeit (Witten und Berlin: Eckart Verlag, 1969); and Oswald Eggenberger, Die Kirchen, Sondergruppen, und religiöse Vereinigungen, 3rd rev. ed. (Zürich: Theologischer Verlag, 1983).

[2] Eggenberger, p. 5.

[3] Eggenberger, p. 7.

[4] Dated, but still the most important German account of Methodism is F. Sommer, et. al., Der Methodismus (Stuttgart: Evangelisches Verlagswerk, 1966); older, but still useful, especially for early German Methodism are: John L. Nuelsen, Theophil Mann, and J.J. Sommer, Kurzgefasste Geschichte des Methodismus von seinen Anfängen bis zur Gegenwart (Bremen: Buchhandlung und Verlag des Traktathauses, G.m.b.H., 1920); Johannes Jüngst, Der Methodismus in Deutschland: Ein Beitrag zur neuesten Kirchengeschichte (Giessen: Verlag von Alfred Töpelmann, 1906); and Christian Maile, 100 Jahre Methodismus in Deutschland, 1833-1933 (Winnenden: Im Selbstverlag der Methodisten-Gemeinde, 1933). For the close connections between American and German Methodism, see Friedrich Wunderlich, Brückenbauer Gottes (Frankfurt am Main: Anker Verlag, 1963).

[5] Henry Boehm, Reminiscences, Historical and Biographical, of Sixty-Four Years in the Ministry, ed. Joseph P. Wakely (New York: Carlton & Porter, 1866), chap. II.

[6] Carl Wittke, William Nast: Patriarch of German Methodism (Detroit: Wayne State University Press, 1959).

[7] Most accounts of the Seventh-Day Adventists in Germany are biased one way or another. W. Mueller, Die Adventisten: Was Man von Ihnen Wissen Muss (Hamburg: Advent Verlag, 1948) is a summary of their doctrinal viewpoints from their side. Hans-Jürgen Twisselmann, Die Adventisten - zwischen Sinai und Golgatha: Ihre Geschichte, Lehre und eine Stellungnahme aus biblischer Sicht (Witten: Bundes-Verlag, 1967) is a criticism of their biblical interpretations. Numerous other books and pamphlets could be mentioned, but space does not permit.

[8] A Roman Catholic, but fairly objective account of the Mormons is Konrad Algermissen, Die Mormonen oder die Heiligen der letzten Tage (Hannover: Giesel, 1928). Of the many works by German speaking Protestants critizing the Mormons, only three will be mentioned: Fritz Blanke, Wer sind die Mormonen? (Zürich: Zwingli Verlag, 1960); Charles Brütsch, Was Haben Wir von den Mormonen

zu Halten? (Zürich: EVZ-Verlag, 1962); and Hans-Jürgen Twissel-mann, Die Mormonen im Schatten ihrer Geschichte (Witten: Bundes-Verlag, 1967).

[9]As in the United States, the Jehova's Witnesses have drawn a great deal of criticism in print. Here only two works can be cited: Konrad Algermissen, Die Zeugen Jehovas (Celle: Verlags-buchhandlung Joseph Giesel, 1949) and Hans-Jürgen Twisselmann, Vom "Zeugen Jehovas" zum Zeugen Jesus Christi (Giessen/Basel: Brunnen-Verlag, G.m.b.H., 1961). Algermissen is only moderately critical, while Twisselmann is extremely so.

[10]An example of the literature written against the Witnesses during the Nazi era is Hans Jonak von Freyenwald, Die Zeugen Jehovas: Pioniere für ein jüdisches Weltreich (Berlin: Buch Verlag Germania Aktien-Gesellschaft, 1936).

[11]Manfred Gebhard, ed., Die Zeugen Jehovas: Eine Dokumentation über die Wachtturmgesellschaft (Leipzig/Jena/Berlin: Urania Verlag, 1970) uses the Witnesses' own writings against them. In 1971, the work was reprinted in West Germany by Verlag Hubert Freistühler in Schwerte.

Contributors

Axel, Larry E.: Ph.D., Associate Professor of Philosophy, Department of Philosophy, Purdue University, West Lafayette, Indiana. - Publications: Ed., with Creighton Peden, Creative Freedom: Vocation of Liberal Religion (New York, 1982); ed., with William Dean, The Size of God: The Theology of Bernard Loomer in Context (Macon, Georgia, 1986); about 20 book chapters and articles on liberal religious thought in America, the "Chicago School," and process theology. Editor, with Creighton Peden, of the American Journal of Theology & Philosophy.

Backman, Milton V., Jr.: Ph.D., Professor of Church History and Doctrine, Department of Church History, Brigham Young University, Provo, Utah. - Publications: American Religions and the Rise of Mormonism (Salt Lake City, 1970); Joseph Smith's First Vision (Salt Lake City, 1971); Christian Churches of America: Origins and Beliefs (New York City, 1983); The Heavens Resound: A History of the Latter-day Saints in Ohio, 1830-1838 (Salt Lake City, 1983); Eyewitness Accounts of the Restoration (Salt Lake City, 1986); 5 pamphlets and 17 articles dealing with religion in early America, especially the history of Mormonism.

Barrett, J. Edward: Ph.D., Professor of Philosophical Theology, Department of Religion, Muskingum College, New Concord, Ohio. - Publications: How Are You Programmed? (Richmond, 1971); Faith In Focus (Washington, D.C., 1981); finalist in essay contest published in How Peace Came to the World (Cambridge, 1986); and more than 20 scholarly articles. Associate Editor of American Journal of Theology and Philosophy.

Brumm, Ursula: Dr. phil., Professor of Amerikanistik (American Literature, American Studies), John F. Kennedy Institut, Freie Universität Berlin. - Publications: Die religiöse Typologie im amerikanischen Denken: Ihre Bedeutung für die amerikanische Literatur und Geistesgeschichte (Leiden, 1963), translated as American Thought and Religious Typology (New Brunswick, N.J., 1970); Puritanismus und Literatur in Amerika (Darmstadt, 1973); Geschichte und Wildnis in der amerikanischen Literatur (Berlin, 1980); and about 40 articles dealing with American and English authors and aspects of American intellectual and literary history in German and American academic journals, critical anthologies, and Festschriften. Member of the editorial board of Early American Literature.

Buczynska-Garewicz, Hanna: Ph.D., Dr. habil., Professor of Philosophy, Department of Philosophy, College of the Holy Cross, Worcester, Massachusetts. - Publications: Charles S. Peirce (1966); Wartosc i Fact (1970); Uczucia i Rozum w swiecie wartosci (1975); Znak,

Znaczenie, Wartosc (1975); Znak i Oczywistosc (1981); and about 70 articles in Polish, English and German dealing with phenomenology, semiotics and moral philosophy.

Cobb, Larry R.: Ph.D., Professor of Public Administration, Slippery Rock University, Slippery Rock, Pennsylvania. - Publications: "The Dynamics of Freedom and Justice," in J.A. Broyer and Wm. Minor, eds., Creative Interchange (Carbondale, 1982); "A Freshman Program: Learning How to Learn," in J. Katz, ed., Teaching as Though Students Mattered (San Francisco, 1985); "Society: Modes of Knowing, Modes of Being," in Religion and Intellectual Life (1986). Coauthor of research reports: "Training and Professional Interests of Political Scientists in Pennsylvania," cited in PS, 1971; "Freshman Experimental Studies" in the Final Report (FIPSE Project # 0029, 1971) and "Bureaucracy" (FIPSE Project, 1982); Excellence in Public Higher Education (APSCUF, Harrisburg; ERIC (ED 247 821, 1985) and Faculty Development: An Agenda for Reform. (APSCUF, Harrisburg, 1986).

Collison, Gary: Ph.D., Assistant Professor of English, Department of English, Pennsylvania State University at York, York, Pennsylvania. - Publications: Several articles on American Transcendentalism, Unitarianism, and anti-slavery in academic journals and collections of criticism.

Comstock, Gary: Ph.D., Assistant Professor of Religious Studies, Philosophy Department, Iowa State University, Ames, Iowa. - Publications: Ed., Is There A Moral Obligation to Save the Family Farm? (Ames, 1986), and half a dozen articles on hermeneutics and ethics in academic journals.

Dapice, Ann N.: Ph.D., Director of the Institute for Values Inquiry and Lecturer, College of Arts and Sciences and the College of Human Development, The Pennsylvania State University, Ogontz Campus, Abington, Pennsylvania. - Publications: Several papers on the unfolding of values presented at professional meetings.

Dean, William: Ph.D., Professor of Religion, Gustavus Adolphus College, St. Peter, Minnesota. - Publications: Coming To: A Theology of Beauty (Philadelphia, 1972); Love Before the Fall (Philadelphia, 1976); American Religious Empiricism (Albany, New York, 1986); ed., with Larry Axel, The Size of God: The Theology of Bernard Loomer in Context (Macon, Georgia, 1987); 12 articles in theology and the philosophy of religion, particularly the empirical tradition in American religious thought and process theology.

Dörfel, Hanspeter: Dr. phil., Professor of English, Pädagogische Hochschule Ludwigsburg. - Publications: Ed., with Dieter Zeh, Modern Drama, Scenes of Conflict on the Stage: Student's Book (Paderborn, 1980), Teacher's Book (Paderborn, 1982); several articles dealing with individual American and British authors, with aspects of teaching literature and with curriculum questions in various critical anthologies and academic journals.

Ferré, Frederick: Ph.D., Professor of Philosophy and Head, Department of Philosophy, University of Georgia, Athens, Georgia. - Publications: Language, Logic and God (New York, 1961, and Chicago, 1981); Exploring the Logic of Faith (New York, 1962); Basic Modern Philosophy of Religion (New York, 1967); Shaping the Future (New York, 1976); ed., William Paley's Natural Theology (New York, 1962); ed., Comte: Introduction to Positive Philosophy (Indianapolis, 1970); ed., with Joseph Kockelmans and John E. Smith, The Challenge of Religion Today (New York, 1982); ed., with Rita Mataragnon, God and Global Justice (New York, 1985); chapters and entries in 20 books, anthologies, and encyclopedias; more than 40 articles on philosophy of religion, philosophy of science, language analysis, epistemology, and metaphysics in various scholarly journals. General Editor of Research in Philosophy and Technology.

Freese, Peter: Dr. phil., Professor of American Studies, Department of English, Universität Paderborn. - Publications: Die Initiationsreise: Studien zum jugendlichen Helden im modernen amerikanischen Roman (Neumünster, 1971); Die amerikanische Kurzgeschichte nach 1945: Salinger, Malamud, Baldwin, Purdy, Barth (Frankfurt, 1974); ed., Die amerikanische Short Story der Gegenwart: Interpretationen (Berlin, 1976); ed., Growing up Black in America: Stories and Studies of Socialization (Paderborn, 1978; 5th rev. ed., 1984); Teacher's Book (Paderborn, 1978; 2nd ed., 1979); ed., Bernard Malamud, 'The Assistant' (Paderborn, 1982; 2nd ed., 1985); Teacher's Book (Paderborn, 1983); ed., with Manfred Pütz, Postmodernism in America: A Critical Anthology (Darmstadt, 1984); ed., Teaching Contemporary American Life and Literature in the Advanced German EFL-Classroom (Paderborn, 1986); half a dozen other books; and about 100 articles dealing with American literature and history and with aspects of teaching American Studies in Germany in academic journals, critical anthologies and various Festschriften. Series editor of Texts for English and American Studies and the Paderborner Universitätsreden.

Freywald, Carin: Dr. phil., Akademische Oberrätin, Department of English, Universität Münster. - Publications: Untersuchungen zur Symbolik in William Faulkners Kurzgeschichten (Frankfurt/M., 1983); various articles and reviews on Hemingway, Faulkner, and Fitzgerald.

Friedl, Herwig: Dr. phil., Professor of American Literature, Universität Heidelberg. - Publications: Die Funktion der Bildlichkeit in den kritischen und theoretischen Schriften von Henry James (Heidelberg, 1972); Anfänge einer literarischen Karriere: Edith Whartons frühe Lyrik (MS, 1979); Begegnungen mit dem Neohumanismus: Edith

Wharton und William Cracy Brownell (MS, 1979); ed., with Roland Hagenbüchle, American Transcendentalism (Amerikastudien/American Studies, 1983); ed., with Dieter Schulz, E. L. Doctorow: A Symposium (Heidelberg, 1987); about 20 articles dealing with individual authors of 19th and 20th century American literature and aspects of the history of ideas in America in academic journals and Festschriften.

Garrison, George R.: Ph.D., Associate Professor of Philosophy and Black Studies, Department of Anthropology, Black Studies and Women Studies, University of Northern Colorado, Greeley, Colorado. - Publications: with E.M. Madden, "William James - Warts and All," American Quarterly (Summer, 1977); "Historical Traditions in Civil Dissent ...," Black Law Journal (Fall, 1983); "Afrocentrism, Ethnocentrism and Self-Determination: The Case of the African," Proceedings of the 12th Annual Third World Conference (August, 1986); "Afro-American Philosophy: The Early Beginnings and the Afro-centric Substratum," The Journal of the Society for the Study of Black Philosophy (forthcoming); "The Philosophical Evolution of Malcolm X: The Philosophy of Elijah Muhammad, Black Nationalism and Orthodox Sunni Islam," Afro-American Journal of Philosophy (forthcoming); and others dealing with the ideas of individual Afro-Americans and the intellectual and cultural tradition of Africa and the African Diaspora.

Gay, William C.: Ph.D., Associate Professor, Department of Philosophy, University of North Carolina at Charlotte, Charlotte, North Carolina. - Publications: With Michael A. Pearson, The Nuclear Arms Race (Chicago, 1987); ed., Philosophy and the Debate on Nuclear Weapons Systems and Policies, a special double issue of Philosophy and Social Criticism (1984); "Nuclear War: Public and Governmental Misconceptions" in Michael Fox and Leo Groarke, eds., Nuclear War: Philosophical Perspectives (New York, 1985); and 12 articles on other aspects of the nuclear debate and on various themes in continental philosophy, several reviews and bibliographies.

Geiger, Annamaria: Dr. phil., M.A., Hochschulassistentin, Fachbereich Erziehungswissenschaften, Abteilung Englische Sprache, Literatur und Landeskunde und ihre Didaktik, Universität Göttingen. - Publications: Britischer Kontextualismus und Fremdsprachenunterricht. Darstellung und Bedeutung für die sprachpraktische Ausbildung des Englischlehrers (Berlin, 1979); with S. Johnson-Fricke and G. Schwibbe, Youth and Politics in the U.S. (München, 1984); with S. Johnson-Fricke, English for Language Teaching (Heidelberg, 1984); 14 articles on various aspects of teaching foreign languages and cultural studies as well as on the specific topic of American born-againism.

Hampsch, George H.: Ph.D., Professor of Social and Political Philosophy, Department of Philosophy, College of the Holy Cross, Worcester, Massachusetts. - Publications: Theory of Communism (New

York, 1965, and London, 1966); about 35 articles in the areas of social and political philosophy, Marxist studies, peace studies, philosophy of war, and international relations in academic journals and anthologies. Some publications have been translated into German, Spanish, Polish and Chinese.

Hardwick, Charles D.: Ph.D., Professor of Religious Studies, Department of Philosophy and Religion, The American University, Washington, D.C. - Publications: Faith and Objectivity: Fritz Buri and the Hermeneutical Foundations of a Radical Theology (The Hague, 1972); Religious Truth in the Absence of God (Washington, D.C., 1981); about 20 articles and papers dealing with existential philosophy and contemporary theology.

Herget, Winfried: Dr. phil., Professor of American Studies, Department of English, Johannes Gutenberg-Universität Mainz. - Publications: Untersuchungen zur Wirklichkeitsdarstellung im Frühwerk Joseph Conrads (Saarbrücken, 1965); ed., with George H. Williams, Norman Pettit, Sargent Busch, Jr., Thomas Hooker. Writings in England and Holland, 1626-1633 (Cambridge, Mass., 1975); ed. with H. Meyer, Texte zur Amerikakunde (Saarbrücken, 1977); ed., Studies in New England Puritanism (Frankfurt, 1983); ed., with Klaus Peter Jochum and Ingeborg Weber, Theorie und Praxis im Erzählen des 19. und 20. Jahrhunderts: Studien zur englischen und amerikanischen Literatur zu Ehren von Willi Erzgräber (Tübingen, 1986); ed., with Karl Ortseifen, The Transit of Civilization from Europe to America: Essays in Honor of Hans Galinsky (Tübingen, 1986); about 20 articles dealing with Puritanism, 19th and 20th century American literature (Hawthorne, Dickinson, Olson, Updike, Oates), modern American drama, American English, and rhetoric. Series editor, with Renate Schmidt-von Bardeleben, of Mainzer Studien zur Amerikanistik.

Hill, Samuel S.: Ph.D., Professor of Religion, Department of Religion, University of Florida, Gainesville. - Publications: Southern Churches in Crisis (New York, 1967); Religion and the Solid South (Abingdon, 1972); The South and the North in American Religion (Georgia, 1980); with D.E. Owen, The New Religious-Political Right in America (Abingdon, 1982); ed., and contributor Encyclopedia of Religion in the South (Mercer, 1984); Handbook of Denominations in the United States (Abingdon Press, 1985); about 25 articles dealing with religion in America, the American South, and politics and religion in recent America.

Kelly, Eugene: Ph.D., Associate Professor, Center for General Studies, New York Institute of Technology, Central Islip, New York. - Publications: Max Scheler (Twayne, 1977); with L.E. Navia, Ethics and the Search for Values (Prometheus, 1979); with N. Capaldi and L.E. Navia, An Invitation to Philosophy (Prometheus, 1980); with L.E. Winters, Continental Philosophy and the Arts (University Press of America, 1983); several articles on social philosophy and aesthetics in various journals.

Kurtz, Ernest: Ph.D., Director of Education and Research, Guest House, Lake Orion, Michigan, and Lecturer in American Religious History, Department of Theology, Loyola University of Chicago. - Publications: Not-God: A History of Alcoholics Anonymous (Center City, 1979); Shame and Guilt: An Historical Perspective for Professionals (Center City, 1981); Shame: Understanding and Coping (Center City, 1982); Ninety Meetings, Ninety Days (Minneapolis, 1984); 8 articles dealing with Alcoholics Anonymous, with shame, and with religion in the American South in academic journals and encyclopedic anthologies.

Lang, Bernhard: Dr. theol., Professor of Religious Studies, Universität Paderborn. - Publications: Monotheism and the Prophetic Minority (Sheffield, 1983); Wisdom and the Book of Proverbs (New York, 1986); ed., Anthropological Approaches to the Old Testament (Philadelphia, 1985); and 11 more books in German, in the fields of comparative religion and biblical studies. Editor of Internationale Zeitschriftenschau für Bibelwissenschaft und Grenzgebiete.

Leonard, Bill J.: Ph.D., Professor of Church History, The Southern Baptist Theological Seminary, Louisville, Kentucky. - Publications: Word of God Across the Ages (Nashville, 1981); ed., Early American Christianity (Nashville, 1983); contributing ed., Foxfire 7 (New York, 1982); The Nature of the Church (Nashville, 1986); about 50 articles dealing with American religious studies, Southern religion, and Christian spirituality.

Martin, John E.: M.A., Wissenschaftlicher Oberrat, Seminar für Englische Sprache und Kultur, Universität Hamburg. - Publications: "Approaches to the Reality of the Slave Family in Uncle Tom's Cabin and the Work of Eugene Genovese," in H.-H. Freitag and P. Hühn, eds., Literarische Ansichten der Wirklichkeit (Frankfurt/Main, 1980); "Martin Eden, a London Superman Adventurer: A Case Study of the Americanization of European Ideology," in C. Uhlig and V. Bischoff, eds., Die Amerikanische Literatur in der Weltliteratur (Berlin, 1982); "The Portrayal of Women and Men in Henry James' The Portrait of a Lady and Marilyn French's The Women's Room," in H. Bock, ed., Frau und Mann in Literatur und Gesellschaft (Hamburg, 1982); "The Conflict between the Artist and Second Generation Puritanism in Nathaniel Hawthorne's The Scarlet Letter," in G. Dose, ed., Interessante Werke der englischsprachigen Literatur (Hamburg, 1987).

McGraw, John G.: Ph.D., Associate Professor and Chairman, Department of Philosophy, Concordia University, Montreal. - Publications: Various articles including areas in philosophy of religion, philosophical anthropology, philosophy of sport, and futures studies; currently engaged in writing a two-volume work on loneliness and related phenomena.

Mikelson, Thomas J.S.: Candidate for Th.D. Degree, Harvard University. - Publications: Assistant Editor, The Thought of Paul Tillich (New York, 1985), ed. by James Luther Adams, Roger L. Shinn, and Wilhelm Pauck; with James Luther Adams, "Legitimation and Social Action," in Encyclopedia of Religion (New York, 1987); and other articles and book reviews. Currently working on a dissertation, "The Concept of God in the Theology of Martin Luther King, Jr.," Harvard University.

Miller, David Lee: Ph.D., Professor of Philosophy, Department of Philosophy, University of Wisconsin-La Crosse, La Crosse, Wisconsin. - Publications: Buddhist Themes in Wieman's View of Creative Interchange (Carbondale, 1982); On Individuality: A Critical Essay (La Crosse, 1983); Buddhism and Wieman on Suffering and Joy (Albany, 1984); The Task of Philosophy in the Humanities (La Crosse, 1984); The Experience of Creative Interchange (West Lafayette, 1986); Some Meanings of the Earth: A Process Perspective (The Hague, 1986).

Milligan, Charles S.: Ph.D., Th.D., Professor of Philosophy of Religion, Division of Philosophy, Theology and Ethics, The Iliff School of Theology, Denver, Colorado. - Publications: Contemporary Philosophy of Religion (Denver, 1971); ed., William H. Bernhardt: A Functional Philosophy of Religion (Denver, 1968); The Cognitive Quest for God and Operational Theism (Denver, 1972); some 30 articles on contemporary philosophy, theology, ethics and social problems in various journals and books. Editor of The Iliff Review.

Peden, Creighton: Ph.D., Fuller E. Callaway Professor of Philosophy, Augusta College, Augusta, Georgia. - Publications: Wieman's Empirical Process Philosophy (Washington, D.C., 1977); with Charles Hartshorne, Whitehead's View of Reality (New York, 1981); ed., with Donald Chapman, Philosophical Reflections on Education and Society (Washington, D.C., 1978); ed., with Donald Chapman, Critical Issues in Philosophy of Education (Washington, D.C., 1979); ed., with Larry E. Axel, Creative Freedom: Vocation of Liberal Religion (New York, 1982); ed., Philosophy for a Changing Society (Reynoldsburg, Ohio, 1983); over 75 articles dealing with American liberal religious thought and social philosophy in academic journals and anthologies. Editor, with Larry E. Axel, of the American Journal of Theology & Philosophy.

Pütz, Manfred: Dr. phil., Professor of Amerikanistik, Department of English, Universität Augsburg. - Publications: Motivation im englischen und amerikanischen Roman des neunzehnten und zwanzigsten Jahrhunderts (Cologne, 1972); The Story of Identity: American Fiction of the Sixties (Stuttgart, 1979; rpt. Munich, 1987); Ralph Waldo Emerson: A Bibliography of Twentieth-Century Criticism (Frankfurt, 1986); ed., Ralph Waldo Emerson: Die Natur und Ausgewählte Essays (Stuttgart, 1982); ed., Benjamin Franklin: Autobiography (Munich, 1983, rpt. Zürich, 1985); ed., with Peter Freese, Postmodernism in American Literature: A Critical Anthology (Darmstadt, 1984); about 30 articles dealing with aspects of American literature, history, and philosophy in American, English, and German academic journals and critical anthologies.

Rich, Gregory P.: Ph.D., Assistant Professor of Social Science, Department of History and Philosophy, Grambling State University, Grambling, Louisiana. - Publications: "Softening Up Hard Determinism," Philosophia, 15 (1985); "Preferential Hiring and Equal Opportunity," in Tom Hawkins, ed., Excellence and Equality, Proceedings of the 29th Annual Meeting of the South Atlantic Philosophy of Education Society, 12-13 Nov., 1984 (Spartanburg, S.C., 1984); "Is Pacifism Justifiable?," in Frederick Broadhurst, ed., Peace and War 1984: Power and Moral Responsibility, a Symposium, Selected Proceedings of a Symposium Held by East Carolina University and the Honor Society of Phi Kappa Phi, 21-22 Feb., 1984 (Greenville, N.C., 1984).

Roth, John K.: Ph.D., Russell K. Pitzer Professor of Philosophy, Department of Philosophy, Claremont McKenna College, Claremont, California. - Publications: Freedom and the Moral Life: The Ethics of William James (Philadelphia, 1969); with Frederick Sontag, The American Religious Experience (New York, 1972); American Dreams (San Francisco, 1976); with Frederick Sontag, God and America's Future (Wilmington, 1977); with Robert H. Fossum, The American Dream (Durham, 1981); ed., The Moral Philosophy of William James (New York, 1969); ed., The Moral Equivalent of War and Other Essays (New York, 1971); ed., The Philosophy of Josiah Royce (Indianapolis, 1982); ed., with Robert C. Whittemore, Ideology and American Experience (Washington, D.C., 1986); more than 100 articles and reviews dealing with American philosophy, religion, and culture.

Schwarz, Hans: Dr. theol., Professor of Systematic Theology and Contemporary Theological Issues, Institut für Evangelische Theologie, Universität Regensburg. - Publications: On the Way to the Future (Minneapolis, 1972, rev. ed. 1979); The Search for God (Minneapolis, 1975); Our Cosmic Journey (Minneapolis, 1977); Beyond the Gates of Death (Minneapolis, 1984); Divine Communication (Philadelphia, 1985); Verstehen wir das Glaubensbekenntnis noch? Der gemeinsame Glaube der Christen (Freiburg, 1986); Kurs: Die christliche Kirche, 3 vols. (Göttingen, 1986); several other books on issues in systematic theology; and more than 50 scholarly articles in English, German, Greek, and Hungarian on issues in theology with special attention to the relationship between theology and the natural sciences.

Shaw, Marvin C.: Ph.D., Professor of Religious Studies, Department of History and Philosophy, Montana State University, Bozeman, Montana. - Publications: The Paradox of Intention (forthcoming); articles on William James, George Santayana, John Dewey and Henry

Nelson Wieman in Journal of Religion, American Journal of Theology and Philosophy, Encounter (U.S.A.), Faith and Freedom (U.K.), Zygon: Journal of Religion and Science.

Speak, David M.: Ph.D., Associate Professor of Political Science, Department of Political Science, Public Administration and Criminal Justice, Georgia Southern College, Statesboro, Georgia. - Publications: Living Law: The Transformation of American Jurisprudence in the Early Twentieth Century (New York, 1986); with George H. Cox, Jr., "Contemporary Doctrines of Civil Death," in Susette Talarico, ed., Courts and Criminal Justice: Emerging Issues (Sage Publications, 1985); "The Notion of Rhetoric as a Uniquely Political Compound," The Journal of the North Carolina Political Science Association (now Politics and Policy), 1 (1979).

Steinkraus, Warren E.: Ph.D., L.H.D., Professor of Philosophy, State University of New York, College at Oswego, Oswego, New York. - Publications: Philosophy of Art (1974, repr. 1982); with G.R. Malkani, A Discussion of the Law of Karma (India, 1966); ed., New Studies in Berkeley's Philosophy (1966, repr. 1981); ed., New Studies in Hegel's Philosophy (1971); ed., Representative Essays of B.P. Bowne (1980); co-ed., with K. Schmitz, Art and Logic in Hegel's Philosophy (1980); over 70 articles in professional journals on history of philosophy, social thought, philosophy of religion, and aesthetics. Contributor of essays to 5 volumes and to one Festschrift on Paul Schilpp. Book Review Editor for Idealistic Studies.

Trulove, Sarah Chappell: M.A., Assistant Director for Programs and Publications, Joyce and Elizabeth Hall Center for the Humanities, University of Kansas, Lawrence, Kansas. - Publications: With James Woelfel, "Mary Wollstonecraft," in University of Kansas Western Civilization Program Student's Manual (Lexington, 1986); "Dorothee Soelle," supplementary volumes on twentieth-century biographies, Encyclopedia of World Biography (New York, forthcoming).

Turner, Donald Lloyd: M.A., Lecturer, Department of English, Universität Paderborn. - Publications: ed., Religion and Society in Contemporary America (Heidelberg, 1984); ed., God's Own Country: Religion in America (Paderborn, 1987); various articles on religion in America as a subject in the German EFL-classroom.

Woelfel, James: Ph.D., Professor of Philosophy and Religious Studies and Director, Western Civilization Program, University of Kansas, Lawrence, Kansas. - Publications: Bonhoeffer's Theology: Classical and Revolutionary (Nashville and New York, 1970); Borderland Christianity: Critical Reason and the Christian Vision of Love (Nashville and New York, 1973, and London, 1974); Camus: A Theological Perspective (Nashville and New York, 1975); Augustinian Humanism: Studies in Human Bondage and Earthly Grace (Washington, D.C., 1979); about 45 articles on issues in the philosophy of religion, existentialist thought, modern Western religious thought, and religion and literature in academic journals, encyclopedias, books of essays, and special journal issues.